Politics and populism across modes and media

Linguistic Insights

Studies in Language and Communication

Edited by Maurizio Gotti,
University of Bergamo

Volume 265

PETER LANG
Bern · Berlin · Bruxelles · New York · Oxford

Ruth Breeze / Ana M. Fernández Vallejo (eds.)

Politics and populism across modes and media

PETER LANG
Bern · Berlin · Bruxelles · New York · Oxford

Bibliographic information published by die Deutsche Nationalbibliothek
Die Deutsche Nationalbibliothek lists this publication in the Deutsche Nationalbibliografie; detailed bibliographic data is available on the Internet at ‹http://dnb.d-nb.de›.

Library of Congress Cataloging-in-Publication Data
A CPI catalog record for this book has been applied for at the Library of Congress.

"The editors of this volume acknowledge the support of the Spanish Ministry of Economy and Competitiveness (MINECO), through project FFI2015-65252-R "El demos en el imaginario de la nueva política: el debate sobre la voluntad popular en el discurso público en Europa".

ISSN 1424-8689
ISBN 978-3-0343-3707-6 (Print)
E-ISBN 978-3-0343-3724-3 (E-PDF)
E-ISBN 978-3-0343-3725-0 (EPUB)
E-ISBN 978-3-0343-3726-7 (MOBI)
DOI 10.3726/b16306

Wabernstrasse 40, CH-3007 Bern, Switzerland
bern@peterlang.com, www.peterlang.com

Table of Contents

Ruth Breeze and Ana M. Fernández Vallejo

Introduction: Politics, populism, media

Politics is inextricably bound up with discourse and communication. From the earliest times, the sphere of the political has been understood as a social arena in which power and influence can be garnered, and possible collective futures shaped, through persuasion – and persuasion is conducted through symbolic systems of social communication, that is, through languages. In Chilton's words (2004: 19), through language, individuals have the capacity to "communicate, compare, align or dissent from one another's mental representations of the present, future and possible worlds". Language enables us to engage in dialogue with others, and through this, to share and negotiate visions and goals: together, these discursive activities form the essence of the human activity that we call 'politics'.

There is, of course, nothing new about this. Since Aristotle's definition of the human being as a 'political animal' that is distinguished from the other animals precisely by his/her power of speech, it has been generally accepted that politics is interconnected with language not just superficially, but in its very essence. However, in more recent times with the rise of the different forms of mass media, attention came to focus anew on politics and language, looking not just at the rhetoric used to shape the message, but also at the means used to convey this to a wider public. For many years, the focus was on the press, radio and television, and the way politicians and their audiences adapted to these different media (and vice versa). Since the advent of digital communication, the relationship between new media and politics has now become a focus of intense interest and speculation on the part of politicians and academics alike. Currently, it seems that the symbiosis between the two spheres is such that political activity is almost inseparable from media communication (Engesser *et al.* 2017; Strömback/Esser 2014; Esser/Strömback 2014). Politicians and parties who have a strong media presence, or who attract lively media attention, are more visible, trigger stronger reactions, and perhaps receive more support, than those that do not. The study of this intersection between politics and the media is perceived to be particularly important. In a positive sense, it involves crucial ideals, values and aspirations, such as informed democracy, citizens' empowerment and social debate. But importantly, on the negative side, experience has also taught us that this synergy between politics and the media is increasingly likely to be open to manipulation, propaganda, polarization effects, and so on.

If we examine recent research trends concerning politics and the media in more detail, it is clear that most academic interest is currently centring on the so-called 'new media', particularly the Internet and social media, on the grounds that these have wrought swift and radical changes in the way people communicate and interact on a daily basis, not least as far as politics is concerned (Enli 2017). On the one hand, mainstream politicians and parties have adapted quickly to this new scenario, investing considerably in online communication tools and strategies. On the other, Internet-based affordances have made it much easier for new political movements to find supporters and gain ground quickly. Recent examples, such as the US, French and Italian election campaigns of 2017–2018, suggest that digital media make it easier for "outsider" candidates to attract sufficient public attention to launch themselves into mainstream politics. From a slightly different angle, online activism has also been studied in contexts as different as the Arab Spring and the Brexit referendum, showing that digital tools can be effective when it comes to gaining critical mass in order to organise protests or sway public opinion. However, the follow-up and ongoing consequences of such phenomena are far from predictable, and controversy still rages concerning the degree to which campaigns and movements conducted through digital media are open to manipulation (Jansen 2010; Penney/Dadas 2013; Gibson 2013; Bennett 2018).

Against this background, the extension of this association between politics and media to take in the phenomenon of populism becomes clear. The term populism has enjoyed huge popularity in recent years, and is open to various differing interpretations. In discourse analysis, it is generally understood that the common core of populist messages, be they principally right, left or nationalist-oriented, lies in a loose or 'thin' ideology that posits a notion of popular sovereignty: populist discourse assumes the existence of two homogeneous units, 'the people' and 'the elites', which are placed in antagonism to each other, such that the former's rights and aspirations need to be defended against those of the latter (Mudde 2004; Stanley 2008). Importantly, this basic pro-people/anti-establishment stance is highly open and flexible in ideological terms, proving to be applicable to both the right and the left, to Trump and Syriza, to Marine Le Pen, Movimento Cinque Stelle, Podemos and Chávez, as well as to regional nationalisms of various kinds. Perhaps for this reason, contemporary understandings of populism have come to centre primarily on the notion of discourse, performance and style (Moffitt 2016; Macaulay 2019), on the one hand, and on disentangling the relationship between populist discourse and other ideological trends, such as nationalism or socialism (de Cleen/Stavrakakis 2017), on the other.

Within the perspective of this discursive-performative understanding of populism, it is clear why the media (of all kinds) play a key role in its generation and propagation: populism feeds off media attention, and the new media in particular give populists enormous potential for performing to ever wider audiences (Llamas Saíz 2018). As Wodak (2015) and Moffitt (2016) have pointed out in their different ways, what unites populists is their ability to 'perform' in such a manner that they attract the public eye, engage popular identities, and arouse strong reactions of a highly affective nature, triggering politically operative emotions such as fear (Wodak 2015), anger (Wagner 2014; Breeze 2019a) and sadness (Rico *et al.* 2017). The digital media (YouTube, Twitter, websites, comments pages and discussion boards, Facebook, etc.) notoriously lend themselves to the transmission of radical political messages, in that they are open to the widest possible range of users, are subject to very few controls, and are often multimodal, allowing users to combine images, video and words to create striking emotive messages. According to many researchers, social media are an ideal resource for populist politicians because of the preference for what is "polarised, simplistic and emotional" (Enli 2017: 222). Moreover, since in many cases it is possible to gain ever-wider audiences through rapid snowball effects, there is a premium on sending high impact messages, even if this means sacrificing important qualities such as reliability, truthfulness and respect for others. At the same time, public trust in the (new and old) media is being undermined by issues surrounding the topic of 'fake news', and by the allegations that bots and other technical innovations are being used systematically to influence public opinion on the social media. All of this has serious consequences for the way the public receive, consume and produce digital messages, as well as for the way politics is conducted on a regional, national and transnational level.

In response to these social and political phenomena, a vast volume of research has focused on populist (and other) politicians' uses of digital media (Graham *et al.* 2014), and on the 'mediatisation of politics' (Esser/Strömback 2014), with some suggestion that we are truly witnessing a profound transformation of political life (Gerbaudo 2018). Much of the specific analysis has centred on high-profile campaigns (i.e. Obama and Trump, the Brexit referendum) or popular movements (i.e. the Arab Spring). Less attention has been paid, however, to the similarities and differences that emerge across cultures and political systems as populists movements harness the power of the digital media across the world.

To carry out such research, two things are necessary: close attention to the actual textual and multimodal characteristics of the messages; and a well-founded understanding of the social and political background to the movements, parties and audiences in the different countries concerned. This volume is intended to contribute to our knowledge of these issues by providing case studies based on the uses of digital and other media in populist politics in various parts of Europe, the Americas, Africa and the Middle East, and Asia. The chapters each provide an overview of the context of each study, including the political scenario from which they emerge, but importantly, they also pay particular attention to the linguistic/discursive, multimodal and media effects that characterise the messages and interactions produced. Our aim is not only to bring together a collection of papers that illustrate the workings of populism across modes and media, but also to show explicitly how the specific mode and medium used has a bearing on the nature of the messages and the way people receive them and interact with them in the digital sphere.

The selection of chapters presented in this volume thus covers a wide range of countries, parties, and movements, including some, like Pakistan, Romania and Puerto Rico, that have received little attention so far from scholars interested in populism and politics in the media. Although all the chapters here focus on events in the last few years, their geographical and ideological scope is immense, ranging from Imran Khan's successful election campaign promoting a modernising agenda in Pakistan, in 2018, to the public outcry over Nicolás Maduro's attempt to further undermine democracy in Venezuela by setting up a Constituent Assembly entirely loyal to himself, in 2017. The discursive data under consideration are also highly diverse. First, from the politicians and parties themselves, this volume includes analysis of speeches delivered live and relayed through YouTube and social media, campaign posters and television spots, politicians' official webpages, and also their personal or party Twitter, Facebook and Instagram accounts. Importantly, these analyses are not confined to profiling how populist leaders and/or parties themselves communicate, but they also consider what other parties have to say about them, and how mainstream politicians use a variety of means to delegitimise populist actors in the eyes of the public. Second, from the perspective of the general public and grass-roots movements, these chapters also consider reactions from and interactions between members of the public on Twitter and in reader comments pages in diverse settings, illustrating the growth of public resistance to populist messages, on the one hand, but also showing how popular movements can gather momentum and become politically operative, on the other.

The theoretical frameworks used to inform the studies presented here, and the methodologies applied to analyse the data, are mainly based on linguistic approaches to discourse analysis, yet within this, they represent a variety of different approaches. Many studies are designed to incorporate mixed (quantitative and qualitative) approaches (Fernández Vallejo; Schmidt) to social media analysis, including some that exploit the potential of corpus assisted discourse analysis (Schmidt; Bhatia/Ross; Aiezza; Napolitano; Hassan). Other chapters prioritise qualitative analysis with a view to gaining an in-depth understanding of online political discourses (Badarneh; Meléndez; Nadeem; Rovenţa-Fruműşani/Ştefănel; Breeze). The interpretive frameworks used include systematic linguistically grounded approaches to discourse analysis (Ayerbe Linares), approaches informed by the theory of discursive illusions (Bhatia/Ross), theories of identity (Aiezza; Breeze) or theories of politeness and language aggression (Breeze), as well as studies focusing on the use of first and second person devices to create a more intimate style of communication (Hassan). Finally, some studies clearly adopt a macro-perspective to interpretation of data, looking at the digital phenomena in the wider scope of entitlement and inequality, freedom and disenfranchisement, democracy and disillusionment (Meléndez; Badarneh; Rovenţa-Frumuşani/Ştefănel; Fernández Vallejo).

1 Populist performers and performances

The first overarching theme of this book concerns politicians' media performances. In this, chapters analysing Donald Trump's approach to communication, as one of the most visible examples of the 'populist style' found across new and old media, form an important element, as we see in the chapters by Aditi Bhatia and Andrew S. Ross, Maria Cristina Aiezza, Antonella Napolitano and Aline Schmidt. But importantly, readers also have the opportunity to compare his performances with those of other leaders, such as Imran Khan in Pakistan, analysed here by Saqlain Hassan, Tsipras in Greece, studied by Giorgos Venizelos, or Salvini in Italy, investigated by Maria Cristina Aiezza. This opens up the scope for comparisons on a political level, placing a question mark over certain value judgements that condemn populism in its entirety. However, it also draws our notice to aspects of the way politicians and people behave in the media that seem to transcend national and cultural boundaries. These chapters amply illustrate the features identified by Moffitt (2016) and others as characteristic of populism, namely a dichotomous view of society in which 'the people' is pitted against a corrupt or treacherous 'elite'. An urgent sense of crisis, generated by dramatic use of language, is omnipresent in discourses across the political spectrum. However, the elements of 'bad manners' (Moffitt 2017) and perhaps also 'exclusionary discourse' (Wodak 2015) appear to be more strongly associated with those on the right, and here in particular by Salvini and Trump, with their diatribes against external 'others' such as migrants. Thus de Cleen and Stavrakakis' (2017) argument that left-wing populism (in their view, populism proper) and right-wing nationalist populism (which they would term 'nationalism') are essentially different receives some support from the present data on a discursive level (see also Breeze 2019b).

At the same time, the chapters in this volume serve to add some nuances to the above discussion concerning the nature and uses of populist discourse. The first of these contributions concerns the attitude that mainstream political parties often adopt towards their new populist rivals. Miguel Ayerbe Linares's chapter shows clearly that established parties in Germany and Austria adopt powerful strategies to delegitimise parties such as AfD and FPÖ, evoking highly negative historical connotations to undermine their credibility. As we might predict, however, once a populist party attains power, the picture changes: in Austria, the FPÖ's coalition partner, the ÖVP, carefully refrains from using inflammatory allusions of this kind. From a slightly different perspective, Daniela Rovenţa-Frumuşani and Adriana Ştefănel's chapter on Romania shows how in cultures with little recent tradition of informed public debate, populist strategies seem to become contagious across the spectrum. Their chapter provides insights into the proliferation and generalisation of populist discourses in a post-communist setting. A further contribution in this sense is about whether or not populists' strategies change when they come to power. In the case of Tsipras, Giorgos Venizelos brings multimodal evidence into play to illustrate the shift in Syriza's messages from its years in opposition to its years in power. By contrast, Antonella Napolitano's chapter on the White House website in the Trump era suggests that populist discourses and performances can persist after power has been secured, maintaining a strong personalist approach to politics and keeping alive the construct of the state that is under attack.

2 People and populism in the media

The second major strand in this volume is the discursive analysis of popular responses to political events or leaders, and the phenomenon of grass-roots political movements that gain momentum through digital media. These chapters also fall into two identifiable but overlapping categories: those which can be primarily understood as popular reactions to populist leaders, and those which could be classified as bottom-up popular movements that might gain momentum in order to become operative. Of course, the former can also become politically operative, but on the basis of the evidence presented here, their nature in these two concrete cases seems mainly to be reactive.

Looking at the first category, we can see that leaders such as Ensour in Jordan and Maduro in Venezuela identify as populists, justifying their grip on power by claiming to speak for 'the people', but that their claims, and their legitimacy in general, are strongly questioned in social fora. In the case of Jordan, long-standing anti-elite and anti-corruption discourses are mobilised in online fora as people exert themselves in the public performance of attacking, refusing and ridiculing Prime Minister Ensour's populist claims. Similarly, in Venezuela, as Fernández Vallejo shows, citizen participation in politics through social media such as Twitter becomes increasingly intense when it comes to countering Maduro's claims to represent 'the people', leading to strong polarisation of online exchanges. In a rather different vein, Meléndez's chapter illustrates the constraints on political development in Puerto Rico, showing how divergent readings of political events fail to attain critical mass, and suggests ways in which social media might in the long term provide a vehicle through which citizens' consciousness could be raised and a heightened awareness of civic rights, duties and identities might come into being.

Regarding the second strand, addressing more proactive forces from below, Nahla Nadeem considers the strategies used in social media during the Arab Spring, documenting ways in which contributors respond to each other across national frontiers with messages of support and encouragement, and build common ground on the strength of shared cultural values and identities, airing similar social grievances. Her chapter explores the way that grass-roots movements can gather momentum and come to play an active role in events. In the contrasting case of Puerto Rico, Víctor A. Meléndez analyses the way citizens communicate their dissatisfaction on social media, and illustrates the convergence between ideological systems, political actors, and so on, in order to bring out both the opportunities and the limitations of this sphere. In his view, the limitations operating in this socio-political scenario are so profound that political protest rarely transcends the virtual sphere to crystallise in action. In a very different context, Ruth Breeze looks at the way contributors to newspaper reader comments pages clash over far-right politics in the United Kingdom. Her analysis suggests that contributors appear to derive enjoyment from these risk-free skirmishes, but also that discursive sparring of this kind may well encourage extremism, by strengthening participants' convictions and identities, and perpetuating their entrenched positions. The dynamics of right-wing user-generated comment is further analysed on a more theoretical level in a stimulating chapter by Aline Schmidt, who relates the social media discourses of Trump supporters to Weber's theory of charismatic authority.

3 Modes and media effects

In all of this, it is evident that the various media themselves, and the different modes of communication that they afford (visual, auditory, written or spoken language), play a crucial role in the generation and diffusion of political messages. Starting with the more informal media like Twitter or the comments forum, which are generally associated with a vast proliferation of user-generated content, we can observe that Twitter and comments pages seem to serve as a particularly suitable vehicle for launching unbridled attacks: users employ these media for sharpening antagonism, airing aggressive language, venting rage or frustration, and so on. These media thus serve as an ideal tool for politically engaged citizens who want to stir up antagonisms (against elites, or against political rivals and stigmatised 'others') (Breeze; Fernández Vallejo; Badarneh; Meléndez). They also provide suitable channels for populist politicians who want to create the sensation of communicating directly with the electorate (Aiezza; Bhatia/Ross; Rovenţa-Frumuşani/Ştefănel), and for leaders and supporter groups who aspire to projecting and perpetuating charismatic authority (Schmidt). Moreover, as Aditi Bhatia and Andrew

S. Ross illustrate, these social media also lend themselves to the propagation of 'fake news', because the social cybersphere demands very little accountability. A more positive aspect of the same phenomenon is that the social media are also being used for building solidarity and cementing allegiances with like-minded people or fellow sufferers (Nadeem; Breeze; Schmidt; Meléndez). At the same time, we can observe that these same weapons in the hands of mainstream parties can be used to stigmatise competitors, particularly so-called populist rivals, to electoral ends (Ayerbe Linares; Rovenţa-Frumuşani/Ştefănel).

The potential of Twitter and online interactions through fora has tended to distract researchers' attention away from other media that offer equally interesting forms of political communication that operate through a considerable repertoire of modes. Video-based platforms such as YouTube offer affordances that permit the transmission of particularly powerful messages, both exploiting and enhancing traditional political genres. For example, As Giorgos Venizelos and Saqlain Hassan both show, YouTube has become the logical successor of television for campaign spots, and provides a way for classic election events such as speeches to be projected into the living rooms or mobile phones of the entire population, perhaps with a corresponding modification of tone and manner towards the cultivation of private intimacy rather than public impact. Multimodal genres like posters still have a role to play in illustrating parties' demands and joining different claims with a view to generating a hegemonic discourse. At the same time, new platforms such as Instagram are taking on a role as the vehicle for multimodal messages (Venizelos). With the increasing number of digital affordances available, it is likely that these transformations in political communication point the way for many more to come.

In all of this, we should not forget that one essential area in which media affordances converge with populist strategies is that of transmitting emotion. As Ana M. Fernández Vallejo, Maria Cristina Aiezza, Aditi Bhatia and Andrew S. Ross, Nahla Nadeem and Muhammad Badarneh all indicate in their chapters in different ways, social media such as Twitter lend themselves to the expression of negative emotions such as anger, and to the venting of frustration. That means that for politicians like Trump and Salvini, Twitter provides an ideal channel for stirring up negative feelings against antagonists. However, online media are not only about negativity, and social media also offer enormous potential for the sharing of positive feelings, for offering support and creating a collective identity. Positive emotions are sensed when participants share feelings of solidarity and positive identity (Nadeem), as well as when leaders encourage the generation of positive affect through highly personal discourse accompanied by strategic use and subtle redeployment of cultural symbols (Hassan; Schmidt). To this we can add two observations that take us in slightly different directions. First, we should not forget that insulting language and verbal attacks are not just used to incite and enrage others, but that precisely these negative phenomena can also be a means towards creating solidarity with the in-group (Schmidt; Breeze). Second, we should not consider that the use of emotions is the exclusive prerogative of populists: we must not forget that mainstream politicians also indulge in similarly emotive strategies – both positive and negative – in the social media and elsewhere (Ayerbe Linares; Rovenţa-Frumuşani/Ştefănel).

To conclude this section, we would like to add a few words of caution. Media are conducive to populism, but their influence is certainly not one-way or deterministic (Mazzoleni 2014). Moffitt (2018: 34–38) has drawn our attention to the grave dangers inherent in interpreting populists' direct style in social media communication as meaning that they are somehow truly 'in touch' with 'the people'. On the one hand, mediatisation is always a matter of degree, and new strategies and uses evolve in parallel with new technological affordances, giving a temporary advantage to those who are more adept at spotting their potential and fine-tuning their applications (Strömbäck/Esser 2014). As these chapters show, so-called non-populists are quite capable of using populist strategies and techniques when they perceive that it is in their interest to do so. At the same time, we must remember that these media are precisely that: media, that is, channels through which messages are expressed. The messages that are transmitted through them may certainly be adapted to exploit the technological potential of the medium in question, and the limitations of the medium may have an impact on the nature of the message (Gallardo Paúls 2017), but the essential message remains independent from the medium. Political discourses emerge from the wider societal debates about the way that political life can and should be conducted. So while we should not ignore the huge potential of social media to revitalise the public sphere, we should be aware that they provide not only a forum for greater citizen participation and positive solidarity-building, but also a fertile ground for the rise of populist, exclusionary and even authoritarian discourses (KhosraviNik 2017). Precisely for this reason, volumes such as this are needed to keep apace with developments in politics and populism across modes and media in contrasting settings from around the world.

4 Concluding remarks

Finally, the editors would like to acknowledge their gratitude to a number of institutions and people. This volume is one of the outcomes of the DEMOS project (MINECO FFI2015-65252-R, 2016–2018), which focused on the representations of the people in politics across Europe and beyond (see also the volumes Zienkowski/Breeze 2019, and Llamas Saíz (ed.) 2018). We would like to express our indebtedness to the Ministry of Economy and Competitiveness for funding this project and making this book possible. Several of the chapters published here had their origin in papers presented at the conference "In the name of the people", held at the University of Navarra in November 2018, and we would like to thank all the participants at that conference for their feedback and encouragement, particularly Benjamin de Cleen, Majid KhosraviNik, Massimiliano Demata, Andreas Musolff, Monika Kopytowska, Carmen Sancho Guinda, Sam Bennett and Beatriz Gallardo Paúls. Our thanks also go to members of the GradUN project at the University of Navarra, for their support and help with the DEMOS project in general and this volume in particular: our particular gratitude goes first of all to Manuel Casado, and then to our fellow researchers Carmen Llamas, Inés Olza, Jan Zienkowski, Dámaso Izquierdo, Eleonora Esposito, Ricardo Jiménez and Sarali Gintsburg. We also acknowledge our special debt to the Instituto Cultura y Sociedad at the University of Navarra for providing the infrastructure – and the personal and professional support – needed to carry out projects of this kind.

References

Bennett, Sam 2018. New Crises, Old Habits. Online Interdiscursivity and Intertextuality in UK Migration Policy Discourses. *Journal of Immigrant and Refugee Studies* 16/1-2, 140-160.

Breeze, Ruth 2019a. Emotion in Politics: Affective-Discursive Practices in Ukip and Labour. *Discourse & Society* 30/1, 24-43.

Breeze, Ruth 2019b. Positioning the People and Its Enemies: Populism and Nationalism in Afd and Ukip. *Javnost – the Public* 26/1, 89-104.

Chilton, Paul 2004. *Analysing Political Discourse. Theory and Practice*. London: Routledge.

De Cleen, Benjamin / Stavrakakis, Yannis 2017. Distinctions and Articulations: A Discourse-Theoretical Framework for the Study of Populism and Nationalism. *Javnost - The Public* 24/4, 301-425.

Engesser, Sven / Ernst, Nicole / Esser, Frank / Büchel, Florin 2017. Populism and Social Media: How Politicians Spread a Fragmented Ideology. *Information, Communication & Society* 20/8, 1109-1126.

Enli, Gunn 2017. New Media and Politics. *Annals of the International Communication Association* 41/3-4, 220-227.

Esser, Frank / Strömback, Jesper (eds) 2014. *Mediatization of Politics*. Basingstoke: Palgrave Macmillan.

Gallardo Paúls, Beatriz 2017. Pseudopolítica en la red: indicadores discursivos de desideologización en Twitter. *Pragmalingüística* 25, 189-210.

Gerbaudo, Paolo 2018. *The Digital Party: Political Organisation and Online Democracy*. London: Pluto Press.

Gibson, Rachel 2013. Party Change, Social Media and the Rise of 'Citizen-Initiated' Campaigning. *Party Politics* 21/2, 183-197.

Graham, Todd / Jackson, Dan / Broersma, Marcel 2014. New Platform, Old Habits? Candidates' Use of Twitter during the 2010 British and Dutch General Election Campaigns. *New Media & Society* 18/5, 765-783.

Jansen, Fieke 2010. Digital Activism in the Middle East: Mapping Issue Networks in Egypt, Iran, Syria and Tunisia. *Knowledge Management for Development Journal* 6/1, 37-52.

KhosraviNik, Majid 2017. Social Media Critical Discourse Studies (SM-CDS). In Flowerdew, John / Richardson, John (eds) *Routledge Handbook of Critical Discourse Studies*. London: Routledge, 582-596.

Llamas Saíz, Carmen (ed.) 2018. *El análisis del discurso político: géneros y metodologías*. Pamplona: EUNSA.

Macaulay, Marcia 2019. Bernie and the Donald: A Comparison of Left- and Right-Wing Populist Discourse. In Macaulay, Marcia (ed.) *Populist Discourse: International Perspectives*. Cham: Palgrave Macmillan, 165-196.

Mazzoleni, Gianpietro 2014. Mediatization and Political Populism. In Esser, Frank / Strömbäck, Jesper (eds) *Mediatization of Politics*. Basingstoke: Palgrave Macmillan, 42-56.

Moffitt, Benjamin 2016. *The Global Rise of Populism: Performance, Political Style and Representation*. Stanford: Stanford University Press.

Moffitt, Benjamin 2017. Transnational Populism? Representative Claims, Media and the Difficulty of Constructing a Transnational People. *Javnost – The Public* 24/4, 409-425.

Moffitt, Benjamin 2018. Populism 2.0: Social Media and the False Allure of 'Unmediated' Representation. In Fitzi, Gregor / Mackert, Juergen / Turner, Bryan S. (eds) *Populism and the Crisis of Democracy*. London: Routledge, 30-46.

Mudde, Cas 2004. The Populist Zeitgeist. *Government and Opposition* 39/4, 541-563.

Penney, Joel / Dadas, Caroline 2013. (Re)Tweeting in the Service of Protest: Digital Composition and Circulation in the Occupy Wall Street Movement. *New Media & Society* 16/1, 74-90.

Rico, Guillem / Guinjoan, Marc / Anduiza, Eva 2017. The Emotional Underpinnings of Populism: How Anger and Fear Affect Populist Attitudes. *Swiss Political Science Review* 23/4, 444-461.

Stanley, Ben 2008. The Thin Ideology of Populism. *Journal of Political Ideologies* 13/1, 95-110.

Strömbäck, Jesper / Esser, Frank 2014. Mediatization of Politics: Towards a Theoretical Framework. In Esser, Frank / Strömbäck, Jesper (eds) *Mediatization of Politics*. Basingstoke: Palgrave Macmillan, 3-28.

Wagner, Markus 2014. Fear and Anger in Great Britain: Blame Assignment and Emotional Reactions to the Financial Crisis. *Political Behavior* 36: 683-703.

Wodak, Ruth 2015. *The Politics of Fear. What Right-Wing Populist Discourses Mean*. London: Sage.

Zienkowski, Jan / Breeze, Ruth (eds) 2019. *Imagining the Peoples of Europe: Populist Discourse across the Political Spectrum*. Amsterdam: John Benjamins.

Section 1 Politicians across Modes and Media

Aditi Bhatia and Andrew S. Ross

Trumpian tweets and populist politics: A corpus-assisted discourse analytical study

1 Introduction

Donald Trump's election to the highest office in the United States of America in November 2016 signified a major victory for populist politics, highlighting the effectiveness of his rhetoric. Trump has been largely labelled a populist due to his "appeal to 'the people' against both the established structure of power and the dominant ideas and values of the society" (Canovan 1999: 3; cf. Skonieczny 2018), and he has continued to travel in this direction since his inauguration as President. A distinctive feature of Trump's campaign and Presidency has been his prolific use of the social media platform, Twitter; and it can be argued that his adoption of this platform as his primary vehicle of communication with the American people, coupled with his atypical style of political communication, is perhaps the most visceral example of his populist rhetoric. Recently, it has been highlighted that in comparison to traditionally organised and managed political Twitter campaigns, Trump's use is very much spontaneous and non-traditional, and manifests in what Enli (2017: 54) has termed his "amateurish yet authentic style" of "gut-feeling tweeting". Such unusual social media engagement by a politician in power has rarely been encountered, and as such presents an opportunity for investigation to better understand both the popular appeal, and the linguistic and discursive construction, of this new hybrid form of socio-political rhetoric.

2 Political communication via social media and Twitter

Social media has demonstrated an increasing presence within the political domain in recent years, enabling an "explosion of grass-roots participation, allowing individuals to express their opinions more openly and freely" (Gil de Zúñiga *et al.* 2014: 613) towards the broader public. There are also significant benefits for politicians and political organisations to utilising social media, and the micro-blogging application Twitter is among the most highly utilised and effective. The appeal of Twitter to politicians and political campaigns can be narrowed down to its function as "an awareness system that allows for an immediate, fast, and widespread dissemination of information" (Maireder/Ausserhofer 2012: 306) in such a manner that Larsson and Moe (2011: 741) state it makes a significant contribution to the "broadening of public debate". Numerous studies have pointed to the effective way that Twitter enables a quicker and cheaper method of circulating information and gauging public opinion (Conway/Kenski/Wang 2015; Gil de Zúñiga *et al.* 2012; Small 2011). With further regard to political campaigning – which is of course relevant to the current study – Jensen (2017) has outlined three main ways that Twitter provides a higher degree of empowerment in the communication process. Firstly, the dialogic relationship with the public is broadened with a more diverse audience. Second, through the "retweet" function selected posts and comments can be shared and disseminated to an even wider audience. Third, campaign managers have utilised the platform as a way to engage members of the public in helping with campaigns on their own terms and in their own time (i.e. without the need for management or employment). Furthermore, through activities such as 'live-streaming' political events and debates Twitter is able to display the various perspectives and opinions of viewers.

This foregrounding of the utilisation of Twitter in the political sphere is of relevance to the current chapter as it is from this foundation that Trump developed his own signature use, which represented a significant deviation from the way that we have come to understand political Twitter use.

3 The tweeting of Donald Trump

In the last three years a number of studies have been conducted on the influence of social media on politics, and more specifically on the 2016 US elections. Although Twitter was a feature of both the Clinton and Trump campaigns, it has been noted that Trump's engagement with the platform represented a new style of Twitter use due to the unmediated and unorthodox way he utilises it (Ross/Rivers 2018a). In relation to this, Sclafani (2017), for instance, has suggested the need for a closer examination of Trump's rhetoric due to the contradictory effect of his mean tweets and his perceived popularity as an authentic and likeable political leader. One key conclusion Sclafani's study offers is that Trump's exploitation and repetition of specific linguistic expressions and discourse markers has resulted in a sort of linguistic brand. Evidence of this has been highlighted in Ross and Rivers's (2018a) study focusing on Trump's persistent use of accusations of 'fake news' levelled at mainstream media outlets such as *The New York Times* and *The Washington Post* at the same time as being guilty of spreading disinformation himself. Further to this, Trump's communication style has ramifications beyond himself, forcing his "'interpreters'- his press secretary, spin doctors, and other surrogates- who are often called upon to provide metadiscursive commentary on the president's language... [to] come under scrutiny and... subsequently become objects of parody themselves" (Ross/Rivers 2018a: 85) (cf. Chilton 2017). Hall, Goldstein and Ingram (2016: 71) posit that Trump's political success can be attributed in part to "comedic entertainment" arising from his unconventional political style, more specifically "his use of gesture to critique the political system and caricature his opponents" working to create a public spectacle. Further, Ott's (2017: 59) study reveals how Twitter privileges discourse that is "simple, impulsive, and uncivil" and so it remains safe to assume that the parallel between Trump's erratic and raw public discourse and Twitter's logic for to-the-point communication makes Trump a "man of his technological moment".[1] Trump's informal

1 <http://billmoyers.com/story/donald-trump-the-emperor-of-social-media/>

political style, crude political grandstanding and spontaneous use of Twitter can be said to contribute to the erosion between the public and private sphere, offering listeners, voters, fans, and critics alike public displays of private identity. As Lakoff (2005: 174) has argued, the public increasingly insists on

> interpreting public figures as private friends or family members, looking to their public performances for indications about their private selves and personalities... we expect their utterances to sound unrehearsed and off-the-cuff... [e]ven though on one level most of us are aware that what we are seeing is not the off-the-cuff discourse of daily intimacy, many of us persist in reading it as if it were...

We aim to continue this line of research into Trump and Twitter, but unlike previous studies, we hope to combine a quantitative approach to data collection with a qualitative approach to data analysis in order to offer a richer understanding of how Trump employs Twitter to reformulate modern day presidential discourse. More importantly, by drawing on Bhatia's (2015) multi-perspective framework of the Discourse of Illusion, we hope to offer more insight into the discursive process through which Trump constructs socio-political reality for younger supporters, the politically uninitiated, and those simply out of patience with typical 'politician types'.

4 Analytical framework: The discourse of illusion

Creators of discursive illusions (typically powerful groups in society), with access to proliferative media (e.g. mass/social media), often employ particular linguistic resources, in order to persuade audiences of the legitimacy of their conceptualisations of reality. In this way, collective illusions arise when specific conceptualisations of reality (be they of an event or issue) become recognised by a consenting audience as the dominant framework within which understanding of that reality operates. Collective illusions thus become a challenge to disprove because they represent 'the truth' for a particular social group.

The Discourse of Illusion framework argues that subjective versions of reality offered as narratives of truth are persuasive because they touch on core human weaknesses (cf. Vallee 2000), such as fear, prejudice and doubt, resonating with audiences because the truth offered aligns with their pre-existing ideologies. In arguing such, we elevate the earlier notion of dominant framework to dominant representations [or versions] of specific instances of reality, proliferated through various multimodalities, that proceed to constitute the hegemonic discursive framework through which understanding and action is formed. What is of concern here is not necessarily the falsity or subjectivity of the offered versions of reality, but rather the process through which they acquire a status of 'truth'.

To closely explore how discursive illusions are realized, the paper draws on a combined analysis incorporating dimensions of historicity, linguistic and semiotic action, linked to an account of some of the social effects of these actions:

1. Historicity: the recontextualisation of past experiences into present day action is critical to not only gauging how perceptions change over time, but how "how participants enrich the here-and-now of action by connecting it to the past" (Leudar/Nekvapil 2011: 66). To explain this, we borrow from the concept of structured immediacy (ibid), with a focus on what we refer to as "the unconscious or conscious reconceptualization of historical antecedents in an attempt to situate and present specific instances of current reality, often in relation to the future" (Bhatia 2015: 52). Analysis at this level involves looking at temporal references, invocation of past events or sociocultural/political history, and recontextualisation of present occurrences in terms of these past events. In doing so, we discover how situating current activities in history through reference to the past " 'thicken' the descriptions of people and activities – providing them with meanings they would not have had otherwise" (Leudar/Nekvapil 2011: 80).
2. Linguistic and semiotic action: it is through these that we discursively construct our subjective versions of reality, most evident in the use of metaphorical rhetoric, to analyse how the framework borrows elements of critical discourse analysis (CDA), focusing in particular on critical metaphor analysis (Charteris-Black 2004, 2014), which "aims to identify the intentions and ideologies underlying language use" (Charteris-Black 2005: 26). The emphasis here is on the speaker or writer's intention in the creation and diffusion of metaphor by blending both cognitive and pragmatic perspectives. Analysis at this level involves looking at various metaphorical representations which

can "bring to a discourse event traces of previous uses and of previous discourse events" (Candlin/Cameron 2003: 27).

3. Social impact: the language and actions of an individual or group engenders many categories and stereotypes, which can be analysed through Jayyusi's (1984: 183) concept of categorisation that explicates how people "organize their moral positions and commitments round certain category identities". Analysis at this level involves identifying three classes of membership categories: self-organised groups (united by common beliefs, interests and commitments); type categorisation (predicting actions believed to be "embedded in the features of that categorisation" [Jayyusi, 1984: 24]); and individual descriptor designators (assigning labels with both an ascriptive and descriptive function to 'types' of people in those groups). Put together, analysis of categorisation at these levels reveals the ideologies behind the positive or negative representation of self and other groups in the context of complex issues.

5 Data collection

Data collection for the current chapter took place across a period beginning on 29 June, 2016 and ending on August 21, 2017 and focused solely on Trump's tweets. The data is drawn from the final five months of the 2016 Presidential campaign when Trump was the Republican Party's nominated candidate and Clinton was Democratic Party candidate, through to nine months following his election victory. As such, the data adheres to Twitter's 140-character limit that was in place at the time, and not the current 280-character limit. To collect the data, we utilised Anthony and Hardaker's (2017) software application 'FireAnt', a Twitter data collection and analysis tool which enables the collection of up to a maximum of 3,000 tweets from the tweet history of any particular user at one time. It is possible to perform multiple operations with different date ranges to develop a larger corpus of tweets, but at the time of our data collection we performed one single operation which yielded the maximum 3,000 original tweets (i.e. excluding retweets), which in turn established a research corpus of 55,512 words.

When conducting a corpus analysis, traditionally the most common type of analysis is a keyword analysis, which involves a research corpus (i.e. the dataset of Trump's tweets) being compared to a much larger reference corpus that reflects language use in general (Branum/Charteris-Black 2015) – an example of such a corpus would be the British National Corpus. In the current study, however, a more acute methodology known as a comparative keyword analysis is used, where the research corpus is compared to a more specific "discourse reference corpus" in order to observe how language is used within similar contexts. The discourse reference corpus used in the study is known as the Political Discourse Reference Corpus (PTDC), developed by Ross and Rivers (2018b) for use in a previous study of Trump's rhetoric on Twitter (Ross/Rivers 2018a), but that could be applied to any corpus-based study of political Twitter use. The PTDC is comprised of 205,303 original tweets made by current US politicians with a total of 4,659,381 words. Details of the corpora can be seen in Tab. 1.

Upon completion of the data collection, the research corpus was loaded into AntConc (Anthony 2016), another corpus analysis software application, which enabled us to carry out the comparative keyword analysis. The analysis generated a keyword list, with keywords being those that occur "with unusual frequency in a given text" (Scott 1997: 236) when compared to a reference corpus such as the PTDC. Ross and Rivers (2018a: 4) point out that "this does not necessarily equate to high frequency – the emphasis is on unusual frequency". For instance, the most frequently occurring word may be a function word such as 'the', which would not represent unusual frequency and thus would not rank highly in the results of the analysis. As a result of this, all function words were removed from the results, and content words were analysed for their rhetorical function and use. In keyword lists, the results are typically presented in order of their "keyness", which is a statistic determined by the use of a chi-square test conducted automatically

Tab. 1: Details of the research corpus and discourse reference corpus (PTDC).

Corpus	Content	Total Tweets	Total Words
Research	Trump tweets	3,000	55,512
Discourse reference (PTDC)	Original tweets from US politicians	205,303	4,659,381

by the software. According to Branum and Charteris-Black (2015), this indicates any statistically significant frequency differences (i.e. unusualness) between the corpora. The top 25 results from the comparative keyword analysis are presented in Tab. 2.

Tab. 2: Results of the comparative keyword analysis.

Rank	Frequency	Keyness	Keyword
1	153	1220.131	crooked
2	307	1142.600	hillary
3	224	901.115	clinton
4	133	766.931	maga
5	108	724.488	fake
6	83	705.502	americafirst
7	88	698.220	draintheswamp
8	61	518.501	imwithyou
9	142	486.628	media
10	64	467.638	makeamericagreatagain
11	52	442.001	bigleaguetruth
12	347	436.430	thank
13	145	309.960	again
14	81	308.375	cnn
15	43	289.634	dishonest
16	93	282.377	bad
17	33	280.501	crookedhillary
18	38	274.161	trumppence
19	196	270.117	trump
20	32	251.611	melania
21	181	232.563	america
22	46	232.433	totally
23	46	222.795	tickets
24	459	213.440	great
25	62	210.912	pence

Note: Software used calculates keyness by chi square

Another useful tool for our analysis was the concordance tool, which presents data within a keyword in context (KWIC) display in order to highlight the word within its original context. Being able to observe the surrounding text of each word was critical to our analysis and meant we were not relying on frequency alone. Fig. 1 shows an example of the KWIC display for the keyword "crooked".

Once we had determined the keyword list, we were able to use the results as "the basis of a qualitative investigation" (Charteris-Black 2014: 541) of the tweets, analysing them manually to demystify the creation of discursive illusions through them. The results indicated that among the top ten most frequently used terms were the clusters "Crooked Hillary Clinton" and "Fake Media/News" along with one of the most commonly used hashtags associated with Trump's campaign – "#draintheswamp". Thus, due to their unusually high degree of frequency in Trump's rhetoric in comparison to typical political rhetoric on Twitter, we focused our analysis on these three areas in the following sections.

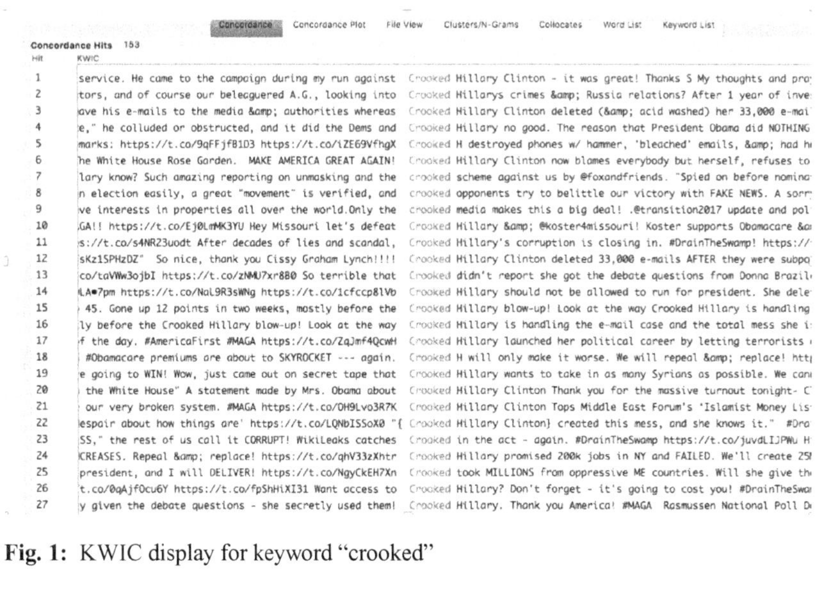

Fig. 1: KWIC display for keyword "crooked"

6 Analysis and discussion

Trump's election campaign, and agenda since he was elected to office, ran on several key issues, including immigration laws, a border wall, and free trade. Based on the results of the comparative keyword analysis, we focus here on three such issues that have propped up his agenda since he entered American politics, including Hillary's tenure as Secretary of State and Trump's overall evaluation of her character (Crooked Hillary), unfair lobbying and corruption in the federal government (#draintheswamp), as well as negative coverage and misinformation in the press (Fake News or Fake Media).

6.1 Crooked Hillary

During a speech in April 2016, Trump emphatically labelled his opponent Hillary Clinton as 'crooked' in order to bolster general perceptions of Clinton's untrustworthiness. Trump's rhetorical strategies of branding his opponents proved effective in creating a political narrative of heroes and villains. His enemies were 'sloppy', 'crooked', 'little', 'crazy'. etc.[2] In labelling his enemies, Trump demonstrated his own default goodness: he was not corrupt or unstable. His given monikers often served the purpose of enforcing existing perceptions of the individuals concerned or creating new representations of them. To demonstrate, let us consider the tweets below that recontextualise Hillary Clinton's present credibility and future actions in terms of her history.

> TWEET 1 Crooked H destroyed phones w/ hammer, 'bleached' emails; had husband meet w/AG days before she was cleared- & they talk about obstruction? (15/6/2017)
>
> TWEET 2 So terrible that Crooked didn't report she got the debate questions from Donna Brazile, if that were me it would have been front page news! (1/11/2016)

---

2 <https://www.theguardian.com/us-news/shortcuts/2018/apr/17/presidents-nicknames-slimeball-comey-former-fbi-director>

TWEET 3 Wow, just came out on secret tape that Crooked Hillary wants to take in as many Syrians as possible. We cannot let this happen – (24/10/2016)

TWEET 4 Did Crooked Hillary help disgusting (check out sex tape and past) Alicia M become a U.S. citizen so she could use her in the debate? (1/10/2016)

In the tweets, we see Trump draw on Clinton's past ('destroyed phones', 'bleached emails') to justify assumptions about her questionable actions in the present ('got the debate questions', 'wants to take in as many Syrians as possible', 'help Alicia M become a citizen'). In doing so, he not only portrays her as unscrupulous but, also, simplifies more complex political issues, such as an open-doors immigration policy, women's rights, and the Syrian civil war, reconceptualising them within a simplistic narrative that more keenly fits the actions of the main protagonists and antagonists of his illusory story.

For example, the first tweet comments on the following issues: firstly, Hillary's use of a personal email account for communication about official security matters during her tenure as Secretary of State (2009–2013) causing much debate about whether she had violated federal laws or protocols; secondly, the consequent investigation into her responses during the 2012 Benghazi attacks; and thirdly, a chance encounter between Obama's Attorney General and Bill Clinton on an airport tarmac (June, 2016) while the former was investigating the Benghazi response. All three issues, complex and not entirely interconnected, are efficiently condensed into the metaphors 'bleached emails' and 'destroyed phones', ending with the summation that questions the Clinton's overall credibility. Trump adopts a fairly reductionist cause and effect template to reconceptualise socio-political situations, resulting in, for laymen at least, a more palatable understanding of issues that otherwise become muddied and convoluted by partisan reporting. For example, in Tweet 3, Trump references a 'secret tape' filmed by Project Veritas in conversation with a Clinton aide, whose comments on Islamophobia were taken out of context. Although, there is no official policy referenced in the tape, and Clinton is herself not present on it, by invoking the metaphor of 'Crooked Hillary' in conjunction with amplifiers like 'wow' and adjectives like 'secret', Trump creates a discursive illusion about her agenda to flood the US with ISIS-led refugees, by effect portraying himself as the populist leader who, aligned with the cause of the vulnerable population through the uniting pronoun 'we', will not 'let this happen'.

Within these tweets, the misnomers become both a metaphor for and a categorisation of the characters involved. For example, the metaphor 'Crooked Hillary' soon became a negative representation of Clinton, a basis for doubting her decisions and actions, and also a means of aligning her with the corrupt elite, including 'Donna Brazile'. In identifying her as crooked, Trump is able to attribute to her actions typical of such types of people ('destroyed', 'bleached', 'before being cleared', 'didn't report', 'secret tape is out', 'use her in debate'). These actions work together to invoke images of a suspicious, untrustworthy, immoral candidate.

The actions mentioned might pertain to different issues, and many are possibly taken out of context, but within Twitter's tight character count, and presented with very colloquial summations of judgement ('so terrible', 'cannot let this happen', 'wow', 'they talk about obstruction?') they serve the purpose of linking events, issues, characters and actions. Inevitably, social media becomes the space in which political performance is produced and played out. In Kolehmainen's (2017: 1) words, elections are really just "affairs of performance and narrative… they involve selling a story to the voting audience… a story of the country, the candidate, and of the policies, issues, and ideologies they represent".

6.2 Fake news

The 2016 elections also birthed the 'fake news' effect. Labelled 2017's word of the year,[3] and deemed one of the "greatest threats to democracy, free debate and the Western order" (ibid.), the debate about fake news circulated in the news cycles more than actual news. Essentially understood as news that deliberately spreads disinformation, the hashtag became a favourite tool of Trump's in countering negative press about

3 <https://www.telegraph.co.uk/technology/0/fake-news-exactly-has-really-had-influence/>

himself. Consider the following tweets within which Trump employs the strategy of enemification (labelling opponents hyperbolically as enemies) to discredit media outlets that negatively represent him.

TWEET 5 Only the Fake News Media and Trump enemies want me to stop using Social Media (110 million people). Only way for me to get the truth out! (1/8/2017)

TWEET 6 With all of its phony unnamed sources & highly slanted & even fraudulent reporting, #Fake News is DISTORTING DEMOCRACY in our country! (16/7/2017)

TWEET 7 The Fake News Media has never been so wrong or so dirty. Purposely incorrect stories and phony sources to meet their agenda of hate. Sad! (13/6/2017)

TWEET 8 The fake news media is going crazy with their conspiracy theories and blind hatred. @MSNBC & @CNN are unwatchable. @foxandfriends is great! (15/2/2017)

In identifying fake news media not only in general terms as his 'enemies' but more specifically in the forms of CNN and MSNBC, Trump proceeds to type categorise them ("predicting actions" believed to be "embedded in the features of that categorisation" [Jayyusi 1984: 24]). Using capitals and exclamation marks to mimic a virtual shout, he emphatically attributes to CNN and MSNBC negative actions such as 'distorting democracy', 'fraudulent reporting', spreading 'phony stories', 'conspiracy theories and blind hatred'. Based on these actions, traditional media like CNN, are represented to be inherently agenda-driven, 'wrong' and 'dirty', reinforcing common popular dislike against propaganda-driven reporting.

As previously mentioned, exaggeration, recontextualisation, and supposed spontaneity, performed on Twitter and other social media sites, have given rise to a sort of 'post-truth era'[4] in which societies no longer share a common "cohesive sense of a shared reality" but, instead, pick and choose from the buffet of real and falsified facts provided by mainstream and alternative sources of information, to boost their favoured versions of reality (Kolehmainen 2017: 3). Overwhelmed with

4 <https://www.nytimes.com/2016/08/24/opinion/campaign-stops/the-age-of-post-truth-politics.html>

different 'truths', and contradictory facts, social media becomes then "a mirror whose image is an imagined and fabricated one, a conglomerate of stories of how and what we fantasize" (Hotz-Davies/Kirchhofer/Leppänen 2009: xii). It is this truth which lends the highly ironic tone to Trump employing words and phrases that fall into the semantic category of falsehood: 'phony', 'highly slanted', 'fraudulent', 'distorting', 'incorrect', 'blind'. In fact, there has been much debate about the facticity of his own narrative. Thus, typical of discursive illusions, we find the categorisation of both Donald Trump and CNN, MSNBC reversed when the latter claim:

> President Donald Trump is consistent about almost nothing. Which is what makes his long-running war on truth and facts all the more remarkable. The President's lack of concern for established facts is long and well-documented... Trump has said 8,718 false or misleading things in his first 759 days in office. That's, roughly, 11.5 lies or misleading statements a day. Every day. Of late, Trump has expanded his war on truth to those who do the work of fact-checking him.[5]
>
> President Donald Trump put his long-promised border wall at the center of the government funding debate on Tuesday, repeating the frequently fact-checked falsehood that it's already under construction no fewer than eight times while making a host of questionable new assertions... Trump's claims, made on Twitter and during a testy public spat with Democratic leaders at the White House... The White House did not respond to a request for more clarity[6]

We see here journalists from both news outlets accuse Trump of the same disregard for the truth that he accuses them of, and while he claims in tweet 5 that Twitter is the only way for him to 'get the truth out', in the extracts above CNN and MSNBC both claim it is in fact their news medium that is 'fact-checking' and seeking 'more clarity' amidst Trump's 'war on truth'. But, perhaps, because of the stereotypical expectations people have from partisan news media, information circulating on Twitter not only reaches listeners faster but also appears more authentic. In other words, people's expectations of Twitter contrast with their expectations concerning traditional media, namely that

---

5 <https://edition.cnn.com/2019/02/19/politics/donald-trump-fact-checking/index.html>

6 <https://www.nbcnews.com/politics/politics-news/fact-check-trump-constructs-false-misleading-claims-about-his-border-n946651>

these will act as gatekeepers in picking and choosing which aspects of the on-going political drama to report on, how to interpret it, and how the interactants involved should be evaluated. In this vein, Jungherr (2014: 241) argues that traditional media covers "items that allow the personalization of politics, the illustration, staging, and dramatization of political contest (for example through horserace coverage), and negativity". By contrast, Twitter is perceived as a space for "self-expression and public interactions between users… [becoming] a channel for getting political information and interacting with political elites, as well as a platform for expressing political convictions as well as the exchange about political topics" (2014: 242). By its very nature, then, Twitter encourages spontaneity and authenticity, while traditional media demonstrates strategy and calculation. It is, therefore, easy to understand why the word on Twitter may come across as more genuine and credible.

6.3 Drain the swamp

The part of the Make America Great Again (MAGA) narrative that most convincingly portrayed Trump as a populist hero was #draintheswamp. Echoing the cries of Ronald Regan from the 1980s, the swamp, of course then a literal reference to the bog-like state of Pennsylvania Avenue,[7] is now a metaphorical reference to Washington DC and its corrupt elite. The following tweets illustrate part of the discursive illusion that Trump and his campaign created about their being the only solution to ridding the Capitol of its elite sell-outs who work against the interest of the American people.

TWEET 9 'State works hard, and illegally, for Clinton' #DrainTheSwamp (19/10/2016)

TWEET 10 @HillaryClinton loves to lie. America has had enough of the CLINTON'S! It is time to #DrainTheSwamp! (20/10/2016)

TWEET 11 Crooked @HillaryClinton's foundation is a CRIMINAL ENTERPRISE. Time to #DrainTheSwamp! (20/10/2016)

7 <https://www.newyorker.com/news/news-desk/draining-the-swamp>

TWEET 12 I WILL DEFEAT ISIS. THEY HAVE BEEN AROUND TOO LONG! What has our leadership been doing? #DrainTheSwamp (20/10/2016)

In these tweets, we see Trump's version of reality, in which he identifies the self-organised group of corrupt Washington elites, specifically Hillary Clinton and the State department, attributing to them the quality of lawlessness ('illegally', 'lie', 'criminal'). In doing so, Trump by default fills the opposite role of the lawless vs lawful category-pairing, representing himself as law abiding, and by implication, not corrupt. Use of the strong verb 'love' in tweet 10 depicts Clinton as a habitual liar, denying her actions any justification, by implying she has a history of deception, and will continue to do so, unless she is stopped. Repetition of 'it is time to' in tweets 10 and 11 discursively constructs the 2016 elections into a historic illusionary moment, the results of which have the potential to lead to a "dramatic crisis of existing practices" (Sewell 1996: 843). In other words, repetition of the phrase emphasises the importance of making the right decision in the elections, the key moment, for the discontinuity in routine practice, to the extent that it becomes history-making. Manipulation and negotiation of Clinton's past to predict the future, and justify present accusations and assumptions (both in the hashtags #CrookedHillary and #draintheswamp) in this way demonstrates the manner in which the meaning of socio-political issues is creatively rendered through ideologically solid connections between the past and present (in this case through the historical conditioning of the present to predict the future) (Leudar/Nekvapil 2011; cf. Bhatia 2015).

Again, Trump recontextualises otherwise complex issues like the Syrian civil war, the intricate nature of Jihad and terrorism including ISIS, and the philanthropic efforts of the Clinton Foundation, into a reductionist and consolidated narrative. The State department is represented as working for the Clintons, instead of the government elected by the people, and too involved in criminal wrong-doing to prevent ISIS from threatening the world in general, but American lives more specifically. Use of capital letters and exclamatory questions emphasises the key parts of the narrative, including 'I WILL DEFEAT ISIS', which with its lack of hedge, writes Trump into the MAGA narrative with the "swagger any cowboy of the Old West would recognize. He refuses to apologize for being a man… he doesn't play by the rules of the other elites- he blazes his own trail".[8]

Nonetheless, typical of the discourse of illusion, truth is often a contested entity, generating a multitude of representations. Media commentators accused Trump of the same elite pandering that he accused Hillary Clinton of during, and since, the 2016 elections:

> Donald Trump promised to "drain the swamp" while running for office. Voters gave him the opportunity to follow through when they propelled him to the White House. Instead, he surrounded himself with people who saw his victory as an opportunity to enrich themselves by selling the promise of access or influence… Trump voters who wanted to rid Washington of sellouts should be most upset, but no one wants to admit that the person they voted for was misrepresenting his intentions.[9]

In the preceding extract, Trump is accused of squandering the historic opportunity he fought for (election win) by bolstering the same corrupt practices that he offered himself as a cure to. Use of phrases and words that connote falsification of the truth ('instead he surrounded himself with', 'enrich themselves by selling', 'misrepresenting his intentions') crack the hero myth, portraying Trump as just as susceptible to corruption and manipulation by the crooked elite as Clinton.

7 Conclusion

This chapter made an attempt to shed light on how Trump's election run for and eventual victory in attaining the most powerful office in the world ushered in a new age of social media-enabled populism. Claiming his twitter is not presidential,[10] Trump used this social media platform

8 <https://www.washingtontimes.com/news/2016/jun/28/donald-trump-and-resurrection-american-cowboy/>

9 <https://www.theatlantic.com/ideas/archive/2018/05/trumps-washington/560105/>

10 <https://www.independent.co.uk/news/world/americas/us-politics/the-twitter-president-how-potus-changed-social-media-and-the-presidency-a8164161.html>

to share his narrative about what was wrong with the world, and how he could fix it, "without the filter of a traditional media he claims not to trust. The White House was obliged to clarify that his tweets also represent presidential statements, and should carry the same imprimatur as a comment issued by his press office" (ibid). To his supporters, use of an informal platform without PR censorship implied authenticity and sincerity; the colloquial language and non-traditional use of punctuation, a translation of otherwise stiff, evasive political discourse; and lack of regard for political etiquette and facts simply meant he was cutting straight to the point. As Hall, Goldstein and Ingram (2016: 71) have posited, the "exaggerated depictions of the sociopolitical world that Trump crafts with his hands to oppose political correctness and disarm adversaries accrue visual capital in a mediatized twenty-first-century politics that is celebrity driven".

The framework employed enabled us to more closely analyse, not the truthfulness of his statements, but rather the process through which he crafted a unique story around the toils and troubles of Washington DC, and the consequent effect on the American people. The manipulation of history to condition the present, and the use of metaphors to both categorise opponents and conceptualise events, worked to create a convincing hero narrative. In representing himself as the saviour of the American people, as the solution to the country's woes, Trump, by default, assigned himself as the positive counterpart in the most common category-pairs he uses to position himself and his opponents: lawful vs. lawless; honest vs. corrupt; factual vs. deceptive. Trump used his tweets as a tactical device to frame events, divert attention from negative publicity, or attack an opponent, and in doing so remaining in 'constant control of the news cycle'[11].

Use of the Discourse of Illusion framework assisted by corpus methods proved an especially apt approach to the plethora of data under investigation, dealing as it does with the growth and change of perceptions over time, and consequently the usage of narrative constructs, the meanings of which are dynamic and subject to change in terms of their social contexts. What the Discourse of Illusion brings to light is the struggle between competing narratives in society to conceive and

11 <https://twitter.com/GeorgeLakoff>

generate a dominant representation of events that will become associated with the understanding of certain socio-political issues, in an effort to maintain moral, social, or political superiority.

References

Anthony, Laurence 2016. AntConc (Version 3.4.4) [Computer software]. Tokyo, Japan: Waseda University. Available at <http://laurenceanthony.net>

Anthony, Laurence / Hardaker, Claire 2017. *FireAnt* (Version 1.1.4) [Computer software]. Tokyo, Japan: Waseda University. Available at <http://www.laurenceanthony.net>

Bhatia, Aditi 2015. *Discursive Illusions in Public Discourse: Theory and Practice*. London, New York: Routledge.

Branum, Jens / Charteris-Black, Jonathan 2015. The Edward Snowden Affair: A Corpus Study of the British Press. *Discourse & Communication* 9/2, 199-220.

Candlin, Christopher / Cameron, Lynne 2003. *Metaphor in Educational Discourse*. Australia, Australia/Oceania, London : Continuum.

Canovan, Margaret 1999. Trust the People! Populism and the Two Faces of Democracy. *Political Studies* 47/1, 2-16.

Charteris-Black, Jonathan 2004. *Corpus Approaches to Critical Metaphor Analysis*. Berlín: Springer.

Charteris-Black, Jonathan 2005. *Politicians and Rhetoric. The Persuasive Power of Metaphor*. Basingstoke: Palgrave Macmillan.

Charteris-Black, Jonathan 2014. Political Style: A Study of David Cameron. In Stockwell, Peter / Whiteley, Sara (eds) *The Handbook of Stylistics*. Oxon: Routledge, 536-557.

Chilton, Paul 2017. Toward a Neuro-Cognitive Model of Socio-Political Discourse, and an Application to the Populist Discourse of Donald Trump. *Langage et société* 2, 237-249.

Conway, Bethany A. / Kenski, Kate / Wang, Di 2015. The Rise of Twitter in the Political Campaign: Searching for Intermedia Agenda-Setting

Effects in the Presidential Primary. *Journal of Computer-Mediated Communication* 20, 363-380.

Enli, Gunn 2017. Twitter as Arena for the Authentic Outsider: Exploring the Social Media Campaigns of Trump and Clinton in the 2016 Us Presidential Election. *European Journal of Communication* 32/1, 50-61.

Gil de Zúñiga, Homero / Jung, Nakwong / Valenzuela, Sebastián 2012. Social Media Use for News and Individuals' Social Capital, Civic Engagement and Political Participation. *Journal of Computer-Mediated Communication* 17/3, 319-336.

Gil de Zúñiga, Homero / Molyneaux, Logan / Zheng, Pei 2014. Social Media, Political Expression, and Political Participation: Panel Analysis of Flagged and Concurrent Relationships. *Journal of Communication* 64, 614-634.

Hall, Kira / Goldstein, Donna M. / Ingram, Matthew B. 2016. The Hands of Donald Trump: Entertainment, Gesture, Spectacle. *HAU: Journal of Ethnographic Theory* 6/2, 71-100.

Hotz-Davies, Ingrid / Kirchhofer, Anton / Leppänen, Sirpa. 2009. Introduction. In Hotz-Davies, Ingrid *et al.* (eds) *Internet Fictions*. Newcastle: Cambridge Scholars Publishing, xii.

Jayyusi, Lena 1984/2014. *Categorization and the Moral Order (Routledge Revivals)*. London: Routledge.

Kolehmainen, Pekka 2017. Social Media Narratives as Political Fan Fiction in the 2016 Us Presidential Election. *European Journal of American Studies* 12/2, 1-19.

Jensen, Michael J. 2017. Social Media and Political Campaigning: Changing Terms of Engagement? *The International Journal of Press/Politics* 22, 23-42.

Jungherr, Andreas 2014. The Logic of Political Coverage on Twitter: Temporal Dynamics and Content. *Journal of Communication* 64/2, 239-259.

Lakoff, Robin T. 2005. The Politics of Nice. *Journal of Politeness Research* 1/2, 173-191.

Larsson, Anders O. / Moe, Hallvard 2011. Studying Political Microblogging: Twitter Users in the 2010 Swedish Election Campaign. *New Media & Society* 14, 729-747.

Leudar, Ivan / Nekvapil, Jiří 2011. Practical Historians and Adversaries: 9/11 Revisited. *Discourse & Society* 22/1, 66-85.

Maireder, Axel / Ausserhofer, Julian 2012. Political Discourses on Twitter: Networking Topics, Objects and People. In Weller, Katrin *et al.* (eds), *Twitter and Society*. New York: Peter Lang, 305-318.

Ott, Brian L. 2017. The Age of Twitter: Donald J. Trump and the Politics of Debasement. *Critical Studies in Media Communication* 34/1, 59-68.

Ross, Andrew S. / Rivers, Damian J. 2018a. Discursive Deflection: Accusation of "Fake News" and the Spread of Mis- and Disinformation in the Tweets of President Trump. *Social Media + Society*. <https://doi.org/10.1177/2056305118776010>

Ross, Andrew S. / Rivers, Damian J. 2018b. *Political Twitter Discourse Corpus (PTDC)*. <https://www.damianrivers.com/ptdc/>

Sclafani, Jennifer 2017. *Talking Donald Trump: A Sociolinguistic Study of Style, Metadiscourse, and Political Identity*. New York: Routledge.

Scott, Mike 1997. PC Analysis of Key Words – and Key Key Words. *System* 25, 233-245.

Sewell, William H. 1996. Historical Events as Transformations of Structures: Inventing Revolution at the Bastille. *Theory and Society* 25, 841-881.

Skonieczny, Amy 2018. Emotions and Political Narratives: Populism, Trump and Trade. *Politics and Governance* 6/4, 62-72.

Small, Tamara 2011. What the Hashtag? A Content Analysis of Canadian Politics on Twitter. *Information, Communication & Society* 14, 872-895.

Vallee, Virginia 2000. The Roots of Sound Rational Thinking. Available at <http://www.plusroot.com>

Giorgos Venizelos

Populism and the digital media: A necessarily symbiotic relationship? Insights from the case of Syriza

1 Introduction

An avalanche of literature suggests that there is an intimate interaction between populism and the digital media[1]. This relationship has been well-studied from a variety of perspectives and disciplines, including political communication, media and culture studies, and political party research (see Blumler/Gurevitch 1995; Boomgaarden/Vliegenthart 2009; Ellinas 2010; Esser/Strömbäck 2014; Tronconi 2015; de Vreese *et al.* 2018). In brief, this abundant literature perceives the successful diffusion of populist discourse as something that is closely related to the processes of political mediatisation. In the most recent years, respective research moved from the point of studying digital media as an extraneous tool in political practices to the recognition of the key role that technological means of communication play in the rise and dominance of populist actors. On the supply side of political discourse, 'populist parties are said to be more dependent on media and communication because they have weaker party organisation compared to the old, traditional parties' (Aalberg *et al.* 2017: 6–7). On the demand side, it seems that the more media outlets adopt a market logic the more they are attracted by dramatic and alarmist discourses to host in their headlines (Mazzoleni/Stewart/Horsfield 2003). As Mazzoleni (2003: 3) puts it in a chapter named 'The media and the growth of neo-populism in contemporary democracies', "a full understanding of the populist

1 The author wishes to thank Marco Deseriis for his useful comments.

phenomenon cannot be achieved without studying mass communication perspectives and media-related dynamics, especially not without using a comparative approach."

This 'shift' in academic research, from the media as an external to the media as an integral part of populism, reflects the extent to which the mediatisation of politics is embedded in everyday socio-political practices. Relevant transformations in political party structures and organisation has even resulted in framing them as 'digital' or techno-political parties (Gerbaudo 2019; Deseriis 2017a, 2017b). However, while the use of digital media is no longer regarded as a foreign body to politics, this, I argue, is not a feature of populism alone.

This chapter has a motivation that is conceptual in nature and aims to disentangle, prior to any potential entanglement, the objects of 'populism' and 'digital politics'. In its vast majority, political communication research and especially the strain that originates from Europe, views negatively the mediatised diffusion of populist messages as it is perceived to downplay the quality of democracy (see Blumler/Gurevitch 1995; Mutz/Reeves 2005; Mazzoleni 2014). This point of view, which one could investigate through the lenses of what an emerging strain in the literature calls antipopulism (Ostiguy 2017; Stavrakakis/Katsambekis 2018), comes as no surprise. Until very recently, in Europe at least, 'populism' received an axiomatically pejorative framing which loaded the concept with a highly charged normative content. The chapter enquires into the relationship between the digital media and populism, which is (pre)supposed to be symbiotic. It argues that the hegemonically pejorative and normatively loaded understanding of populism, interwoven with a conventionally sceptical framing of the digital media as untrustworthy, scandalous, 'fake-y' forms of communication, has two effects. It not only reinforces further an allegedly strong link between the two but also assumes a type of relationship that is necessarily negative. While there is an evidently a strong interaction between populism and the digital media, it is critical to wonder whether all populists use and capitalise upon technological advancements on the one hand, and whether all users of respective decision-making and information-spreading media are indeed populist on the other hand. Arguably, the interaction between the two is not a consequence of any essential 'nature' in populism;

rather, technological advancements are available to all political actors, amongst them populists too.

To scrutinise this suggested normative affinity, the chapter draws on the case of the left-wing populist party of Syriza (2012–2019) and brings it into a comparative perspective. It shows that the party fits neither in a framework of an exclusionary populism nor in the family of techno-populist parties. While Syriza shares with other parties the populist structure in its discourse, its organisational structure does not share the digital philosophy behind many other populist parties. Rather, although Syriza indeed communicates its message through certain standard forms of digital media, like any actor, it primarily organises its activities in traditional arenas and through conventional methods.

The chapter begins with a theorisation of the digital media while it also brings contemporary empirical examples into comparative perspective. It draws on the 2011 movement mobilisations in the Arab world, Europe and the US, the so-called digital or techno-populist parties that emerged out of them, as well as more conventional political actors in order to make sense of the multiplicity of technologies of communication, and their array of methods of use.

Enquiring through the Essex School's research programme, the chapter builds a bridge between discourse theory in populism research and anti-essentialist strains in communication studies. It defines populism through the discourse-theoretical perspective as an object of study that contains its own formal criteria for classification, and expands the applicability of the discursive approach into the realm of visuality and aesthetics in order to relate further with the theme of this book. The second section tests empirically the abovementioned theoretical expectations. It begins by outlining the organisational transformations and dynamics of Syriza across time in order to examine the extents to which Syriza is comparatively similar to its digital counterparties. It considers campaigning material such as posters, and campaigning spots that were communicated in the period between 2012 and 2015 when Syriza was in the opposition, as well as the digital accounts such as Facebook, Twitter and Instagram of the (now) Prime Minister Alexis Tsipras. The chapter applies a discourse-analytical methodology to elaborate on the populist nature of Syriza as well as visual analysis in the respective resources.

2 Digital politics in comparative perspective

While the suggested relationship between the digital media and populism is often presented as symbiotic, it should be perceived as more complex. Before any theoretical or empirical association between the two is established, a conceptual clarification and disentanglement must take place. This section begins by defining the digital media and looks at a variety of instances applying distinct forms of techno-politics.

2.1 The digital media

Drawing on Enli's (2017: 220) historically-relative approach on the 'new media' one could define this age's equivalent, the digital media, as:

> communication technologies that enable or facilitate user-to-user interactivity and interactivity between users and information, and the main point in the definition is that the one-to-many model of traditional mass communication is challenged by the possibility of many-to-many communication via the Internet.

These are "those digital media that are interactive, incorporate two-way communication and involve some form of computing [...] it is very easily processed, stored, transformed, retrieved, hyperlinked and, perhaps most radical of all, easily searched for and accessed" (Logan 2016: 4). These broad definitions suggest that the concept of digital media should not be restricted to a medium-centric conceptualisation as it cannot be defined by the use of one single platform. Rather, digital media could also be perceived as a form of relationship that is decentralised (as it does not occur from a single locus) and heterogeneous (it is diffused from multifaceted types of media). Inductively, as empirical investigations show, digital media include social media such as Twitter, Facebook and Instagram; messaging apps such as WhatsApp and Telegram; and online platforms used as organising as well as decision-making tools which are often developed on (and often put forward values of) Free and Open Source networks (Juris 2012; Gerbaudo 2012, 2017, 2018; Wolfson 2014; Deseriis 2017a). Numerous examples indicate that the use of contemporary political practices is 'entrenched in the use of information and communication technologies' (Mattoni/Ceccobelli 2018: 2). Crucially however, the nature of the actor, the goals pursued and the methods used vary.

To begin with party-political discourse, the literature suggests that the media is used to increase interactivity between the receivers (the 'audience', 'the citizens', or the 'voters') and the sender (the politician or 'political entrepreneur') (Heiss/Schmuck/Matthes 2018). It has to be stressed right from the beginning that this affinity between politics and technology is nothing new in political practices. Media-mogul Silvio Berlusconi entered the Italian political scene spectacularly in 1994; he introduced himself in a rather unusual way with respect to how politics was once perceived in Italy and gathered media attention on his persona, and most often on his non-political life (Pellizzetti/Colombo 2009). Gradually, political mediatisation became normalised. Podemos' leader Pablo Iglesias for example, presents his own 'counter hegemonic television project' - *La Tuerka* - which is broadcast via its YouTube channel (Rendueles/Sola 2018: 36). The most current and widely spoken-about example that illustrates the affinity between media and populism is indeed that of the US president Donald Trump. His excessive use of Twitter, as well as simplified method of presenting governmental 'updates' on his presidential channels, fit well into the picture of communicating politics via the internet (Boczkowski/Papacharissi 2018). Yet, while Trump *stereotypically* impersonates 'the ideal-type' of a technologically-driven populist, one has to trace this trend in American politics back to the current president's predecessor. Barack Obama introduced personalised political communication and the commodification of digital media as tools in his 2008 and 2012 campaigns (see Bimber 2014). In essence, Obama, who is not conventionally described as a populist leader, made a breakthrough towards the digital political campaigning era by initiating what later would be called a 'super-brand' (Klein 2018) or 'hyperleader' (Gerbaudo 2018).

Digital media are not available to politicians alone. In the last decade, they became a key organising and decision-making tool for the social movements across the globe. The Arab Spring and the examples of the Tahrir Square protests in Egypt and the Jasmine revolution in Tunisia (Lotan *et al.* 2011), as well as the repertoire of protests that followed these in Europe and the US, such as the Kitchenware Revolution in Iceland, the Indignados in Spain (Calzada 2017) and the Occupy Movement, respectively (Kavada 2015), exemplify a new era that is highly characterised by the introduction of social media and web-platforms in social movement practices. As Gerbaudo (2017: 135) shows, activists in the 2011 protest cycles were "heavily influenced by 'internet freedom' movements, and the open-source software movement", while at the same time "they collaborated with hacker groups (such as Anonymous) that supported the protest wave with a number of connected 'ops', from OpTunisia and OpEgypt to direct declarations of support for Occupy."

Techno-politics, as Deseriis (2017a: 442) labels it, pursues online political deliberation and decision making processes while it relies on the development of Free and Open Source Software. According to Deseriis there are two variants within this political culture. The first, the leaderless-technocratic variant "attribute[s] to the network itself the task of producing a shared political line". The second variant, the leaderist-*populist* one, "endows political leaders with the task of synthesizing different and conflicting positions that may emerge from the network" (2017a: 442).

While the techno-political character does not automatically translate into populism, a plethora of these movements presented characteristics that did resemble populism: they pursued a mass - as opposed to class-specific - political vision which was pursued via targeting and subverting the 'commonplaces' of the mainstream and corporate social media. Most importantly, these movements articulated claims for 'popular sovereignty' against traditional 'elites', be those autocracies in the Arab world or established technocratic political parties in the 'West' (Sitrin/Azzellini 2014; Aslanidis 2016). Due to their ambition "to occupy the digital mainstream", via the means of "Facebook and Twitter as means of mass mobilisation", these projects were also labelled as 'cyber-populist' (Gerbaudo 2017: 137).

Many of these movements formed the core, became the inspiration, or even triggered the next phase of new parties that emerged in the following years. Thanks to their dedication in the development of online decision-making tools and their reliance on the new forms of technology as the primary means of organisation, these parties were also described as 'technopopulist' or 'digital parties'. These parties could be seen as the best manifestation of the close interaction between populism and digitalism. Digital parties aim "to a deliver a new politics supported by digital technology; a kind of politics that [. . .] professes to be more democratic, more open to ordinary people, more immediate and direct, more authentic and transparent" (Gerbaudo 2018: 4). In this sense there is a clear resemblance to the populist discourse that pursues incorporation of the marginalised sectors, and popular participation as remedy to the technocratic post-democracy of the last two decades. The digital or techno-populist parties present themselves as "the solution to the democratic deficit that has turned political institutions into the preserve of technocrats and self-serving politicians" (ibid.). At the same time, "they respond to a generalised distrust towards traditional political parties caused by the effects of the Great Recession, by promising to deliver a democracy matching contemporary social and technological conditions" (ibid.). As Deseriis (2017a: 442) contends, the eruption of the global financial crisis in 2018 and the widespread frustration at the ruling elites "propelled a new generation of 'technoparties' such as the Five Star Movement (Movimento Cinque Stelle or M5S) in Italy, Podemos in Spain, and the Pirate Party in Iceland". Most recently, we also observed "France Insoumise in France, [and] campaign organisations such as Momentum, driving the surge in popularity of Corbyn's Labour Party in the United Kingdom" (Gerbaudo 2018: 4). These parties' aim to achieve a "government of the people, by the people, for the people" is felt to be achievable by means of information communications technology (Deseriis 2017a: 441).

With this aim in mind, the M5S developed Rousseau, an online platform "where registered members can discuss and vote about various political issues concerning the internal and external activities of the organisation" (Gerbaudo 2018: 2). With 140,000 members it consists of "one of the world's largest online platforms for political participation and collaborative law-making" (Deseriis 2017b: 47). Rousseau allows party members to participate in the writing of national and regional laws proposed by parliamentarians or regional councillors respectively, participate in primary elections for party candidates as well as vote in referendums (Gerbaudo 2018: 116). It can be said that the M5S is a paradigmatic example of a digital party which does not simply rely on technology but incorporates technology within its own political philosophy and structures. In the case of Podemos, the digital tools Consul and Participa were used, which were self-described as "the most complete citizen participation tool for an open, transparent and democratic government" (Gerbaudo 2018: 121). In the case of Podemos, however, citizens' assemblies and physical meetings also have an important presence. In this sense we can say that Podemos applies a double method of political participation into its structure which makes it less techno-populist than the M5S, and hybrid in nature.

2.2 Populism

After this overview of the current literature it becomes obvious that there is a 'theoretical expectation' for a splice between populism and the new technological forms of communication (Manucci 2017). There are arguably two reasons for this professed association. First, both populism and digital media are perceived as a disruption to the hitherto hegemonic orders (on the one hand, the political one and on the other hand, that of the media and communication outlets). The collapse of their dominance has resulted to an extent to the association of populism with the digital media. Second, the stylistic features of populist actors: e.g. 'the colloquial and emotional language', 'controversial content', 'black and white rhetoric', 'dramatization', 'spectacularisation', 'personalisation' (ibid.). These features seem indeed to resemble the theories of Pierre Ostiguy and Benjamin Moffitt which make them compatible with populism. Ostiguy (2017: 2) observes that populist politicians 'frequently use language that includes slang or folksy expressions and metaphors, are more demonstrative in their bodily or facial expressions as well as in their demeanor, and display rawer, culturally popular tastes'. In opposition to non-populist, or anti-populist politicians who present a standard, conventional, perhaps conservative or moderate or restrained image, populism flaunts the low in that it is "transgressive, improper, and antagonistic" (ibid.). In Moffitt's (2016: 3) vocabulary, populism is a "political style that is performed, embodied and enacted across a variety of political and cultural contexts." To establish a link with the politics of 'the average citizen', populist political style puts forward a "symbolically mediated performance made to audiences that are used to create and navigate the fields of power that comprise the political, stretching from the domain of government through to everyday life" (ibid: 28).

Critically, one must wonder whether the supposed newness of both populism and the digital media, the 'low' political style and the disruption they pose to the hegemonic practices suffice to define populism. To scrutinise the relationship between populism and the new tools of communication and diffusion of political messages, it is not enough to define those tools only. The excessive focus on the literature in this area may lead us to disregard the advances in the field of populism - indeed, this is nothing strange in academic research. Thus, one must not neglect to define populism in a rigorous way as well.

Despite the conventional perception that views the rise of populism as a product of political mediatisation, "it is feasible to create a definition that is able to accurately capture the core of all major past and present manifestations of populism" (Mudde/Rovira Kaltwasser 2017: 5). This chapter defines populism as a people-centric and – synchronically - an anti-elitist discourse that pursues a dichotomic representation of the socio-political field between 'Us' (the marginalised, the underdog, 'the people') and 'Them' (the establishment, the 1 %, the elite); the former are perceived as the rightful social majority while the latter as an illegitimate minority that suppresses the enjoyments of the former (Stavrakakis/Katsambekis 2014; de Cleen/Stavrakakis 2017). The juxtaposition of the people against the elite then provides a set of formal characteristics for the identification of populist phenomena.

In the discourse-theoretical perspective the focus of this analysis of populism shifts from the content of the latter's rhetoric (which ideology? which policy? which demands?) to a particular logic of articulation of those contents: how are these demands brought together? How are they linked to seemingly asymmetrical identities (Laclau 2005a; de Cleen/Glynos/Mondon 2018)? Laclau's concept of the 'chain of equivalence' is critical in understanding the process of collective identity formation (Laclau 2005b). Populism as a mode of identification pursues "the establishment of linkages between a series of initially heterogeneous unsatisfied demands, which enter into relations of equivalence thus forming a collective identity [. . .] through the opposition towards a common enemy (the power bloc, the establishment)" (Stavrakakis/Katsambekis 2014).

When populism is studied as a discursive logic it serves in bridging the gap between communication and populist studies. In their contribution to political communication studies, Reinemann *et al.* (2016: 14) understand populism as "a set of features or elements of communicative messages". This anti-essentialist shift is compatible with the research programme deployed by the Essex School (Laclau/Mouffe 2000; Howarth/Norval/Stavrakakis 2000; Glynos/Howarth 2007) in that it allows for the disentanglement of the phenomenon of populism from the normatively and ideologically charged content ascribed to it throughout the long decades of anti-populist and western-centric theorisations, and captures the core criteria and formal characteristics of the phenomenon. Crucially, it resembles the ontological stance taken by Laclau (2005a: 33) who argued that "the political practices do not express the nature of social agents but, instead, constitute the latter". There is an ontological priority on the practices over the agent, so to speak.

Put simply, it is not the a priori labelling of an actor as populist that defines its subsequent practices as populist too. Rather, depending on whether the practices can be defined as populist in association with the formal criteria described above, an actor can be rightfully defined as populist. Similarly, it is not the use of new media practices that define an actor as a populist but rather the diffusion of communication that represents society as being divided among 'the people' as the suppressed majority and 'the elite' as the illegitimate minority who denies the former's enjoyment.

To recap through the words of communication scholars "populism is understood as features of political communication rather than characteristics of the actor sending the message" (de Vreese *et al.* 2018: 3). There is an additional merit of the anti-essentialist discourse-oriented perspectives which is of primer importance for the empirical analysis that follows. Elements of discourse are not restricted solely to language but expand towards multimodal visual and aesthetic material such as videos and images which are in fact mediated by discourse.

3 The case of Syriza

Having defined both digital media and populism and having set the context in a comparative perspective, one can observe how the degree of digitalism varies from party to party, and how the techno-political aspirations, or the simple use of technologies, may or may not be accompanied by populism. The case of Syriza, with which this chapter will be dealing from now on, reinforces this view against the theoretical expectations that perceive the relationship between populism and the new forms of technology as necessarily symbiotic.

Syriza is a paradigmatic case of left-wing populist discourse in the southern European periphery that has received a tremendous media, scholarly and public attention over the last few years. It shook and reshaped the Greek political arena by disrupting the 40 years of bi-partisan rule between the centre-right New Democracy and the centre-left PASOK, and played a critical role in the re-politicisation of Greek society as well as in the shift in political party identification. Due to its rapid, multilevel transformations, Syriza has attracted the attention of political party scholars (Spourdalakis 2014; Katsourides 2016; Aslanidis/Rovira Kaltwasser 2016). Finally, concerning its political vision Syriza was in the spotlight of domestic and international commentators and intellectuals who either sided with it, framing it as a vision for a progressive Europe (Douzinas 2017; Sheehan 2017), or against it, perceiving it as a threat to Europe and democracy and placing its leader Alexis Tsipras amongst the top 10 most dangerous politicians in Europe (Spiegel 2012; Žižek 2018). Despite the particularity of the party, which turns it into a unique case study, and its classification as a populist party (Stavrakakis/Katsambekis 2014), Syriza bears little resemblance to its digitalised counterparts such as Podemos, the M5S and the Pirate Parties. This comparative discontinuity provides an additional core reason to justify the consideration of Syriza in this analysis.

I will begin by providing a historical account of Syriza's emergence as a relevant populist party, then move on to a 'classic style' discourse analysis followed by a visual-discursive analysis for purposes of triangulation.

3.1 Syriza's historical trajectory and organisational dynamics

The analysis of the relationship between Syriza and the new forms of media technology must take account of the nature of the party, its political trajectory and internal architecture, which arguably determine the contemporary organisational dynamics of Syriza, one part of which is the use (or not) of new forms of technological communication. Although this chapter focuses on the period 2012–2015 when Syriza served as the axiomatic opposition party in the Greek parliament, as well as 2015–2019, when the party governed the country, it is necessary to go back in time in order to capture how its historical evolution and political foundations have influenced its present organisational philosophy.

Syriza was founded as a coalition of various Left parties in 2004. Rooted in the Eurocommunist current, and being a splinter-party of the orthodox Communist Party of Greece (KKE), Syriza's predecessor (Synaspismos 1991–2004) attempted to incorporate the varied ideological tendencies on the left of social democracy, which is typical of the anti-totalitarian Left. Organisationally, then, Synaspismos had a decentralised character and provided a political edifice for the several sectorial components of the Greek anti-Stalinist and radical left, while sympathetic to the extra-parliamentary Left. Ideologically it could be located between the social-democratic PASOK and the communist KKE (Balampanides 2015). At this time, the fringe party Syriza addressed 'class' and 'the Left'. But following the December 2008 uprising and given the young nature of its supporters, Syriza placed 'youth' at the core of its political project and consequently its discourse (Katsambekis 2015). "This party transformation, however, had an unintended generational effect; triggering the learning and training of a younger generation of members in grassroots activism, both at the international (anti-globalization mobilizations) and domestic level (student movements)" (Kouki/González 2018: 130).

When the crisis erupted in 2009, Greece experienced a repertoire of contentious actions including general strikes, mobilisations, contentious forms of politics and intense resistance to the government's 'stability policies', as well as open assemblies, as part of the 'square movements', also known as the Aganaktismenoi (Diani/

Kousis 2014). "Democratic accountability was challenged, as were labour rights [. . .]; pension cuts undermined the health of the elderly reductions in public health, tax increases, and cuts in welfare benefits were not accompanied by national security programs" (della Porta *et al.* 2017: 40). Popular frustration was channelled against the political establishment, which opened a window of opportunity for Syriza to rise.

By this time, "Syriza's membership was already naturally active in most mobilisations. . .. Even if none of these protest events or spaces were the product of the party's steering, Syriza was present in most social struggles publicly supporting anti-austerity claims" (Kouki/ González 2018: 130). As activists often explain, Syriza was welcomed by most of the movements as it was perceived as a 'clean' party, "a party that was open and sharp about supporting the protests"; after all, "it had never governed, and thus it had never proven itself untrustworthy". Its members were perceived as ordinary citizens rather than politicians (GR3, GR7, GR11).

The analysis so far describes a type of party that built upon and benefited from grassroots mobilisations. There is indeed something 'uncommon' here, which is a revived dynamic between movements and parties (Goldstone 2003; della Porta *et al.* 2017), also conceptualised as movement-parties: those are political entities that put forward a relationship between contentious politics as hitherto expressed by social movements which make demands from below on the one hand, and on the other hand, political parties which are located in the locus of representational politics but embrace the demands of the former (della Porta *et al.* 2017). However, while these organisational dynamics can be understood as 'uncommon' with respect to the ways political parties have been transformed in the last two decades, Syriza's identity by 2015 resembles little of the techno-political 'newness' of the digital parties such as the M5S in Italy, Podemos in Spain and the Pirate Parties comparatively. Arguably, the more 'traditional' character of Syriza's organisational structures is a key factor that hampered the possibilities for an equally techno-political party. Perhaps, the political culture in Greece may have not provided a fertile ground – or even a necessity - for a such a digitally oriented party transformation.

3.2 The populist Syriza

Syriza's discourse under the leadership of Alexis Tsipras played a paramount role in its trajectory from the margins of the political spectrum to the capturing of power. It shifted the blame for the crisis ascribed to the Greek citizens by the internal and international elites towards the pro-austerity establishment. "Syriza managed to provide anti-memorandum protesters with an alternative, coherent narrative of the crisis and thus gave them an organized political outlet and parliamentary representative" (Kouki/González 2018: 132). Speeches at rallies, and representations in the campaigning material, show how Syriza linked particularistic identities, struggles and demands into a symphony of collective representation resembling Laclau's theory of the chains of equivalences. A paradigmatic example of populist instance can be identified in Tsipras' speech a day before his election in January 2015:

> No one can intimidate or blackmail a wounded people, a people who have been betrayed and humiliated. This coming Sunday, it is not the lenders or their representatives here who will be speaking. This Sunday, the Greek people will speak. And they will give the clearest answer: down with the memoranda; down with subjugation. The blackmail is over! (Tsipras 2015a).

'The people' in the case of Tsipras and Syriza is not homogenous or monist as conventional perceptions on populism put forward (cf. Mudde 2004; Müller 2016); nor is the excluded 'other'. 'The Greek people' as a signifier resembles little of the proclaimed 'nationalist' character un-rigorously ascribed to populism when it is labelled 'nationalist populism' (cf. Taguieff 2013; Eatwell/Goodwin 2018). In fact, this perspective reflects the mainstream understanding of populism that is habituated by the politics of closure revolving around the nodal point 'the nation'.

In the case of Syriza, one could observe a polymorphic and inclusive chain of equivalence that includes 'the many', 'youth', 'the world of labour', 'pensioners', 'those who suffer'. The political adversary is not represented by the immigrant, as in the case of nationalist populism, but rather by 'the bankers', 'the oligarchs', 'corruption', 'the New Democracy and PASOK coalition', 'the ancient régime', 'the establishment', (political/economic) 'thieves', 'scandals', the 'internal' and 'external troika' (Tsipras 2015b).

The ideological orientation of Syriza's discourse is enunciated by Tsipras' definition of the 'vision for the homeland' which reinforces further the characterisation of solidarity-based left-wing populism: "we must protect the 99 % of society that is looted by the memorandum. We must detect the 1 % which has to pay as it has systematically evaded taxation" (Tsipras 2015a). Tsipras (2015a) states that:

> No one should be left out in the cold in the cruelty of winter, no one abandoned by the cruelty of the state, no one attacked by the cruelty of the bankers [. . .] no elderly person should be abandoned with a meagre pension, in poverty and in the cold, facing a humiliating death [. . .] no citizen left undefended in the desperation of unemployment [. . .] no one living in the dark because their power supply has been cut off.

3.3 Visual analysis

Syriza's populist communication is not a subject to discourses pronounced at rallies alone. Nor is the populist agenda communicated through a sole medium. In order to relate better with the theme of this book I now turn towards "the much neglected 'visual analysis' inspired by the 'Power of Images' (Mitchell 2007) in political conflict" (Doerr/Mattoni/Teune 2013). As Doerr, Mattoni and Teune (2013: xi) argue, "the presence and relevance of images in mobilisations [. . .] is no novelty. Encounters with social movements [and politics in general I must add] have always been intrinsically tied to the visual sense." Importantly, they go on, "activists articulate visual messages, their activities are represented in photos and video sequences and they are ultimately rendered visible or invisible in the public sphere." Thus, vision is not independent from discourse but rather mediated by it. Images convey messages which are rooted in a pre-existing culturally related context; the processing of those images is filtrated by the very same meaning that is shared and structured in the form of language.

3.4 Syriza in opposition (2012–2015)

Let us initiate this analysis from the May 2012 elections. The poster that is located on the left in Fig. 1 reads: "either us or them . . . together

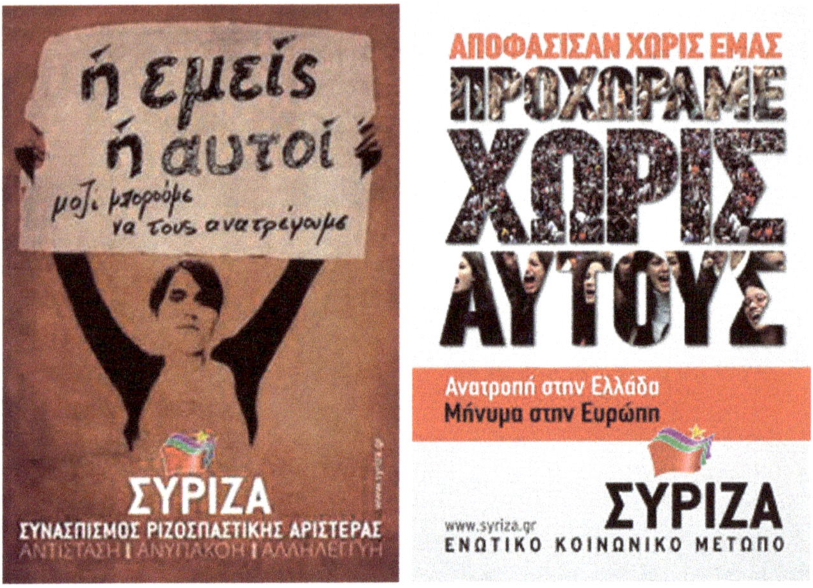

Fig. 1: Syriza's 2012 election campaign posters.

we can overthrow them", and below "Syriza. Coalition of the Radical Left: Resistance, Disobedience, Solidarity". The second poster, located on the right-hand side, reads: "They decided without us. We move on without them. Upheaval in Greece. Message to Europe" (Syriza 2012). Evidently, the populist polarisation is present, accompanied by the revolutionary aspect in populism: the collision with the establishment and the desire for change prevail in these two posters.

Two years later, in the European elections of May 2014, Syriza launched the posters one can see in Fig. 2. They are evidently vibrant, colourful and hopeful. Within the emotive sphere, this aesthetic is not irrelevant to the conditions that prevailed in Greece, or to Syriza's proclamation that it would reverse the general mood of depression and distress. This is best evident in the changing audio-visual scenes exposed in Syriza's one-minute campaigning spots. The screenshot in the left spot portrays numerous signs reading 'For Sale' or 'For Rent'. It narrates a widespread situation where people lived in fear of losing their homes during the crisis (Syriza 2015a). The screenshot on the right

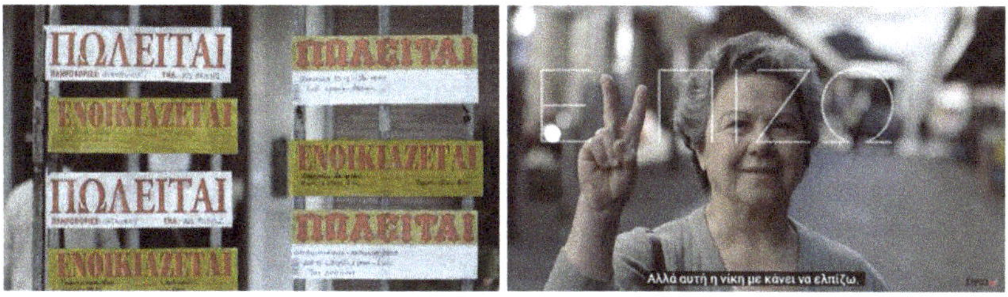

Fig. 2: Stills from Syriza's January 2015 election campaign spots.

portrays a female pensioner receiving "300 euros per month which are not enough even for basic medication" (Syriza 2015a). In the end, the scenario is completely overturned. The melancholy music and colours change to an optimistic mood and a phrase which communicates that "this coming victory allows me to hope. Greece moves forward. Europe is changing. Hope is coming" (ibid.).

At the level of collective identity formation, the posters in Fig. 3 portray the different social groups that composed Syriza's 'chain of equivalence': manual workers, youth, pensioners, people with disabilities and children. Respectively, the messages that the posters communicate: "we vote for jobs and wages", "...for our dreams and rights", "...for pensions and dignity", "...for healthcare and social security", "...for the future of our children", while the last two posters read "our patience is over". Evidently, the 'identities' that are portrayed in the posters are in line with the subjects that Syriza addressed at rallies in

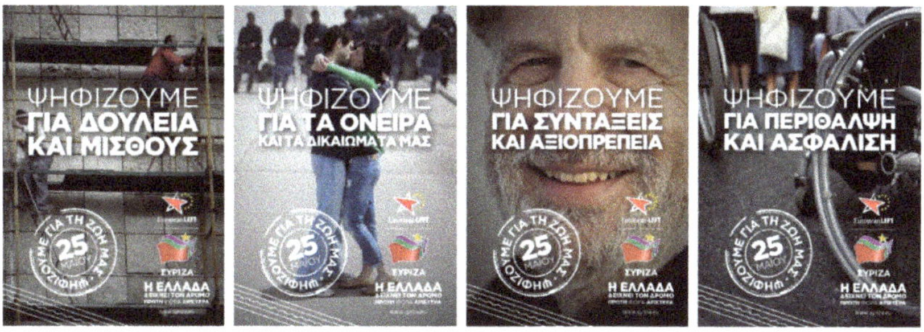

Fig. 3: Syriza's posters from the 2014 European election campaign.

Omonoia Square or the parliament as the main opposition party, which have been analysed above.

The central demands that are visually illustrated in the posters for the same European elections (see Fig. 4) reflected the general social and economic conditions in Greece which the United Nations characterised as being in a state of 'humanitarian crisis'. Applying only a loose comparison, this also highlights a continuity between these demands and the political vision articulated by Tsipras. In order, the posters read: "our fridge is empty…", "our power supply is cut off…", "our medication has run out…"; while the last poster portrays a black and white hand joined, reading "we vote for justice and equality", providing a visual representation of an inclusive populism.

Drawing on the theory of populism, and the minimal criteria that classify it, one could clearly see the metonymy that the political enemy takes on for Syriza. On the left of Fig. 5, we see a poster prepared for the visit of the German Chancellor Angela Merkel in Athens in April 2014, portraying her with the then Greek Prime Minister and New Democracy leader, Antonis Samaras. They are shown together as an ensemble presented as the enemy, reading "No more – Thank you". What that slogan refers to can be found in the poster on the right: "Memoranda – Never Again".

The analysis of the above visual material is evidently coherent with the left-populist discursive of Syriza. Beyond the discursive analysis presented above, the formal characteristics of populism are evident in aesthetic and visual representations which are indeed discursively mediated and comprehended. Syriza continues to divide the Greek socio-political space in two, between the many and the few; additionally, there is a systematic co-articulation of seemingly asymmetric identities that are brought into discursive equivalence.

3.5 Syriza in Government (2015–2019)

Syriza's victory in the January 2015 election brought the party to power for the first time in its history. With the exception of a few campaigns such as that on the Referendum where the Greek citizens were called

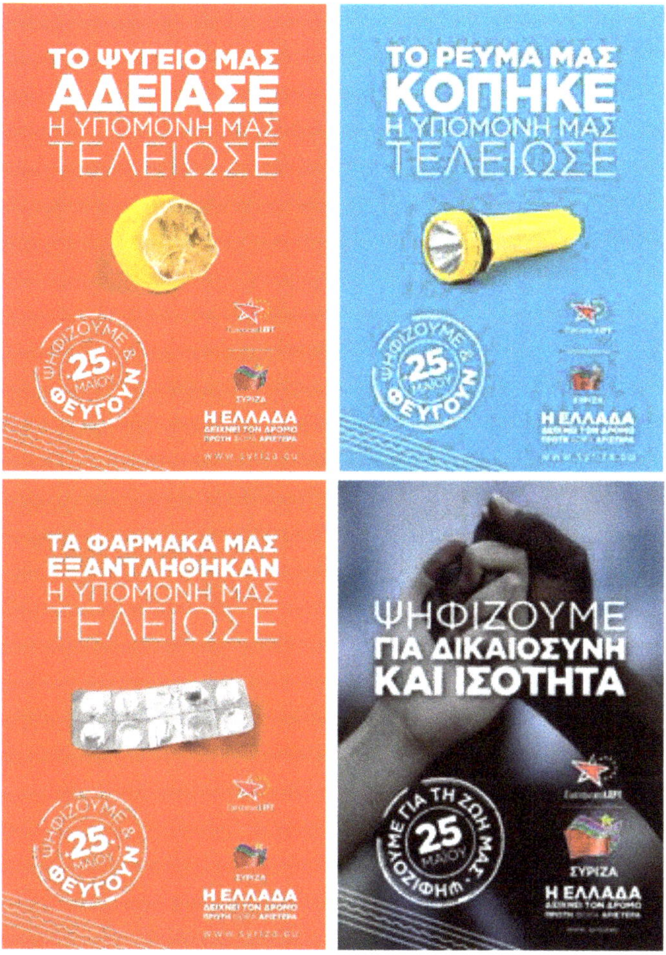

Fig. 4: 2014 European election campaign posters: Syriza's central demands.

to decide with a 'Yes' or 'No' (the latter is also known as OXI), and the campaign for the re-election of Alexis Tsipras after his resignation and the snap elections in September 2015, the diffusion of discourses through the means of traditional campaigning such as posters as already analysed was significantly weaker. Additionally, the relative centralisation of communication around the figure of Tsipras himself shifted the

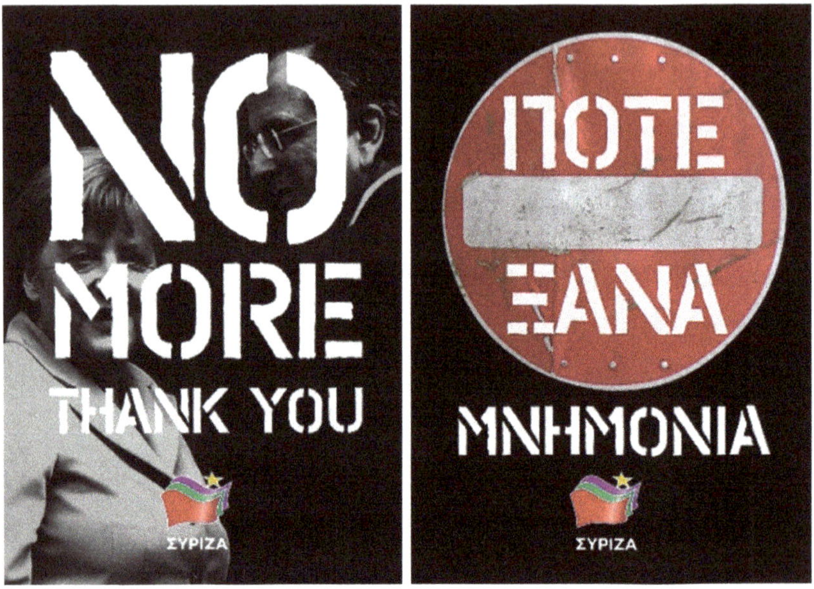

Fig. 5: Syriza's posters for Angela Merkel's visit to Athens, 2014.

focus of the analysis to other forms of media which are of interest for this chapter and were employed by the Greek Prime Minister and his strategists.

Like other politicians, populists or not, Alexis Tsipras uses social media, both before and after his election. He maintains a Facebook account where he is followed by around 438,000 people, Twitter where he is followed by 519,000 people on his 'Greek' account which is the one he used to use as party leader, around 307,000 people on his 'international account', while as of 31 August 2017 he also employs Instagram, where he is followed by 32,642 people (Fig. 6).

Let us turn to the analysis of a few posts from Instagram which is undoubtedly one of the most expressive media for visual analysis of those mentioned above. Following the trends of the current era, the Greek Prime Minister uploads 'stories' from his political missions abroad, for example in Moscow, but also domestic events in various cities, and from various activities such as Christmas celebrations.

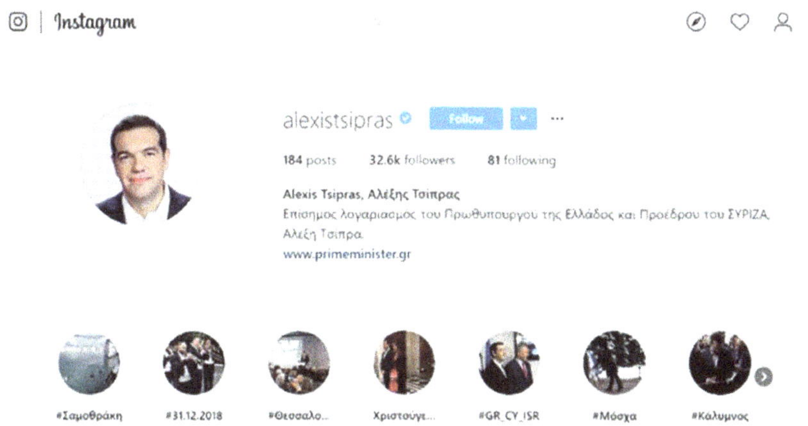

Fig. 6: Tsipras' account in Instagram.

In his own Instagram post shown in Fig. 7, the Prime Minister is located in a pub; he holds a pint of beer, he appears joyful and relaxed, without a full suit on and, as always, without a tie. This is a picture that can be interpreted as representing common man rather than a conventional politician. On the caption of the post it reads: "At a pub in London after the end of the Western Balkan Summit to watch the

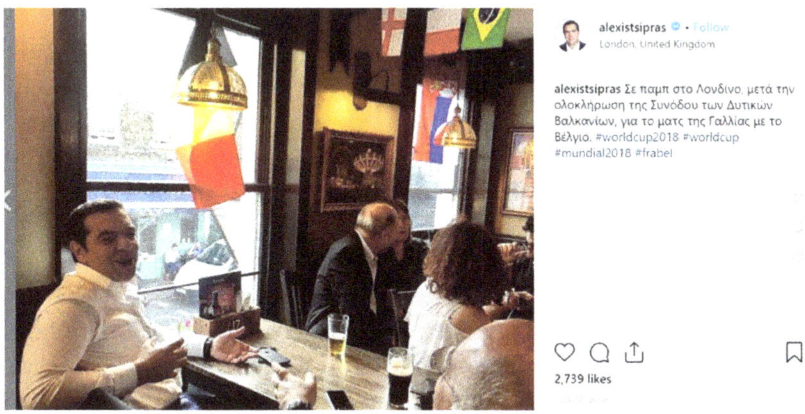

Fig. 7: Instagram post: Tsipras relaxes in a London pub.

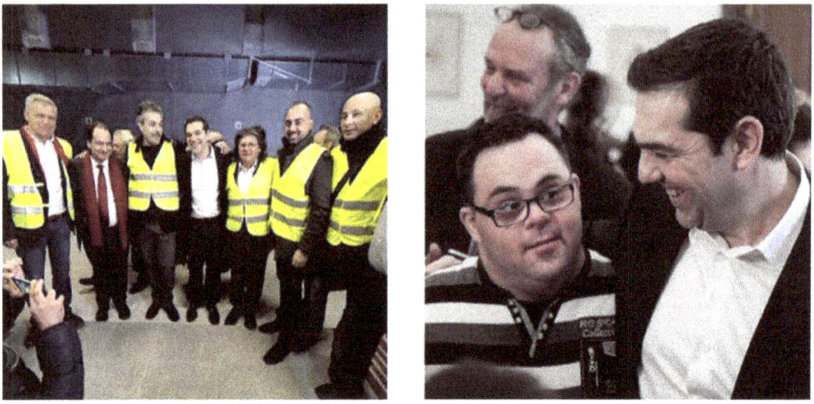

Fig. 8: Images from Tsipras' Instagram pages: meeting 'the people'.

match between France and Belgium", followed by the relevant hashtags '#worldcup2018', '#worldcup' '#mundial2018', '#frabel'.

In other posts Tsipras is photographed with a group of workers at the Thessaloniki Metro works (Fig. 8, left), which can again be interpreted as a self-representation as one of the people, and especially as one of the workers (Tsipras 2018a, Fig. 8, left). He is also shown with people with Down syndrome (Tsipras 2018b) (Fig. 8, right) and hosting children at Maximou Palace for the Christmas carols (Fig. 9), thus presenting a human and accessible persona.

In other posts (Fig. 10), the Greek Prime Minister uploads a photo of himself wearing a basketball T-shirt with Thanassis Antedokoumpo's name: he is a black Greek basketball player who was a victim of racist slurs. Tsipras stood in solidarity with the player, giving the following caption: "respect and pride for those who were born and raised in Greece and made the country their own home. No tolerance for hatred and racism" (Tsipras 2018c).

Alexis Tsipras' presence on social media, and especially on Instagram, projects an ordinary, accessible man. The representations that appear on the photos fit perfectly with Ostiguy's spatial positioning of populism in the politico-cultural 'low' region. Yet, drawing back on the core conceptualisation of populism as performative instance, one can also observe how the use of social media by a populist like

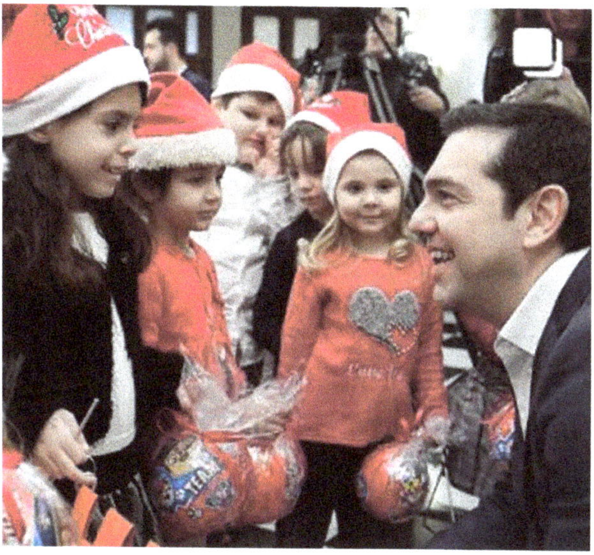

Fig. 9: Image from Tsipras' Instagram pages: hosting children at Maximou palace.

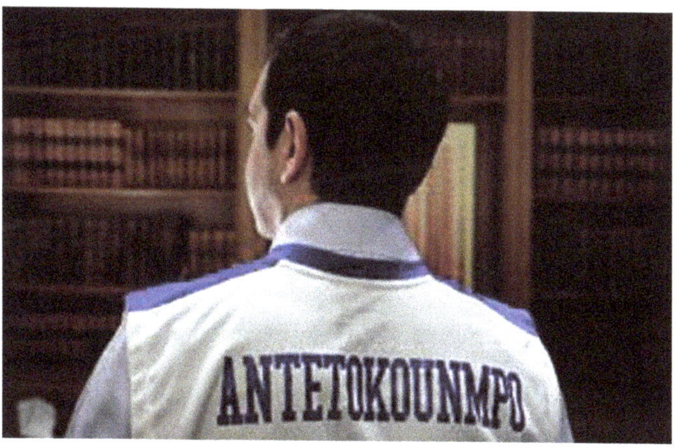

Fig. 10: Tsipras wearing Thanassis Antedokoumpo's basketball kit.

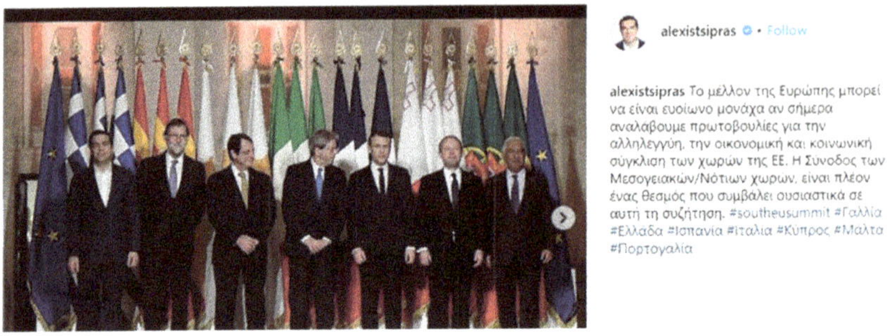

Fig. 11: Tsipras with other European leaders.

Alexis Tsipras can be employed for the communication of non-populist messages. In the photo in Fig. 11, Tsipras appears among the six state leaders in the official-unofficial cooperation between the North European and Mediterranean countries. This highly institutional and summit-like setting, as well as the fact that all leaders are men, resembles a conventional political frame. Undoubtedly, this setting is located on Ostiguy's 'high' point of the axis. Yet it has to be stated that Tsipras is the only man not wearing a tie: an accessory of political conventionalism.

4 Conclusions

This chapter enquired into the professed symbiotic relationship between populism and the new media. While conventionally the new media are perceived as a vehicle used by populists to spread a 'fragmented ideology' (Engesser *et al.* 2017), this chapter has argued that things are far more complex. Prior to any potential association between populism and the new forms of communicational interactivity, decision-making and organisation, a conceptual disentanglement of the two is critically necessary.

This chapter investigated empirically the case of the Greek party Syriza, which has been characterised as a paradigmatic instance of left-wing populism. In contrast to political parties in its morphological vicinity (i.e. parties such as the Spanish Podemos and the Italian M5S, which also emerged out of the crisis of representation in the context of the recession and embody profound populist characteristics), Syriza's digital techno-political features were constrained only at the level of communication. More specifically, unlike the highly digitalised M5S, which incorporated technology at the core of its structures, for example, or Podemos, which supplemented this with some traditional means of organisation, Syriza presented a more traditional character rooted in social movements and conventional party structures. Arguably, its political trajectory, emanating from a conventional-like type of party rooted in the eurocommunist current, coupled with the more traditional forms used to express political indignation in Greece, provided neither the need nor the fertile ground for the development and adoption of digital forms of organisation.

In fact, the use of digital elements was not absent. However, it was restricted to the sphere of social media, which is considered as standard in contemporary political practices. The use of digital media was a tool for political communication rather than a foundational principle embedded in the party's organisational core to promote participation and decision-making processes. Syriza used YouTube, Twitter and Facebook, while it also put forward an evidently vibrant, youthful aesthetic in its political posters to capitalise on its appeal. In his transition from Syriza's leader in opposition to the Prime Minister of Greece, Alexis Tsipras employed the social media to communicate political messages that fit both the low politico-cultural axis reflecting the populist style, but also the high level on the very same axis, which resembles conventional non-populist politicians. In this sense, to describe Syriza as a techno-political populist party must be insufficient. The content of Syriza's discourse also challenges the strict association between populism and the extreme right, illiberalism and monism, since Syriza's populism is clearly expressed through a leftist discourse that is pluralistic and democratic in nature.

The selection of a relatively negative case, that is, a case of populism that is not boldly fuelled by digital media, is not random. In fact, this chapter aimed at challenging the association between populism and the media which is often taken for granted. Society has entered into a new era that is strongly characterised by technological innovation, and this undeniably influences the sphere of politics too. This is nothing new, but it is most evident at the moment, as the digitalised forms of politics are slowly outnumbering the 'analogue' ones. Social media, web platforms, decision-making and organising tools are not available solely to populists but to any political actor who has the capacity and desire to utilise them.

References

Aalberg, Toril / Esser, Rank / Reinemann, Carsten / Strömbäck, Charles / de Vreese, Claes H. (eds) 2017. *Populist Political Communication in Europe*. New York: Routledge.

Ant1 News 2016. Tsipras plays...basketball with Galis at Maximou Palace! [Ο Τσίπρας παίζει... μπάσκετ με τον Γκάλη στο Μαξίμου!]. July 6.

Aslanidis, Paris 2016. Populist Social Movements of the Great Recession. *Mobilization: An International Quarterly* 21/3, 301-321.

Aslanidis, Paris / Rovira Kaltwasser, Cristóbal 2016. Dealing with Populists in Government: The Syriza-Anel Coalition in Greece. *Democratization* 23/6, 1077-1091.

Balampanides, Giannis 2015. Ευωρκομμουνισμός: Απο Την Κομμουνιστική Στην Ριζοσπαστική Αριστερά [Eurocommunism: From the Communist to the Radical Left]. Athens: Polis.

Bimber, Bruce 2014. Digital Media in the Obama Campaigns of 2008 and 2012: Adaptation to the Personalized Political Communication Environment. *Journal of Information Technology & Politics* 11/2, 130-150.

Blumler, Jay G. / Gurevitch, Michael 1995. *The Crisis of Public Communication. Communication and Society*. London /New York: Routledge.

Boczkowski, Pablo J. / Papacharissi, Zizi (eds) 2018. *Trump and the Media*. Massachusetts: MIT Press.

Boomgaarden, Hajo G. / Vliegenthart, Rens 2009. How News Content Influences Anti-Immigration Attitudes: Germany, 1993–2005. *European Journal of Political Research* 48/4, 516-542.

Calzada, Igor 2017. Do Digital Social Networks Foster Civilian Participation among Millennials? Kitchenware Revolution and 15m Democratic Regeneration Cases. *Glocalism: Journal of Culture, Politics and Innovation* 3.

De Cleen, Benjamin / Glynos, Jason / Mondon, Aurelien 2018. Critical Research on Populism: Nine Rules of Engagement. *Organization* 1/13, 1-13.

De Cleen, Benjamin / Stavrakakis, Yannis 2017. Distinctions and Articulations: A Discourse Theoretical Framework for the Study of Populism and Nationalism. *Javnost - The Public* 24/4, 301-319.

Della Porta, Donatella / Fernández, Joseba / Kouki, Hara / Mosca, Lorenzo 2017. *Movement Parties against Austerity*. Cambridge: Polity Press.

Deseriis, Marco 2017a. Technopopulism: The Emergence of a Discursive Formation. Triplec: Communication, Capitalism & Critique. *Open Access Journal for a Global Sustainable Information Society* 15/2, 441-458.

Deseriis, Marco 2017b. Direct Parliamentarianism: An Analysis of the Political Values Embedded in Rousseau, the "Operating System" of the Five Star Movement. *JeDEM - eJournal of eDemocracy and Open Government* 9/2, 47-67.

De Vreese, Claes H. / Esser, Frank / Aalberg, Toril / Reinemann, Carsten / Stanyer, James 2018. Populism as an Expression of Political Communication Content and Style: A New Perspective. *International Journal of Press/Politics* 23/4, 423-438.

Diani, Mario / Kousis, Maria 2014. The Duality of Claims and Events: The Greek Campaign against the Troika's Memoranda and Austerity, 2010-2012. *Mobilization* 19/4, 387-404.

Doerr, Nicole / Mattoni, Alice / Teune, Simon 2013. Toward a Visual Analysis of Social Movements, Conflict, and Political Mobilization. In Doerr, Nicole / Mattoni, Alice / Teune, Simon (eds) *Advances in the Visual Analysis of Social Movements*. Bingley: Emerald.

Douzinas, Costas 2017. *Syriza in Power: Reflections of an Accidental Politician*. Cambridge, UK: Polity.

Eatwell, Roger / Goodwin, Matthew J. 2018. *National Populism: The Revolt against Liberal Democracy*. London: Pelican.

Ellinas, Antonis 2010. *The Media and the Far Right in Western Europe: Playing the Nationalist Card*. New York: Cambridge University Press.

Engesser, Sven / Ernst, Nicole / Esser, Frank / Büchel, Florin 2017. Populism and Social Media: How Politicians Spread a Fragmented Ideology. *Information, Communication & Society* 20/8, 1109-1126.

Enli, Gunn 2017 New Media and Politics. *Annals of the International Communication Association* 41/3-4, 220-227.

Esser, Frank / Strömbäck, Jesper (eds) 2014. *The Mediatization of Politics*. London: Palgrave Macmillan.

Gerbaudo, Paolo 2012. *Tweets and the Streets: Social Media and Contemporary Activism*. London: Pluto Press.

Gerbaudo, Paolo 2017. *The Mask and the Flag: Populism, Citizenism and Global Protest*. London: C Hurst & Co.

Gerbaudo, Paolo 2018. *The Digital Party: Political Organisation and Online Democracy*. London: Pluto Press.

Glynos, Jason / Howarth, David 2007. *Logics of Critical Explanation in Social and Political Theory*. London: Routledge.

Goldstone, Jack A. 2003. *States, Parties, and Social Movements*. Cambridge: Cambridge University Press.

Heiss, Raffael / Schmuck, Desiree / Matthes, Jörg 2018. What Drives Interaction in Political Actors' Facebook Posts? Profile and Content Predictors of User Engagement and Political Actors' Reactions. *Information, Communication & Society*, 1-17.

Howarth, David / Norval, Aletta / Stavrakakis, Yannis 2000. *Discourse Theory and Political Analysis: Identities, Hegemonies and Social Change*. Manchester: Manchester University Press.

Juris, Jeffrey S. 2012. Reflections on #Occupy Everywhere: Social Media, Public Space, and Emerging Logics of Aggregation. *American Ethnologist* 39/2, 259-279.

Katsambekis, Giorgos 2015. ΣΥΡΙΖΑ 2004-2012: απο τη Νεολαία στο Λαό [Syriza 2004–2012: From the Youth to the People]. In Θεωρία του Λόγου: Δημιουργικές Εφαρμογές [Discourse Theory: Creative Applications]. Athens: Gutenberg, 215-248.

Katsourides, Yiannos 2016. *Radical Left in Government: The Cases of SYRIZA and AKEL*. London: Palgrave Macmillan.

Kavada, Anastasia 2015. Creating the Collective: Social Media, the Occupy Movement and Its Constitution as a Collective Actor. *Information, Communication & Society* 18/8, 872-886.

Klein, Naomi 2018. *No Is Not Enough: Defeating the New Shock Politics*. London: Penguin.

Kouki, Hara / Fernández González, Joseba 2018. Syriza, Podemos and Mobilizations against Austerity: Movements, Parties or Movement-Parties? In Roose, Jochen / Sommer, Moritz / Scholl, Franziska (eds) *Europas Zivilgesellschaft in Der Wirtschafts- Und Finanzkrise*. Wiesbaden: Springer Fachmedien Wiesbaden, 123-140.

Laclau, Ernesto 2005a. What's in a Name? In Panizza, Francisco (ed.) *Populism and the Mirror of Democracy*. London - New York: Verso.

Laclau, Ernesto 2005b. *On Populist Reason*. London/New York: Verso.

Laclau, Ernesto / Mouffe, Chantal 2000. *Hegemony and Socialist Strategy*. London/New York: Verso.

Logan, Robert K. 2016. *Understanding New Media*. New York: Peter Lang.

Lotan, Gilad / Graeff, Erhardt / Ananny, Mike *et al.* 2011. The Revolutions Were Tweeted: Information Flows during the 2011 Tunisian and Egyptian Revolutions. *International Journal of Communication* 5, 1375-1405.

Manucci, Luca 2017. Populism and the Media. In Rovira Kaltwasser, Cristóbal / Taggart, Paul / Ochoa Espejo, Paulina / Ostiguy, Pierre (eds) *The Oxford Handbook of Populism*. Oxford: Oxford University Press, 467-488.

Mattoni, Alice / Ceccobelli, Diego 2018. Comparing Hybrid Media Systems in the Digital Age: A Theoretical Framework for Analysis. *European Journal of Communication* 33/5, 540-557.

Mazzoleni, Gianpetro 2003. The Media and the Growth of Neo-Populism in Contemporary Democracies. In Mazzoleni, Gianpetro / Stewart, Julianne / Horsfield, Bruce (eds) *The Media and Neo-Populism: A Contemporary Comparative Analysis*. London: Praeger Publishers, 1-20.

Mazzoleni, Gianpetro / Stewart, Julianne / Horsfield, Bruce (eds) 2003. *The Media and Neo-Populism: A Contemporary Comparative Analysis*. Westport, United States: Praeger Publishers.
Mazzoleni, Gianpetro 2014. Mediatization and Political Populism. In Esser, Frank / Strömbäck, Jesper (eds) *The Mediatization of Politics*. London: Palgrave Macmillan, 42-56.
Mitchell, W. J. T. 2007. *Picture Theory: Essays on Verbal and Visual Representation*. Chicago: University of Chicago Press.
Moffitt, Benjamin 2016. *The Global Rise of Populism: Performance, Political Style, and Representation*. Stanford, California: Stanford University Press.
Mudde, Cas 2004. The Populist Zeitgeist. *Government and Opposition* 39/4, 542-563.
Mudde, Cas / Rovira Kaltwasser, Cristóbal 2017. *Populism: A Very Short Introduction*. Oxford: Oxford University Press.
Müller, Jan-Werner 2016. *What Is Populism?* Pennsylvania: University of Pennsylvania Press.
Mutz, C. Diana / Reeves, Byron 2005. The New Videomalaise: Effects of Televised Incivility on Political Trust. *American Political Science Review* 99/1, 1-15.
Ostiguy, Pierre 2017. Populism: A Socio-Cultural Approach. In Rovira Kaltwasser, Cristóbal / Taggart, Paul / Espejo Ochoa, Paulina / Ostiguy, Pierre (eds) *The Oxford Handbook of Populism*. Oxford: Oxford University Press, 73-97.
Pellizzetti, Pierfranco / Colombo, Furio 2009. *Fenomenologia di Berlusconi* [The Phenomenology of Berlusconi]. Roma: Manifestolibri.
Reinemann, Carsten / Aalberg, Toril / Esser, Frank / Strömbäck, Jesper / de Vreese, Claes H. 2016. Populist Political Communication: Toward a Model of Its Causes, Forms, and Effects. In Aalberg, Toril / Esser, Rank / Reinemann, Carsten / Strömbäck, Charles / de Vreese, Claes H. (eds) *Populist Political Communication in Europe*. New York: Routledge, 22-36.
Rendueles, César / Sola, Jorge 2018. The Rise of Podemos: Promises, Constraints, and Dilemmas. In García Agustín, Óscar / Briziarelli, Marco (eds) *Podemos and the New Political Cycle*. Cham: Springer International Publishing, 25-47.

Sheehan, Helena 2017. *The Syriza Wave: Surging and Crashing with the Greek Left*. New York: Monthly Review Press.

Sitrin, Marina / Azzellini, Dario 2014. *They Can't Represent Us! Reinventing Democracy from Greece to Occupy*. London: Verso.

Spiegel 2012. Europe's 10 Most Dangerous Politicians. <http://www.spiegel.de/international/europe/ten-politicians-who-worsen-the-euro-crisis-with-aggressive-rhetoric-a-848762.html>, accessed August 25, 2018.

Spourdalakis, Michalis 2014. The Miraculous Rise of the "Phenomenon Syriza." *International Critical Thought* 4/3, 354-366.

Stavrakakis, Yannis / Katsambekis, Giorgos 2014. Left-Wing Populism in the European Periphery: The Case of Syriza. *Journal of Political Ideologies* 19/2, 119-142.

Stavrakakis, Yannis / Katsambekis, Giorgos 2018. The Populism/Anti-Populism Frontier and Its Mediation in Crisis-Ridden Greece: From Discursive Divide to Emerging Cleavage? *European Political Science*, 1-16.

Syriza 2012. Syriza Campaign Posters.

Syriza 2015a. Συνταξιουχοι: Τηλεοπτικό Σπότ Συριζα [Pensioners: Syriza's TV Spot]. <https://www.youtube.com/watch?v=2wAJYeL-H3U&list=PLeD_6gbqIpFFuGkn3GldaMNzP5zjtE1fN&index=9>, accessed December 6, 2017.

Syriza Campaign Spot 2015b. ΕΝΦΙΑ Και Πληστειριασμοι [Enfia and Auctions]. <https://www.youtube.com/watch?v=I_gfmIqnxDw&list=PLeD_6gbqIpFFuGkn3GldaMNzP5zjtE1fN&index=8>, accessed February 15, 2017.

Taguieff, Pierre 2013. Ο Νέος Εθνικολαϊκισμός [Le Nouveau National-Populisme]. Translated by Pantazopoulos, Andreas / Iliadeli, Anastasia. Athens: Epikentro.

Tronconi, Filippo 2015. *Beppe Grillo's Five Star Movement: Organisation, Communication and Ideology*. Farnham, England: Ashgate.

Tsipras, Alexis 2015a. Speech at Omonoia Square. January 22. <https://www.youtube.com/watch?v=ytB7z1zExYY>

Tsipras, Alexis 2015b. Ομιλία Του Πρωθυπουργού Στις Προγραμματικές Θέσεις Της Κυβέρνησης [Prime Minister's Speech at the Governments Programmatic Theses]. August 2. <https://primeminister.gr/2015/02/08/13322>

Tsipras, Alexis 2018a. "Με Τον Υπουργό Υποδομών, Χρήστο Σπίρτζη Και Εργαζόμενους Του Μετρο Θεσσαλονίκης..." [with the Development Minister, Christos Spirtzis, and the Workers of Thessaloniki Metro]. Instagram. <https://www.instagram.com/p/Br-p2Wbg1nF/>, accessed February 20, 2019.

Tsipras, Alexis 2018b. Carols from the Greek Association for down Syndrome. Instagram, December 29. <https://www.instagram.com/p/Br-HiGiAyFu/>, accessed October 3, 2019.

Tsipras, Alexis 2018c. Instagram Post Antedokoumpo. <https://www.instagram.com/p/BqNAtmWA9G6/>, accessed January 15, 2019.

Wolfson, Todd 2014. *Digital Rebellion: The Birth of the Cyber Left.* Urbana: University of Illinois Press.

Žižek, Slavoj 2018. Should the Left's Answer to Rightist Populism Be a "Metoo"? Part1. *Philosophical Saloon.* <http://thephilosophicalsalon.com/should-the-lefts-answer-to-rightist-populism-really-be-a-me-too-part-i/>, accessed October 15, 2018.

Antonella Napolitano

Achieving results for the American people. A corpus-assisted CDA of the White House website under Trump's presidency

1 Introduction

1.1 What is populism?

The consequences of globalisation and financial crisis, the feeling of uncertainty about the future, the fear of immigration and terrorism have generated a growing disillusionment with politics and a distrust of the elites. Minorities, subjects who are perceived as *other* from the original group, have been seen as a threat to the people's legitimate rights and culture. The idea that citizens should exercise direct political power is being understood in a radical sense, leading to support for populist leaders who present themselves as part of *the people*. This trend has culminated in extreme manifestations such as Brexit, or the election of Donald Trump in the United States (see also Demata 2018).

Despite its recent upswing, populism does not represent a new phenomenon. It is commonly viewed as an approach framing politics as a struggle between the will of the common people and a conspiring elite. Albertazzi and O'Donnell (2008: 3) define populism as:

> an ideology which pits a virtuous and homogeneous people against a set of elites and dangerous *others* who are together depicted as depriving (or attempting to deprive) the sovereign people of their rights, values, prosperity, identity and voice.

Regardless of their policy positions, some elements seem to be present in the populist persuasive discourse, namely:

> Manichaean outlook; identification of Good with the will of the people; identification of Evil with a conspiring elite; [. . .] an emphasis on systemic change and an anything-goes attitude toward minority rights and democratic procedure (Hawkins 2010: 33).

Populism can indeed be understood as comprising certain key elements: an appeal to the people; anti-politics, anti-elitism, anti-establishment; a belligerent ethos and simple language that foster a sense of closeness with the disenchanted audiences; the exploitation of crises of democratic representation and the promotion of vague forms of direct democracy (Block/Negrine 2017). While different kinds of populism display common features, populism is actually an extremely heterogeneous political phenomenon, as the individual populist actors can be, for instance, conservative or progressive, religious or secular.

> Given that populism is a thin-centered ideology, addressing only a limited set of issues, almost all populist actors combine populism with one or more other ideologies, so-called host ideologies (Mudde/Rovira Kaltwasser 2017: 21).

Considering that populist traits are identified in various policies, movements, and actors, populism could be viewed merely as an empty word. Nevertheless, the term is today still in the spotlight particularly due to the resurgence of so-called populists in the 21st century, both on the right, such as Trump and the Italian Matteo Salvini, and on the left, mainly in Latin America, such as Bolivia's Evo Morales and Venezuela's Hugo Chávez. It has been argued that right-wing populists tend to be more *exclusionary*, as they omit migrants or ethnic minorities from their ideal virtuous people, while left-wing populists would have a more inclusive concept of *the people* (Rice-Oxley/Kalia 2018). However, arguably the "most successful populists today are on the right, particularly the radical right", politicians who "like Marine Le Pen in France, Viktor Orbán in Hungary, and Donald Trump in the US, combine populism with [anti-immigrant] nativism and authoritarianism" (Mudde in Molloy 2018). Wodak (2015: 25–26) describes three central concepts in right-wing populist discourses: the existence of a *pure people*, which represents a central community living in the *Homeland*, which constitutes the second concept, and an antagonistic *Other*, consisting of, for instance, the elites, minority groups or immigrants. The *People* appears to be constructed as a single, homogenous group, which is situated against an *Other*, in an *us* versus *them* logic (Panizza 2017: 409–410).

The contemporary populist communication style is influenced by the character of our era, in which politics is mediatised and affected by the complexity and fluidity of media (Chadwick 2013). Successful populists have been recognized for their savvy use of media communication, while conventional politicians have found it increasingly difficult to communicate with voters. Populism may therefore be investigated as a political communication style enacted for the construction of identity and power. Populist actors use words, signs, and images to connect with the people and to demonise the other (Block/Negrine 2017: 179). Populists all tend to resort to a similar kind of rhetoric to win over their audiences. For instance, they often use short, simple slogans and direct language and refer to *the will of the people* or describe the virtuous masses as *ordinary*, *hard-working* or *taxpaying*. The politicians of the 'evil elite' are questioned in their fundamental dignity as political actors but also attacked as persons. Some academics argue that populism necessarily has a performative character, as

> [c]harismatic populists need crowds, a stage, the limelight, usually coupled with a plain-speaking approach that everyone will understand (Hawkins in Rice-Oxley/Kalia 2018).

Clearly, "populists are dividers, not uniters" (Mudde in Friedman 2017): populism divides society into two homogenous and antagonistic groups: the pure people and the corrupt elite. The United States, which forms the object of the present study, is a liberal democracy, a system based on pluralism, on the idea that different interests and values are legitimate and respected. Populists are essentially not pluralist, as they consider just one group, *the people*, as legitimate. Trump, in particular, has been considered a typical example of a populist leader. He empathised with the anger and frustration of the working class who felt neglected by the elites. Trump exploited many Americans' discontent with a multicultural society, blaming migrants for stealing American jobs, and portraying refugees, South Americans and Muslims as criminals and security risks. His slogans promised to put 'America First', acting in the interest of the American people, and to 'Make America

Great Again', restoring the state to its former glory (see, e.g. Napolitano/Aiezza 2018). Especially from the day of his inauguration, Trump shifted from promoting his leadership to presenting himself as a vehicle of the interests the Americans and as a paternalistic leader who will do things for his people (Mudde in Friedman 2017; Napolitano 2018; Williams 2018).

1.2 The White House website

The present study focuses on the United States context and the discourses constructed under the current presidency through the materials published on the White House website, <www.whitehouse.gov>. The first White House website was launched in the early days of the web, in 1994, under President Clinton, when only 2 % of American households had access to the Internet (Clinton 2001). The platform aimed to provide a single point of access to virtually all government information available on the Internet. The site has been reorganised under each following president, has evolved along with the technological development of the Internet and adapted to new portable devices (Trump 2018). Nowadays, it also includes participative functions and live multimedia streaming (Axios 2014).

The website collects different types of official documents authored by multiple figures. In particular, the Office of the Press Secretary is responsible for writing the statements and memoranda that are published on the website. The Press Office works alongside the Office of Communications to produce and divulge the presidency's message, for instance by collaborating in the writing of speeches, such as the inaugural address. The Communications Director, in particular, is responsible for the development and promotion of the presidential agenda and manages its media campaign (Liptak 2017).

At the time of writing this paper, the position of White House Communications Director is vacant after Bill Shine resigned on March 8, 2018. He was the sixth person to have held the top communications post in Trump's administration in just over two years, which reflects a much higher turnover compared to the previous presidencies

(Riley-Smith/Sabur 2019). President Trump had indeed had problems in filling the post since the beginning of his term (Gstalter 2019). Moreover, Trump may be said to have enacted a *foxification* of the White House as he has hired many of Fox News talents (Collins/Darcy 2018).

Immediately after the presidency was transferred from Barack Obama to Donald Trump, a digital shift of power also took place online, as the White House website was dramatically reorganised to emphasise the new administration's priorities. The topics highlighted in the new website drastically underscored the differences between the two presidencies. Obama's White House website hosted information on issues such as Civil Rights, Climate Change, LGBT Rights, Healthcare, Immigration, Education and the Iran Deal. Initially, Trump's White House website listed instead just six issues scattered with *America First* slogans: America First Energy Plan, America First Foreign Policy, Bringing Back Jobs And Growth, Making Our Military Strong Again, Standing Up With Our Law Enforcement Community, Trade Deals Working For All (Glenza/Borger 2017).

Another of the changes sadly introduced in the White House is the banning of the Spanish language from the website, which is currently an English only site. When the users try to access the link <www.whitehouse.gov/espanol>, they are presented with this message "404 - PAGE NOT FOUND. That page cannot be found, or is located on an archived web page". The ideological decision seems to be consistent with President Trump's criticism of the widespread use of Spanish in the United States (see Fox News 2017). The Trump White House site has indeed been expanded over the past year. At the time of writing, it includes Economy & Jobs, Budget and Spending, Land & Agriculture, Veterans, Education, Law and Justice, Energy & Environment, Healthcare, Immigration, Infrastructure & Technology, National Security & Defense, Foreign Policy, Social Programs. Nevertheless, some topics have not been re-introduced: Civil rights, Climate change, Disabilities, Equal pay, Reducing gun violence, Urban and economic mobility, Women (Robertson 2018).

The homepage of the White House website under Trump's presidency looks to be similar to a blog, with the latest news or *posts* in evidence and direct links to the most relevant issues in the presidential agenda. The main issues highlighted in the menu at the top of the page under Trump are Economy, National Security, Budget, Immigration, and The Opioid Crisis. Like the sites of his predecessors, this website collects an array of online resources relating to a variety of issues, divided into news, presidential actions and briefing and statements. The site also maintains a symbolic continuity with his predecessors, through the White House logo and the images and information about the White House building itself. Such elements constitute traditional symbols of political legitimation and authority. The website also establishes contact with its audience primarily through a newsletter subscription and social media links (see also Chadwick 2001).

2 Aims and purposes

The present research analyses the political discourse constructed through official government communications during Trump's US Presidency. The investigation focuses on the representation and promotion of the US leader and political actions as a champion of the American people and its will, in contrast with its enemies. The study explores how the official documents published on the White House contribute to Trump's populist and nativist rhetoric. More specifically, the paper investigates the discursive construction of the national in-group and of its out-group and the promotion of actions aimed at safeguarding the American interest against *others*.

3 Data and methods

This study considers the online texts published on the current White House website from the beginning of Trump's office, i.e., February 20 2017, until October 31 2018, about the *hot topics* of National

Security & Defense (228 texts, 178,902 tokens, 8,741 types) and Immigration (123 texts, 155,111 tokens, 7,030 types). The corpus comprises a total of 351 articles (amounting to 334,013 tokens and 11,147 types).

The research investigates the different kinds of texts published on the White House website considering the role of this official channel in the construction of the official institutional discourse under one administration.

The investigation integrates qualitative and quantitative perspectives of analysis. Critical Discourse Analysis (see, e.g. Wodak 2009) provides a useful framework for the study of political speeches and documents, as it aims to critically investigate how social inequality, domination, and power abuse are produced and reproduced and how power relations are legitimised in language use. More specifically, the study analyses the discursive construction of the identity of the leader and his people, through the representation of the nation and the construction of its others, all to endorse the presidential policies. The Discourse-Historical Approach developed by Ruth Wodak and her colleagues (see, e.g. Reisigl/Wodak 2001, 2016), in particular, is an interdisciplinary methodology based on critical discourse analysis which provides a set of analytical tools useful in the analysis of ideology in populist discourse. The approach was applied, for instance, to investigate the discursive representations of minority *out-groups* in racist and anti-Semitic discourses (Reisigl/Wodak 2001). In their analysis of racist discourse, Reisigl and Wodak (2001, 2016) identified the strategies adopted in the construction of social actors, objects and events (including nomination, predication, argumentation, perspectivisation and intensification/mitigation).

The present study is supported by Corpus Linguistics (see, e.g. Baker *et al.* 2013) tools, in order to identify trends in language usage which may be suggestive of discourses. In particular, the documents were analysed through the corpus analysis suite *AntConc 3.4.4* (Anthony 2014). Texts were also part-of-speech tagged and examined through the online corpus query tool *SketchEngine* (Kilgarriff *et al.* 2014).

Tab. 1: Main references to the in-group.

Word	Freq.	%
we	4,406	1.32
our	3,166	0.95
United States	1,829	0.55
people	1,103	0.33
country	1,056	0.32
America	551	0.16
us	511	0.15
nation	466	0.14
u.s.	366	0.11
Americans	194	0.06

4 Analysis

As a starting point of the study, the most frequent words, present at least 100 times in the whole corpus, were identified. It was, therefore, possible to categorise them in three macro-areas: terms referring to *us*, the in-group, the people; those defining the *other*, the enemy; terms referring to corrective and legal actions towards the other (see also McEnery 2006). The following paragraphs analyse in more detail the discourses associated with such categories.

4.1 The in-group

Among the most frequent terms referring to the American people (collected in Tab. 1), first-person plural personal references *we* and *our* ranked the highest. Personal references represent some of the fundamental linguistic structures which allow the speakers to define our in-group, conveying a feeling of *we-ness* (Chilton 2017) as opposed to the excluded out-group. It was therefore deemed worthwhile to focus on the possessive adjective *our*, considered as a particularly significant linguistic resource used to define the national attributes.

Tab. 2: Right-hand collocates of *our*.

Word	Freq.	%	Word	Freq.	%
Country	301	0.09	families	45	0.01
border	266	0.08	economy	45	0.01
nation	214	0.06	strategy	41	0.01
military	130	0.04	enforcement	39	0.01
security	126	0.04	interest	39	0.01
national	123	0.04	life	37	0.01
system	123	0.04	way	37	0.01
communities	122	0.04	forces	36	0.01
allies	116	0.03	efforts	35	0.01
partners	82	0.02	freedom	35	0.01
people	73	0.02	homeland	35	0.01
defense	61	0.02	southern	33	0.01
citizens	46	0.01	current	30	0.01

The collocates of *our* in the corpus were thus retrieved. Tab. 2 shows the main right-hand collocates of the adjective. The most frequent elements defined as *our* in the documents include references to the nation such as *our country*, *our nation*, *our people* and *our families* but also mentions of *our border* and *our security*.

Tab. 3 shows the main left-hand collocates of *our*. As revealed in the data, the majority of verbs tend to be linked to the protection of a country under external attacks, such as *protect*, *secure*, *defend* on one side and *threaten* and *enter* on the other. The linguistic opposition between *us* and the *other* seems to reiterate the America First promise made by Trump to his voters. Nevertheless, Trump's speaking in the name of *his* people is also particularly stressed as many of his opponents attack his *America First* mentality as "outdated, obsolete, and dangerous". As Michael Quigley (14/11/2017) of the Democratic Party stated (Quigley 2017), it:

> paints a picture that is blatantly un-American. "America First" sends a signal to the global community that the United States no longer wants to carry the torch of freedom and democracy, which shines brighter through inclusion and collaboration.

Tab. 3: Left-hand collocates of *our*.

Lemma	Freq.	%
protect	142	0.04
secure	126	0.04
enforce	64	0.02
support	63	0.02
need	57	0.02
defend	51	0.02
threaten	43	0.01
keep	41	0.01
strengthen	34	0.01
rebuild	34	0.01
ensure	33	0.01
enter	33	0.01

The clusters including the adjective *our* in the corpus were also obtained. Of particular relevance were the collocations linked to the actions the US need to take for the people's sake, in particular *protect our country/nation/families*, *secure our border/s*, *enforce our immigration laws*, as represented in the following examples from the official documents on the White House website:

(1) SECURE BORDERS, SECURE COMMUNITIES: Securing our borders will help safeguard the safety of our communities and curb the flow of illegal drugs into the United States (Immigration. Fact Sheets 02/02/2018).
(2) THE PRESIDENT: It's time to support our police, to protect our families, and to save American lives (Immigration. Remarks 16/08/2018).

These actions are presented as the necessary response to external subjects that *threaten our* (*national*) *security/way of life*, as in (3):

(3) President Donald Trump will not rest and will not relent until we destroy ISIS at its source so it can no longer threaten our people or threaten our allies or freedoms around the world (National Security & Defense. Remarks 09/06/2017).

Since the notion of *the people* is so central in populist discourse, it is interesting to comment on the collocational pattern for the word *people* itself. By the word *people*, the texts mainly refer to US citizens defined as the *American people* (252, 0.08 %), the virtuous group requiring the President to provide protection and security, as exemplified by frequent clusters such as *protect* (*the safety and security of*) *the American people*. In particular, when connoted as *great* (23, 0.007 %) and *incredible* (15, 0.004 %), the term *people* is referred to the armed forces, such as army, veterans, police officers, border patrol agents, praised as defenders of the nation:

(4) We're also deeply honored to be joined today by family members of four fallen Border Patrol agents — Luis Aguilar, Nicolas Ivy, Rohelio Martinez, and Brian Terry. And I just met the folks and the people and the children, and these are incredible people. Could I ask you to stand, please? What incredible people (Immigration. Remarks 20/08/2018).

The people and its protectors are presented in antithesis to the immigrant subjects defined e.g. as *bad* (8, 0.002 %) and *horrible* (3) people who illegally enter the national territory to commit crime (see also Charteris-Black 2018):

(5) They mind it when it happens to them. They don't mind it when they have to watch it on television. Have waged an unprecedented assault on American law enforcement — our greatest people — threatening ICE and Border Patrol for performing their duties admirably and for defending our country from horrible people and horrible, horrible events and crimes (Immigration. Remarks 20/08/2018).

4.2 The out-group

Among the most frequent words in the corpus, a considerable section relates specifically to the *Others*, subjects different from the in-group and to their actions threatening its values and life. As evident in Tab. 4, these subjects are connected to issues such as immigration, gangs (as in (7)), foreign regimes (as in (6)), and terrorism (as in (8)).

(6) With each chemical attack that goes unpunished, dangerous regimes see an opportunity to expand their arsenal (National Security & Defense 14/04/2018).

Tab. 4: Main references to the out-group.

Lemma	Freq	%	Lemma	Freq	%
they	1,776	0.53	ISIS	170	0.05
immigration	1,077	0.32	armed	168	0.05
their	874	0.26	drug	160	0.05
them	606	0.18	problem	156	0.05
alien	507	0.15	Syria	151	0.05
criminal	488	0.15	risk	147	0.04
threat	394	0.12	terrorism	145	0.04
illegal	388	0.12	refugee	144	0.04
foreign	380	0.11	chemical	137	0.04
terrorist	315	0.09	emergency	136	0.04
ms-13	284	0.09	nuclear	133	0.04
gang	256	0.08	dangerous	132	0.04
attack	240	0.07	bad	117	0.04
immigrant	224	0.07	kill	113	0.03
weapon	202	0.06	Afghanistan	112	0.03
Korea	195	0.06	threaten	111	0.03
enter	189	0.06	Iraq	109	0.03
Iran	181	0.05	migration	103	0.03
regime	177	0.05	Mexico	100	0.03
crime	176	0.05			

(7) Ranchers, border residents are having to deal every single day with the threat of gangs and other criminal organizations coming straight through their property, right around their families, endangering the lives as they are trafficking through (Immigration. Remarks 06/08/2018).

(8) Jihadist Terrorist Organizations, such as ISIS, threaten all civilized people in every corner of the world. These national security challenges also require a dramatic rethinking of American foreign policy from the previous decades (National Security & Defense. Remarks 02/12/2017).

In his characterisation of social actors and their actions, Trump exploits argumentations that are distinctly imbued with populist motifs. His reliance on fear and his battle against immigration are typical topics of right-wing nativist populism, which were once connected to fringe movements such as the Tea Party, but have now become part of mainstream American politics (Wodak 2015).

The President's emphasis on border control and his construction of the identity of the *other* in relation to the national borders is connected to bordering practices and the process of alienisation (Demata 2017: 275). Ideological discourse typically constructs an *other* subject, who is represented as having negative characteristics, opposed to the moral and social norms of a presumed majority. Considering the frequency list, an issue which seemed to be particularly relevant in the discourse of the Trump administration is the naming of the immigrant subjects. The most frequent adjective/noun used by the current administration to refer to immigrants is *alien*. Immigration is a particularly sensitive lexical area, in which, for political correctness, euphemisms are often preferred in order to show respect towards the rights of the human being. Expressions such as *undocumented immigrants* have, for instance, been favoured by many. Nevertheless, it is true that the American law does define these subjects as *alien*, attributing to the term the meaning of "any person, not a citizen or national of the United States" (USA 1952). Nonetheless, the word is also negatively connoted as somehow dehumanising people. It is relevant to note that the CNN declared that it had received an email from the Justice Department requiring the channel to use the phrase *illegal aliens* instead of *undocumented* immigrants (Kopan 2018). This terminological requirement seems to be in line with the trend identified in the corpus.

To further investigate the usage of the term *alien* in Trump's era documents, the immediate right and left collocates were obtained. The main R1 collocates of the term in the corpus were: *child* (42, 0.013 %), *family* (15, 0.004 %), *crime* (11, 0.003 %), *gang* (9, 0.003 %), *minor* (8, 0.002 %). *Alien* is thus used as an adjective defining above all children and families and then crime and criminals, as in the examples:

(9) The Secretary shall not, however, detain an alien family together when there is a concern that detention of an alien child with the child's alien parent would pose a risk to the child's welfare (Immigration. Executive Orders 20/06/2018).

(10) But under federal law, all unaccompanied alien children, regardless of nationality, they have to go before a judge. They cannot be subject to expedited removal proceedings (Immigration. Remarks 23/05/2018).

The strong association of the term with unaccompanied minors who were forced to abandon their native countries seems to be particularly insensitive, especially considering the recent US policies which separated children from their parents at the border with Mexico.

Among the collocates of the term *alien*, several are represented by past participles used as adjectives, namely *convicted* (8, 0.002 %), *apprehended* (6, 0.002 %), *charged* (5, 0.001 %), *backed* (4, 0.001 %), *incarcerated* (4, 0.001 %), *affiliated* (2, 0.001 %). These terms are employed to refer mainly to the US legal actions against foreign subjects who violated the law both as criminals or as simple immigrants, as in the example:

(11) In just the last few days our Nation's ICE officers have arrested 153 criminal aliens in south Texas, 84 criminal aliens in the Pacific Northwest, and 31 criminal aliens in Long Island, New York – these arrests include aliens convicted of robbery, burglary, aggravated assault, sexual assault against a child, smuggling, drug dealing, and many more (National Security & Defense. Statements & Releases 07/04/2017).

As shown in (11), one of the strategies exploited in ideological discourse is the inclusion of figures (see van Dijk 2005) from official sources about immigration and criminality to display objectivity and lend credibility to the danger represented by immigrants.

The left-hand collocates of the term *alien* were also examined to investigate the main attributes associated with them. The main qualifiers referring to these subjects in L1 position are, again, *illegal* (136, 0.04 %), *criminal* (125, 0.04 %), *unaccompanied* (37, 0.01 %), as in the example:

(12) As a result, dangerous criminal aliens are released back into American communities, where they have the potential to commit further crimes. [...] President Trump has acted to strengthen the country's ability to enforce the laws and stop illegal aliens at the border and has directed the hiring of 10,000 additional ICE agents and 5,000 additional Border Patrol agents (Immigration 16/05/2018).

The immigrant people seem to be further dehumanised by being defined based on the policies applicable to their case as *removable* (13,

0.004 %), *resident* (3, 0.001 %), *deportable* (2, 0.001 %), *foreign-born* (2, 0.001 %) as in:

(13) Limited categories of aliens are currently subject to expedited removal, which erodes border integrity and control by impeding the ability of the Federal Government to efficiently and quickly remove inadmissible and deportable aliens from the United States (Immigration. Statements & Releases 08/10/2017).

The three-word clusters of the term *alien** were also identified, showing, again, how the word is mainly adopted for *unaccompanied alien children* (31, 0.009 %) or criminals, such as *dangerous criminal aliens* (12, 0.004 %), *illegal alien crime* (11, 0.003 %), *criminal illegal aliens* (9, 0.003 %). Furthermore, it is found in the cluster *an illegal alien* (19, 0.006 %) in reports of single cases of illegal immigrants who committed crimes, which, by accumulation, strengthen the idea of immigrants as a threat.

By continually defining them as *criminals* and *illegal*, these discourses construct immigrants crossing borders as the out-group. Mexican immigrants, in particular, are viewed as murderers, rapists or drug traffickers. Immigrants are described as *illegal* for several reasons: they enter the country illegally; some of them already have a criminal record; most of them are expected to commit crime. Other groups of social actors are also constructed as *others* and evoked by Trump in his anti-immigration discourse. In particular, we see mention of *terrorists*, mainly *Muslim terrorists*, and *refugees*, especially from Syria (Demata 2017: 279–280).

4.3 Corrective actions

Amongst the most frequent terms in the corpus, a large group of words refers to legal actions and measures aimed at protecting the people and at stopping the other from invading the country (Tab. 5).

The protection of the American border seems to be particularly relevant, with great importance given to the infamous wall on the Southern border with Mexico intended to prevent illegal immigrants from entering the USA. This seemingly absurd and impractical plan became one of the central motifs of Trump's campaign which evidently helped him

Tab. 5: Main references to corrective actions.

Lemma	Freq.	%	Lemma	Freq.	%
security	1,698	0.51	removal	138	0.04
law	1,120	0.34	prevent	135	0.04
border	951	0.28	identify	125	0.04
defense	743	0.22	benefit	124	0.04
enforcement	472	0.14	lottery	123	0.04
policy	464	0.14	enforce	120	0.04
visa	295	0.09	implement	119	0.04
secure	254	0.08	restriction	118	0.04
safety	253	0.08	chain	115	0.03
wall	225	0.07	authorize	115	0.03
sanctuary	220	0,07	remove	110	0.03
arrest	213	0.06	patrol	108	0.03
safe	210	0.06	legal	107	0.03
fight	208	0.06	combat	105	0.03
stop	178	0.05	control	104	0.03
loophole	148	0.04	freedom	101	0.03
guard	138	0.04	measure	101	0.03

achieve consensus. Illegal Mexican immigrants in the USA were constructed as a threat, accused of stealing American jobs and committing criminal activities. In his discourse on immigration, Trump stressed, therefore, the need for a physical barrier to stop illegal immigrants from accessing the country, in order to prevent crime and social danger. The plan to build a wall on the border with Mexico addresses the sense of insecurity generated by the perception of dangers, real or projected, coming from outside the nation and putting it under threat. The idea of immigrants, *aliens*, crossing the American border, created in his people a sense of insecurity and danger: Trump skilfully connected illegal immigration, the American borders and the integrity of the nation-state. Already in his pre-electoral manifesto, *Immigration Reform that Will Make America Great Again*, Trump had created a relationship between the supposedly fallen state of the USA and the immigration policies under his predecessor. In the text, Trump stressed the idea that "the absence of borders pre-empts the very existence of a nation" (Demata 2017: 287), as evident from its main points:

1. A nation without borders is not a nation. There must be a wall across the southern border.
2. A nation without laws is not a nation. Laws passed in accordance with our Constitutional system of government must be enforced.
3. A nation that does not serve its own citizens is not a nation. Any immigration plan must improve jobs, wages and security for all Americans. (Trump 08/2015).

In the official documents on the White House website, when Trump's words were reported, these were, as always, very straightforward and direct, offering a testimony of the informalisation of politics the President embodies. Trump seems, therefore, to give voice to what angry ordinary people say or would say without being intimidated by official roles and contexts.

(14) Q Is there any agreement without the wall? THE PRESIDENT: No, there wouldn't be. You need it. John, you need the wall. I mean, it's wonderful – I'd love not to build the wall, but you need the wall (Immigration. Remarks 09/01/2018).

(15) THE PRESIDENT: They wanted it so badly – San Diego. They wanted it so badly. And I said, you know, if we build it, we will lose a big constituency, because there won't be anybody saying, "We want the wall." But we had to build it. So I know they're very happy about it (Immigration. Remarks 16/08/2018).

(16) BORDER SECURITY: Build a southern border wall and close legal loopholes that enable illegal immigration and swell the court backlog (Immigration. Fact Sheets 08/10/2017).

As evident in (16), a significant issue appearing in the corpus is the attack against those practices in current immigration law that are considered as legal loopholes and threats to the national security, namely the visa lottery, chain immigration, and sanctuary cities. Sanctuary cities, in particular, are jurisdictions that limit their cooperation with the national government's effort to enforce immigration law. Trump's presidency constructed these cities as supporting criminality by releasing dangerous criminals and empowering violent cartels such as MS-13, by refusing to turn over incarcerated criminal aliens to Federal authorities:

(17) Hundreds of sanctuary jurisdictions release dangerous criminals and empower violent cartels like MS-13 by refusing to turn over incarcerated criminal aliens to Federal authorities (Immigration. Statements & Releases 08/10/2017).

(18) The sanctuary cities like to say they're protecting immigrant communities. These criminal aliens are going to go back into the very communities they live in. They're going to victimize those very immigrant communities (Immigration. Remarks 02/02/2018).

Visa Lottery is the US programme which randomly selects 50,000 foreign nationals per year to apply for permanent residence (green cards) in the United States. The process was criticised by the President for being based on chance instead of personal abilities and for importing into the US criminals and unwanted elements, as Trump stated in his colourful language:

(19) Each year, the diversity visa lottery program randomly selects up to 50,000 foreign nationals to apply for permanent residence (green cards) in the United States. Many of them have absolutely no ties to the United States, and are not required to have special skills or much education. Randomly selecting foreign nationals from around the globe, including from state sponsors of terrorism, and admitting them into the United States invites large amounts of fraud and does not serve the national interest (Immigration 01/02/2018).

(20) We have the visa lottery, where we take people by lottery from countries. Now, just – you know, from a business standpoint, do you think they're giving us their finest? We get some real beauties out of the lottery. These countries – I mean, they're not stupid. They give us people that they do not want. And we have to take them (National Security & Defense. Remarks 20/10/2018).

Through chain immigration, foreign nationals who permanently resettle in the US have the possibility to bring over their foreign relatives, who will then be able to do the same. Trump also attacked this process for not being based on merit and as favouring the arrival of criminals and terrorists. Several times, the documents report single cases of criminal actions committed by subjects who entered the US through these immigration programmes:

(21) Under chain migration, foreign nationals can come to the United States and bring in unlimited numbers of foreign relatives. A single immigrant can begin a chain that could ultimately bring in dozens of increasingly distant relations. Because these individuals are admitted solely on the basis of family ties – not skill or not merit – most of this immigration is lower-skilled, putting considerable strain on federal welfare. Moreover, because there are no real selection criteria, the current system is totally incompatible with national security. This week, a terrorist exploded a pipe bomb on a busy subway passage during rush hour in New York City, injuring innocent Americans. This individual arrived through chain migration (Immigration. Statements & Releases 16/12/2017).

4.4 Comparing Trump's and Obama's White House websites

It would have been interesting to investigate, together with Trump's White House, the archived Obama's era site, as a means to gather insights of the changes in the two Presidents' positions and communicative strategies on immigration and security. A parallel comparison of the materials published on the two websites about these specific issues would, however, require a particularly time-consuming cataloguing, as Obama's website does not organise documents by topic but by text type. Nevertheless, in order to obtain a general representation of linguistic tendencies in the two websites, Google Searches of some relevant terms were launched on the websites <https://www.whitehouse.gov/> and <https://obamawhitehouse.archives.gov/> (on March 30 2019). It is important to bear in mind that Obama remained in office for 96 months while, at the time of writing article, Trump's presidency has lasted 25 months.

As evident from Tab. 6, in eight years as president, the term *alien** was mentioned only on 345 occasions on Obama's website and, most of the times, it was actually included in direct quotes of the American law. The high use in Trump's website of terms like *immigrant**, *illegal alien**, *illegal immigrant** and *our border* reflects and confirms his construction of an external enemy, typical of nativist political strategies. It is also worthwhile to contrast the results of the searches of *our people/people's* and *Americans*. Their high presence in Trump's documents seems to testify, on the other hand, the stronger branding of Americans as the in-group defended by the current President.

Tab. 6: Frequencies of a selection of terms related to the out-group and the in-group in Trump's and Obama's White House websites.

Terms	Frequencies in Trump's White House website (time span 25 months)	Frequencies in Obama's White House website (time span 96 months)
immigrant*	1,810	2,370
alien*	663	345
illegal alien*	293	120
illegal immigrant*	214	148
our border	578	251
our people/'s	1,615	1,713
Americans	15,400	21,700

5 Conclusions

Populism celebrates the people, conceived as a numerous and homogenous whole. The construction of an identity for the people is enacted in opposition to its enemies who are depicted as threatening it. Right-wing populism is often connected to nativist tendencies, which identify the pure people with the native inhabitants of a homeland, menaced by the immigrant others. The *body politic* is thus often integrated with *border politics*. In his discourse, Trump represents himself as a paternalistic leader who will provide solutions for the nation's evils, defending the United States against dangers coming from inside and outside its borders. Trump creates the image of weak border security, a frontier constantly penetrated by malicious criminal subjects who represent a threat to the nation, its interests, and its values. The president exploits the popular frustration for economic and social issues to rely on a *politics of fear*: fear of aggression by strangers, of losing jobs and rights, of compromising old traditions and values (Rydgren 2007). Right-wing populist parties offer facile solutions to these challenges, through simplifications which may be easily understood and retained by the masses. They tend therefore to construct the other as a scapegoat for the current problems, relying on traditional stereotypes and images of the enemy. Ethnic, religious and linguistic minorities are hence represented as a scapegoat for the current problems. Fear of the other is thus exploited by politicians who claim to speak and act on behalf of the nation to justify their tough policies on security and immigration matters (see Wodak 2015).

The present study aimed at exploring how the institutional White House website contributes to the representation of the present US president as a champion of the rights of the American people against its enemies. The official documents construct a state under attack by multiple subjects who often reach the US territory through immigration processes. Immigrants are thus continually associated with Mexican criminal gangs and Islamic terrorism. The nation and its borders are thus depicted as needing to be protected by policies designed *in the name of the people*. These arguments are exploited to justify a necessity to enforce, strengthen and change the American immigration law. This political strategy also involves addressing practices which are currently favouring immigration and thus compromising Trump's project of American greatness.

The institutional discourse analysed is developed through official publications available to and addressing the whole nation. Nevertheless, the presidential discourse gives the impression of justifying xenophobia, empowering and protecting only white Americans, while enabling them to consider Latino or Muslim minorities as *un-American* and as unwelcome. It would be meaningful to further examine the evolution of the concept of the US national identity over time, especially in connection with security and immigration discourses. On that account, it would therefore be useful to compare more systematically the official documents produced under Trump's office with those archived on the websites of the previous US presidencies.

References

Albertazzi, Daniele / O'Donnell, Duncan 2008. Introduction: The Sceptre and the Spectre. In Albertazzi, Daniele / O'Donnell, Duncan (eds) *Twenty-First Century Populism: The Spectre of Western*

European Democracy. Basingstoke, UK, and New York: Palgrave Macmillan, 1-11.

Anthony, Laurence 2014. *AntConc 3.4.4*. Tokyo: Waseda University.

Axios, Ashleigh 2014. Welcome to the White House: Then and Now. *The White House. President Barack Obama*. <https://obamawhitehouse.archives.gov/blog/2014/10/24/welcome-white-house-then-and-now>

Baker, Paul / Gabrielatos, Costas / McEnery, Tony 2013. *Discourse Analysis and Media Attitudes: The Representation of Islam in the British Press*. Cambridge: Cambridge University Press.

Block, Elena / Negrine, Ralph 2017. The Populist Communication Style: Toward a Critical Framework. *International Journal of Communication* 11, 178-197

Chadwick, Andrew 2001. The Electronic Face of Government in the Internet Age: Borrowing from Murray Edelman. *Information, Communication & Society* 4/3, 435-457.

Chadwick, Andrew 2013. *The Hybrid Media System: Politics and Power*. Oxford: Oxford University Press.

Charteris-Black, Jonathan 2018. *Analysing Political Speeches: Rhetoric, Discourse and Metaphor*. London: Palgrave.

Chilton, Paul 2017. "The People" in Populist Discourse: Using Neuro-Cognitive Linguistics to Understand Political Meanings. *Right-Wing Populism in Europe & USA: Contesting Politics & Discourse beyond 'Orbanism' and 'Trumpism'. Special Issue of Journal of Language and Politics* 16/4, 582-594.

Clinton, William Jefferson 2001. Frequently Asked Questions. *The White House*. President William Jefferson Clinton. <https://clintonwhitehouse4.archives.gov/WH/html/faq.html>

Collins, Kaitlan / Darcy, Oliver 2018. Former Fox News President Accepts Top White House Job. *CNN*. <https://edition.cnn.com/2018/06/27/politics/bill-shine-donald-trump-communications-director/index.html>

Demata, Massimiliano 2017. "A Great and Beautiful Wall". Donald Trump's Populist Discourse on Immigration. *Journal of Language Aggression and Conflict* 5/2, 274-294.

Demata, Massimiliano 2018. "I Think That Maybe I Wouldn't Not Be Here If It Wasn't for Twitter." Donald Trump's Populist Style on Twitter. *Textus, English Studies in Italy* 31, 67-90.

Fox News 2017. White House Takes down All Spanish-Language Content from Its Website. *Fox News*, 23 January. <https://www.foxnews.com/us/white-house-takes-down-all-spanish-language-content-from-its-website>

Friedman, Uri 2017. What Is a Populist? *The Atlantic*, 27 February. <https://www.theatlantic.com/international/archive/2017/02/what-is-populist-trump/516525/>

Glenza, Jessica / Borger, Julian 2017. White House Website Switches over to Trump's 'America-First' Policy Agenda. *The Guardian*, 20 January. <https://www.theguardian.com/us-news/2017/jan/20/white-house-website-trump-policy-agenda>

Gstalter, Morgan 2019. The Five Trump Communications Directors Who Have Come and Gone. *The Hill*, 8 March.

Hawkins, Kirk A. 2010. *Venezuela's Chavismo and Populism in Comparative Perspective*. New York: Cambridge University Press.

Kilgarriff, Adam / Baisa, Vít / Bušta, Jan / Jakubíček, Miloš / Kovvář, Vojtěch / Michelfeit, Jan / Rychlý, Pavel / Suchomel, Vít 2014. The Sketch Engine: Ten Years on. *Lexicography* 1, 7-36.

Kopan, Tal 2018. Justice Department: Use 'Illegal Aliens', Not 'Undocumented'. *CNN*, 25 July. <https://edition.cnn.com/2018/07/24/politics/justice-department-illegal-aliens-undocumented/index.html>

Liptak, Kevin 2017. Shaping Trump's Messaging as He Looks to Fill Communications Director Post. *CNN*, 7 August. <https://edition.cnn.com/2017/08/07/politics/white-house-communications-director/index.html>

McEnery, Tony 2006. *Swearing in English: Bad Language, Purity and Power from 1586 to the Present*. London/New York: Routledge.

Molloy, David 2018. What Is Populism, and What Does the Term Actually Mean? *BBC News* 6 March. <https://www.bbc.com/news/world-43301423>

Mudde, Cas / Rovira Kaltwasser, Cristóbal 2017. *Populism: A Very Short Introduction*. Oxford: Oxford University Press.

Napolitano, Antonella 2018. Another Brick in the Wall: A Critical Discourse Analysis of the Political Discourse of Division. In Diglio, Carolina / Napolitano, Antonella / Perilli, Fabio (eds) *Identity, Language and Diversity, Between Walls and Bridges*. Naples: Paolo Loffredo Iniziative Editoriali, 471-498.

Napolitano, Antonella / Aiezza, Maria Cristina 2018. The Press War in the Post-Truth Era: A Corpus-Assisted Cda of the Discourse of Us Political Analysts on Trump's Figure and Policy. *Textus, English Studies in Italy* 31, 91-118.

Panizza, Francisco 2017. Populism and Identification. In Rovira Kaltwasser, Cristóbal / Taggart, Paul / Ochoa Espejo, Paulina / Ostiguy, Pierre. *The Oxford Handbook of Populism*. Oxford and New York: Oxford University Press, 406-425.

Quigley, Mike 2017. Trump's "America First" Foreign Policy Is Blatantly Un-American. *Congressman Mike Quigley*, 14 November. <https://quigley.house.gov/media-center/speeches/quigley-trump-s-america-first-foreign-policy-blatantly-un-american>

Reisigl, Martin / Wodak, Ruth 2001. *Discourse and Discrimination. Rhetorics of Racism and Antisemitism*. London and New York: Routledge.

Reisigl, Martin / Wodak, Ruth 2016. The Discourse-Historical Approach (Dha). In Wodak, Ruth / Meyer, Mike (eds) *Methods of Critical Discourse Studies*. London: Sage, 23-61.

Rice-Oxley, Mark / Kalia, Ammar 2018. How to Spot a Populist. *The Guardian*, 3 December. <https://www.theguardian.com/news/2018/dec/03/what-is-populism-trump-farage-orban-bolsonaro>

Riley-Smith, Ben / Sabur, Rozina 2019. White House Communications Director Bill Shine Resigns. *The Telegraph*, 3 August. <https://www.telegraph.co.uk/news/2019/03/08/white-house-communications-director-bill-shine-resigns/>

Robertson, Adi 2018. Trump's White House Website Is One Year Old. It's Still Ignoring Lgbt Issues, Climate Change, and a Lot More. *The Verge*, 20 January. <https://www.theverge.com/2018/1/20/16909218/trump-white-house-website-update-lgbt-climate-change-disabilities-one-year-anniversary>

Rydgren, Jens 2007.The Sociology of the Radical Right. *Annual Review of Sociology* 33, 2412-2462.

Trump, Donald 2015. Immigration Reform That Will Make America Great Again. *Donald J. Trump*. <https://assets.donaldjtrump.com/Immigration-Reform-Trump.pdf>

Trump, Donald 2018. *The White House*. President Donald John Trump. <https://www.whitehouse.gov/>

USA (United States of America) 1952. *Definitions. Immigration and Nationality Act*. 8 U.S.C. 1101.
van Dijk, Teun A. 2005. Politics, Ideology and Discourse. In Wodak, Ruth (ed.) *Elsevier Encyclopedia of Language and Linguistics: Politics and Language*. Oxford: Elsevier, 728-740.
Williams, Donovan E. 2018. Populism in the Era of Donald Trump. *IOL. Independent Online*, 10 August. <https://www.iol.co.za/news/opinion/populism-in-the-era-of-donald-trump-16493780>
Wodak, Ruth 2009. *The Discourse of Politics in Action: Politics as Usual*. Basingstoke: Palgrave Macmillan.
Wodak, Ruth 2015a. Right-Wing Populism Is Surging on Both Sides of the Atlantic – Here's Why. *The Conversation*, 25 November. <http://theconversation.com/right-wing-populismis-surging-on-both-sides-of-the-atlantic-heres-why-47876>
Wodak, Ruth 2015b. *The Politics of Fear: What Right-Wing Populist Discourses Mean*. London: Sage.

Miguel Ayerbe Linares

Talking about populists in Twitter: Politicians' linguistic behaviour in comments about populists in Germany and Austria

1 Introduction

The role of the social media in politics has been under close scrutiny for over twenty years (Altheide 2004; Dahlgren 2009; Strömback/Esser 2009; Nahon *et al.* 2011; Chadwick 2013, 2014; Groshek/Engelbert 2013; Klinger/Svensson 2015; Broersma/Graham 2016; Chadwick *et al.* 2016; Enli 2016, 2017; Graham *et al.* 2016; Nahon 2016). According to some experts, the advent of social media has wrought fundamental changes in the relationship between politicians and the citizens they represent since, as Engesser *et al.* suggest (2017: 1110), these media offer a direct channel of communication from politicians to ordinary people, lessening the intermediary role formerly played by the traditional media, and the rules that these imposed. However, the changes brought by social media amount to more than simply facilitating politicians' access to their audiences: they also allow the audiences to participate actively, or in other words, they enable citizens to take part in public political debate (Gil de Zúñiga *et al.* 2014: 613; Skoric *et al.* 2016: 1818; Enli 2017: 221).

Regarding the relationship between social media and populism, which forms the framework for the present study, previous authors have analysed populists' communication strategies, the way they present themselves, and even the way they interact with their audiences. Bobba (2018), Engesser *et al.* (2017), and Groshek and Engelbert (2013) draw attention to the growing academic bibliography on the use of resources like Facebook and Twitter in the political sphere, but they contrast this with the relative paucity of studies within the same area on the relationship between populism and social media, and the manifestations of populism in Internet. In this context, Engesser *et al.* (2017) concretely mention studies by Bartlett (2014), and Groshek and Engelbert (2013). However, in a relatively short period of time, a sizeable volume of studies on the relationship between populism and social media has now come into being, such as Bobba (2018), Mazzoleni and Bracciale (2018), Postill (2018), Bracciale and Martella (2017), and Ernst *et al.* (2017) and Gerbaudo (2018). Hameleers *et al.* (2018) have produced large-scale studies of the communication strategies of populist political parties in Europe from a comparative perspective covering 16 countries, while smaller-scale surveys are to be found in papers such as that by Ernst *et al.* (2017). There is thus a growing volume of studies analysing the way political parties in Europe use the Internet and social media to communicate, transmit their own ideas, exert an influence, and reach the public in general or like-minded audiences in particular. The volumes edited by Aalberg *et al.* (2017) and Zienkowski and Breeze (2019) also present a useful overview of the different ways in which populists currently communicate, looking at countries in northern, southern, eastern and western Europe.

On a different level, it is also important to take account of work by Ott (2017), about the attitudes that are encouraged by social media, as well as the papers by Stieglitz and Dang-Xuan (2013) and Thelwall, Buckley and Paltoglou (2011) on the role of the emotions and impulsiveness in social media. In fact, it is widely acknowledged that the use of Twitter is often governed by impulse, and that users may fail to consider the consequences and implications of the comments that they publish in this medium. This holds for the contents of what they say, as well as for formal aspects such as grammar and spelling. However, the story does not end here. Impulsiveness and uncivil communication, in Ott's words (2017: 61–62), may lead to attitudes and comments that cross the borderline from the domain of the purely negative to the terrain proper of offensiveness and aggression.

A considerable amount of attention has now been paid to the way different populist parties present themselves in the social media, how they try to influence voters, how they convey their ideas, and the arguments and strategies they use to do all this. The moment has come to ask ourselves what image populist parties have in the worldview of other political groupings, as evidenced in social media. In other words, still within the area of the relationship between populism and social media, it is important to turn the question around, and see what happens when populists are not seen as the active subject of social media communication, but rather as the object of discussion. How do political groups who are not populist talk about populist parties and populism in the social media? Contributions are needed that can explore this perspective. Previous studies have drawn attention to the particular interest of populists in this type of media in order to establish direct contact with citizens. Work by Engesser *et al.* (2017: 1113), Enli *et al.* (2017: 222), Krämer (2014: 45), Kriesi (2014: 363), Canovan (2002: 34), and Taggart (2002: 67) has considered this issue: some populists are opposed to any kind of intermediary between politicians and voters, while others consider that this is the way to establish more direct contact without external entities imposing rules or controlling the messages that can be sent. However, we should also reflect on whether this kind of behaviour is peculiar to populist political formations, or whether similar phenomena are to be found in the actions of non-populist political groups when they appear in social media such as Facebook and Twitter.

In this, it is important to bear in mind that social media are by no means the exclusive preserve of populists and their supporters, but are actually open to all political parties, be they socialist, liberal, ecologist (green) or right-wing. It is reasonable to assume that all these different types of party want to reach their respective audiences more directly, influence public opinion, discredit other parties, etc. In this sense, we can safely assume that populism itself is one of the topics that are hotly disputed in these forums, above all if we take into account the enormous expectations that populist parties have generated in the last two or three years, in the election campaigns that have been held in different parts of Europe. Given the real possibility that these populist groups may form part of a government, it is understandable that other parties would try to counteract their influence through all available means – which, of course, include the social media.

All these political formations must necessarily be aware of the possibilities that the social media offer for direct contact, without mediating institutions, but also without the need to follow the normal rules of politeness and good style. These other parties are likely also to use the social media in order to send messages, appeal to the emotions of potential supporters, and to criticise and/or discredit rival parties.

The aim of the present chapter is to analyse how the mainstream political parties in Germany and Austria talk about the right-wing populist parties (*Alternative für Deutschland* (AfD) and *Freiheitliche Partei Österreichs* (FPÖ)) and their main representatives, in the social media, and in concrete, in Twitter: how do they refer to them, how do they describe them, how do they handle them? What is their linguistic behaviour towards these right-wing populist parties? Do we find aggression and offensive behaviour, in terms of form and/or content, as Ott (2017) suggested? In the second half of 2017, general elections were held in Germany and Austria, and the populist parties (AfD and FPÖ, respectively) aroused great expectation, as the possibility arose that AfD would hold seats in the *Bundestag*, and that the FPÖ would obtain enough votes to form a coalition government. As we now know, both of these predictions were to come true after those elections.

2 Methodology

The aim of this study is to analyse the linguistic behaviour of the other German and Austrian parties when commenting on the right-wing populist parties AfD and FPÖ, and their main representatives, in Twitter. I analyse the national Twitter accounts of the parties CDU and SPD in Germany, and SPÖ and Die Grünen in Austria. Comments from the Twitter accounts of prominent party members that were re-tweeted through the party account were also taken into consideration. The period of analysis encompasses June 2018 to January 2019, that is, a period after the new governments had been formed in the wake of the general elections of 2017.

The study is essentially qualitative, based on the analysis of comments tweeted by politicians in the non-populist parties concerned from the parties' Twitter accounts on a national level. As comments published in this medium contain different resources, including words, emoticons, photos, videos and other symbols, I limit my present study to language data. More concretely, I analyse the nouns, adjectives and verbs used to refer to populist parties and their members, and also their actions. I also search for expressions, possibly metaphorical, that are used to refer to them when the party's official name is not used (AfD or FPÖ), or when individuals are not given their proper name (Alexander Gauland, Alice Weidel or Heinz-Christian Strache, Norbert Hofer, Herbert Kickl). In the case of Austria, since the FPÖ formed a coalition with the conservative ÖVP, this party itself became an object of criticism because of its pact with the populists, with attacks levelled particularly at leader Sebastian Kurz, currently Chancellor of Austria. In the present context, it is important to note that criticisms of Kurz were often similar to attacks on the Vice Chancellor, Hans Christian Strache, a member of the FPÖ.

The analysis of these Twitter attacks on the different parties are explained separately, starting with Germany, then moving on to Austria. The Twitter account of each party is examined separately, as there may be major differences in each party's behaviour when talking about the populists in the country concerned. A distinction will be made between the treatment of AfD and FPÖ as political formations, in terms of nouns, adjectives and verbs, as well as between their members. In other words, I analyse the lexical categories used by mainstream parties to characterise populists and their actions.

In addition to this, I also examine other morphological aspects of the linguistic handling of these parties, such as word formations (derivation and composition), as well as reduced forms. Similarly, I take into account communicative strategies of different kinds, such as implicit references, omissions, comparisons, identifications, etc. I contrast the attitude of the two different parties towards the populist party, in each case, in order to find possible similarities; and finally I compare the results from the two countries in order to establish whether or not their handling of the populists is different (bearing in mind that the populists formed part of the government in Austria, but remained a minority with no decisive political influence in Germany). As a result, through this last comparison, I hope to ascertain whether the treatment of the AfD in Germany is qualitatively different from the handling of the FPÖ in

Austria, given the fact that the latter party later became part of a coalition government.

3 The AfD in German parties' Twitter accounts

3.1 ***Comments in the CDU's Twitter account***

Within the time frame of the present study, only six comments on AfD were published in the CDU's Twitter account. The only expression used to identify the party *Alternative für Deutschland* is its abbreviation, AfD:

(1) Wir lehnen Koalitionen und ähnliche Formen der Zusammenarbeit sowohl mit der Linkspartei als auch mit der AfD ab (@CDU Deutschlands, 17.12.2018). [We reject coalitions and similar forms of collaboration with both the left party and with AfD]

Regarding nouns for referring to AfD members, more variety is present: *Populisten* (3 times), *Extremen* (once), *Radikalen* (once), which are used in exactly the same contexts, which implies that these terms function as synonyms.

This idea is supported by the fact that in 4 out of 6 comments the CDU uses the noun *Zusammenarbeit* to talk about its attitude towards the AfD, that is, its refusal to work together with this group. This noun appears in the same sentences as the nouns used to refer to populist politicians. This is, in fact, practically the CDU's only message concerning the AfD in Twitter:

(2) Nur Volker #Bouffier hat eine Zusammenarbeit mit den Populisten von links und rechts ausgeschlossen! (@CDU Deutschlands, 24.10.2018) [Only Volker #Bouffier has excluded collaboration with the populists from left and right]

As far as verbs are concerned, we only find verbs with a meaning associated with exclusion or rejection concerning the possibility of working together: *ablehnen*, *ausschließen*. When a verb with this meaning is not used, the negative adjective *kein* is placed before *Zusammenarbeit* or *Populisten*.

3.2 ***Comments in the SPD's Twitter account***

A much larger number of comments were found in the SPD's account than in that of the CDU: 37 comments over the same time period. To refer to the AfD itself, two nouns are used: AfD (8 times) and *Rechtspopulismus* (once). Regarding nouns denoting populist politicians, we find 7 different terms: *(neue) Nationalisten*, *die Rechten*, *politische Gegner*, *Rechtspopulisten*, *Spalter*, *Hetzer*, *Feinde*. The most frequent were: *Rechtspopulisten* [right-wing populists] (5 times) and *Hetzer* [agitators] (3 times). These nouns can be classified in two groups: those which are simply a political label (*Rechtspopulisten*, *politische Gegner*, *Nationalisten*, *die Rechten*), while, on the other hand, we have nouns that seem to indicate judgements about people (*Spalter* [people who cause division], *Hetzer*, *Feinde* [enemies]):

(3) Die Rechtspopulisten sind unsere Feinde! (@SPD Parteivorstand, 24.12.2018) [The right-wing populists are our enemies!]

The use of *Spalter*, *Hetzer* and *Feinde* presents a striking contrast to the comment re-tweeted by Andrea Nahles (SPD) condemning the physical attack suffered by Frank Magnitz, a member of the AfD, on 7 January:

(4) Die AfD ist ein politischer Gegner unserer toleranten und friedlichen Gesellschaft. Aber wer die Partei und deren Politiker mit Gewalt bekämpft, verrät diese Werte und gefährdet unser Zusammenleben. (@SPD Parteivorstand, 8.01.2019). [The AfD is a political opponent of our tolerant and peaceful society. But someone who combats this party and its politicians using violence betrays these values and places our life together at risk]

It is worth discussing some aspects of this tweet at greater length, since it contrasts notably with what we normally find. In the first place, *Gegner* [opponent] is a more positive term when compared to *Feind* [enemy], since it makes reference to a competitor or rival who does not necessarily pose any danger. *Feind*, by contrast, has a very hostile loading, representing a danger that is more or less serious. This term would not be used in the language of sporting competitions, for example, except as a metaphor to speak of someone who is going to take away a trophy in a fair fight. In the SPD's comments, *Gegner* is only used to refer to the AfD in this case, where the discourse is softened, probably in order to express solidarity with the victim of the attack. Secondly, the populists are here referred to as *Politiker* [politicians], and this is the only time that this is the case, since they are mostly presented as enemies (*Feinde*), people who cause division (*Spalter*) or agitators (*Hetzer*), that is, everything except politicians like the others.

Some of the nouns used reveal how the SPD understands the AfD and its members or followers. AfD's actions are described as *Angriffe* [attacks] and *Bedrohung* [threats], and as intended to inspire fear:

(5) Rechtspopulisten bedrohen Europa. (@SPD_Parteivorstand, 9.12.2018) [Right-wing populists threaten Europe]

(6) Die AfD aber lebt davon, Ängste zu schüren und hat kein Interesse an Lösungen. (@SPD_Parteivorstand, 30.11.2018) [The AfD lives from stoking fears and has no interest in solutions]

Unlike the CDU, the SPD includes some adjectives referring to AfD politicians and their supporters:

(7) Wenn das Mikro aus ist, ist die Sprache der Gaulands, Weidels und Storchs noch Hasserfüllter und Menschenverachtender als wenn es an ist. (@SPD_Parteivorstand, 30.11.2018) [When the microphone is off, the language used by Gauland, Weidel and Storch is even more full of hate than when it is on]

(8) Die Jugendorganisation der AfD Baden-Württemberg ist durchsetzt mit rechtsradikalen und verfassungsfeindlichen Kräften. (@SPD_Parteivorstand, 16.11.2018) [The AfD BadenWürttemberg's youth organisation is packed with right-wing extremist forces that are hostile to the constitution]

These examples also contain expressions such as *hasserfüllt* [filled with hatred], *menschenverachtend* [contemptuous of people], *rechtsradikal* [right-wing extremist], *verfassungsfeindlich* [anticonstitutional]. In a similar tone, they also use verbs like *sägen* [to saw], or *bedrohen* [to threaten].

On another level, some comments build associations between AfD and reprehensible occurrences in the past, such as the persecution of the Jews, particularly during the National Socialist regime:

(9) Lassen wir nicht zu, dass neue Nationalisten den alten Ungeist in Europa wieder entfesseln! (@SPD_Parteivorstand, 30.11.2018) [Let's not allow the new nationalists to unleash the old demon in Europe again!]

(10) Die Juden sind angeschuldigt worden, sie würden die Pest verbreiten. Genau das Gleiche machen Sie heute mit den Flüchtlingen. (@SPD_Parteivorstand, 22.11.2018) [The Jews were accused of spreading the plague. They are doing exactly the same today with the refugees]

The first of these quotations seems to be attributing to AfD a return (*wieder*) to the kind of disaster (*Ungeist*) caused by the National Socialists in the period before the Second World War. The second appears to be equating AfD's stance in favour of controlling immigration to the persecution of the Jews, a subject that is still extremely sensitive in Germany.

On the other hand, the SPD does not portray the AfD as an isolated phenomenon that represents a threat to Germany and to Europe. One comment situates the AfD in the same group as conservatives and big corporations:

(11) Kampfansage an Großkonzerne, Rechtspopulismus, Konservative! (@SPD_Parteivorstand, 2.12.2018) [Declaring battle on big business, right-wing populism, conservatives!]

Finally, we have to mention the use of a communicative strategy which is normally associated with populist discourse: the use of the antithesis "us versus them" (Albertazzi/McDonnell 2008: 3; Rooduijn 2014: 727; Engesser *et al.* 2017: 1112):

(12) Entweder wir entscheiden über die Zukunft Europas oder die anderen. Entweder wir oder die Le Pens, die Salvinis, die Gaulands, die Orbans. (@SPD_Parteivorstand, 1.12.2018) [Either we decide the future of Europe or the others will. Either we do it, or the Le Pens, the Salvinis, the Gaulands, the Orbans]

3.3 ***Comparison between CDU and SPD in Germany***

Apart from the quantitative difference in the number of comments by each political group, in the case of the CDU we can note that the noun

Populist prevails over words of a more evaluative nature presenting a value judgement, such as *Radikaler* [radical] or *Extreme* [extremist]. They do not use descriptive adjectives or verbs with negative connotations or aggressive undertones to talk about the AfD. Their attitude towards the AfD seems to be mainly reduced to their refusal to contemplate cooperation (*Zusammenarbeit*) with them. In short, the CDU's comments are almost always characterised by a certain moderation, with very few value judgements. Moreover, the CDU does not use communicative strategies that directly or indirectly evoke associations between the AfD and the crimes of the past.

The SPD's comments, by contrast, are more derogatory and aggressive, using highly charged nouns and adjectives that would be inappropriate in a more formal medium. Something similar is the case with verbs. Similarly, they employ the strategy of referring to highly negative events in the past, such as the Holocaust, which are still very sensitive issues today.

Finally, neither of these two parties regards the AfD as an isolated group on the margins of politics, as if it were on the fringes of democracy.

4 The FPÖ in Austrian parties' Twitter accounts

4.1 ***Comments in the SPÖ's Twitter account***

Rather than using the official abbreviation, the SPÖ refer to the FPÖ using derogatory terms such as *Faschismus* [fascism], *Rechtsextremismus* [right-wing extremism], *Arbeiterverräter* [traitor to the workers], *Klassenkampf* [class struggle], *rechtspopulistische Illusion der völligen Abschottung* [right-wing populist illusion of complete isolation], *Gipfel des Hasses* [peak of hatred], to name but a few:

(13) Von Beginn an war die SPÖ treibende Kraft zur Verbesserung der sozialen Lage und der Rechte der BürgerInnen sowie im Kampf gegen Faschismus und Rechtsextremismus (@SPOE_at, 1.01.2019) [From the outset, the SPÖ

was the driving force behind the improvement of the social situation and rights of citizens, as well as in the struggle against fascism and right-wing extremism]

When it comes to specific people, particularly Sebastian Kurz (ÖVP) and Hans Christian Strache (FPÖ), their surnames generally appear in association with concepts that are negative and even dangerous for Austria:

(14) Er (Kickl) ist damit eines des größten Sicherheitsprobleme unseres Landes (@SPOE_at, 7.09.2018) [He (Kickl) is thus one of the biggest security problems for our country]
(15) Kickl ist ein Problem für diese Republik (SPOE_at, 24.09.2018) [Kickl is a problem for this republic]

Apart from this, the SPÖ uses wordplay to criticise members of the government. Examples can be found such as *Schweigekanzler* [Chancellor of silence], *Konzernkanzler* [Business Chancellor]. Other examples include *(Un)sozialministerin* [Minister of the (Un)Social]. Nonetheless, as far as other nouns are concerned, the doubt arises as to whether the socialist SPÖ applies these terms to Kurz and the Vice-Chancellor Strache because it regards them as populists, or because it aims to criticise big business and defend workers' rights. In the latter case, we can suppose that it would use these nouns for all the leaders of other parties, whether they are populists or not:

(16) Danke, Konzernkanzler #Kurz und ArbeitnehmerInnenverräter #Strache! (@SPOE_at, 1.09.2018) [Thank you, Business Chancellor #Kurz and worker-betrayer #Strache!]

Negatively connotated nouns are also used to refer to the FPÖ's actions and measures, such as *Gesetzesraub* [legal theft], *Lohnraub* [salary theft], *Obszönität* [obscenity], *Schweinerei* [dirty business], *Hetze* [agitation]:

(17) Der Tausch 12-h-Tag gegen Nichtraucherschutz war schon ein Junktim von hoher Obszönität (SPOE_at, 3.11.2018) [The exchange of the 12-hour day for protection for non-smokers was a highly obscene package]

Regarding verbs for describing the FPÖ's actions and measures, and those of Chancellor Kurz, the list is long and varied (around 30 different verbs are used), including some with particularly violent connotations that are hardly appropriate in this context: *peitschen* [to whip], *fesseln* [to tie up], *angreifen* [to attack], *gefährden* [to endanger], *enteignen* [to expropriate], *spalten* [to divide], *verraten* [to betray], *drohen* [to threaten], *diffamieren* [to defame], *beleidigen* [to insult], etc.:

(18) Er (Kickl) setzt sie (freie Medien) unter Druck und diffamiert JournalistInnen. (@SPOE_at, 4.11.2018) [He (Kickl) puts them (the free media) under pressure and slanders journalists]

On another level, we can perceive the use of different strategies to delegitimise the FPÖ. One of them already familiar from the German data consists of building associations between the FPÖ and negative aspects of the past, such as National Socialism, perhaps with the idea that society needs to learn the lessons of recent history and prevent such disasters from happening again:

(19) Heute jähren sich #Novemberpogrome ggn [gegen] JüdInnen zum 80. Mal. Die unmenschlichen Taten konnten nur geschehen, weil eine Politik d [der] Spaltung & d [des] Hasses geführt wurde. Dubkelste [Dunkelstes] Kapitel unserer Geschichte verpflichtet nicht nur zu erinnern, sondern zu handeln. Nie wieder Faschismus! (SPOE_at, 9.11.2018) [Today is the 80th anniversary of the November pogroms against Jews. These inhuman acts could only happen because there was a politics of division and hatred. The darkest chapter in our history obliges me not only to remember, but to act. Never again fascism!]

Another strategy, also observed above, consists of using the dichotomic approach often attributed to populists, 'people up there', 'us against them':

(20) Dieser Klassenkampf von oben ist nicht hinnehmbar! (SPOE_at, 16.06.2018) [This class struggle from above is not acceptable!]
(21) Wir sind die WIR-AG (AktienGesellschaft "PLC") die anderen sind die ICH-AG! (SPOE_at, 29.09.2018) [We are the WE-PLC, the others are the I-PLC]

In other cases, the "Ö" is omitted from the abbreviated name of the two governing parties, ÖVP and FPÖ, which is short for Austria in both cases (*Österreich*), perhaps as a way of saying that these parties do not represent Austria, since, in the SPÖ's view, they attack and betray the citizens and the country itself:

(22) VP/FP vergrößern die Probleme, die sie vorgeben zu lösen (SPOE_at, 26.08.2018) [VP/FP magnify the problems that they pretend to be solving]

Similarly, we should mention the parody of literary genres such as folk-tales and the use of rhyming couplets:

(23) 60 Stunden hackeln gehn, wenn's der Chef verlangt,
was er dir mit null Überstundenzuschlägen dankt.
Sagst du einmal nein, ist's kein Problem,
Job ist weg, das wirst doch verstehn! (SPOE_at, 19.06.2018)
[Work for 60 hours when the boss tells you to,
and he shows his gratitude with zero overtime rates.
If you once say no, it's no problem,
your job is gone, as you can understand!]
Es war einmal ein selbsternannter Kämpfer des kleinen Mannes (SPOE_at, 19.06.2018) [Once upon a time there was a self-declared fighter for the small man]

*4.2 **Comments in Die Grünen's Twitter account***

In the Twitter account of the Austrian ecological party, the same nouns appear as above to refer to the FPÖ, such as *Populismus*, *Rechtspopulismus*, and some more derogatory nouns such as *Faschismus*. Since the FPÖ has formed a coalition with the ÖVP, which is a more conservative party, various descriptions appear to indicate this coalition: *Schwarz-Blau* [black-blue], *Türkis-Blau* [turquoise-blue], made up of the colours associated with these parties[1]. These composite names are often used to criticise the measures and actions of the coalition:

(24) Schwarz-Blau raubt Kindern technisch und kalt ihre Zukunft (@BirgitHebein, 17.06.2018) [Black-blue robs children using technology and kills their future]

---

1 Black is traditionally associated with the ÖVP and, since 2017, so is turquoise. Blue is the traditional colour of the FPÖ.

As for people in the FPÖ, they are almost always called by their surname *(Heinz-Christian) Strache*, *(Norbert) Hofer*, *(Herbert) Kickl*:

(25) Kurz-Strache können das nicht kübeln! (@Gruene_Austria, 9.12.2018) [Kurz-Strache can't ignore that]

This party also uses official titles, such as *Minister*, *Innenminister*, *Vizekanzler*, with or without the person's name:

(26) Der österreichische Innenminister #Kickl bedient sich am ungarischen Vorbild #Orban! (@Gruene_Europa, 25.09.2018) [The Austrian Home Secretary #Kickl is following the example of his Hungarian role model#Orban!]

Nouns conveying negative evaluation are also used to refer to members of the FPÖ, both collectively and as individuals: *Alpennationalisten* [Alpine nationalists], *Freiheitlichen* [freedom fans], *Rechtsextremen* [right-wing extremists], *Verschwörungstheoretiker* [conspiracy theorists], *Gefahr für die Rechtsstaatlichkeit* [danger for the rule of law]; some of which are reinforced by the use of adjectives: *gefährliche innenpolitische Bombe* [dangerous domestic policy bomb], *Knecht der Starken* [slave of the strong]:

(27) Kickl und seine Behörden sind eine Gefahr für die Rechtsstaatlichkeit! (@m_steinkogler, 29.11.2018) [Kickl and his authorities are a danger for the rule of law!]

The nouns and adjectives used to describe the attitudes of the populists and their associates (here, the ÖVP) dwell on what is undemocratic, hostile and motivated by hatred: *gesteuerte Hetze* [organised defamation], *geschürter Hass* [incited hatred], *Missachtung der Demokratie* [scorn for democracy], *menschenfeindliche Realität* [reality hostile to human beings], *geplante demokratiefeindliche Änderungen* [planned changes against democracy]:

(28) Wie müssen die menschenfeindliche Realität von #türkisblau beenden! (@Gruene_Austria, 17.11.2018) [We must put an end to the inhuman reality of #turquoise-blue!]

Regarding verbs, we find many with a negative meaning that is quite inappropriate in the political sphere, being used to describe the actions of people within the coalition and, particularly, members of the FPÖ: *stehlen* [to steal], *rauben* [to rob], *angreifen* [to attack], *schweigen* [to silence], *pfeifen* [to whistle, not care], *aushöhlen* [to hollow out], *drohen* [to threaten], *ignorieren* [to ignore], *zerstören* [to destroy], *(Angst) schüren* [to whip up (fear)], *(auseinander) dividieren* [to sow division]:

(29) Diese Regierung höhlt nicht nur die Demokratie aus, sondern ihre Instrumente und somit den Parlamentarismus (@Gruene_Austria, 29.11.2018) [This government not only hollows out democracy, but does the same to its tools and to the parliamentary system]

When it comes to communicative strategies, Die Grünen also draw on associations with the National Socialist past, as in the following tweet:

(30) Ein neuer Rommel ist das allerletzte, was wir brauchen und haben wollen (@haraldwalser, 3.09.2018) [A new Rommel is the last thing that we need and want]

This was published to criticise comments made by Reinhard Bösch (FPÖ) about the possibility of creating an area for detaining emigrants in North Africa. It establishes a direct connection with General Erwin Rommel (1891–1944) who led the German Wehrmacht campaign in North Africa during the Second World War. The following tweet provides another example of this strategy:

(31) Also in Österreich baut die Regierung Stacheldracht um Flüchtlingskinder und in den USA schreibt sie ihnen Nummern auf die Unterarme (@michaelreimon, 1.12.2018) [So in Austria the government puts barbed wire around refugee children and in the USA they mark numbers on their arms]

This again evokes memories of the war, and of concentration camps where children were also branded with numbers. Even though the tweet attributes this measure to the US government, the association with Nazi concentration camps is clearly established.

4.3 ***Comparison between the SPÖ and Die Grünen***

Both parties' Twitter accounts show evidence of a large number of negatively connoted nouns used to refer to the FPÖ and its members. The same negative load is also found in the verbs used to describe its measures, initiatives and actions. This goes beyond assertions that "they are wrong", "they have acted inappropriately" or "they are making a mistake". The judgements here seem to imply that the FPÖ is acting illegally or violently, by "robbing", "threatening", "tying up", "beating", "putting in danger", and so on. This leads to degradation in terms of content, with a highly emotive negative representation of populist politicians and their actions.

Both parties also apply the strategy of implying links with negative events in the past, particularly National Socialism and the Holocaust, aspects which are still extremely sensitive in Germany and Austria. By arousing fear along these lines, these two parties seek to discredit populists in the eyes of the electorate. Both parties thus present the populists as a danger to society, the rule of law, and democracy.

Despite the similarities, the comments from Die Grünen maintain a certain degree of formality when mentioning figures from the FPÖ who are now members of the government, for example by using their official title (*Vizekanzler Strache*, *Minister Kickl*). In the comments by the SPÖ, by contrast, only the surname is used (*Strache, Kickl*).

5 Conclusion

This analysis of the Twitter accounts belonging to the CDU and SPD in Germany, and the SPÖ and Die Grünen in Austria, focusing on the way they portray the AfD and FPÖ, respectively, has brought several points to light. Notably, there is an imbalance between the two countries as far as comments about the populist party is concerned. The German parties publish far fewer tweets about populists than the Austrian ones do, which could be because the AfD currently does not have a decisive role in German politics. In Austria, the FPÖ later went into coalition with the ÖVP, which might account for its prominence in the Twitter accounts run by the SPÖ and Die Grünen.

Quantity aside, all the Twitter accounts analysed project a negative vision of the AfD and FPÖ, although the type and degree of negative appraisal varies. The conservative CDU is the only party among those studied that does not use a degrading or offensive tone when talking about the populists – something that is abundantly present in the other parties' tweets. The CDU's strongest declaration is its desire not to collaborate with the AfD and its assertion that this party is not needed in the parliament, but the tone is neither aggressive nor insulting. By contrast, the other party not only criticises AfD, but employs nouns, adjectives and verbs that are derogatory and insulting. It is hard to imagine terms of this kind being used by these politicians in other contexts where criticism is frequent, such as in parliamentary debates. In this sense, we can say that this is a style of communication that it not just uncivil, but actually aggressive, along the lines described by Ott (2017).

Regarding communication strategies, both SPD and SPÖ make use of resources generally associated with populists, such as 'the others' and 'the people up there' (Bobba 2018; De Cleen 2019). Moreover, in all three left-wing parties (SPD, SPÖ and Die Grünen) we find the strategy of triggering associations between populism, on the one hand, and National Socialism, the Holocaust and the Second World War, on the other.

This study has also enabled us to determine, along the lines envisaged by Enli (2017), the extent to which the social media constitute an important alternative channel of communication and interaction between parties and their sympathisers. This communication is much more direct than that provided by traditional media such as newspapers, which are constrained by editing practices (Engesser *et al.* 2017): social media cut out the intermediary, bringing sender and recipient much closer to one another (Bobba 2018). This has led to a new concept of communication, since social media facilitate greater spontaneity (Mazzoleni/Bracciale 2018), which may in turn lead to heightened polarisation in which the emotions play a major role (Enli 2017; Engesser *et al.* 2017). The observations made in the present study have tended to confirm the presence of this polarising tendency. On the other hand, the foregoing analysis has also brought out how some of the features identified in the bibliography as being characteristic of populism in the social media, especially Twitter, are also present in the comments made by non-populist parties when referring to populist groups and their followers, in both Germany and Austria. We have seen how mainstream parties also exploit the discursive dichotomy between "us" and "the others", and between "elites" and "working people". These parties also seek to generate fear, even though the contexts they use to do so are different from those used for scaremongering by the populists. Whereas populist discourse often conjures up images of uncontrolled immigration as a potential threat, the non-populist parties build associations with the National Socialist past, the Second World War and the Holocaust to alarm the populace. A further common point is the use of impoliteness and even aggression on the part of mainstream parties when talking about their rivals (Ott 2017). In other words, this chapter has shown how in a media environment characterised by the absence of institutional or editorial intermediaries, the linguistic behaviour and communication strategies found in comments by non-populist parties about their populist rivals in Germany and Austria do not differ greatly from the behaviour and strategies attributed in the bibliography to populists themselves.

References

Aalberg, Toril / Esser, Frank / Reinemann, Carsten / Strömbäck, Jesper / De Vreese, Claes H. (eds) 2017. *Populist Political Communication in Europe*. New York: Routledge.

Albertazzi, Daniele / McDonnell, Duncan 2008. Introduction: A New Spectre for Western Europe. In Albertazzi, Daniele / McDonnell, Duncan (eds) *Twenty-first Century Populism: The Spectre of Western European Democracy*. Basingstoke: Palgrave Macmillan, 1-11.

Altheide, David L. 2004. Media Logic and Political Communication. *Political Communication* 21/3, 293-296.

Bartlett, Jamie 2014. Populism, Social Media and Democratic Strain. In Lodge, Guy / Glenn, Gottfried (eds) *Democracy in Britain: Essays in Honour of James Cornford*. London: Institute for Public Policy Research, 91-96.

Bobba, Giulano 2018. Social Media Populism: Features and 'Likeability' of Lega Nord Communication on Facebook. *European Political Science* (online first), 1-13. doi.org/10.1057/s41304-017-0141-8
Bracciale, Roberta / Martella, Antonio 2017. Define the Populist Political Communication Style: The Case of Italian Political Leaders on Twitter. *Information, Communication & Society* 20/9, 1310-1329.
Broersma, Marcel / Graham, Todd 2016. Tipping the Balance of Power: Social Media and the Transformation of Political Journalism. In Bruns, Axel / Enli, Gunn / Skogerbø, Eli / Larsson, Anders O. / Christensen, Ch. (eds) *The Routledge Companion to Social Media and Politics*. New York/London: Routledge, 89-103.
Canovan, Margaret 2002. Taking Politics to the People: Populism as the Ideology of Democracy. In Mény, Yves / Surel, Yves (eds) *Democracies and the Populist Challenge*. Basingstoke: Palgrave, 25-44.
Chadwick, Andrew / Dannies, James / Smith, Amy P. 2016. Politics in the Age of Hybrid Media: Power, Systems, and Media Logics. In Bruns, Axel / Enli, Gunn / Skogerbø, Eli / Larsson, Anders O. / Christensen, Ch. (eds) *The Routledge Companion to Social Media and Politics*. New York/London: Routledge, 7-22.
Chadwick, Andrew 2014. The Hybrid Media System: Politics and Power. *Public Administration* 92/4, 1106-1114.
Chadwick, Andrew 2013. *The Hybrid Media System*. Oxford: University Press.
Dahlgren, Peter 2009. *Media and Political Engagement*. Cambridge: University Press.
De Cleen, Benjamin 2019. The Populist Logic and the Discursive Construction of 'the People'. In Zienkowski, Jan / Breeze, Ruth (eds) *Imagining the Peoples: Political Discourses across the Political Spectrum*. Amsterdam: John Benjamins.
Engesser, Sven / Ernst, Nicole / Esser, Frank / Büchel, Florin 2017. Populism and Social Media: How Politicians Spread a Fragmented Ideology. *Information, Communication & Society* 20/8, 1109-1126.
Enli, Gunn / Simonsen, Chris-Adrian 2017. 'Social Media Logic' Meets Professional Norms: Twitter Hashtags Usage by Journalists and Politicians. *Information, Communication & Society* 21/2, 1-16.
Enli, Gunn 2017. New Media and Politics. *Annals of the International Communication Association* 41/3-4, 220-227.

Enli, Gunn 2016. "Trust Me, I Am Authentic!": Authenticity Illusions in Social Media Politics. In Bruns, Axel / Enli, Gunn / Skogerbø, Eli / Larsson, Anders O. / Christensen, Ch. (eds) *The Routledge Companion to Social Media and Politics*. New York/London: Routledge, 121-137.

Ernst, Nicole / Engesser, Sven / Büchel, Florin / Blassnig, Sina / Esser, Frank 2017. Extreme Parties and Populism: An Analysis of Facebook and Twitter across Six Countries. *Information, Communication & Society* 20/9, 1347-1364.

Gerbaudo, Paolo 2018. Social Media and Populism: An Elective Affinity? *Media, Culture & Society* 40/5, 745-753.

Gil de Zúñiga, Homero / Molyneux, Logan / Zheng, Pei 2014. Social Media, Political Expression, and Political Participation: Panel Analysis of Lagged and Concurrent Relationships. *Journal of Communication* 64/4, 612-634.

Graham, Todd / Wright, Scott / Jackson, Dan 2016. Third Space, Social Media and Everyday Political Talk. In Bruns, Axel / Enli, Gunn / Skogerbø, Eli / Larsson, Anders O. / Christensen, Ch. (eds) *The Routledge Companion to Social Media and Politics*. New York/London: Routledge, 74-88.

Groshek, Jacob / Engelbert, Jiska 2013. Double Differentiation in a Cross-National Comparison of Populist Political Movements and Online Media Uses in the United States and the Netherlands. *New Media & Society* 15/2, 183-202.

Hameleers, Michael *et al.* 2018. Start Spreading the News: A Comparative Experiment on the Effects of Populist Communication on Political Engagement in Sixteen European Countries. *The International Journal of Press/Politics* 23/4, 517-538.

Klinger, Ulrike / Svensson, Jakob 2015. The Emergence of Network Media Logic in Political Communication: A Theoretical Approach. *New Media & Society* 17/8, 1241-1257.

Krämer, Benjamin 2014. Media Populism: A Conceptual Clarification and Some Theses on Its Effects. *Communication Theory* 24/1, 42-60.

Kriesi, Hanspeter 2014. The Populist Challenge. *West European Politics* 37/2, 361-378.

Mazzoleni, Gianpierto / Bracciale, Roberta 2018. Socially Mediated Populism: The Communicative Strategies of Political Leaders on Facebook. *Palgrave Communications* 4/1, 1-10.

Nahon, Karine 2016. Where There Is Social Media There Is Politics. In Bruns, Axel / Enli, Gunn / Skogerbø, Eli / Larsson, Anders O. / Christensen, Ch. (eds) *The Routledge Companion to Social Media and Politics*. New York/London: Routledge, 39-55.

Nahon, Karine / Hemsley, Jeff / Walker, Shawn / Hussain, Muzammil 2011. Fifteen Minutes of Fame: The Power of Blogs in the Lifecycle of Viral Political Information. *Policy & Internet* 3/1, 1-28.

Ott, Brian L. 2017. The Age of Twitter: Donald J. Trump and the Politics of Debasement. *Critical Studies in Media Communication* 34/1, 59-68.

Postill, John 2018. Populism and Social Media: A Global Perspective. *Media, Culture & Society* 40/5, 754-765.

Rooduijn, Matthijs 2014. The Mesmerising Message: The Diffusion of Populism in Public Debates in Western European Media. *Political Studies* 62/4, 726-744.

Skoric, Marko M. / Zhu, Qinfeng / Goh, Debbie / Pang, Natalie 2016. Social Media and Citizen Engagement: A Meta-Analytic Review. *New Media & Society* 18/9, 1817-1839.

Stieglitz, Stefan Dang-Xuan, Linh 2013. Emotions and Information Diffusion in Scial Media-Sentiment of Microblogs and Sharing Behavior. *Journal of Management Information Systems* 29/4, 217-248.

Strömback, Jesper / Esser, Frank 2009. Shaping Politics: Mediatization and Media Interventionism. In K. Lundby (ed.) *Mediatization: Concept, Changes, Consequences*. New York/Bern/Berlin: Peter Lang, 205-223.

Taggart, Paul 2002. Populism and the Pathology of Representative Politics. In Mény, Yves / Surel, Yves (eds) *Democracies and the Populist Challenge*. Basingstoke: Palgrave, 62-80.

Thelwall, Mike / Buckley, Kevan / Paltoglou, Georgios 2011. Sentiment in Twitter Events. *Journal of the American Society for Information Science and Technology* 62/2, 406-418.

Zienkowski, Jan / Breeze, Ruth 2019. *Imagining the Peoples of Europe: Populist Discourses across the Political Spectrum*. Amsterdam: John Benjamins.

Maria Cristina Aiezza

#AmericaFirst vs #primagliitaliani: A Corpus-Assisted CDA of Trump's and Salvini's Twitter communications

1 Introduction

1.1 Populism and digital communication

In the last decades, the terms *populism* and *populist* have been increasingly applied to describe political groups, leaders, discourses and measures. *Populism* is defined as a political approach appealing to "ordinary people who feel that their concerns are disregarded by established elite groups" (Oxford English Dictionary Online 2019). The growing support for populist positions has been clearly influenced by the consequences of the economic and financial crisis, the impoverishment of the middle class, the loss of credibility of the ruling classes, the inability to face technological changes and the challenges of globalisation, refugee crisis and terrorism. The populist ideology considers society as separated into two homogenous and antagonistic groups, the *pure people* and the *corrupt elite*, arguing that politics should be the expression of the general will of the people. The affirmation of these views is supposed to explain developments such as the election of Donald Trump in the United States, Brexit and the rise of authoritarian parties in Europe. Although such political movements undoubtedly make use of populist rhetoric, in the majority of cases, the support they received is motivated by other ideological factors, especially by nativist interests (Mudde/Rovira 2017; Wodak 2017). Nativism opposes an in-group to a non-native alien group threatening it and aims therefore at "protecting the interests of native-born or established inhabitants against those of immigrants" (Oxford English Dictionary Online 2019). In Western societies, migration and defence of minority rights are thus being scapegoated and semiotised as the cause of policies which have harmed the nation, and especially the lower classes (see KhosraviNik 2017: 58).

The evolution of the Internet into web 2.0 has dramatically transformed our lives and affected contemporary political debate (see e.g. Gallardo Paúls 23/11/2018). The recent changes in the communication framework have involved a democratisation of access to information and content production. This has favoured an informalisation of language and the development of a participatory culture which has eroded the old notion of passive media spectatorship, determining convergence of media producers and consumers (Jenkins 2006: 3). The Internet and social media have enabled users to easily express their emotions and thoughts in the online arena, a digital world where visibility has become the new currency (Ziccardi 2018). We are now experiencing a proliferation of opinions, the diffusion of fake and biased news and hate speech, a tendency to remain enclosed in *echo chambers*, and generally a rebellion against expert knowledge (Orsina 2019: 8). Social media, in particular, show potential for networking, political participation and opinion formation, features which have both favoured and been exploited by populist and nationalist movements.

In the age of the end of ideology (Bell 1960), more than relying on collective action, parties seem to depend on the ability of a single charismatic figure, resulting in the personalisation or *leaderisation* of politics (Novelli 2009). In our postmodern era, we live in a state of permanent campaign, in which propaganda is not only aimed at winning elections, as support needs to be continuously monitored, conquered and managed. Politics thus makes systematic use of marketing techniques and gives a significant role to communication experts (Norris 2000).

Political leaders' media-savvy performance has become crucial to consensus building so that we are experiencing a growing trend towards de-professionalisation and celebrity culture in political discourse (Wodak 2011). Their political model is taking advantage of the disintermediation of the digital era, in which the news media are losing their gatekeeping function and seem to have acquired the "almost bureaucratic function" [my translation] (Giorgino 2019: 24) of reporting the ongoing online conversation between politics and citizens. The autonomous structures of communication offered by owned media (Savar

2013) such as social networks are therefore becoming the channels preferred by politicians to interact with voters, in a similar way to traditional rallies:

> Politicians [...] live in their own universe, in a bubble of words, in a bubble of tweets, of interventions on social media, of 'digital balconies', in which they want to speak directly with the people, outside journalistic mediation, outside independent narration [my translation] (Formigli 16/03/2019).

The storytelling infrastructure of social media platforms "invites observers to tune into events they are physically removed from" (Papacharissi 2015: 4). The microblogging platform Twitter appears to be particularly useful to politicians as it can be accessed anywhere from a smartphone to share news, events, comments and multimedia content. It offers a cheap, immediate and effective way to be in the news and shape public opinion and allows users to launch hashtags with the potential to become viral trending topics. Twitter provides a virtual venue where citizens can interact with politicians and among themselves (see Buccoliero *et al.* 2018).

The architecture of the social medium influences the features of the messages produced. Twitter contents, in particular, typically consist of short phrases and comments, images, videos, and links. The platform seems therefore to promote a public discourse that is simple, uncomplicated and informal. The website allows users to publish impulsively and instantaneously spreads their messages. Tweets are generally designed to make an impact, motivated by narcissism and self-promotion (Ott 2017). They are often characterised by sensationalism, extreme and emotive language and especially by negative sentiment, which proves to be key to popularity on Twitter (Thelwall *et al.* 2011).

The new trends in political communication are easily identifiable in the successful experiences of the last elections and governments in the United States (Demata 2018) and Italy. The specific impact of Twitter on public debate would appear to be higher in the US, where 24 % of the population uses this social network (Pew Research Center 03/2018), as compared to only 12.3 % of Italians (Censis 11/10/2018). Especially in Italy, the platform seems to be more aimed at a public of insiders, and is used mainly by opinion makers, opinion leaders, politicians, think tanks and journalists. However, it is also true that Twitter has acquired considerable relevance in newsmaking practices, as it "has complemented or even substituted traditional press agencies in the diffusion of primary political information and statements commenting on the main events" [my translation] (Giorgino 2019: 57).

1.2 Trump's and Salvini's populism

The present study focuses on the successful social media communication strategies enacted by two political leaders, namely the American Donald Trump and the Italian Matteo Salvini, who have recently ascended to power by riding a populist and nativist wave.

Trump represents an unconventional president, with no prior political or military experience, but who has been well known for years as a successful businessman and a reality show celebrity. He is the epitome of everything the world detests, but also admires about America: wealth, power, confidence, but also crass materialism, arrogance, racism and vulgarity (Thomas 2015). From his independent position, the tycoon was able to take advantage of the growing gap between the white working class and the politicians, intellectuals and media. He presented himself as a champion of the American people against its supposed internal detractors, especially the democratic elites, who were accused of harming national interests and of being unresponsive to issues such as unemployment, inequality, immigration and terrorism (see Inglehart/Norris 2016; Napolitano 2018). However, with Trump, "the US moved backward on human rights at home and abroad" (Human Rights Watch 2017: 591). He attacked the mainstream media, depicting them as the 'enemy of the people' for spreading fake and biased news against him. He launched a campaign of hatred against Mexican immigrants and Muslims refugees, construed as external enemies threatening the US security and economy. He supported foreign autocratic governments militarily, financially and diplomatically, and showed little interest or leadership in promoting human and environmental rights in the world (see Human Rights Watch 2019: 619).

Similar attitudes have been adopted in Italy by Matteo Salvini, the leader of the party once known as *Lega Nord*, the *Northern League*. The League traditionally aimed at the independence of the mythical Padania area, roughly comprising northern Italian regions around the river Po valley. Salvini's greatest intuition was to put aside this separatist dream in order to rebrand his party as a national force. The League passed in a few years from low percentages of consensus, under 5 % in 2013 elections, to 17 % in 2018, thus becoming the third Italian party and stealing from Berlusconi the leadership of the right. Salvini became Interior minister and co-Vice-President of an all-populist government formed in co-operation with the Five Star Movement, in the so-called *Governo del Cambiamento* [*Government of Change*]. Surveys showed that the League's popularity even increased after this, reaching 36 % (Pagnoncelli 19/01/2019). Salvini represented in Italy a sort of *de facto* President of the Government but, like Trump, he did not renounce the freedom of action and expression which is more typical of a party leader. The great increase in the League's popularity can be linked to Salvini's personal strength, communication ability, and responsiveness – at least in words – to social problems such as insecurity, unemployment, and lack of social mobility. Before its transformation, the League used to attack the centralised Italian state as impeding local autonomy and overtaxing the prosperous north. In the new League's narrative, Salvini presented himself as the warrior *Captain*, who would defend the people from threats to the national identity and interests, represented by an overbearing EU, elites, globalisation and immigration (Stille 09/08/2018). Salvini accused Matteo Renzi's Democratic Party of favouring bankers and minorities, while disregarding the real Italian people's needs. Salvini also attacked the EU bureaucrats and bankers for interfering in the Italian politics and economy, while leaving the peninsula alone in dealing with the migration issue. In order to fulfil his political ends, Salvini fostered an atmosphere of *fear of crime*, supporting the idea that lost *law and order* had to be brought back to the country (see e.g. Lee/Farral 2008). These motifs seemed to authorise authoritarian decisions, social exclusion and xenophobia, scapegoating migrants, refugees, Muslim minorities and Roma people.

1.2.1 Trump's and Salvini's social media practices

Twitter has become Trump's favourite sounding board, used to promote his accomplishments, announce events and policies, criticise opponents, compliment supporters. Trump's tweeting style undeniably helped him build his peculiar *brand*. He uses a very basic lexicon (with words such as *bad*, *wrong*), extreme but empty adjectives and adverbs (e.g. *great*, *wonderful, totally*), emphatic language (by means of intensifiers like *very*, *so*, exclamations, question marks, shouty capitalisations), repetitions, oppositions. His messages also contain a large number of offensive comments, nicknames and also contradictions, which appear to be published without considering their consequences or his own institutional role (see Leith 13/01/2017; Demata 2018; Napolitano/Aiezza 2018). He combines political incorrectness, an incendiary attitude, anti-intellectualism and use of the friend/enemy-scheme (Fuchs 2017). Thanks to this style, he managed to embody the archetypal Twitter user, overcoming the striking difference between his gilded life and that of the average American voter, and conveying, instead, an impression of authenticity and closeness to his angry people (Ott 2017). Nevertheless, even when they genuinely sound like his voice, tweets are not always tapped out by Trump himself. West Wing employees apparently ghostwrite some of his messages by mimicking the president's style, also intentionally inserting grammar irregularities (Relman 22/05/2018). The most controversial social media account in the world is co-managed by Dan Scavino, assistant to the president and director of social media, a position that had never existed before (Draper 16/04/2018). Trump's account was created in 2009 at the suggestion of his marketing staff in order to promote an upcoming book. The username chosen was @realDonaldTrump as @DonaldTrump was already being used. From 2009 to 2011, tweets posted on his account included the phrase *From Donald Trump* to distinguish them from those written by his assistants but, by about June 2011, those labels had disappeared. Especially from 2013, Trump's account turned more and more politically charged, and was then to become one of the main tools of Trump's presidential campaign (see BBC News 12/12/2016) and of his subsequent communications.

A similar style is adopted in Italy by Matteo Salvini, who relies on an accurately planned social media strategy. Salvini's communication staff, nicknamed *la Bestia* [*the Beast*] and headed by philosopher and ICT expert Luca Morisi, is made up of about ten young assistants constantly producing posts to feed the politician's personal storytelling on Facebook, Twitter and Instagram. Salvini has the ability to occupy all the communicative spaces: his statements are diffused through "cross-mediality, live streaming, hybridisation of physical and digital channels, *mirroring* between different media" [my translation] (Giorgino 2019: 129). He uses a clear appeal to negative feelings (especially anger and fear) to lower his audience's guard so that it will be more willing to accept his message. He also tends to represent himself as a political martyr to attract sympathy and consensus, especially when attacked for his stubborn approaches to immigration issues. Along with the growth of his political weight, his social media style has also become more complex. Especially at first, he tended to use an angrier language with extensive use of capitalisations, repeated letters, exclamations, such as *Bastaaaaa!* [*Stoooop!*] or *A CASAAAAAAAA!!!* [*GO HOOOOOOOOOME!!!*], while a more articulated language was elaborated ahead of the 2018 political election (see Sclaunich 14/12/2015; Piccinelli Casagrande 15/02/2018). In his Facebook posts, references to *Italy* and *Italians* have increased in recent years, while mentions of the *North*, *Milan* and *Lombardy* have skilfully tended to disappear. His attempt to overcome the local vocation of the League is also shown by the choice of expressions uniting the whole population, such as *da Nord a Sud* [*from North to South*] and *milioni di Italiani* [*millions of Italians*]. The term *home* has often been used to invite immigrants, the government or Renzi to return to their respective places of origin. Attacks on Laura Boldrini (former President of the Chamber of Deputies of Italy mocked for her pro-migrant stances), Strasbourg, lack of security, illegal immigration and terrorism are also often exploited in Salvini's Facebook communicative strategy. Salvini also attempts at constructing a warm, familiar online narration, by greeting his followers daily and publishing pictures and descriptions of his meals with typical local dishes (Poltronieri 17/10/2017).

Salvini's communicative talent is also based on the ability to modify his tone based on the nature of his target public, passing from the extreme tones of social media to the more moderate language of TV talks and institutional seats (Giorgino 2019: 123). His selfies and walkabouts around Italy show the need to shorten the distance between politics and electors, testifying to a politics made "among the people and for the people" (Salvini *et al.* 2016). Salvini constantly takes advantage of news and current events to express his indignation by thundering from his social profiles and repeating his pounding mantras of security and fight against the enemies. He thus exploits his visibility to give official voice to the common people's opinions. He also makes use of the body as a form of communication, by symbolically wearing each time the uniform of a different armed force, or his popular sweatshirts with the name of the place where he is holding a rally.

Both Trump and Salvini condense their politics in their epic slogans. From a marketing perspective, the slogan is one of the main components of an integrated brand identity, summarising the brand message and facilitating its storage in the memory of consumers (Reece *et al.* 1994). The use of slogans in political marketing exploits the human tendency to prefer cognitive shortcuts to careful thought when forming judgments. Politicians try therefore to catch voters through simplification tactics which also include schemes, scripts, stereotypes (Cwalina *et al.* 2008). The construction of/appeal to a national identity is crucial to these political strategies, which tend to create a need "to become what we actually already are (e.g. to become Italian despite being Italian by defending ourselves from others who are not Italian)" [my translation] (Giorgino 2019: 21). In particular, Trump promised to *Make America Great Again* (shortened into *MAGA*), pledging to restore America to its decayed glory and to put *America First*, making political choices only for the benefit of the American people. Similarly, Salvini repeated his motto *Prima gli Italiani* [*Italians First*]. Both criticised their predecessors, accused of putting other interests and subjects *first* (e.g. Charlemagne 26/07/2018).

2 Aims and purposes

Without disregarding the ideological, cultural and historical differences between the two contexts considered, the present study connects the political figures of Donald Trump and Matteo Salvini, by viewing both as populist leaders and communicators. Given their intense activity on social media, the analysis compares their style on Twitter, thus expanding previous studies on the topic. The research investigates both commonalities and peculiarities in their persuasive messages, focusing on the discursive construction of the political leaders as champions of the interests of their people against its numerous enemies. The examination also takes into consideration how the features of the online messages are influenced by the properties of the microblogging platform.

3 Data and methods

The study examines the collection of all the tweets published on the official accounts by Trump, @realDonaldTrump, and Salvini, @matteosalvinimi, from their creation, respectively in 2009 and 2011, until October 31 2018. The corpus is therefore composed of a subcorpus in English and one in Italian (Tab. 3.1).

The analysis combines quantitative and qualitative perspectives of investigation. A Critical Discourse Analysis framework (see e.g. van Dijk 2006) is employed to uncover and compare the construction of populist ideological discourse, based mainly on a positive presentation of the nation, the in-group, and a negative presentation of the out-group, the enemy. Corpus linguistics tools (see e.g. Baker *et al.* 2013) allow the researcher to compare language usage and identify trends which may indicate discourses and ideologies. In particular, the corpus is analysed with the support of both *WordSmith Tools 6* (Scott 2014) and of the

Tab. 3.1: Corpus composition.

User	Dates	Tweets	Tokens	Types	Type/Token
@realDonaldTrump	04/05/09–31/10/18	32,672	921,018	31,062	5.60
@matteosalvinimi	23/03/11–31/10/18	24,866	699,606	27,705	4.79

online corpus query system *SketchEngine* (Kilgarriff *et al.* 2014). The following paragraph shows a selection of representative and significant sets of data within the corpus and compares the use of some features of social media language by the two leaders.

4 Analysis

4.1 The discursive construction of the in-group

The frequency lists for both Trump's and Salvini's corpora were obtained through the *SketchEngine* online tool. Among the most frequent lemmas, it appeared useful to identify and compare the occurrence of content words referring to the nation. As evident from Tab. 4.1, as a whole, references to Italy appeared statistically more often in Salvini's tweets, if compared with Trump's mentions of America. The results are quite meaningful, especially considering that, at least during the first years of his social media communications, Salvini's audience was not the whole Italy but only the north of it, or *Padania*.

In order to quantify the usage of terms referring to the nation over time in the two corpora, a dispersion plot was obtained, offering a visual representation of where a search word is mentioned the most throughout a corpus (Scott 2014). In Trump, references to *America* are quite evenly distributed over time (see Tab. 4.2) but they have intensified since his candidacy, presented on June 16 2015. As for Salvini, mentions of *Italy* (Tab. 4.3) were distinctly fewer during the Northern League era, while they became constant especially since the period leading to the foundation of his national party *Noi con Salvini* [*Us with Salvini*], on December 19 2014. As evident in Tab. 4.4, along with the dropping of the term *Padania*, the word *Italy* was used instead, so that the plots in Tab. 4.3 and 4.4 seem to be one the negative of the other.

Burying for the moment the League's hostility towards Southern Italy, Salvini was able to construe his party as willing to transfer its devotion to the Northern cause to the whole country, in order to fight Italy's

Tab. 4.1: Main references to the in-group.

Trump			Salvini		
Lemma	**Freq.**	**%**	**Lemma**	**Freq.**	**%**
America	1,483	0.16 %	Italia [Italy]	1,838	0.24 %
U.S.	726	0.08 %	italiano [Italian]	1,714	0.26 %
American	614	0.07 %			
US	278	0.03 %			
United States	277	0.03 %			
USA	265	0.03 %			
Americans	262	0.03 %			
U.S.A.	45	0.005 %			
total	3,950	0.43 %	Total	3,552	0.51 %

Words	Hits	per 1,000	Dispersion	Plot
774.293	2.620	3,38	0,802	

Tab. 4.2: Dispersion plot of *America** in Trump's corpus (2009–2018).

Words	Hits	per 1,000	Dispersion	Plot
550.241	3.313	6,02	0,819	

Tab. 4.3: Dispersion plot of *Itali** in Salvini's corpus (2011–2018).

Words	Hits	per 1,000	Dispersion	Plot
550.241	105	0,19	0,308	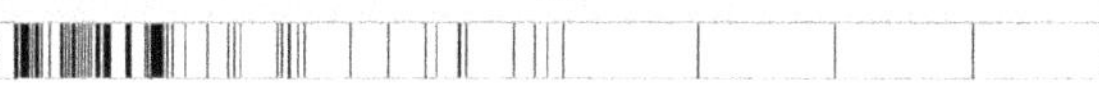

Tab. 4.4: Dispersion plot of *Padan** in Salvini's corpus (2011–2018).

external enemies, as evident from the frequent presence in the corpus of the cluster *da Nord a Sud* [*from North to South*] (88 occurrences, 0.01 %):

(1) #salvini: se lo Stato italiano non difende i confini, lo faremo noi, da Nord a Sud! Patria e terra! #Pontida14 #Lega [#salvini: if the Italian State does not defend our borders, we will do it, from North to South! Homeland and land! #Pontida14 #Lega] (@matteosalvinimi 04/05/2014)

(2) #Salvini: Alle elezioni ci sarà la "#Lega", punto. Senza "Nord". E saremo presenti in tutta Italia. #piazzapulita [#Salvini: At the elections there will be the "#League", full stop. Without "North." And we will be present in the whole Italy. #piazzapulita] (@matteosalvinimi 26/10/2017)

Especially in the light of the new trend of enlarged inclusion which characterises Salvini's political strategy and of Trump's defence of the pure American *brand*, it also appeared particularly relevant to investigate the use of first-person plural deictics in the corpora. Such resources are indeed charged with ideological meanings, as they may appeal to shared intents and values, contributing to the discursive construction of national identities. In particular, the use of the pronoun *our* includes the readers in a group, in this case the nation, while creating a polarisation with an implied *their* connected to the outsiders (see e.g. van Dijk 2006).

Considering the occurrences of the possessive *our* in Trump's corpus, amounting to 3,035 (0.33 %), and of its correspondent *nostr** [*our*] in Salvini's, 1,020 (0.15 %), it is observable that Trump made use of this linguistic resource twice as often as Salvini. Investigating the collocates of *our* may provide evidence of who is considered as part of the in-group and what parts, attributes and interests of the nation are selected and given prominence. The most frequent immediate right collocates of *our* in Trump's and Salvini's corpora were thus obtained and grouped in broad semantic areas. Tab. 4.5 summarises the most frequent collocates of *our* in the two corpora divided by topic. For the sake of convenience and comparability, Salvini's words are only reported in their English translation. Adjectives frequently present in R1 position were concordanced and included in brackets in the table, preceding the noun they commonly pre-modify. As shown in the table, in both corpora, collocates of *our* developed around the thematic areas of nation, defence, economy, politics and future/prospective aims. Nevertheless, the terms also revealed some peculiarities in the discourse constructed by each of the two leaders.

In particular, Trump's tweets produced a thematisation around the issue of defence, relying on key issues to the Republican ideology. He addressed the military, soldiers, veterans and defence, conceived both and as self-defence, as in (3) and as border security, as in (4):

Tab. 4.5: Main R1 collocates of *our* in the two corpora.

	Trump	Salvini
Nation	(great) country, nation, people, flag	country, cities, people, home, culture, traditions, history, grandparents, land, citizens, values, elderly, roots, freedom
Defence	military, vets, (Southern) border, (great/brave/incredible/amazing) troops, marines, veterans, soldiers, second amendment, armed forces, heroes	borders, armed forces, men in uniform
Economy	economy, jobs, farmers, taxes, money, debt, trade	economy, expenses, agriculture, companies, products, workers, farmers, currency
Politics	leader, government, enemy, friend, ally	government, candidate, mayor, ally
Future/aims	children	children, youth, boys, future, plan, idea, programme, proposal, battle, priority, objective

(3) …John is strong on crime and borders, loves our Military, our Vets and our Second Amendment. He will be a star. He has my full and total Endorsement! (@realDonald Trump 27/07/2018)

(4) The migrant 'caravan' that is openly defying our border shows how weak & ineffective U.S. immigration laws are. Yet Democrats like Jon Tester continue to support the open borders agenda – Tester even voted to protect Sanctuary Cities. We need lawmakers who will put America First. (@realDonald Trump 30/04/2018)

Salvini, on his side, surprisingly discovered a common Italian identity based on traditional shared culture, history, values, roots, also echoing some of the topics of Italian fascist imagery. At the same time, he wished to present himself and his party as an innovative force which would create a better country for the future generations. The national identity was constructed above all as a distinction and in opposition to an enemy, especially the immigrant other, who generates a lack of order and security (as in (5)) and is defended by the Italian elites at the expense of traditional values (as in (6)):

(5) #Salvini: Chiedo solo TRANQUILLITÀ, per i nostri figli. È folle negare che un'immigrazione FUORI CONTROLLO porti caos e problemi. #Mattino5 @Mattino5 [#Salvini: I only ask for TRANQUILITY, for our children: It is crazy to deny that an OUT-OF-CONTROL immigration causes chaos and problems #Mattino5 @Mattino5] (@matteosalvinimi 12/02/2018)

(6) Qui Altamura (Bari), lo spettacolo del territorio che si trasforma nella gioia del Natale. Lo dedichiamo a chi vorrebbe cancellare la nostra storia, la nostra civiltà e i nostri valori. Viva il presepe! [Here in Altamura (Bari), the show of the territory transforming itself in the joy of Christmas. We dedicate this to those who would like to erase our history, our civilisation and our values. Long live the nativity scene!] (@matteosalvinimi 19/12/2017)

Salvini linguistically constructs an opposition between *casa nostra* [*our home*] and *casa loro* [*their home*], mainly referring to the immigrants' land of origin, which is generally Africa. The word *loro* is frequently found in co-occurrence with casa [*home*] (75 instances, 0.01 %) and *Paese* [*Country*] (18, 0.003 %) and in clusters linked to the repatriation of immigrants and refugees, such as *rispediamoli/aiutiamoli a casa loro* [*let's send them back to/help them in their own homes*] or *scontino la pena nel loro Paese* [*they shall serve their sentence in their own Country*]. The old slogan of the Northern League *PADRONI A CASA NOSTRA* [*MASTERS OF OUR OWN HOUSE*] has thus been dusted off and transformed into a national mantra against the EU and migrants. Moreover, the idea of *helping them in their own homes* seems to have the only aim of appeasing consciences. It allows the politician and his supporters to reject accusations of egoism and even to pretend to be good Christians, by proclaiming to be willing to aid others, yet without compromising their own interests (Agnoletto 06/09/2017).

4.2 Hashtags

One of the features of Twitter is the possibility to launch trends through the hashtag function. Users incorporate hashtags in their messages to label contents through keywords. Messages thus become searchable by the virtual community and other users can include a hashtag to comment on a topic and demonstrate affiliation (Zappavigna 2012). Comparing the hashtags used by the two politicians, Salvini appeared to make use of this function significantly more often. In Trump, the total number of hashtags amounted to 14,516 (1.58 %), the total types to 2,021, while Salvini used 32,151 total hashtags (4.69 %) and 2,153 different types. The most frequent hashtag inserted by Trump still remained linked to his presidential campaign, i.e. *#Trump2016* (897 instances, 0.1 %). Salvini, on his side, was also particularly self-referential, through the hashtag *#Salvini* (10,175 occurrences, 1.45 %). He continuously quoted himself and his presence on other traditional media, not by inserting his nickname @matteosalvinimi, as would be more usual in Twitter, but through a hashtag, labelling himself and making his name searchable, thus transforming his surname into a topic and a trend.

Most of Trump's hashtags were represented by his slogans, especially his popular *#makeamericagreatagain* (564, 0.06 %) or *#maga* (218, 0.02 %) and *#americafirst* (99, 0.01 %). These mantras have become both his political imperatives and a demand by his supporters, as also represented in the wallpapers of Trump's Twitter profile, which frequently show his audience holding the typical placards with his political slogans such as *Build/Finish the wall.*

In his messages, Trump also tended to hashtag political issues such as *#obamacare* (29, 0.003 %) and enemies, like the well-known *#crookedhillary* (42, 0.005 %). This resort to nicknames represents "public displays of disaffection" (Wahl-Jorgensen 2018) which vilify opponents describing them not only as incompetent but also as intentionally betraying the nation (Hawkins in Rice-Oxley and Kalia 03/12/2018).

Salvini, on his side, tagged his messages with a great variety of topics and issues. In particular, he named political opponents, such as members of the previous government *#renzi* (851, 0.12 %) and *#fornero* (113, 0.02 %) – the latter is the author of a loathed pension reform –, also launching exhortatory or mocking slogan-hashtags, such as *#renziacasa* [*#renzigohome*] (219, 0.03 %) or *#PDclandestino [#illegalDemocraticParty*] (19, 0.003 %). Salvini tagged issues related to the Italian economy and job policies, such as *#flattax* (66, 0.01 %) and *#esodati* [*#pensionreformvictims*] (19, 0.003 %). His hashtags also referred to the European Union, its criticised currency, e.g. *#bastaeuro* [*#stopeuro*] (219, 0.03 %) or *#oltreleuro* [*#beyondeuro*] (51, 0.01 %), and its intrusive representatives, e.g. *#merkel* (22, 0.003 %).

Yet, hashtags present in higher frequency and variety in Salvini's tweets were those opposing immigration, such as *#clandestini* [*#illegalimmigrants*] (159, 0.02 %), and immigrants' rights, like the slogans *#primagliitaliani* [*#italiansfirst*] (349, 0.05 %) and *#noiussoli* [*#nobirthrightcitizenship*] (55, 0.01 %). In particular, migration by sea from Africa was labelled as *#invasione* [*#invasion*] (63, 0.01 %) which needed to be blocked, as in *#stopinvasione* [*#stopinvasion*] (258, 0.04 %), or eradicated, as in *#liberiamoci* [*#letsfreeourselves*] (80, 0.01 %). A series of hashtags also condemned international terrorism, e.g. *#Isis* (19, 0.003 %), connecting the presence of terrorists in the European territory to immigration. Salvini even reproduced the prejudice that assimilates terrorists with the whole of Islam and accused the left of supporting illegal immigration:

(7) #STOPINVASIONE e #stopIslam, oggi in 4 minuti ho smontato tutte le EUROBALLE della sinistra scafista! [#STOPINVASION and @stopIslam, today in 4 minutes I demolished all of the EUROLIES of the alien smuggling left!] (@matteosalvinimi 25/10/2017)

A further alien group in the Italian territory which is harshly despised by Salvini is represented by the *#rom* [*#roma*] people (110, 0.02 %), and their unauthorised camps, which he wishes to destroy through his infamous *#ruspa* [*bulldozer*]. With his unpleasantly playful comments on the issue, as in (8), Salvini promoted a normalisation of xenophobia:

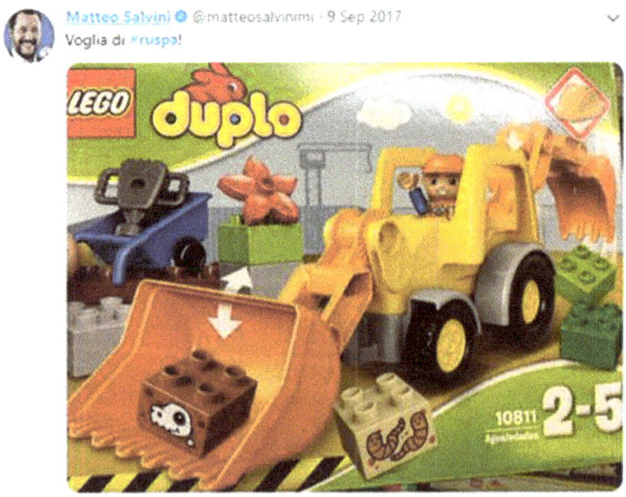

(8) [Wishing on a bulldozer!] (@matteosalvinimi 09/09/2017)

Several hashtags were also related to security issues, denouncing organised crime, as *#lamafiamifaschifo* [*#mafiasucks*] (38, 0.005 %) and requiring harsh penalties, such as *#tolleranzazero* [*#zerotolerance*] (20, 0.003 %). Salvini also showed support for Italian citizens who shot robbers in self-defence, both by launching *jesuisCharlie-like* hashtag trends and by physically meeting them as heroes of the nation, as in (9):

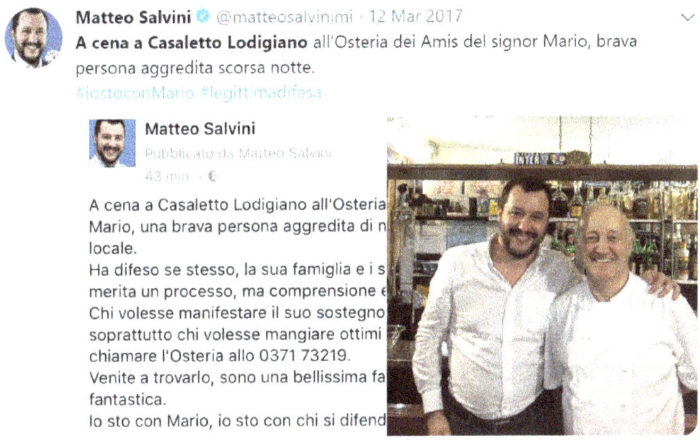

(9) [Having dinner in Casaletto Lodigiano at Osteria dei Amis of Mr Mario, a good man who was assaulted last night #ImwithMario #legitimatedefence] (@matteosalvinimi 12/03/2017)

4.3 @Mentions

Another typical property of Twitter language is the insertion in the messages of the @ symbol followed by a username to mention and/or address users. Both politicians make use of quotes, but Trump employs them in a significantly higher percentage: the total number of @mentions in Trump's corpus is 39,581 (4.3 %, 14,537 total types), while Salvini uses them in 4,005 occurrences (0.57 %, 778 types). Interestingly, the username both leaders quote most often is their own, *@realDonalTrump* and *@matteosalvinimi*. The leaders also mention: traditional media (such as *@FoxNews* or *@CNN* in Trump's tweets and *@rtl1025* radio or *@La7tv* in Salvini's); other politicians (e.g. Trump's adversaries *@BarackObama* or *@HillaryClinton* and Salvini's ally *@MLP_official* – i.e., Marine Le Pen –, and nemesis *@matteorenzi*); opinion leaders; VIPs; common citizens. In Trump's corpus, in particular, most mentions are quotes and responses not addressing public figures but ordinary people who endorsed him and his plan for America, especially before he was elected, as in the examples:

(10) @Jpicc1: @realDonaldTrump Please DO run!! We need a strong leader who will end the embarrassment our current President has caused us!! (@realDonaldTrump 08/04/2015)

(11) @kwcrow: @CommunityJC I agree America is disheartened. I truly believe #Trump can turn this country around. He is the only 1 who can (@realDonaldTrump 09/04/2015)

Donald Trump thus skilfully constructed his candidacy as an urgent request made to him – *personally* – by citizens who cared for America. Trump also paid *shout outs* to his supporters, by publicly mentioning and thanking them, a social media strategy improving brand loyalty and testifying user engagement to the whole digital community (see McCoy 13/11/2013).

Interestingly, among the other populist and authoritarian right politicians praised, Salvini showed support for Trump himself, by mentioning his account and through the use of hashtags such as *#godonaldgo* (10, 0.001 %) or *#trumppresident* (10, 0.001 %), thus further confirming an affinity between the two leaders. Salvini also follows an array of Trump-related Twitter accounts, among which: Donald J. Trump (*@realDonaldTrump*), Official Team Trump (*@TeamTrump*), President Trump (*@POTUS*), and Trump ATeam (*@trumpATeam*).

4.4 Intensification devices

A further feature typical of social media language is the tendency to use intensification devices to emphasise positive or negative statements. The exploitation of typographical resources, emojis and multimedia is supposed to compensate for the lack of the paralinguistic dimension typical of spoken face-to face conversation (Zappavigna 2012: 67). The use of emphatic language has become part of Trump's and Salvini's social style. One of the patterns observed in the corpora under examination is represented by words or whole sentences written in full capital letters (see examples (5) and (7)). In the netiquette, writing in all capitals equals to shouting, and tends therefore to be considered impolite and be chastised. Nevertheless, it has become common practice, chosen to give prominence to some words within a text or to simulate a screaming tone. Capitalised words not only attract the readers' attention, but also increase the force of the statements (see Zappavigna 2012: 184) and appear as an expression of genuine feelings and emotions which the populist leaders share with their angry voters.

The most frequently words *shouted* by the two politicians seem to provide an overview of the main points of their political language. Capitalised words represent their recurring hobbyhorses, slogans, pleas and hashtags, such as Trumps' *MAKE* (294, 0.03 %) *AMERICA* (399, 0.04 %) *GREAT* (557, 0.06 %) *AGAIN* (320, 0.03 %). Interestingly, among the most frequently capitalised words in Salvini's messages, negative terms such as *NON* [*NOT*] (249, 0.04 %), *NO* (244, 0.03 %), *MENO* [*LESS/FEWER*] (155, 0.02 %), *STOP* (65, 0.01 %), and *ZERO* (47, 0.01 %) rank high, signalling a politics which knows and tends to spell out what citizens do not want rather than what they do want (Giorgino 2019: 106).

Emphasis is also obtained through the use of punctuation marks, which are often repeated to simulate the tone of a political protest or of informal conversation. Repeated question marks, multiple exclamation marks and an alternation of the two are present on 1,333 occasions (0.14 %) in Trump's tweets, and in 1,595 occurrences (0.23 %) in Salvini's. Words may be also spelled with repeated letters (generally, vowels) to mimic screaming, conveying different kinds of meanings, such as surprise, exhortation, intensification, contrast or irony. In Salvini's corpus, the words most frequently spelled with repeated letters include *grazie* [*thank you*], *no* and *spettacolo* [*amazing*]. Punctuation expressiveness may be extended by using patterns mixing different resources, as in Salvini's *SVEGLIAAA!!!* [*WAKEUUUP!!!*]. In Trump's corpus, these typographical devices were identified mostly in the past retweets of passionate messages by common people (as in example (10)) supporting his candidacy.

5 Conclusions

Although differing considerably in terms of international relevance, cultural and historical contexts, the discourses constructed by Donald Trump and Matteo Salvini showed similar populist and nativist traits. Furthermore, both statesmen have given proof of a keen ability to exploit social media as a tool for consensus-building.

Contemporary politics is characterised by *hypercommunication*, as it is endlessly enacted through representations in the public sphere and media. Given their frequent and provocative use of social networks, both Donald Trump and, on a smaller scale, Matteo Salvini are regularly under the scrutiny of journalists and academics. The present study represented a further investigation in the area, carried out on the entire collection of the Twitter posts produced by the two politicians. The research aimed to provide further insights into similarities in the contemporary populist discourse developed online across the Atlantic, in terms of motifs and linguistic resources exploited.

Populist political figures impose their own opinion and presence in the news through the daily production of messages which rely on – generally negative – emotions and exploit a friend/enemy logic. This way, they legitimise the need for a strong leader's power and policies. Their right-wing populist rhetoric presents simplistic solutions, by reducing complex issues to dichotomies, pointing to scapegoats as the reasons for the current problems, and relying on a sense of nostalgia for a mythical past before the nation was contaminated by its others. The current political communication framework seems to reward the use of a direct and provocative communicative style, maintaining a firm line, appreciated as conveying the impression of a solid identity and of a political programme based on real facts and needs. This allows a politician to present him/herself as *one of the people*, while constantly testing the norms of civility. Yet, to engage voters and manage consensus, right-wing populist leaders are revitalising nativist tendencies, border narratives and economic fears, thereby putting at serious risk the very principles of democratic institutions. Their rhetoric justifies discriminatory and exclusionary agendas by relying on traditional body politics, portraying a homogenised ideal people and its homeland as threatened by the dangerous *other* (see Wodak 2015; Wodak/Krzyżanowski 2017; Kreis 2017).

Both Trump and Salvini claimed to speak for the people but built followings by demonising unpopular minorities, attacking human rights principles, and fuelling distrust of democratic institutions. The two politicians strategically constructed their electorate over time by showing themselves as both close to the interests of the ordinary people and supported by them. Both showed a tendency for self-promotion, narcissism and self-referentiality (Ott 2017), as they tended to continually reproduce their own online messages and increase their visibility through self-mentions, constructing their own *brand* of proud and confident champions of the national good. In particular, Trump's initial political vocabulary was focused on self-promotion, presenting his presidency as the only solution to the US evils, then to develop his populist discourse by constructing himself as a paternalistic leader who would act on behalf of his people (see Mudde in Friedman 27/02/2017).

Both leaders made use of *shouty*, emphatic language and pounding slogans aimed at generating Internet trends. Yet, Salvini, who is a younger politician and relies on a younger communication team, appeared to master more skilfully the allowances of the medium. He often employed the hashtag function to address an array of political and social issues and exploited typographical creativity to intensify his claims.

Twitter would appear to be a quintessentially democratic medium, as it promotes personal expression, a decentralised public sphere, and allows users to build networks. However, in the populist rhetoric, it has become a powerful amplifier of authoritarianism. Though their tweets, Trump and Salvini construct their own myth in a chaotic and dangerous world, while the media, although with the intent of criticising them, contributes to amplifying their messages (Turner 2018: 143).

The present investigation represented a preliminary study of a vast corpus, covering nearly a decade of posts. The corpus will be further updated and examined, with a more specific focus on the chronological dimension, in order to investigate the evolution of language and policy objectives over time. Moreover, additional studies will focus on the large amount of images and multimedia materials published by the leaders on their Twitter accounts and on the contribution of visuals (see e.g. examples (8) and (9)) to the construction of the populist and nativist discourse in the two countries.

References

Agnoletto, Vittorio 2017. Migranti, Quattro Motivi per Cui 'Aiutiamoli a Casa Loro' È una Balla Spaziale. *Il Fatto Quotidiano*, 06 September. <https://www.ilfattoquotidiano.it/2017/09/06/migranti-quattro-motivi-per-cui-aiutiamoli-a-casa-loro-e-una-balla-spaziale/>

Baker, Paul / Gabrielatos, Costas / McEnery, Tony 2013, *Discourse Analysis and Media Attitudes: The Representation of Islam in the British Press*. Cambridge: Cambridge University Press.

BBC News 2016. Trump on Twitter: A History of the Man and His Medium. *BBC News*, 12 December. <https://www.bbc.com/news/world-us-canada-38245530>

Bell, Daniel 1960. *The End of Ideology: On the Exhaustion of Political Ideas in the Fifties*. Cambridge, MA, and London: Harvard University Press.

Buccoliero, Luca / Bellio, Elena / Crestini, Giulia / Arkoudas, Alessandra 2018. Twitter and Politics: Evidence from the US Presidential Elections 2016. *Journal of Marketing Communications*, 1-27.

Censis 11/10/2018. *15° Rapporto sulla Comunicazione: I Media Digitali e la Fine dello Star System. Sintesi per la Stampa*. Rome: Censis.

Charlemagne 2018. Matteo Salvini, Italy's De Facto Leader, Is Instinctively Authoritarian. *The Economist*, 26 July. <https://www.economist.com/europe/2018/07/26/matteo-salvini-italys-de-facto-leader-is-instinctively-authoritarian>

Cwalina, Wojciech / Falkowski, Andrzej / Newman, Bruce I. 2008. *A Cross-Cultural Theory of Voter Behavior*. New York: Haworth Press.

Demata, Massimiliano 2018. "I Think That Maybe I Wouldn't Be Here If It Wasn't for Twitter." Donald Trump's Populist Style on Twitter. *Textus, English Studies in Italy* 31, 67-90.

Draper, Robert 2018. The Man behind the President's Tweets. *The New York Times Magazine*, 16 April. <https://www.nytimes.com/2018/04/16/magazine/dan-scavino-the-secretary-of-offense.html>

Formigli, Corrado 16/03/2019. Interview. In *TV Talk*. Milan: Rai 3.

Friedman, Uri 2017. What Is a Populist? *The Atlantic*, 27 February. <https://www.theatlantic.com/international/archive/2017/02/what-is-populist-trump/516525/>

Fuchs, Christian 2017. Donald Trump: A Critical Theory-Perspective on Authoritarian Capitalism. *tripleC (Communication, Capitalism & Critique)* 15/1, 1-72.

Gallardo Paúls, Beatriz 23/11/2018. El Entramado Discursivo En La Política Del Siglo Xxi: Simultaneidades, Límites Y Procesos. Conference paper delivered at *In The Name of the People: Representing the People in Twenty-First Century Politics*, University of Navarra, Pamplona, 22–24 November 2018.

Giorgino, Francesco 2019. *Alto Volume: Politica, Comunicazione e Marketing*. Rome: LUISS University Press.

Human Rights Watch 2017. *World Report 2018: Events of 2017*. New York: Associated Press.

Human Rights Watch 2019. *World Report 2019: Events of 2018*. New York: Associated Press.

Inglehart, Ronald F. / Norris, Pippa 2016. *Trump, Brexit, and the Rise of Populism: Economic Have-Nots and Cultural Backlash*. Cambridge, MA: Harvard Kenney School Faculty Research Working Paper Series.

Jenkins, Henry 2006. *Convergence Culture: Where Old and New Media Collide*. New York and London: New York University Press.

Kilgarriff, Adam / Baisa, Vít / Bušta, Jan / Jakubíček, Miloš / Kovvář, Vojtěch / Michelfeit, Jan / Rychlý, Pavel / Suchomel, Vít 2014. The Sketch Engine: Ten Years on. *Lexicography* 1, 7-36.

Kreis, Ramona 2017. The "Tweet Politics" of President Trump. In Wodak, Ruth / Krzyżanowski, Michał (eds) *Right-Wing Populism in Europe & USA: Contesting Politics & Discourse Beyond 'Orbanism' and 'Trumpism'. Special Issue of Journal of Language and Politics* 16/4, 608-618.

Lee, Murray / Farrall, Stephen 2008. Critical Voices in an Age of Anxiety: A Reintroduction to the Fear of Crime. In Lee, Murray / Farrall, Stephen (eds) *Fear of Crime: Critical Voices in an Age of Anxiety*. Oxon, UK, and New York: Routledge-Cavendish.

Leith, Sam 2017. Trump's Rhetoric: A Triumph of Inarticulacy. *The Guardian*, 13 January. <https://www.theguardian.com/us-news/2017/jan/13/donald-trumps-rhetoric-how-being-inarticulate-is-seen-as-authentic>

KhosraviNik, Majid 2017. Right Wing Populism in the West: Social Media Discourse and Echo Chambers. *Insight Turkey* 19/3, 53-68.

McCoy, Julia 2013. Driving Social Media Engagement: 13 Copywriting Hacks. *Express Writers*, 13 November. <https://expresswriters.com/driving-social-media-engagement-13-copywriting-hacks/>

Mudde, Cas / Rovira Kaltwasser, Cristóbal 2017. *Populism: A Very Short Introduction*. Oxford: Oxford University Press.

Napolitano, Antonella / Aiezza, Maria Cristina 2018. The Press War in the Post-Truth Era: A Corpus-Assisted CDA of the Discourse of US Political Analysts on Trump's Figure and Policy. *Textus, English Studies in Italy* 31, 91-118.

Napolitano, Antonella 2018. Another Brick in the Wall: A Critical Discourse Analysis of the Political Discourse of Division. In Diglio, Carolina / Napolitano, Antonella / Perilli, Fabio (eds) *Identity, Language and Diversity, Between Walls and Bridges*. Naples: Paolo Loffredo Iniziative Editoriali, 471-498.

Norris, Pippa 2000. *A Virtuous Circle: Political Communications in Postindustrial Societies*. New York: Cambridge University Press.

Novelli, Edoardo 2009. Leaderizzazione. In Viganò, Dario Edoardo (ed.) *Dizionario della Comunicazione*. Rome: Carocci, 1194-1197.

Orsina, Giovanni 2019. Prefazione a Giorgino, Francesco, *Alto Volume: Politica, Comunicazione e Marketing*. Rome: LUISS University Press, 7-9.

Ott, Brian L. 2017. The Age of Twitter: Donald J. Trump and the Politics of Debasement. *Critical Studies in Media Communication* 34/1, 59-68.

Oxford English Dictionary Online 2019. Oxford University Press. <https://en.oxforddictionaries.com/>

Pagnoncelli, Nando 2019. Sondaggi Europee. Lega Vicina al 36%, Caduta dei 5 Stelle: Sono al 25,4. *Il Corriere della Sera*, 19 January. <https://www.corriere.it/politica/19_gennaio_19/verso-europee-caduta-m5s-che-scende-254percento-lega-al-36-f08fe346-1b68-11e9-a392-0b2e66f10fec.shtml?refresh_ce-cp>

Papacharissi, Zizi 2015. *Affective Publics: Sentiment, Technology, and Politics*. Oxford and New York: Oxford University Press.

Pew Research Center, 03/2018. *Social Media Use in 2018*. Washington: Pew Research Center. <https://www.pewinternet.org/wp-content/uploads/sites/9/2018/02/PI_2018.03.01_Social-Media_FINAL.pdf>

Piccinelli Casagrande, Francesco 2018. I Segreti della Strategia di Matteo Salvini sui Social Network. *Wired*, 15 February. <https://www.wired.it/attualita/politica/2018/02/15/matteo-salvini-strategia-social-network/?refresh_ce=>

Poltronieri, Filippo 2017. Renzi, Grillo e Salvini: Confronto Social. L'Ex Premier Scrive Poco (Ma Ha Molte Interazioni). Il Leader M5s Pubblica Sempre Meno. Il Carroccio? Fa Rabbia. *Il Fatto Quotidiano*, 17 October. <https://www.ilfattoquotidiano.it/2017/10/17/renzi-grillo-e-salvini-confronto-social-lex-premier-scrive-poco-ma-ha-molte-interazioni-il-leader-m5s-pubblica-sempre-meno-il-carroccio-fa-rabbia/3903552/>

Reece, Bonnie B. / Van den Bergh, Bruce G. / Li, Hairong 1994. What Makes a Slogan Memorable and Who Remembers It. *Journal of Current Issues and Research in Advertising* 16/2, 41-57.

Relman, Eliza 2018. Trump's Staff Ghostwrites Some of His Tweets and Inserts Grammatical Errors to Make Them Seem Authentic. *Business Insider*, 22 May. <https://www.businessinsider.com/trump-staff-inserts-grammatical-errors-into-tweets-2018-5?IR=T>

Rice-Oxley, Mark / Kalia, Ammar 2018. How to Spot a Populist. *The Guardian*, 03 December. <https://www.theguardian.com/news/2018/dec/03/what-is-populism-trump-farage-orban-bolsonaro>

Salvini, Matteo / Pandini, Matteo / Sala, Rodolfo 2016 (Digital Edition). *Secondo Matteo: Follia e Coraggio per Cambiare il Paese.* Milano: Rizzoli.

Savar, Avi 2013. *Content to Commerce: Engaging Consumers across Paid, Owned and Earned Channels.* Hoboken, NJ: John Wiley & Sons.

Sclaunich, Greta 2015. Maiuscole, Hashtag e Autocitazioni: Il Salvini Style sui Social Network. *Il Corriere della Sera*, 14 December. <https://www.corriere.it/politica/14_dicembre_15/maiuscole-hashtag-autocitazioni-salvini-style-social-network-d2f34030-8468-11e4-b9cc-80d61e8956c5.shtml?refresh_ce-cp>

Scott, Mike 2014. *WordSmith Tools 6.0.* Oxford: Oxford University Press.

Stille, Alexander 2018. How Matteo Salvini Pulled Italy to the Far Right. *The Guardian*, 09 August. <https://www.theguardian.com/news/2018/aug/09/how-matteo-salvini-pulled-italy-to-the-far-right>

Thelwall, Mike / Buckley, Kevan / Paltoglou, Georgios 2011. Sentiment in Twitter Events. *Journal of the American Society for Information Science and Technology* 62/2, 406-418.

Thomas, Paul 2015. The Greatest Threat to America? Republicans. *The New Zealand Herald*, 17 July. <http://www.nzherald.co.nz/opinion/news/article.cfm?c_id=466&objectid=11482176>

Turner, Fred 2018. Trump on Twitter: How a Medium Designed for Democracy Became an Authoritarian's Mouthpiece. In Boczkowski, Pablo J. / Papacharissi, Zizi (eds) *Trump and the Media*. Cambridge, MA, and London: The MIT Press, 143-150.

Van Dijk, Teun A. 2006. Ideology and Discourse Analysis. *Journal of Political Ideologies* 11/2, 115-140.

Wahl-Jorgensen, Karin 2018. Public Displays of Disaffection: The Emotional Politics of Donald Trump. In Boczkowski, Pablo J. / Papacharissi, Zizi (eds) *Trump and the Media*. Cambridge, MA, and London: The MIT Press, 79-86.

Wodak, Ruth 2011. Disenchantment with Politics and the Salience of Images. In Stocchetti, Matteo / Kukkonen, Karin (eds) *Images in Use: Towards the Critical Analysis of Visual Communication.*

Amsterdam and Philadelphia: John Benjamins Publishing Company, 69-88.

Wodak, Ruth 2015. *The Politics of Fear: What Right-Wing Populist Discourses Mean*. London: Sage.

Wodak, Ruth 2017. The 'Establishment', the 'Elites' and the 'People', Who's Who? *Journal of Language and Politics* 16/4, 551-565.

Wodak, Ruth / Krzyżanowski, Michał 2017. Introduction: Right-Wing Populism in Europe and the USA: Contesting Politics and Discourse beyond 'Orbanism' and 'Trumpism'. In Wodak, Ruth / Krzyżanowski, Michał (eds) Right-Wing Populism in Europe & USA: Contesting Politics & Discourse Beyond 'Orbanism' and 'Trumpism'. *Journal of Language and Politics* 16/4, 471-484.

Zappavigna, Michele 2012. *Discourse of Twitter and Social Media: How We Use Language to Create Affiliation on the Web*. London and New York: Continuum.

Ziccardi, Giovanni 2018. Le espressioni di odio online: Una "valuta" per ottenere consenso. In Vitale, Ermanno / Cattaneo, Fabrizio (eds) *Web e Società Democratica: Un Matrimonio Difficile*. Turin: Accademia University Press, 39-65.

Daniela Rovenţa-Frumuşani and Adriana Ştefănel

The populist contagion. The influence of populist discourses on the political communication of traditional parties in Romania.

1 Introduction

At the turn of the new millennium, Mudde (2004) argued that the growing success of populist parties had triggered the emergence of a "populist Zeitgeist" in Western Europe, a development consisting of the increasing adoption of populist messages, or rhetoric, by mainstream parties and politicians. In fact almost all liberal democracies are affected by some sort of populism either in *discursive style* (Jagers/Walgrave 2007; Mudde 2007; Wodak 2013; Moffitt 2016; Herkman 2016 etc.) or as '*thin ideology*' (Mudde/Rovira Kaltwasser 2013; Stanley 2017). As a modern political ideology, populism has been defined through three main characteristics: *anti-elite* and *anti-establishment attitudes*, and a *belief in the homogeneous virtuousness of the people* (Pirvulescu 2018). In a minimal ideological perspective, defined as a *thin centered ideology*, populism is based not only on the Manichean distinction between 'the pure people' and 'the corrupt elite', but also on the defense of *popular sovereignty* at any cost. Nowadays populism is often considered contagious (e.g., Bale *et al.* 2011). Mudde (2004: 563; 2017: 54) himself explains this contagion at the level of political communication:

> While mainstream political parties may not imitate populist parties in their policies, mainstream politicians do imitate populist politicians in their rhetoric, and not only during election campaigns.

Scholars have defined populism as a type of *political discourse, (thin) ideology, leadership, movement, phenomenon, strategy, style* etc. etc. through several approaches: *ideational* (Mudde 2007;

Mudde/Kaltwasser 2017; Mudde 2017; Hawkins/Rovira Kaltwasser 2017), *political-strategic* (Weyland 2017) and *socio-cultural* (Ostiguy 2017). However, the differences between these are not always clear: "Given that we see these differences as minor, we use the terms 'discourse', 'ideology', 'outlook', and 'worldview' somewhat interchangeably" (Hawkins/Rovira Kaltwasser 2017: 514). Since numerous scholars adopt this view (taking a set of ideas and only in a subsidiary sense their constitution in discourse), we will emphasize the invaluable role of discursive constructions, particularly the rhetoric of polarization. Populism is one instance of a particular level or kind of idea, but something that is not as conscious and programmatic as an ideology. Rather, it always attaches itself to some "host" ideology, as can be seen in the fact that it is possible to compare right-wing "exclusionary" forms of populism in Europe with left-wing "inclusionary" populism in Latin America (Mudde/Rovira Kaltwasser 2017).

We follow an approach that combines Mudde's (2004) *ideology-centered* and Hawkins' (2010) *discourse-centered* understanding of populism. Accordingly, we understand populism as a *discursive manifestation of a thin centered ideology* that is not only focused on the underlying "set of basic assumptions about the world" but in particular on "the language that unwittingly expresses them" (de Vreese *et al.* 2018: 425).

The *ideational approach* to populism stays in close contact with the work of the Argentine political theorist Ernesto Laclau, a pioneer in the study of Latin American populism (Laclau 1977) who later elaborated a political theory on populism (Laclau 2008), (Hawkins/Rovira Kaltwasser 2017: 514). Even if the core concepts of several approaches of populism are discourse (Laclau), political style (Jagers/Walgrave 2007), political framing (Lee 2005), all consider populism to be first and foremost about ideas in general and ideas about people in particular (Mudde 2017: 29). In contrast, for other scholars populism is a *political strategy* through which "a personalistic leader seeks or exercises government power based on direct, unmediated, uninstitutionalized support from large members of mostly unorganized followers" (Weyland 2017: 50). Even if Manichean rhetoric serves as a top down instrument for leaders, the main focus in this approach is the "effective political action" (Weyland 2017: 61), the doing not the saying. This political-strategic definition is not necessarily opposed to a consideration of ideas and rhetoric, but it tends to see the discourse of populists as a less important predictor of their behavior. It privileges organizational features, especially charismatic leadership, outsider status, and top-down and uninstitutionalized organization (Weyland 2001). What this definition fails to notice is that populism is in the first place a *moral* set of ideas that is shared by different constituencies, who have emotional and rational motives for adhering to the Manichean worldview inherent in populism.

Pierre Ostiguy's *socio-cultural* or *performative approach* defines politics in general on the basis of a high-low axis related to two sub-dimensions: i) a socio-cultural axis (ways of speaking, dressing); and ii) a political-cultural dimension (forms of leadership and modes of decision making) (Ostiguy 2017). Populism is defined low on both dimensions: populists speak in a popular manner and present strong leadership.

On the other hand, it is also frequent to read of the presence of a *populist virus* (in the language of *Libération*'s journalists about the situation of the Netherlands in 2002), or a *populist temptation* (in the title of an academic synthesis of the beginning of the millennium), indicating the focus on the people, opposed to disinterested or corrupt elites, represented in heterogeneous discourses in America and Europe. This is why we prefer to speak of populist contagion affecting the discourse/style of many political actors (populists or not) who rely on affectivity, the personalization of action (the charismatic leader) and the sacralization of the people.

"New populisms" need to be rethought within the cleavages of nationalisms, and correlated to the emergence of cultural, ethnic, religious identities, the weakness of the nation-state and the disintegration of the Habermasian public sphere into fragmented public spheres as a result of the digital revolution. The essence of populism in this new context is represented less by fixed ideological content than by a rhetorical modality of recreating collective identities by antagonism (Gherghina/Mişcoiu 2010: 66).

2 Populism. Conceptual delimitations

Although the lack of academic consensus on the concept of populism seems to be the only feature that has been agreed upon, most definitions of populism share references to the antithesis of two antagonistic homogeneous groups, *the pure people* and the *corrupt elite* (Mudde 2004; Albertazzi/McDonnell 2008 *inter alii*), constructing a Manichean polarization.

Following the same discursive dimension Canovan (1981: 4) identified three discursive elements that characterize any form of populism:

i) *the exaltation of the people* characterized as honest, sincere, courageous, moral and wise;
ii) *the call for emancipation*, modernization and even revolt by this same people through the support it should provide to populist leaders who purport to represent it and who should defend the people's interests;
iii) *anti-elitism* as a constitutive element that allows radical criticism of the status quo and the definitive positioning of the populist leader on the side of the masses.

Personalization is another general trend in contemporary politics and populism is certainly no exception to this rule (Mudde/Rovira Kaltwasser 2017: 77). Using Taggart's original observation (Taggart 2000), populism can be thought of as "politics for ordinary people by extraordinary leaders who construct ordinary profiles" (Mudde/Rovira Kaltwasser 2017: 78). If Rosanvallon considers populism the 'inversion of democracy', Laclau, on the contrary, believes that populism fosters a 'democratization of democracy' by permitting the aggregation of demands of excluded sectors. Both interpretations are to a certain extent correct, in the sense that populism can be seen as working as *either* a threat to *or* a corrective for democracy (Mudde/Rovira Kaltwasser 2017: 79).

In fact, populism transgresses spatial boundaries and historical periods as well as ideological cleavages. On the left side of populism one can situate Latin America (where populists favor state-run economies, employ a rhetoric of inclusion based on nationalism, and exploit charismatic authority) (Stefanel 2016: 142). Right-wing populism in Western and Northern Europe organizes its agenda around migrants

(Mudde 2007), while in Central and Eastern Europe it focuses on minorities and religious issues (Corbu *et al.* 2017).

By synthesizing the literature on populism, one can say that to be cataloged as populist a discourse must be characterized by homogenization (*the people* on one side, *elites* on the other, appear as unitary, without cracks, without dissonant voices) and Manichean (the interests of the two groups are perfectly opposed, without possibility of consensus or even of negotiation); the tone and *mise en scène* are emotional and not rational-objective; the proposed solutions are simple, reductionist and utopian; and the emphasis falls on the myths and structures of the imaginary.

3 Populism in Central and Eastern Europe

In the tension between populism and democracy (Mudde/Rovira Kaltwasser 2012), Eastern Europe is the generator of right and extreme right populist parties like *Jobbik* in Hungary (The Movement for a Better Hungary), *Attack* in Bulgaria, *The League for the Family* in Poland, but also left-wing populist parties, such as the *Greater Romania* in Romania. In addition to this, matters are complicated by the fact that many mainstream political parties have adopted a populist discourse, as a result of the fall of ideologies, the need for spectacular media discourse and the Internet revolution. Many social factors also seem to propitiate the rise of populist movements: "identity tensions, partisan rivalries, protest mobilizations" (Chêne *et al.* 2003: 10) have contributed also to favouring populism and even threatening democracy. The effects of exclusion and social fracture cannot be separated from the development of populism.

In order to understand this phenomenon in more depth, we need to consider that the democratization process passes through phases: *liberalization, democratic transition*, and *democratic deepening*. During the first stage of *liberalization*, when an authoritarian regime loosens restrictions and broadens some individual and group rights, populism tends to be *grosso modo* a positive force for democracy (Mudde/Rovira Kaltwasser 2017: 88).

In the stage of *democratic transition*, i.e., the transition from an authoritarian regime to an electoral democracy, populism plays an ambiguous, but still rather constructive role, fostering the idea that the people should elect the rulers (Mudde &Kaltwasser 2017: 89).

During the stage of *democratic deepening*, reforms are completed that are crucial for improving institutions specialized in the protection of fundamental rights and the development of a fully liberal democratic regime. Theoretically, populists are at odds with the process of democratic deepening, as they support an interpretation of democracy based on unconstrained popular will and the rejection of unelected bodies (Mudde/Rovira Kaltwasser 2017: 90). The latter are normally portrayed by populism as illegitimate institutions, which seek to defend the 'special interests' of powerful minorities rather than the 'real' interests of the people.

In most EU countries populism is far from being an electorally decisive force, although it may be a significant one. In the Czech Republic, Estonia, Romania and Slovenia, populist parties are decidedly minor in strength and peripheral to the party systems (Stanley 2017: 158), although there is one exception, Hungary. Populism-in-power has led to processes of de-democratization (e.g., Orbán in Hungary or Chávez in Venezuela) and, in some extreme cases, even to the breakdown of the democratic regime (e.g., Fujimori in Peru) (Mudde/Rovira Kaltwasser 2017: 96).

Some researchers (Shafir 2007; Pirvulescu 2018) consider that in most post-communist East European countries there appears a cleavage between *national-communists* and *traditional nationalists* but also between *neo-populism* (based on ethnic or religious grounds) and a paradoxical 'communist-capitalism' with pro-West orientation (ex-communists advocating liberal capitalism and integration in Europe). This "syncretism of neo-communism, traditional nationalism and populism, creates a movement opposed to liberal currents or to social democracies" (Pirvulescu 2018:5).

As post-communist societies passed through the changes of the double transition (i.e., economic and political) - and in some cases even a third national transition, as new states were formed - new populist actors tried to use the growing political dissatisfaction with a discourse of 'the stolen revolution'. They accused the new democratic elites of being either part of the old communist elite or in cahoots with them. Consequently, they called for a new 'real' revolution to oust the corrupt post-communist elite and finally give power to the people (Mudde/Rovira Kaltwasser 2017: 34).

Since many instances argue that populist actors can be defeated only by adopting part of their populist message - as several western European social democrats have suggested in an attempt to fight off the populist radical right - researchers have emphasized the contagious character of populist rhetoric. This adoption intensifies the "moralization and polarization of politics and society, which fundamentally undermines the foundations of liberal democracy" (Mudde/Rovira Kaltwasser 2017: 116). In fact, it is worth considering that the ideational approach (see above) "might be more fruitful for the empirical investigation of populism in Central and Eastern Europe" (Stanley 2017: 142), since 'political entrepreneurs' are eager to create political ideologies in their search for electoral support.

Concerning the interplay between top-down and bottom-up agents, popular protests have contributed to the fall of communism, but the construction of new democracies was shaped at the top (Stanley 2017: 143). For this reason, in this chapter we will emphasize the role and rhetoric of leaders at extraordinary moments (electoral campaign), as well as in ordinary times.

4 Romanian populism. Post-communist incidences of populism and populist discourse

4.1 The first post-communist years

In the form of "alternative politics" (Shafir 2008: 429), or movements that provide simplified Manichean solutions to the intricacies of democracy, populism has been a "constant presence in Romanian politics, accompanying the country's long journey through transition" (Corbu *et al.* 2017: 326). Numerous analysts (Soare 2010; Gherghina/Mişcoiu 2010, *inter alii*) emphasize that the first post-revolutionary years were strongly marked by populist accents and leaders. In fact populist elements are present in the manifestos and political discourses of the Romanian revolution and in the discourses of the new political formations born immediately afterwards. The name *Front* (FSN-*National Salvation Front*) is preferred to that of Party, with evil reverberations in the post-revolutionary Romanian political imagination, because it marks "the connection with the official, revolutionary genealogy, symbol of a new solidarity" (Soare 2010: 101). Moreover, *the National Salvation Front* and its leader Ion Iliescu frequently used populist discourse both to detach themselves from the *Romanian Communist Party*, from which many leaders came, and to remain in power despite the strong opposition of the 'historical' parties that re-emerged in the early months of 1990.

The myth of the conspiracy, the serious accusations against the leaders of the anti-Communist parties that had taken refuge in the West, the generalization of the negative perception of the Hungarian minority suspected of irredentist aims, the labelling of the protesters in the University Square as *golani* ('hooligans', a term used for educated people, mainly young ones, given this name by nostalgic communists) and the correction of their 'deviance' through citizens characterized by a 'high civic spirit' (but also armed with clubs) are some of the populist nationalist discursive strategies by which the FSN succeeded in retaining part of its electorate, dominated by revolutionary exaltation on the one hand, and solidarity with the party's two leaders (Ion Iliescu the 'father' and Petre Roman the 'son'), on the other.

From the center to the periphery, during the second post revolutionary decade, the populist discourse was radicalized, and the minor partners of the FSN and/or the parties formed in other regions of the country (Transylvania) adopted a nationalist-populist aggressive discourse.

When Ion Iliescu lost the elections in 1996 and the *red quadrilateral* went into opposition, there was a clear dissociation between the PDSR (Social Democrat Party of Romania, heir of the FSN) and the nationalist-populist party *The Greater Romania* led by Corneliu Vadim Tudor. Interest in analysing populism in Romanian politics grew significantly after 2000, when Corneliu Vadim Tudor, managed to enter the presidential election race. He did not win, but his performance definitely sent a warning sign both to other (mainstream) parties and to political scholars about how powerful populist discourse really is during elections. Since then, the literature on populism in Romania has been enriched by analyses dealing with populism during presidential elections (Mungiu-Pippidi 2001; Ietcu-Fairclough 2007) and also parliamentary ones (Gherghina 2010; Gherghina/Soare 2013).

When Vadim Tudor lost the presidential elections in 2000 (since all the democratic forces that supported Ion Iliescu opposed him in the second round), and the European path taken by Romania became increasingly clear, populist discourse seems to have lost ground and taken refuge on the margins of the political sphere, from where it reappeared in force when Traian Băsescu made his ascent to the most important position in Romanian politics - the presidency. Elected mayor of Bucharest in 2000, Traian Băsescu created the conditions for imposing a new kind of 'informal' populism that allowed him to transform the 2004 election into an anti-corruption crusade, and impose himself as a champion of the people. During his first mandate, the main target of his criticism was the political system as a whole, along with the Parliament, defined as a stronghold of corruption. This anti-system attitude sharpened after the first suspension in 2007 (in fact, the Parliament decided that he should be suspended but the referendum gave him back the presidential function a couple of months later). Even though this act was constitutional, it was presented as a reaction of a corrupt system against the leader and, by extension, against the people. The simple fact that he was reinstalled in office by a massive popular vote gave Traian Băsescu's populist discourse scope and substance. From a marginal communication strategy, populist topics became central and populist rhetoric was extensively used in his discourse. *Let's return to the people* became his motto and the 322 MPs who voted for his suspension his personal enemies.

Interestingly, this seems to have triggered a change in the political discourses being used by Romanian parties in general. In the last five years of Băsescu's presidency (2009–2014) populist rhetoric was used not only by Traian Băsescu and his followers, but also by his contesters. At the end of his two mandates, one might say that the true legacy of Traian Băsescu was the popularization of populist rhetoric. Nowadays, politicians, at any level of the political system, adopt it; people enjoy it and vote for those who use it; both politicians and people simply ignore the fact that this type of discourse can come to represent a threat to democracy.

In a suggestive dichotomy, Shafir (2007, 2008) opposed neo-populism from below as *vox populi, vox dei*, represented by the leader of the *New Generation Party* (PNG) George (Gigi) Becali, a good example of what might be called an 'instinctive' neo-populist politician seeking to gain power from below by whatever possible means (donations, discourses focused on Christian values and the constant appeal to the Bible). Modelling himself on Italian Prime Minister Silvio Berlusconi, Becali is a highly successful businessman and Romania's second-richest man (Shafir 2008: 433).

Becali represents a totally different style of neo-populist leader from president Traian Băsescu, whose quest was to pursue neo-populism 'from above' (Shafir 2008: 441). Băsescu presented himself and was considered by some media actors "representative of an 'anti-systemic movement' that is triggering 'social energies' which the 'old system' made up of corrupt political parties is incapable of handling; he was perceived as a head master in front of his pupils" (Saftoiu, ex presidential counselor, in *Evenimentul zilei*, 27 November 2007, apud Shafir 2007: 104). In fact Băsescu represents the popular perception that the established parties are corrupt, that they form cartels and are alienated from the people, etc. But it is clear that "ideology plays second fiddle in neo-populist orchestras, for they are nothing more than "catch-all" bands" (Shafir 2008: 452). While fitting into the generalized pattern of neo-populism, Romania nonetheless appears to be more prone to the long legacy of its exacerbated authoritarianism than its neighbors. At the end of Traian Băsescu's two mandates (2004–2014) it can be said that his true legacy is the enormous popularity of populist rhetoric: politicians at all levels unreservedly adopt this rhetoric, the electorate savour it as a grotesque show because he breaks taboos and uses vulgar words. But the actors on the Romanian political spectrum do not seem to grasp the dangers of this rhetoric for the fragile Romanian democracy.

Other key elements of populism, such as people-centrism, anti-elitism (the ruling elite), and the polarization of society *-us vs them-* are present in Romanian politics, too. Additionally, however, "Romanian populism is characterized by a lack of an ideological cleavage between the right and the left and a strong, Christian-Orthodox, reactionary attitude" (Corbu *et al.* 2017: 328).

As the enthusiasm generated by European integration - the latest project to unite the political class - has been diluted in continuous political scandals, strewn with news of acts of corruption and fabulous arrests, two new waves of populism have successively marked the Romanian political sphere.

4.2 The first populist post-European-integration wave

The first wave was represented by the *Party of the People-Dan Diaconescu* (PP-DD) built on the structure of a private television channel called *Oglinda – The Mirror*, later called OTV, which initially worked from a single room with some static cameras, without a fixed programme but with a moderator (Dan Diaconescu) who was able to speak without interruption about the subjects ignored by the serious television channels, and who was open especially to scandals. Despised by the mainstream press and warned several times by the *National Audiovisual Council* (NAC), from the beginning OTV addressed the people who had directly lost out in the transition (former workers in non-performing factories who became unemployed after 1989) and poorly educated people unable to cope with the difficulties posed by the transition.

The fight against the NAC, defined as the arm of the establishment that wanted to 'silence the voice of the people' (this phrase was launched and reiterated by Dan Diaconescu) has turned into a fight against the entire corrupt system as the audience of the channel has grown. PPP-DD displays a *left-wing nationalistic populism* that makes a number of proposals to the electorate: judgement by a People's Court (this phrase appears in an election poster) of all the rulers who looted Romania, an increase in salaries and pensions, and at the same time the elimination of salaries for ministers, parliamentarians and the president, as well as the exclusion of dignitaries from the Palace of Parliament, the Victory Palace and the Cotroceni Palace (the most symbolic places representing the Parliament, government and presidency).

Ignored and despised by mainstream media and politicians, against the backdrop of an election campaign that pitted two political giants against each other, USL (The Social-Liberal Union) and ARD (Alliance the Just Romania), led by the main government party at this date and strongly supported by the country's president, in the 2012 parliamentary elections PP-DD obtained an unexpected share of 13.99 % of the vote, placing it at a small distance from ARD (16.50 %). This success was fundamentally the result of the change of the voting system (from the vote on lists to the uninominal vote, and the significant role of the 'popular leader').

The success was short-lived: OTV television was shut down by the NAC in January 2013 and Dan Diaconescu was sentenced to five and a half years in prison for blackmailing politicians and businessmen; the parliamentary group was then dissolved, but some members entered other parliamentary parties.

4.3 The second populist post-European-integration wave

If the first populist post-integration wave was supported by outsiders – sectors of the population who lack material and symbolic resources, with a vague understanding of democracy and nostalgia for 'good old days' - and traditional media (above all, television), the second post-integration wave appeared in the online environment being actively supported by educated people, who were cosmopolitan, generally working in multinational companies. These people aspired towards the legitimation of a pro-European policy that had been insufficiently promoted by the political class legitimated by the previous populist wave.

The leader who generated this second wave is an activist known for his actions against the demolition of historical buildings in Bucharest. Unknown in the political sphere, Nicuşor Dan quickly became a symbol of the struggle of ordinary citizens against the political system. His candidacy for mayor of Bucharest (capital of Romania) created a tremendous effervescence in the online community, taking up at the local level the momentum of Barack Obama's 2008 campaign: people who were not politically involved and who did not know each other collaborated to create his election posters, personalities from cultural and civic life posted 'home-made' support clips, well-known rock music performers organized a concert marathon pro bono to collect the signatures necessary to enter the campaign, etc. Even though he obtained only 8.48 % of the votes of Bucharest people, his notoriety allowed him to transform the association *Save Bucharest* into a civic movement and then into a political party – the *Union Save Romania* (USR).

If the inclusion of PP-DD in the area of populism enjoys a broad academic consensus (Gherghina/Mişcoiu 2014; Kessel 2015; Rovira Kaltwasser/Taggart/Espejo/Ostiguy 2017; Norris/Inglehart 2018), the association of USR with this stigmatized category is rather rare. But USR is included in a list of European populist parties in a 2016 study (Boros/Freitas/Kadlot/Stetter 2016), and more recently Antonio Momoc (2018) states that USR promotes a populist discourse on the 'corrupt elite' versus the 'pure people'. At the same time in interviews and press articles the political scientist Alina Mungiu labels USR as populist: "The USR movement is pure populism. Instead of looking for the real solutions that are complicated, it arrives with mythological solutions: we must change the Constitution, we must do miraculous things" (interview given to DC News July 11, 2018).

However, this classification of the USR as populist is disputed. The best argument for the exclusion of the USR from the panoply of populist parties is its pro-European orientation and the absence of nationalistic elements in its discourse. Habituated to Tudor's aggressive nationalist discourse or Gigi Becali's orthodoxism, the researchers rightly hesitate to frame USR in the same category. By following Benjamin De Cleen (2017), we separate the two similar but not identical concepts and affirm that in spite of numerous examples of simultaneous use of discursive elements associated with nationalism and populism, the absence of 'the people as a nation' does not exclude it automatically from the populist category, if the people or its good constituents are seen as the underdog in opposition to an oppressive elite. Another reason for excluding the USR from the populist category is the fact that its discourse is not aimed at a marginal electorate but at an educated, cosmopolitan and sophisticated urban electorate that does not feel represented by the political class, and has so far refused political participation and has taken refuge in the construction of a totally non-political alternative Romania inside or outside national borders. USR reflects in its discourse "the populist rage against the political class due to the fact that the prosecution and punishment of numerous high-ranking officials have not yet alleviated corruption" (Mungiu-Pippidi 2018), and is in consonance with the voice of the street (#rezist) that we have heard more and more intensely since 2012 (Stefănel 2017). The third and rather subjective motive is the perception of populism as the twin brother of democracy (Muller 2016). Or it is just difficult to see in a maths teacher, a French-born French mother of four (Clotilde Armand) or, more recently, the jurist Dan Barna, this normality, this resemblance to the electorate they are addressing. The fact that they have not achieved fortunes in onerous relationships with the state prevents their inclusion in a pantheon of evil that contains Victor Orban, Marine Le Pen, Donald Trump and others. But if we go beyond this unilateral perspective and we accept the ambivalence of the populism/democracy relationship (Mudde/Rovira Kaltwasser 2012) this argument disappears.

Synthesizing the populist literature we can affirm that populist discourse must be homogenous (the people as a unitary whole, without cracks or dissonant voices, the elite another entity without cracks or dissonant voices) and Manichean, dichotomizing (the interests of these groups are irreconcilable without possibility of consensus, or even negotiation); the tonality is emotional-affective and not rational-objective, the proposed solutions are simple, reductionist, utopian and the emphasis falls on the myths and structures of the imaginary. We will demonstrate that this type of discourse used from the beginning by USR is being adopted and adapted by the traditional parties (PSD and PNL) as soon as it proves its attractiveness and efficiency.

The main indicators of populist discourse are: i) the appeal to the people, permanently reconstructed by those who have gained the "hegemonic competition" Mihail Chiru (in Gherghina/Mişcoiu 2010: 164); ii) the anti-establishment orientation, because those who govern are seen as a deeply corrupt social layer with interests opposed to the interests of the people they oppress; iii) the Exceptionality of the Leader as a defining feature of populist discourse that privileges the mythological construction of the Saviour-hero destined to mark the history of his people; iv) the crisis situation or turn in the evolution of society. The populist discourse is oppositional: its Manichean logic privileges the ultimatum tension of the decision *hic et nunc*.

In the context of Romanian electoral discourse we will consider as populist patterns the antonymic structures which oppose not different ideologies but two systems: democrat vs. totalitarian. For the populists the opponents are not democrats and their election does not mean the imposition of an ideology (right or left) but the replacement of democracy with a totalitarian system. In recent Romanian history this topic has had a special weight: either it mobilizes people in favor of the true revolution (in opposition to the false revolution of 1989 which failed in the solution of major societal problems), or it fights against the return to power of the Communists: the moment is crucial and must be treated as such.

5 The web 2.0 era

5.1 New technologies: between the democratization of the political sphere and the exacerbation of populism

If the impact of traditional media, and especially television, has been the subject of much research, studies on new technologies and their impact on politics are only at the beginning. What can be said *ab initio* is the fact that ordinary people are more informed and more active through digital technologies. On the other hand, even if the enthusiasm remains high, there has also been a series of criticisms about the impact of new technologies. The ability to mobilize these media can have a detrimental effect on politics. Crowds can be manipulated towards the destruction of democracy in the name of democracy itself. In a proverbial formulation *the best, (in our case participatory democracy) can be the enemy of the good (representative democracy).*

Some researchers argue that consumer opportunities created by the Internet increase consumerism and promote the market economy, but affect the tolerance of citizens frustrated by the perceived lack of civic values they share with others who are culturally different. It is obvious that the freedom to choose is fundamental, but the choice must be made after collecting a sufficient amount of information and having analysed a wide and varied set of options. Without formal censorship or informal rules of behaviour, the online sphere becomes the space for hard expressions and reductionist-populist divisions between THEM and US.

5.2 The 2014 presidential elections and the appearance of populism 2.0

The absence of the common enemy Traian Băsescu (the outgoing president who was unable to run in the presidential elections due to constitutional constraints), and the temptation to attempt a total conquest of power divided the Social Liberal Union (SLU) one year after the 2012 parliamentary elections. Crin Antonescu, leader of the Liberals, and Victor Ponta, leader of the Social Democrats, who had been partners and even friends, formally separated (Crin Antonescu surprisingly withdrew from politics), and Klaus Iohannis, Mayor of Sibiu, and Victor Ponta embarked on the race to the Presidency.

In the first round of the 2014 presidential elections the populist discursive elements were rather associated with the marginal candidates. For example, Monica Macovei, Minister of Justice, launched herself as an independent candidate with a discourse focused on objectives of the type "be at the service of a single master- 'the citizen'", and on negating the role played by the parties.

In the second round, the two remaining candidates (Klaus Iohannis and Victor Ponta) programmatically used populist rhetoric to win over the electorate. What distinguished the two candidates despite the same populist recipe was the massive use of social media: in the first place, Facebook was used to powerful effect by one of the actors (Klaus Iohannis). Klaus Iohannis received 6,288,769 votes (54.43 %) while Victor Ponta earned 5,264,383 votes (45.56 %). This difference of more than a million votes has been attributed to the change in voting patterns as digital platforms triggered a massive mobilization of the undecided electorate. For the first time, a participatory campaign carried out by ordinary people acting as electoral agents led to the Iohannis's victory online and then offline. This mobilization was based on three objectives:

5.2.1 The mobilization of the diaspora and its influence in Romania

In an atmosphere of widespread discontent due to the defective organization of elections outside Romania, the diaspora's inability to participate in the vote (endless queues, few polling divisions, etc.), candidate Klaus Iohannis discusses this electoral problem in 80 % of his Facebook postings:

> Appeal to Romanians from the Diaspora TELEPHONE TO PARENTS, BROTHERS, FRIENDS, NEIGHBOURS WHO ARE IN THE COUNTRY TO HAVE A VOTE AND EXPRESS YOUR VOTE AS WE DO NOT HAVE THE PERMISSION TO EXERCISE THIS RIGHT (comment on the Facebook page of Klaus Iohannis, 12 November 2014, written in capital letters).

This discursive strategy created a divide between the diaspora seen as united, formed by those who have left the country and those who support or think like them, and the political elite who seek continuity of power in their own interest and not modernization and the "job well done" supported by Klaus Iohannis (and, he claims, by ordinary citizens).

On the Facebook page of Klaus Iohannis the people are the diaspora and the Romanians within the country who are in solidarity with those who have left. We can consider that this category of the diaspora prevented from exercising its constitutional right is a populist concept as there is no such diaspora, but rather clusters of individuals with very different characteristics (emigrants of the communist period, the first emigrants of the 1990s, the brain drain, as well as offenders, beggars, prostitutes). Starting from the empirically unfounded reality that the diaspora votes to the right, the liberal Klaus Iohannis assumed the role of spokesperson for the people who traveled 500 km to vote, and for the thousands of Romanians who failed to vote on November 2nd (the messages quoted are taken from the electoral debates posted in video format on Iohannis's Facebook page).

5.2.2 The uniqueness of the moment: "Now or never" as the central theme of online communication

In a democratic system, elections represent moments of choice between several candidates with visions and projects concerning the evolution of society in the short and long term. But on the page of the liberal candidate Klaus Iohannis the elections appear as a moment of identity crisis of the country, of a total rupture between present and future, and thus the moment for a fundamental decision for the history of the country. The choice is not conceived as an option between two political programs, equally democratic and European, but between democracy and communism, between East and West.

In the comments on the Facebook page, the crisis of the official message becomes a crucial moment: either the recovery of the values of the 1989 Revolution confiscated by the beneficiaries (crypto-communists) of the Revolution installed in power, or a true revolution which will be accomplished after the victory of Klaus Iohannis, who will become the president of Romania.

> I would say that all the diaspora must unite and go to the country to make the revolution! Just like the young people of 1990 have removed Ceausescu, let's go, too, to take away the power of this individual (Victor Ponta)-message on Iohannis's FB page 7 November

The uniqueness of the moment is signaled by the countdown (the days remaining until the elections when Romania will be the country of the "job well done").

5.2.3 The two Romanias and the discursive construction of an online community as an electoral strategy

In a latent form in the publications of Klaus Iohannis, but manifestly in the comments of the fans, the image of two different Romanias and with opposite interests is configured (see Tab. 1). On one side, the people who vote for Klaus Iohannis, the young people who desire a future for themselves and their children, and on the other the Romania of Victor Ponta and of his voters, "living in the mud"- in poverty and misery (comment on the Facebook page of Klaus Iohannis, see image 1). One of the comments attracts the attention to this cleavage.

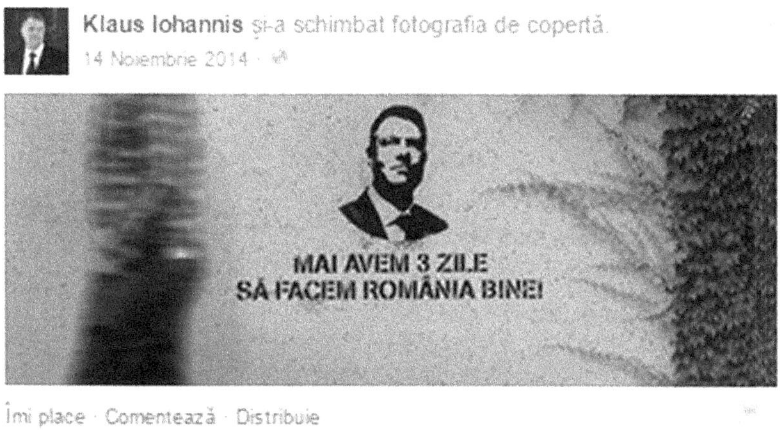

Image 1: Photo on Klaus Iohannis's FB page during the electoral campaign.

Tab. 1: The two Romanias.

People voting for Ponta (for the Social Democrats)	People voting for Iohannis (for the liberals)
Uneducated people	Students and intellectuals
Roma people who have received money for the vote	People who believe in change
Thieves who want to be protected when they steal	Optimistic and honest people
Corrupt politicians	People convinced by facts and not by words
Old communists who let themselves be manipulated by the media (Antena 3 etc.)	People who believe in democracy
'Stupid people' who believe that Ponta is a real Romanian	People who like seriousness, order and discipline

Between these two Romanias all the bridges are down, and any act of aggression (verbal, and even physical) is accepted. Democratic norms apply only within the community, and dialogue is allowed between those who express the same opinion. The gap between *us* and *them* cannot be bridged.

These images (the negative portrait of Ponta's voters and the positive one of the Iohannis voters) have the role of triggering the spiral of silence (Noelle-Neumann 1974), to consolidate the confidence of the voters for Klaus Iohannis in the decision taken and to make them understand the importance of the vote they will give.

In terms of the pragmatic-discursive system (Jagers/Walgrave 2007), used in equal measure by the leaders of the populist and mainstream parties (Gherghina/Soare 2013), Romanian populism has many characteristics of European populism (focus on the people, *anti establishment* philosophy, a Manichean vision of society). However, it also has its own particularities, such as right-left ambivalence, the reactionary religious component and the absence of Islamophobia (Corbu *et al.* 2017: 336). Unfortunately, all these differences fall beyond the scope of the present chapter

6 Conclusion

The political transitions in Eastern and Central Europe, the ensuing globalized economic crisis particularly affecting the Eurozone, the emergence of a *cyberdemocracy* and a public *hypersphere* (Levy 2011), and the extension of market mechanisms in all spheres of life, together determine permanent reconfigurations of the social world, giving rise to ambiguities and hybridizations.

By presenting themselves as "breaking with the ordinary course of representative democracy" (Lévy 2011), populist discourses and mobilizations invite us to look for the principle of their emergence, and investigate their media representation in the online and offline press, with a view to understanding the extent to which these phenomena change the relationship between the people and democracy.

At a moment when "time has no more patience" (to use the famous words of the Romanian writer Marin Preda), populist mobilizations function as warning signs for outdated governors, tending to bypass the heavy institutional procedures (given the difficult and ineffective action of "democratic" political mediation).

In line with recent analyses showing that populist communication consists in the explicit construction of the in-group of the people, a political operation *par excellence* (as Ernesto Laclau would say), our analysis shows how the opinion of the antagonistic camps consolidates and a rhetoric of opposition emerges (Sanders *et al.* 2017), illustrating the functioning of populist rhetoric as a symptom of current political communication. If populists are posing legitimate questions about the current state of liberal democracies (Mudde/Rovira Kaltwasser 2017), the omnipresence of populist discourses in Romanian political communication may be playing the same indexical alerting role (transgressing ideological borders, media systems -TV vs. online-, leaders and parties).

The populist leaders and the leaders of the mainstream parties alike massively appeal to populist discourses –simplifying but pregnant, spectacular and challenging (using myths and symbols with messianic or nationalistic connotations (Corbu *et al.* 2017: 333)). What is noteworthy is the *continuity of the populist discourse in the absence of strong populist parti*es and the contribution of the classical and new media in the dissemination of this type of discourse, a phenomenon which would require a thorough analysis (Ștefănel 2017) especially in Central and Eastern European countries and in a cross-regional perspective.

References

Albertazzi, Daniele / McDonnell, Duncan 2008. Conclusion: Populism and Twenty-First Century Western European Democracy. In Albertazzi, Daniele / McDonnell, Duncan (eds) *Twenty-First Century Populism*. Basingstoke & New York: Palgrave Macmillan, 217-223.

Bale, Tim / van Kessel, Stijn / Taggart, Paul 2011. Thrown around with Abandon? Popular Understandings of Populism as Conveyed by the Print Media: A UK Case Study. In *Acta Politica* 46/2, 111-131.

Boros, Tamas / Freitas, Maria / Kadlot, Tibor / Stetter, Ernest 2016. *The State of Populism in the European Union 2016*. FEPS – Foundation for European Progressive Studies.

Canovan, Margaret 1981. *Populism*. New York: Harcourt Brace Jovanovitch.

Corbu, Nicoleta / Balaban, Delia / Negrea-Busuioc, Elena 2017. Romania: Populist Ideology without Teeth. In Aalberg, Toril / Esser, Frank / Reinemann, Carsten / Strömbäck, Jesper / de Vreese, Claes H. (eds) *Populist Political Communication in Europe*. New York: Routledge, 326-338.

Chêne, Janine / Ihl, Olivier / Vial, Éric / Waterlot, Ghislain 2003. *La tentation populiste au cœur de l'Europe*. Paris: La Découverte.

De Cleen, Benjamin 2017. Populism and Nationalism. In Rovira Kaltwasser, Cristóbal / Taggart, Paul / Ochoa Espejo, Paulina / Ostiguy, Pierre (eds) *Handbook of Populism*. Oxford: Oxford University Press, 435-460.

De Vreese, Claes / Esser, Frank / Aalberg, Toril / Reinemann, Carsten / Stanyer, James 2018. Populism as an Expression of Political Communication Content and Style: A New Perspective. *The International Journal of Press Politics* 23/4, 423-438.

Gherghina, Sergiu / Mişcoiu, Sergiu 2010. *Partide si personalitati populiste in Romania postcomunista*. Iasi: Institutul European.

Gherghina, Sergiu / Mişcoiu, Sergiu / Soare, Sorina (eds) 2013. *Contemporary Populism: A Controversial Concept and Its Diverse Forms*. Newcastle: Cambridge Scholars Publishing.

Gherghina, Sergiu / Mişcoiu, Sergiu 2014. A Rising Populist Star: The Emergence and Development of the PPDD in Romania. *Debatte* 22/2.

Hawkins, Kirk A. 2010. *Venezuela's Chavismo and Populism in Comparative Perspective*. Cambridge: Cambridge University Press. DOI: <https://doi.org/10.1017/CBO9780511730245>

Hawkins, Kirk A. / Rovira Kaltwasser, Cristobal 2017. The Ideational Approach to Populism. *Latin American Research Review* 52/4, 513-528. DOI: <https://doi.org/10.25222/larr.85>.

Herkman, Juha 2016. Construction of Populism. Meanings Given to Populism in the Nordic Press. *Nordicom Review* 37, 147-161. doi:10.1515/nor-2016-0029.

Ietcu-Fairclough, Isabela 2007. Populism and the Romanian 'Orange Revolution': A Discourse Analytical Perspective on the Presidential Election of December 2004. *Studies in Language & Capitalism* 2/1, 31-74.

Jagers, Jan / Walgrave, Stefaan 2007. Populism as Political Communication Style: An Empirical Study of Political Parties' Discourse in Belgium. *European Journal of Political Research* 46/3, 319-345.

Kessel, Stijn van 2015. *Populist Parties in Europe. Agents of Discontent?* London: Palgrave Macmillan.

Laclau, Ernesto 1977. *Politics and Ideology in Marxist Theory*. London: London Humanities Press.

Laclau, Ernesto 2008. *La raison populiste*. Paris: Seuil.

Lévy, Pierre 2011. L'Hypersphère publique. *Medium* 29, 203-219.

Moffitt, Benjamin 2016. *The Global Rise of Populism: Performance, Political Style and Representation*. Stanford: Stanford University Press.

Momoc, Antonio 2018. Populism 2.0. Digital Democracy and the New Enemy of the People. *Communication Today* 1, 55-77.

Mudde, Cas 2004. The Populist Zeitgeist. *Government and Opposition* 39/14, 541-563.

Mudde, Cas 2007 *Populist Radical Right Parties in Europe* Cambridge: Cambridge University Press.

Mudde, Cas / Rovira Kaltwasser, Cristóbal 2012. Populism and (Liberal) Democracy: A Framework for Analysis. In Mudde, Cas / Rovira Kaltwasser, Cristóbal (eds) *Populism in Europe and the Americas: Threat or Corrective for Democracy?* Cambridge: Cambridge University Press, 1-27.

Mudde, Cas / Rovira Kaltwasser, Cristóbal 2013. Exclusionary vs. Inclusionary Populism: Comparing Contemporary Europe and Latin America. *Government & Opposition* 48, 147-174.

Mudde, Cas 2017. Populism: An Ideational Approach. In Rovira Kaltwasser, Cristobal / Taggart, Paul / Ochoa Espejo, Paulina / Ostiguy, Pierre (eds) *The Oxford Handbook of Populism*. Oxford: Oxford University Press, 27-48.

Mudde, Cas / Rovira Kaltwasser Cristobal 2017. *Populism. A Very Short Introduction*. Oxford: Oxford University Press.
Muller, Jan-Werner 2016. *What Is Populism*? Philadelphia: University of Pennsylvania Press.
Mungiu-Pippidi, Alina 2001 The Return of Populism. The 2000 Romanian Elections. *Government and Opposition* 36/2, 230-252.
Mungiu-Pippidi, Alina 2018. Romania's Italian-Style. Anticorruption Populism. *Journal of Democracy* 29/3, 104-116.
Noelle-Neumann, Elisabeth 1974. The Spiral of Silence. A Theory of Public Opinion. *Journal of Communication* 24/2, 43-51.
Norris, Pippa / Inglehart, Roland 2018. *Cultural Backlash: Trump, Brexit, and the Rise of Authoritarian-Populism*. Cambridge: Cambridge University Press.
Ostiguy, Pierre 2017. Populism: A Socio-Cultural Approach. In Rovira Kaltwasser, Cristobal / Taggart, Paul / Ochoa Espejo, Paulina / Ostiguy, Pierre (eds) *The Oxford Handbook of Populism*. Oxford: Oxford University Press, 73-100.
Pirvulescu, Cristian 2018. What about Populism? Is the Populism a "Thin" Ideology or a Neutral Political Instrument? Proceedings of the 4th ACADEMOS Conference 2017. Bologna: Filodiritto.
Sanders, Karen / Canel, Maria J. / Hurtado, Molina / Zoragastua, Jessica 2017. Populism and Exclusionary Narratives: The 'Other' in Podemos' 2014 European Union Election Campaign. *Journal of European Communication* 32/6, 352-367.
Shafir, Michael 2007. Vox Populi, Vox Dei and the (Head)Master's Voice: Mass and Intellectual Neo-Populism in Contemporary Romania. In Nekvapil, Václav / Staszkiewicz, Maria (eds) *Populism in Central Europe*. Prague: AMO Asociace Pro Mezinárodni Otázky, Association for International Affairs, 81-108.
Shafir, Michael 2008. From Historical to "Dialectical" Populism: The Case of Post-Communist Romania. *Canadian Slavonic Papers/ Revue canadienne des slavistes* L/3-4, 425-469.
Soare, Sorina 2010. Genul şi speciile populismului românesc. O incursiune pe tărâmul Tineretii fără bătrâneţe *şi al* Vieţii fără de moarte. In Gherghina, Sergiu / Miscoiu, Sergiu (eds) *Partide şt personalităţi populiste în România postcomunistă*. Iaşi: Institutul European, 87-118.

Stanley, Ben 2017. Populism in Central and Eastern Europe. In Rovira Kaltwasser, Cristobal / Taggart, Paul / Ochoa Espejo, Paulina / Ostiguy, Pierre (eds) *The Oxford Handbook of Populism*. Oxford: Oxford University Press, 140-161.

Ștefănel, Adriana 2016. Notes on Populism. *Revue Roumaine de Philosophie* 60/1, 141-149.

Ștefănel, Adriana 2017. Some Populist Discursive Aspects of the #Rezist Movement. In Adi, Ana / Lilleker, Darren (eds) *#Rezist Romania's 2017 Anti-corruption Protests: Causes, Developments and Implications*. Berlin: Quadriga University of Applied Sciences, 116-123.

Taggart, Paul 2000. *Populism*. Philadelphia: Open University Press.

Weyland, Kurt 2001. Clarifying a Contested Concept. Populism in the Study of Latin American Politics. *Comparative Politics* 34/1, 1-22.

Weyland, Kurt 2017. Populism: A Political Strategic Approach. In Rovira Kaltwasser, Cristobal / Taggart, Paul / Ochoa Espejo, Paulina / Ostiguy, Pierre (eds) *The Oxford Handbook of Populism*. Oxford: Oxford University Press, 48-73.

Wodak, Ruth / Mral, Brigitte / KhosraviNik, Majid 2013. *Right-Wing Populism in Europe: Politics and Discourse*, London New York: Bloomsbury Academic.

Saqlain Hassan

Populism and popularity in Imran Khan's 2018 election speeches

1 Introduction

Since the turn of the 21st century, the term populism has been omnipresent in discussion of the political landscape, to the extent that some researchers have spoken of a "populist Zeitgeist" (Mudde 2004). In the broadest sense, populism has often been understood as an approach to politics intended to "get the support of ordinary people by giving them what they want" (Cambridge Dictionary Online 2008). However, recent understandings of populism have moved away from references to substantive policy to a focus on political communication style (Moffitt 2016). According to Drake, populism "uses political mobilization, recurrent rhetoric, and symbols designed to inspire the people" (quoted from Dornbusch/Edwards 1990: 248). One important aspect of this rhetoric was identified by Mudde (2004), who defines populism as a phenomenon based on the distinction between two groups within a society: the poor and the corrupt elites. Along similar lines, Rodrik (2017) sees populism as a medium that carries a "diverse set of movements" but argues that these essentially contain an anti-establishment element: a struggle against the corrupt practices of ruling elites. Similarly, Hadiz and Chryssogelos (2017) observe that populism is driven by the growing imaginings concerning the antagonism between people and elites, and relate the rise of populism to corruption in the powerful institutions that are responsible for maintaining social, economic, and political life. Corruption leads to resentment against the elite, and populist politicians are particularly adept at taking advantage of this discursive divide (Jagers/Walgrave 2007; Kriesi 2014; Venizelos in this volume).

At the same time, it is important to remember that populism is not the same in Europe as in Latin America or Asia. Populism inevitably takes its influence from culture and context (Gidron/Bonikowski 2013). In some parts of the world, xenophobia seems to provide part of the force behind populism, but in others, such as developing countries, inequality in social spectra has been found to be the main cause underlying the emergence of populism. The essence of populism in each case is hidden in the message to be conveyed, and populist leaders typically choose words aimed to reach people's emotions, both positive and negative (Breeze 2019). Today, as in the past, they can do so through speeches delivered to live audiences, but the power of the speech has been greatly enhanced through the additional help of different media, such as electronic, print, and social media (Ekstrom/Patrona/Thornborrow 2018). Arguably, the availability of digital media is one of the decisive factors in the current rise of populism, since media such as YouTube or Twitter allow politicians to communicate more directly with ordinary people, bringing new political messages to a wider audience than ever before. Astute politicians have learnt to use these media effectively, by targeting people's areas of interest, arousing their emotions, and conveying clear messages that attract attention and inspire support. Populists are generally adept at exploiting the affordances of digital media and projecting their personalities and ideologies in ways that appeal to large sectors of society.

1.1 Populism in West and East

The history of populism is often traced back to the xenophobic Farmer's Alliance (1840s), in the United States, and to Latin American populism in the mid-20th century (Taggart 2000). The recession of 2008 is widely thought to have sparked a new wave of populism in Europe and America fuelled by resentment against social elites and big business (Mudde/Kaltwasser 2017). Subsequently, Trump's victory and the Brexit campaign both came to be associated with reactions to austerity measures implemented in the wake of the financial crisis. Moreover, the term 'globalization' also swiftly came into the discussion after these crises, and right-wing populists in the west were quick to seize on the negative aspects of globalization to advertise their populist claims. Public fears over migration exacerbated the sense of alienation and distrust among many sectors of society, driving voters to follow the far right. Galston (2018) provides the following analysis of populism:

> It has eaten into support for traditional centre-right parties while dealing a knock-out blow to the center-left. The result is the end of the centre-left/centre-right duopoly that has dominated European politics since the end of World War II. Party systems throughout Europe have fragmented, and most have shifted toward the right.

It has eaten into support for traditional centre-right parties while dealing a knock-out blow to the centre-left. The result is the end of the centre-left/centre-right system that has dominated European politics since the end of World War II. Party systems throughout Europe have fragmented, and most have shifted toward the right.
Galston's diagnosis is that the left in Europe paid no attention to migration, which gave the right a chance to win over the lower earning groups. Right- and left-wing populisms have both greatly affected the results of elections in the previous decade, and the upshot of this has often been a shift in western politics from left to right.

On the other hand, the approach to populism in South Asian countries such as Pakistan, India, and Bangladesh is somehow different from that of their European counterparts because in these countries immigration is not a major political headache. The issues addressed by populism in these countries are different: countering elites, issues related to minorities, poverty, and corruption (Kurlantzick 2018). In this context, the family dynasties in Pakistani politics (i.e. the Bhutto and Sharif families) form an obvious target for populist campaigns. This study aims to fill an important research gap by addressing populism in Pakistan, where a charismatic leader uses populist communication strategies to promote an essentially modernizing agenda. I will begin by discussing the history of populism in Pakistan, and then go on to analyse how Imran Khan aimed to target the civilian establishment and the status quo in order to promote his forward-looking ideology.

1.2 Populism in Pakistani politics

Pakistan came into being on August 14, 1947, after the British announced the division of the united India into two parts, one with a Muslim majority and the other with a Hindu majority. The political history of Pakistan encompasses both democracy and dictatorship. The initial two decades in Pakistan were mainly dominated by conspirators and dictators. The 1970 election brought a sea-change in Pakistani political history when Zulfiqar Ali Bhutto secured a victory in West Pakistan and Sheikh Mujeeb-ur-Rehman in East Pakistan. Their clash to secure the control of Pakistan resulted in the separation of East Pakistan (now Bangladesh). Bhutto, who held power from 1973 to 1977, was the first populist leader in Pakistan to stand against the elites and the establishment (both civilian and army) and asserted the moral rights of the nation against capitalists and feudalism by introducing his political slogan 'food, clothes, and shade' (Zahoor 2017).

Over the next decades, the conservative Pakistan Muslim League (Nawaz) and the more progressive Pakistan People's Party alternated in power. However, widespread corruption and failure to make economic progress led to unrest. In 2013 a relatively new party named Pakistan Tehreek Insaf (PTI), founded by Imran Ahmed Khan Niazi (now 66 years old), managed to secure 7.5 million votes, coming second overall. Khan is an Oxford graduate, former captain of the Pakistan cricket team, commentator, philanthropist, and owner of the University of Namal and Shaukat Khanum Memorial Hospital. His political career started when he launched his political party on 25 April 1996, with his slogan "end corruption, clear out the political mafias" (Delcan 2005). After defeat in his first election in 1996, in 2002 and 2013 he was elected member of the national assembly. His 126-day march in 2014 against vote-rigging in the 2013 election helped him to advertise his political agenda, and from then on, the people started coming to his rallies. In the election of 2018, his party secured victory and he is now serving as the 22nd prime minister of Pakistan. Khan's political style is very different from that of Bhutto (Milam 2018), but he has generally been described as an excellent communicator with a populist style which is dominated by progressive views such as promoting women's rights, religious freedom, freedom of expression, and getting rid of corruption.

This chapter uses corpus-assisted discourse methodology to analyse Khan's approach to convincing people in the 2018 election campaign, addressing the following questions: How does Khan's communication style persuade people to support his political ideology? What discursive strategies does he employ to build empathy with a multicultural and multilingual society?

1.3 Pakistan's general election in 2018

The 2018 election campaign was marked by massive media attention, as representatives of the different political parties vied for attention in their speeches. Politics is always about the relationship between leaders and people (Brown/Gilman 1960), and during election campaigns politicians devise careful strategies to convince the people to choose them on voting day (Lagerwerf/Boeynaems/Egmond-Brussee/Burgers 2015). Political speeches can create a bond between the people and the leader, but only if the leader can work magic through his words to engage with the way people are thinking and bring about changes (Peetz 2018). Along these lines, to reach people's hearts the major political parties and strong contenders for the prime ministership in Pakistan, such as the Pakistan People's Party (PPP), Pakistan Muslim League Nawaz (PMLN), Pakistan Tehreek Insaf (PTI), and the coalition of all the religious parties called Muttahida Majlis Amal (MMA), all came up with tempting manifestos and approaches.

Pakistan is facing numerous problems such as an energy crisis, economic decline, public health problems, terrorism, a complex foreign policy, and many internal issues. Previously, during earlier election campaigns, the political parties promised a variety of solutions to these problems. In the 2018 election, Pakistan Tehreek Insaf led by Imran Khan introduced the concept of 'accountability of all corrupt politicians' to get rid of hereditary politicians and political dynasties; Khan also used arguments derived from Sharia Law to justify women's rights and the rights of minorities, while supporting the maintenance of good relations with other Muslim countries.

2 Methodology

2.1 Analytical approach

This study uses corpus-assisted discourse (CAD) methodology (Baker 2006) to analyse an election speech delivered during the campaign and broadcast on YouTube. Discourse analysis in combination with corpus linguistics provides powerful tools to investigate discourse in context (Partington *et al.* 2013; Taylor 2014). Using CAD methodology helps the researcher to detect recurring patterns in discourse, but also to understand speaker/writer intentions behind communicative acts (Koteyko 2014). Moreover, CAD studies are largely tailored to analyse a discourse within context by applying both qualitative and quantitative tools (Siiner 2018). Analysing the language used in political campaigns is an important aspect of corpus studies on political discourse (van Dijk 1998). Previous studies have used such mixed corpus-based approaches to analyse political speeches, focusing on the use of metaphors (i.e. Lu/ Ahrens 2008), on the targeting of different audiences (Rante Carreon/ Svetanant 2017) or on ideology and power (Sharififar/Rahimi 2015).

2.2 Materials

Almost all of Khan's speeches are in Urdu when he addresses in Pakistan, but some of them are translated and uploaded by different users in different blogs on internet. For the present study an extract from his speech delivered in Lahore ('Minare-Pakistan': the monument of Pakistan) during his 2018 election campaign was downloaded from Pakistan Tehreek Insaf's official online blog.[1] The speech was originally delivered in Urdu language but translated into English by the blogger, and the translation was verified as correct by the researcher. The document was uploaded to Sketch Engine (Kilgarriff *et al.* 2014). The speech

1 Pakistan Tehreek-e-Insaf: see <http://www.insaf.pk>.

consisted of 4,903 tokens in running text and 382 sentences with a TTR (type/token ratio) of 25.70.

2.3 Procedure

The analysis was carried out using the tools in Sketch Engine. The new version of this platform allows its users to obtain word sketches, parallel word sketches, keywords, concordances, and collocations, among other aspects. The concordances of frequently occurring lemmas and keywords were obtained and analysed qualitatively.

3 Results

The results are divided into two main categories. We will look first at how Khan made use of certain personal forms as part of his strategy and how he delivered his message (3.1). Secondly, we will examine some frequent keywords and their concordances to find out more about the key concepts in Khan's speech (3.2).

3.1 Personal verb forms in Imran Khan's speech

In many languages, personal pronouns have an interpersonal function in discourse, and they help to project a strong, personal relationship between the speaker and the listener. One well known strategy in political communication consists of switching between politicians' individual and collective identities: politicians need to project both their personal identity and charisma, and the collective identity of their party and/or the social group they claim to represent, and this is achieved in English by careful manoeuvring with shifting pronouns 'I', 'we', 'you', and 'they' (Bramley 2001). Although all politicians use personal pronouns or forms in their speeches, the frequent use of these (particularly first and second person pronouns and verb forms) has often been associated with populist leaders, as it seems to be characteristic of a more emotive, and personal style of communication. Populist politicians often emphasise their own personality and feelings in order to connect with large audiences and build empathy: when Hugo Chávez said "I am not an individual, I am the people", he was inviting the people of Venezuela to share his emotions and place their trust in him. As Li (2002) suggests, the interpersonal function of first and second person forms encourages listeners to respond to the speaker in a more sympathetic way and to share his/her feelings.

For the sake of comprehensibility, the data presented in this study are from the official translation of Imran Khan's speech into English, but since the original is in Urdu, it is important to understand how pronouns and verb forms work in the Urdu language. Urdu is an SOV language that hails from the family of Indo-Aryan languages mainly under the Arabic and Persian influence. There is no gender-specific pronoun in Urdu like English 'she'. The verb in Urdu ending with inflections such as feminine ی (y, i), masculine ا (a), or plural ے (ai or e) indicates the person who is the subject of the verb, just as a pronoun does in English (i.e. he, she, they, you, we). Tab. 1 shows that Imran Khan made frequent use of personal forms: the first person, equivalent to English 'we' and 'I', is especially prominent in this speech, and the second person you is surprisingly common, while possessives are also found. These results suggest that this highly personal language is part of his strategy for connecting with his audiences. In the original speech delivered in Urdu, Imran Khan used three personal forms in abundance, namely (میں , آپ , ہم). Firstly, میں ('mei') 'I' indicates the first-person singular, and ('meray' میرے) 'my' is its possessive form, frequently found in the phrase میرے پاکستانیوں 'My Pakistanis'. Secondly, 'aap'آپ is the honorific form of the second person 'you'. Khan in his speech avoided the use of familiar informal you (تم 'tum'), which can be used to address people of lower social status (see Schmidt 1999), and replaced this by formal you (آپ 'aap'), the honorific form, in nominative and oblique cases (accusative, genitive, dative, and ergative) (Schmidt 1999: 17), accompanied by frequent use of 'your/s' ('aap kay'اپ کے), 'you all' (آپ سب 'aap sub'), and 'you people' ('aap log'آپ لوگ). Khan frequently directed himself to the audience as 'we' ('ham' ہم), a form often used to indicate that

Tab. 1: Person and possessive in Imran Khan's Speech.

Person/possessive	Frequency	Frequency/ Million
First person		
I (میں)	132	23,268.11
We (ہم)	125	22,034.2
My (میرے)	37	6,552.12
We/us (ہمیں)[a]	24	4230.57
Our (ہمارے)	50	8,813.68
Second person		
You (آپ)	52	9,166.23
Your (اپ کے)	14	2,467.83
Third person		
They (وہ)	22	3,878.02

[a] Though Indo-European in origin, Urdu is not a nominative/accusative language, but rather an absolutive/ergative language. This means that the oblique pronoun ہمیں, usually translated as 'us', may have the role of the English subject pronoun, 'we', in some constructions.

the speaker is part of a particular social group (Schmidt 1999: 17), and he also made use of 'our', particularly ('humien'ہمیں) accusative, and ('hamarien'ہمارے) genitive. Apart from these, he also used third person plural ('woh' وہ) 'they' to point to others. Always bearing in mind the linguistic differences, the present study follows Alavidze (2017), in analysing personal forms used in the context of populist politics. Tab. 1 shows the occurrences of personal forms in Khan's speech with their normalized frequency per million words.

On the other hand, in order to triangulate our findings, it is useful to compare Khan's discursive style with that of one of his major rivals in his 2018 election campaign, and so we will compare his speech with one by his counterpart Bilawal Bhutto Zardari, the chairman of the Pakistan People's Party. He is also an Oxford graduate, and was a strong contender for the prime ministership in the election 2018. His speech was retrieved in English from the Pakistan People's Party's online blog. The speech was originally delivered in Urdu but translated by the blogger, and this translation was also verified as correct by the researcher. The speech consists of 1,425 words with a type/token ratio of 38.56 in 68 sentences. Tab. 2 shows personal pronouns used by Bilawal Bhutto in his speech.

Tab. 2 shows that Bilawal Bhutto used few personal forms in comparison with Khan. He mainly communicated with first-person plural (ہم) 'we' and its cases such as (ہمیں used commonly as object 'us' and nominative 'we') to discuss both his party's position and the nation. In his speech he used the first-person plural ہمیں as nominative 'we' to address the nation. The possessive (ہمارے) 'our' is used to discuss the people in general to create a sense of unification, as in the following example:

(1) When we say 'ALL OUR PEOPLE' we mean everyone, and particularly those whose voices are heard less.

In what follows, I will focus on Khan's use of personal forms, showing how these configure his own particular populist style, and bringing out differences from Bilawal's style where appropriate.

Tab. 2: Personal pronouns in Bilawal Bhutto's speech.

Personal forms	Frequency	F/million
First person		
I		
We (ہم)	40	24,464.82
We/us (ہمیں)	15	4,186.44
My		
Our (ہمارے)	26	15,902.14
Second person		
You		
Your		
Third person		
They		

3.1.1 *Personal form: We*

The extensive use of the first-person plural 'we' (ہم) is striking. By using 'we', Khan is positioning himself discursively with the ordinary people of Pakistan, to build a sense of solidarity and evoke a feeling of national unity.

(2) We will have one uniform education system. One uniform curriculum to make one nation.

Importantly, using a strategy identified in the discourse of other leaders described as having a populist style (Moffitt 2016), he places himself on the side of the people to convince them about the wrongdoings of the previous governments, leading to bankruptcy in some institutions:

(3) Today we are at what we call a 'crossroad'. Currently we are on a path to destruction. Rich getting richer. Poor getting poorer.

By comparison, in his speech Bilawal Bhutto used 'we' (ہم) to mean his party, what his party could do after winning the election, and what his party has done in their earlier period in office (2008–2013):

(4) We have previously not only made laws and ratified Conventions, we have also now proposed provisions to further safeguard personal freedoms.

Like Khan, Bilawal occasionally also uses the oblique first-person plural pronoun, represented in the English translation here as nominative (ہمیں), to speak in terms of 'We, our party and our people' to instil a sense of unity and a tradition of attachment to the people:

(5) We have to fulfil Benazir's promise. We have to save Pakistan

3.1.2 *Personal form: I*

Khan in his speech repeatedly uses the first person singular form 'I' (میں) to emphasize his personal commitment to and investment in the project he proposes:

(6) As long as there is last drop of blood in me, I will fight for your rights. No one can stop me.
(7) I promise that I will protect the people's tax money.

3.1.3 Personal forms: I and we

The frequent juxtaposition of 'I' and 'we' helps to build a discursive bond between Khan as an individual political leader and his identification with the people of Pakistan and the country's problems:

(8) We lack money to run the country, we are indebted. Today I claim I will collect money right from this nation, we will not need any external debt.
(9) I claim today we will have to bear no external debt, no bowing before other countries, if we ensure transparency.

3.1.4 Personal forms: I and you

Khan's frequent use of the plural form 'you' is particularly noticeable. In Urdu the plural 'you' (اپ) is the honorific form used to address many people. Here, Khan is addressing his live audience directly, as though this were a conversation among friends or an appeal to a group of people present, but we should remember that he is also addressing his virtual audience through YouTube and social media, where the impact of using 'you' may be even stronger. Importantly, the use of second person 'you' is generally combined with first person 'I' in Imran Khan's speech, conjuring up a relationship that is both close and direct:

(10) Today I want you all to ask yourself why was this great country founded?
(11) I am telling you that we will run Pakistan like it has never been run before and we will start with ourselves.!

3.1.5 Possessive: My

Another interesting choice he made in his speech was the use of a phrase میرے پاکستانیوں 'my Pakistanis' (which occurred five times in the speech, with a frequency of 881.37 per/million and an MI (mutual information) score of 2.21) with great enthusiasm to project his love for the people and people's love for him. In this example, by reminding people of their generosity to his projects in the past, he is subtly suggesting that they will respond generously to his call to them today:

(12) First of all, I want to thank you my Pakistanis. Whenever I called you. You never disappointed me. I am greatly thankful. Whenever I asked you for money be it for Shaukat Khanam Memorial Hospital or the Namal University. You always gave me more and more.

3.1.6 Possessive: Your

In his speech, Khan made several uses of possessive 'your' to make the people feel that he belongs to them. This is especially characteristic in the phrase آپ کا کپتان 'Your Kaptaan' (used once in the speech), which recalls his legendary cricketing career as Captain of the national team, and draws on his popularity as a sporting hero in Pakistan to win people's hearts:

(13) My speech is going to be a little longer today so if you have less stamina than your Kaptaan, please hold up. My Pakistanis listen to me carefully.

3.1.7 Personal forms: We, they and them

Khan is famous in Pakistan because he is one of the few politicians who have been campaigning against the corrupt elites for a longer period of time. In the hope of a better Pakistan, people have flocked to his rallies to praise his brave intentions against discredited ruling elites. He uses the third person plural forms 'they'/'them' (nominative and oblique cases) to target his rivals. He frames them as wholly responsible for the current bad situation within Pakistan and its economic downfall. The framing of other leaders as 'they' helps to establish a dichotomy between 'us' and 'them', while also emphasizing his election agenda of accountability:

(14) All rulers who have come so far, they spend money on themselves. The way our ruling elite spends money, how will anyone pay tax? People don't pay taxes, because they see how our ruling elite spends that money [on themselves].

In Imran Khan's discourse, the root cause of all the problems in Pakistan is framed as corruption within the ruling elites (hidden from the eyes of common people), which has led to the economic downfall that has caused the problems of unemployment, inflation, and foreign debt:

(15) My point is that what we have seen in Pakistan so far, the way the ruling elite has lived off the country's taxes, I will end this. We have to escape this economic crisis. No one is coming to save us. We will strengthen the anti-corruption institutions.

In short, this analysis of Khan's approach to using personal forms sheds light on the way he projects alliances between himself and the people against the corrupt elites. These findings echo those of other authors such as Bramley (2001) that the use of 'I' allows a politician to construct a strong identity as an individual, 'we' to construct his identity as a member of a group, 'you' to address a particular group, and 'they' to point to the others, often the antagonists. By integrating skilful use of personal forms and possessives, Imran Khan's populist discourse style helps him to shift between his identity as an individual and his role as one of the people, to show the viewers his positive qualities and to create a sense of bonding and affective unity.

3.2 Imran Khan's keywords: Building a new political agenda

Although Imran Khan does not have the reputation of being a pious Muslim, he speaks about religion surprisingly often in his speeches. Analysis of his speech reveals that he gave particular prominence to the lemma 'Medina' (used 7 times with 1,233.93 F/M) as a strategy to amalgamate his vision of Islamic simplicity and to legitimise his modernising programme in the eyes of the Muslim population. Medina (a city in the Arabian Peninsula) was the first Islamic state and base for the first Muslim migrant community, who went there from Mecca under the leadership of the prophet Muhammad. By using Medina as his image of the ideal state, Khan introduces Islamic utopianism into Pakistani politics. To put the concept of a utopia in an Islamic context, we have to understand that its main features are grounded in the Quran, Islamic pacifism, and Prophetic traditions that feature Medina as a model utopian state (Sargent 2010). Like other utopian models defined by studies on cultures elsewhere, Medina is often understood as an idealised place that shares qualities different from the real world, containing a diverse society that gives opportunity to everyone (Balasopoulos 2010; Brake 2016; Fernando *et al.* 2018). Here, Khan holds up the Islamic state of Medina as an example of good governance, embodying key features such as: justice and uprightness, education and awareness, tolerance, equality, brotherhood, dignity, power, and reformation of behaviour and attitude.

In this political campaign, Imran Khan made careful use of this image of Medina in order to attract and hold people's attention. He knows that discussing and respecting religion is important for politicians in Pakistan. For the people to accept your authority and identify with you, it is necessary to express and enact shared religious affiliation. Imran Khan drew on the notion of Medina to introduce the concept of a welfare state for the first time in the history of Pakistani politics, and also to project a culturally acceptable model of a plural society. Khan exemplified the characteristics of Medina as guidelines for a successful individual:

(16) It means even if you are not Muslim, but you have either of the principles of Medina's state, justice, equality, unity and education, you'd succeed.

It is a common belief in Pakistan that the name Pakistan is strongly associated with the first pillar of Islam - the Islamic testimony of faith, also known in the Muslim world as *kalima shahada*: "there is no God but Allah and Prophet Muhammad is the messenger of Allah". The first pillar of Islam is at the centre of Muslims' religious identity, which compels them to establish their belief in Allah and the prophet Muhammad (Cady/ Simon 2006; Daniels 2017). In Pakistani society, references to *kalima shahada* are associated with a famous poetic-cum-political slogan, going back to a couplet introduced by a poet named Asghar Sodai in 1944, during the days of Pakistan's independence movement. The slogan was "What does Pakistan mean? - There is no God but Allah". Imran Khan in a similar sense goes back to this foundational belief to reassert that this country came into being to rejuvenate the golden Islamic era:

(17) This country was supposed to be a replication of Medina.
(18) Briefly, I want to describe the kind of Pakistan I want to see. Look, my inspiration is the Prophet Muhammad, the city of Medina that he founded, how it was based on humanity.

Additionally, Khan is keen to discuss the rights of minorities in Pakistan, and he gives the example of Medina to legitimise his programme of tolerance:

(19) Even the model welfare state of Medina had equal rights for all including Jews and Christians.

Similarly, Medina also plays a role in Khan's discourse on corruption: Medina, he tells us, would make sure of merit in every aspect of life. Interestingly, Imran Khan actually uses the English word 'merit', represented in Urdu as (میرٹ), even though there is no shortage of quasi-synonyms (اہلیت رکھنا - مستحق - حقدار) in Urdu, emphasising the use of this expression as meaning getting the right people for the right jobs. He constantly criticised the previous governments for not maintaining the tradition of merit in Pakistan as was the case in Medina:

(20) And then there was Merit in Medina.
(21) Hazrat Khalid bin Walid caused most damage to Muslims in Ohad. But when he came to the fold of Islam, he got the title 'Saifullah' and appointed General of Islamic battles because of MERIT.

Importantly, Khan talks about equality and justice. This was one of his main agendas during his election campaign. He wants to create such a state in which the prime minister will be in court for any misdeed, just as was the case in Medina, where even the prophet's daughter was subject to the law:

(22) Our Prophet said even if his daughter Fatima steals, her hands should be chopped.

Moreover, Khan has won popularity with the lower classes of society in Pakistan because he talks about their rights. During his 2018 election campaign he constantly criticised the previous government for not doing anything for the depressed people in Pakistan. He promised to build five million houses for the poor people and create jobs for them. His promise to facilitate improved circumstances for the oppressed people is also founded discursively on what the state of Medina did:

(23) The state of Medina took responsibility for the destitute. The orphans, the widows, the elderly. The prophet led by example. He was Sadiq and Ameen.[2]

2 Sadiq (truthful) and Ameen (honest) are the two qualities mainly linked to the personality of the Prophet Muhammad.

> Such Muslims then ruled for 700 years. But when Muslims let go of the system based on justice, they got defeated by Halaku Khan.[3] The last Caliph bowed before Halaku Khan and begged for mercy. To which Halaku replied "If only you had spent your gold [that is] in godowns[4] upon your people. You wouldn't have had to beg for your life today!"

Holding up Medina as his exemplary state, Imran Khan dreams of a country that will replicate these ideal Medina-like features. And for that purpose, he introduced his election slogan with the name of (نیا پاکستان) "Naya Pakistan" - a new Pakistan. There will be justice, equality, merit, access to rights, and women's rights:

> (24) This system cannot propel us any further unless we stand up to the tyrant against it. Naya Pakistan is only possible if we stand with the oppressed.

Moreover, he talked about women's rights publicly in a huge gathering, which is not easy for a politician who claims to represent a multicultural country, since discussing this issue poses a contradiction to some of the cultural norms of certain sub-cultures (in some places in Pakistan women are not given their shares in property and they are not allowed to take decisions on their own). It is hard to know how the people would react to his ideas in terms of positive appreciation and votes if he focused on Sharia Law, for example. The lemma 'خواتین' (women) occurred 7 times (1,882.23 F/M) in the original Urdu version of his speech and the cluster (خواتین کے حوقوق) 'women's rights' occurred twice. The following extract illustrates his bold but careful handling of the issue of women's rights, using the emotional strategy of expressing gratitude to his mother in order to frame women's education positively:

> (24) We will ensure through legislation (Sharia Law) that women get their due right.

---

3 Halagu Khan or Halaku Khan was an emperor of Mongol and the grandson of Genghis Khan (a Mongolian emperor). In 1259 his army defeated the Ayyubids in Gaza and in 1260 took control of Damascus, Syria (Runciman 1987; Meri 2005).

4 Colloquial expression meaning vaults or underground storerooms, often used in discussions of political corruption to refer to politicians who store their personal fortunes in Swiss bank accounts. Here, Khan is also criticizing people who never do charity, which is an act against the laws created by God defined in the Quran.

(25) Today I promise Pakistani women three things. My party will ensure we educate our girls. Educated mothers raise educated nation. Whatever I am today is because of my mother. We will open every 2 out of 1 schools for girls. For every 100 colleges, 70 will be for women. We will educate our women. After education, we will empower our women legally. We will replicate Khyber PakhtunKhwa government styled women's police stations[5] so women are encouraged to report crimes. Also we will ensure through legislation that women get their due right.

These examples illustrate how Imran Khan integrated his patriotic and religious views in a populist style that is more left than right, in order to build legitimation for his modernising agenda. His populist discourses helped him to gain power for the centre-left and to secure a good position in the election. In particular, his discourse drawing on the cultural model of Medina also helped him to influence people by appealing to their religious loyalties and their deep-seated emotions.

4 Conclusions

This CAD study was designed to analyse one election speech by Imran Khan that exemplifies his approach to addressing the nation during the recent 2018 election, in which his party was victorious. The examples used in this chapter shed light on the way one politician builds a populist style in order to further a progressive agenda in a Muslim country. Imran Khan's speech undoubtedly contains many of the key features of populism as defined by Mudde (2004), Moffitt (2016), and Mudde and Rovira Kaltwasser (2017), including powerful claims to represent 'the people', built on emotional bonds and projections of national/cultural unity, and strong antagonism towards corrupt 'elites'.

---

5 Khyber PakhtunKhwa is one of the four administrative provinces of Pakistan. Since 2013 it has been governed by Khan's party, who have implemented a modernization policy covering issues such as education, health, and 'women's complaint desks' at police stations.

Previous studies have illustrated populist discourses used by right-wing politicians, such as in Trump's victory or the Brexit referendum. These cases show the results of right-wing populism fueled by fear and hostility towards immigrants (Inglehart/Norris 2016). Populism in western countries (mainly Europe and the USA) is characteristically most strongly associated with right-wing parties (Wodak 2015). But it is clear that the situation in Asian countries such as India and Pakistan is quite different. To connect with huge grass roots electorates, there is vast potential in left-wing populism, and Imran Khan represents a moderate, progressive example of this.

Politicians need certain metaphors or concepts to help people understand their plans, particularly if these are new or controversial (Lu/Ahrens 2008). As we have seen, Imran Khan′s populist discourse mainly revolves around a notion of Islamic simplicity, associating potentially controversial issues such as the welfare state, tolerance and women's rights with the concept of Medina, an idealised Islamic state. In his election campaign he uses this powerful image to win over simple people, since it is compatible with their religious and nationalist loyalties.

On the other hand, we have also observed Khan's highly skilled use of personal forms to reinforce his populist discursive strategy, as compared to rivals in the 2018 election such as Bilawal Bhutto Zardari. To boost his personal credibility, he stresses his alignment with the people and insists on the value of accountability and the need to punish the corrupt elite by careful positioning using first and second person verb forms, pronouns and possessives: 'I', 'you', 'your', 'we', 'my', 'our', positioned against the third person plural 'they'. Pakistan has a political system that has traditionally been mainly dominated by the elites and important families, and Imran Khan's populism is striking in its rejection of the established elite and the corrupt status quo. By reinforcing the dichotomy between us and them, Khan underlines his own commitment to the people and positions himself against the discredited elites. As Alavidze (2017: 355) concluded: "pronouns as pragmatic markers need to be considered as linguistic 'bullets' used by politicians to achieve their goals".

We may also speculate that new media affordances have influenced Imran Khan's populist style of communication. Like Zulfiqar Ali Bhutto before him, Khan managed to exploit a populist style to achieve a major election victory. However, if we compare his performance in this speech to that of Bhutto in 1975/76, we see enormous differences in the way media affordances are exploited. Zulfiqar Ali Bhutto was known for his enthusiastic manner of delivering speeches on a dais in front of a huge gathering: in his dramatic and impassioned performances, it was common for microphones to be smashed. Bhutto inspired generations with his oratory, embedding the kinesthesia of nationalism without any fast medium of communication. By contrast, in a different media age, Khan inspired popularity by denouncing the elites and corrupt mafia, this time inspiring people through his personalised, persuasive speeches with the help of digital affordances such as Facebook, Twitter, and YouTube. The speech analysed by this study, which Khan delivered on 29 April 2018, received more than 3 million views[6] and a vast volume of appreciation on YouTube, which shows that Khan was able to take great advantage from the new digital media that help to secure him popularity with massive audiences both within Pakistan and around the globe.

In sum, Imran Khan´s populist style is characterised by the skilled management of personal forms to convey closeness to his audiences and encourage them to identify with his vision for Pakistan. He uses personal forms to evoke emotions towards different issues such as nationalism, pluralism, religion, and corruption (Proctor/Wen Su 2011). Khan's discursive approach seemed to bring new hope to the Pakistani electorate since he managed to speak for the oppressed, while offering real hope to disadvantaged groups. In a seeming contradiction to his own life experience and personality as a western-educated member of the social elite, his campaign was dominated by appeals to traditional religious beliefs. But his vision of Islam is enlightened, that is, he found a way of using Sharia to justify women's rights, or Medina to justify a plural society. His main agenda during his election campaign was to convince the ordinary people that he was speaking for the oppressed against the oppressor, and it is to be hoped that he can hold a strong enough consensus to usher in a process of peaceful reform.

6 User's views are calculated for all the videos uploaded on YouTube after the speech. Retrieved: 24/02/2019, from; <https://www.youtube.com>.

References

Alavidze, Maia 2017. The Use of Pronouns in Political Discourse. *International Journal of Arts and Sciences* 9/4, 349-356.

Baker, Paul 2006. *Using Corpora in Discourse Analysis*. London: Continuum.

Balasopoulos, Antonis 2010. Ruth Levitas, the Concept of Utopia. *The European Journal of American Studies* 2, 1-5.

Brake, Brittany P. 2016. *Political Utopias of the Renaissance: An Analysis of Thomas More's Utopia, Johann Valentinus Andreae's Christianopolis, and James Harrington's the Commonwealth of Oceana*. PhD thesis, Western Michigan University.

Bramley, Nicolette R. 2001. *Pronouns of Politics: The Use of Pronouns in the Construction of 'Self' and 'Other' in Political Interviews*. PhD thesis, Australian National University. <http://openresearch-repository.anu.edu.au>

Breeze, Ruth 2019. Emotions in Politics: Affective-Discursive Practices in UKIP and Labour. *Discourse and Society* 30/1, 24-43.

Brown, Roger / Gilman, Albert 1960. The Pronouns of Power and Solidarity. In Sebeok, Thomas Albert (ed.) *Style in Language*. Cambridge, Mass: MIT Press, 253-276.

Cady, Linell / Simon, Sheldon W. 2006. *Religion and Conflict in South and Southeast Asia: Disrupting Violence*. London: Routledge.

Cambridge Dictionary Online 2008. <https://dictionary. cambridge.org/>

Daniels, Timothy P. 2017. Sharia Dynamics: Islamic Law and Sociopolitical Processes. *Contemporary Anthropology of Religion*. London: Palgrave Macmillan, 1-27.

Delcan, Walsh 2005. When You Speak Out, People React. *The Guardian*, 30 September.

Dornbusch, Rudiger / Edwards, Sebastian 1990. The Macroeconomics of Populism. *Journal of Development Economics* 32/2, 247-277.

Drake, Paul 1982. Conclusion: Requiem for Populism? In Conniff, Michael L. (ed.) *Latin American Populism in Comparative Perspective*. Albuquerque: University of New Mexico Press.

Ekstrom, Mats / Patrona, Marianna / Thornborrow, Joanna 2018. Right-Wing Populism and the Dynamics of Style: A Discourse-Analytic Perspective on Mediated Political Performances. *Palgrave Communications* 4/1, 83-83.

Fernando, Julian W. / Burden, Nicholas / Ferguson, Adams / O'Brien Lean V. / Judge, Madeline / Kashima, Yoshihisa 2018. Functions of Utopia: How Utopian Thinking Motivates Societal Engagement. *Personality and Social Psychology Bulletin* 44/5, 779-792.

Galston, William A. 2018. The Rise of European Populism and the Collapse of Center-Left. Brookings Blogs. <https://www.brookings.edu/blog/order-from-chaos/2018/03/08/the-rise-of-european-populism-and-the-collapse-of-the-center-left/>

Gidron, Noam / Bonikowski, Bart 2013. Varieties of Populism: Literature Review and Research Agenda. Working Paper Series, *Weatherhead Center for International Affairs*, Harvard University: No. 13–0004.

Hadiz, Vedi R. / Chryssogelos, Aneglos 2017. Populism in World Politics: A Comparative Cross-Regional Perspective. *International Political Science Review* 38/4, 399-411.

Inglehart, Ronald F. / Norris, Pippa 2016. Trump, Brexit, and the rise of populism: Economic have-nots and cultural backlash. HKS Working Paper No. RWP16–026.

Jagers, Jan / Walgrave, Stefaan 2007. Populism as Political Communication Style: An Empirical Study of Political Parties' Discourse in Belgium. *European Journal of Political Research* 46, 319-345.

Kilgarriff, Adam / Baisa, Vit / Butsa, Jan / Jakubicek, Milos / Michelfeit, Jan / Rychly, Pavel / Suchomel, Vit 2014. *Lexicography ASIALEX* 1/7.

Koteyko, Nelya 2014. *Language and Politics in Post-Soviet Russia*. London: Palgrave Macmillan.

Kriesi, Hanspeter 2014. The Populist Challenge. *West European Politics* 37/2, 361-378.

Kurlantzick, Joshua 2018. Southeast Asia's Populism Is Different but Also Dangerous. *Council on Foreign Relations*. <https://www.cfr.org/article/southeast-asias-populism-different-also-dangerous>

Lagerwerf, Luuk / Boeynaems, Aamber / van Egmond-Brussee, Charlotte / Burgers, Christian 2015. Immediate Attention for Public

Speech: Differential Effects of Rhetorical Schemes and Valence Framing in Political Radio Speeches. *Journal of Language and Social Psychology* 34/3, 273-299.

Li, Donghui 2002. *Revisiting the Use of Personal Pronouns (PP) and Related Issues in C-E/E-C Translation*. Paper presented at First Tsinghua-Lingnan International Symposium on Translation Studies, Tsinghua University, Beijing. <https://commons.ln.edu.hk>

Lu, Wei-Lun L. / Ahrens, Kathleen 2008. Ideological Influences on Building Metaphors in Taiwanese Presidential Speeches. *Discourse and Society* 19/3, 383-408.

Mazzoleni, Gianpietro 2008. Populism and the Media. In Albertazzi, Daniele / McDonnell, Duncan (eds) *Twenty First Century Populism*. London: Palgrave Macmillan

Meri, Josef W. (ed.) 2005. *Medieval Islamic Civilization: An Encyclopedia*. London: Routledge.

Milam, W. 2018. Return of Populism in Pakistan? *The Friday Times*, 3 September. <https://www.thefridaytimes.com>

Moffitt, Benjamin 2016. *The Global Rise of Populism: Performance, Political Style and Representation*. Stanford: Stanford University Press.

Molloy, D. 2018. What Is Populism, and What Does the Term Actually Mean? *BBC News*, 6 March. <https://www.bbc.com/news/world-43301423>

Mudde, Cas 2004. The Populist Zeitgeist. *Government and Opposition* 39/4, 541-563.

Mudde, Cas / Rovira Kaltwasser, Cristóbal 2017. *Populism: A Very Short Introduction*. Oxford: Oxford University Press.

Omar, Waraich 2017. Pakistan's Populist Triumph. *The Atlantic*, 27 July. <https://www.theatlantic.com>

Partington, Alan / Duguid, Alison / Taylor, Charlotte 2013. *Patterns and Meanings in Discourse: Theory and Practice in Corpus-Assisted Discourse Studies (CADS)*. Amsterdam/Philadelphia: John Benjamins Publishing.

Peetz, Julia 2018. In Politics, Speeches Matter – but Even Donald Trump Couldn't Make the State of the Union Watchable. *The Conversation*, 1 February. <https://theconversation.com/>

Proctor, Katarzyna / Wen Su, Lily I. 2011. The First Person Plural in Political Discourse: American Politicians in Interviews and in a Debate. *Journal of Pragmatics* 43/13, 3251-3266.

Rante Carreon, Jonathan / Svetanant, Chavelin 2017. What Lies underneath a Political Speech? *Open Linguistics* 3, 638-655.

Rodrik, Dani 2017. *Populism and the Economics of Globalization*. HKS Working Paper No. RWP17–026.

Runciman, Steven 1987. *A History of the Crusades*. Cambridge: Cambridge University Press.

Sargent Lyman, T. 2010. *Utopianism: A Very Short Introduction*. Oxford: Oxford University Press.

Schmidt, Ruth Laila 1999. *Urdu: An Essential Grammar*. London: Routledge.

Sharififar, Massoud / Rahimi, Elahe 2015. Critical Discourse Analysis of Political Speeches: A Case Study of Obama's and Rouhani's Speeches at UN. *Theory and Practice in Language Studies* 5, 99–110, 343–349.

Siiner, Maarja 2018. Corpus Assisted Discourse Analysis of Presentations of 'Dementia', 'Aging' and 'Elderly Immigrants' in Norwegian Media 1995–2015. Centre for Multilingualism in Society across the Lifespan. <https://www.hf.uio.no/multiling/english/projects/>

Taggart, Paul 2000. *Populism*. Philadelphia: Open University Press.

Taylor, Charlotte 2014. Investigating the Representation of Migrants in the UK and Italian Press: A Cross-Linguistic Corpus-Assisted Discourse Analysis. *International Journal of Corpus Linguistics* 19/3, 368-400.

Van Dijk, Teun A. 1998. Editorial: Discourse and Ideology. *Discourse & Society* 9/3, 307-308.

Wodak, Ruth 2015. *The Politics of Fear*. London: Sage.

Zahoor, Muhammad A. 2017. Zulfikar Ali Bhutto: Political Behavior and Ouster from Power. *Journal of the Punjab University Historical Society* 5/2, 99-110.

Section 2 People, Politics and Politicians across Modes and Media

Aline Schmidt

The discursive construction of Trump's charisma on Twitter and Reddit

1 Introduction

The 2016 US presidential election has precipitated the 'Trump Phenomenon' as a symptom of a complex set of changes in socio-political culture and structure, a shift in the loci of authority and trust, and social media democratization. While studies in sociology and political science have focused on socio-demographic factors and longitudinal macro-level transformations to explain the electoral success of underdog Donald Trump (e.g., Fuchs 2017; Norris/Inglehart 2018), there is still the need to address the micro-political interactions on the discursive plane to investigate how Donald Trump's power was initially legitimized in the public sphere at the onset of his presidential bid.

The work presented here is embedded within the larger research project of my PhD thesis in which I approach the emergence of Trump's cult of personality as a charismatic relationship building on Max Weber (1958, 1968). In the present study, I analyze the pre-election phase as a particularly critical period for semiotic charismatization. I specifically focus on discursive practices on social media which are constitutive of the idiosyncratic manifestation of Trump's charisma in the contemporary United States. Both Trump's use of Twitter and the creative exploitation of semiotic resources by online hard-core Trump supporters on the subreddit r/The_Donald demonstrate how the specific affordances of social media enable the construction of Trump as a charismatic leader. I explore the discursive dimension of Weberian charismatic authority, which offers an explanation of the success of the Trump campaign as an irrational, affective phenomenon of our time that rests on mediated social interaction.

2 Trump's charisma and social media

The Trump campaign has been treated as a charismatic phenomenon more or less explicitly in recent sociological studies (Hochschild 2016; Wagner-Pacifici/Tavory 2017; Joosse 2018). This line of research offers valuable ethnographic descriptions of the charismatic effects Trump exerted on his followers (Hochschild 2016), and these studies place Trump's electoral success in the context of political insecurity and social unrest as a means "to rupture and transform forms and structures of the political" (Wagner-Pacifici/Tavory 2017: 19). The element of disruption, revolution and a radical anti-establishment agenda are constitutive of the societal and political function of charisma as a "collective coping mechanism" (Bligh/Kohles 2009: 487) for social crisis.

In order to highlight the particularities of charisma and not to conflate the concept as an individual's ability "to interest a certain number of people in the glitter of his [sic!] personality" (Geertz 2001: 122), I return to Weber's original outline of charisma. Charisma is that dimension of political authority that is socially legitimized on the basis of a collective belief in an individual's extraordinariness, "regardless of whether [it] is actual, alleged, or presumed" (Weber 1968: 295). Extraordinariness is understood as literally *out of the ordinary*, and denotes "supernatural, superhuman, or at least specifically exceptional powers or qualities" (Weber 1968: 241) of an individual.

At its core, charisma is a socially constructed relationship (Couch 1989; Rauer 2009). Weber foregrounds relationality over personality when he emphasizes the followers' collective role in attributing charisma: "[w]hat alone is important is how the individual is actually regarded by those subject to charismatic authority, by his 'followers' or 'disciples'" (Weber 1968: 242). Followers are powerful in ascribing charisma because they form a community of belief oriented towards the leader and accept the "duty" (Weber 1968: 242) to devote themselves to the charismatic's mission. At the same time, every formation of political authority "attempts to establish and to cultivate the belief in its legitimacy" (Weber 1968: 213). This means that political actors claim extraordinary qualities in social performance and aim to forge a personal, emotional connection. Charisma must therefore be understood as a social relationship that only becomes manifest through active validation of the leader's charismatic performance by the people (Rauer 2009; Joosse 2014) based on their experience of personal connection.

From a functional perspective, charisma challenges existing power and knowledge structures and seeks to redefine and reshape social reality. From a discourse analytical perspective, in which discourse is seen as a social practice that is both constitutive of and constituted by social structures, situations and relationships (Fairclough *et al.* 2011), charismatization is inevitably a social-semiotic process negotiated in discursive practice. Turning to the players of this relationship, I thus extrapolate three processes that are interlinked and facilitate charismatization. First, the social performance of the individual claiming charismatic authority; secondly, the formation of a charismatic community; and thirdly, the community attributing charisma. This chapter is devoted to the first two of these.

2.1 Social media and charisma

Since I conceive of charisma as a relational, interpersonal concept, it is indispensable to consider the factors that influence this relationship, i.e., to account for those discursive contexts that facilitate affectedness, community-formation, self-representation and thus enable charismatization (cf. Couch 1989: 266). Meyrowitz suggests that unidirectional audiovisual media can forge "para-social" bonds (1985: 120) that resemble face-to-face communication, and in the past the role of mass media as charisma boosters has been addressed (Glassman 1986; Häusermann 2001). Particularly in the context of digitalization, where political participation is democratized through social media, I argue that social media can even be more powerful tools in enabling discursive charismatization processes. Critical Discourse Studies have begun to address the link between social media "as the realm of affects, connections and personal sharing" (KhosraviNik 2018: 67) and the affective turn in politics (KhosraviNik 2017, 2018; Engesser *et al.* 2017). While charismatics derive their power from their "knowledge of the emotional organization of society" (Wasielewski 1985: 218), social media bear a new "multiaxial" (Williams/Delli Carpini 2004: 1212) meaning-making environment whose emotional and disruptive potential can be exploited for charismatization. The inbuilt systems of social media platforms lend themselves to bridging physical distance, emotion-directed communication, and community-building, and thus create the technological conditions under which charisma can thrive.

2.2 Twitter and Reddit

Donald Trump's activity on Twitter during the 2015/2016 presidential primary contests epitomizes the effective use of virtual networked platforms as a new "opportunity structure for political actors" (Gainous/Wagner 2013: 106; cf. Unger *et al.* 2016: 226) to amplify their own messages. Twitter functions as Trump's virtual megaphone to the people, allowing him to spread his message, "unmediated by traditional media gatekeepers" (Gainous/Wagner 2013: 106). Turner (2018: 148) notes that:

> as mid-century authoritarians could use radio to broadcast their voices into the intimacy of the family living room, so now Trump can use Twitter to insert himself into the company of a user's chosen conversation partners

which highlights the sense of intimacy, authenticity and immediacy associated with Twitter.

Trump's self-proclaimed 'serious supporters' organized online on the subreddit r/The_Donald[1] in a virtual 'neverending rally'. Reddit[2]

1 <https://www.reddit.com/r/The_Donald/>

2 At time of writing, Reddit is ranked the sixth most popular site in the USA (Alexa 2019). Based on its user numbers, it is not a fringe medium, but part of mainstream Internet culture. It has been subject of controversy because of its mild censorship standards, and it presents a breeding ground for racist, misogynist, and right-wing movements, serving as a bridge between the web's 'dark corners' 4chan and 8chan and mainstream media (Wendling 2018: 57).

is a social news aggregation website and discussion board on which users can register anonymously and individually subscribe to topics they are interested in. It is organized into user-generated subreddits, or 'communities of interest' (Topinka 2018), dedicated to a specific topic. Throughout the campaign, r/The_Donald was particularly controversial and impactful, receiving repeated media attention (Alba 2016; Sarlin 2016). Trump's social media advisors have been said to monitor the subreddit to target social media trends (Schreckinger 2017). At 780,000 members (as of November 2019), this subreddit is fairly small by Reddit standards, but its members are highly productive and active[3] (Wendling 2018). r/The_Donald has regularly hosted 'AMAs' ('Ask Me Anything'), where users can ask celebrities questions, e.g., Milo Yiannopoulos, Ann Coulter, or Roger Stone. Trump himself participated in an AMA in July 2016 and addressed his followers directly on the site prior to the final Clinton-Trump debate (Sankin 2016).

This chapter aims to explore online spaces of charismatization on Twitter and Reddit. The interplay of these platforms presents a novel field of research on how political power is discursively claimed by Trump and actively authenticated by a devoted group of followers. Discourse analysis of social media practices on Twitter and r/The_Donald is used to outline the linguistic dimensions of charisma by integrating leader and follower perspectives and offering an appropriate level of contextualization. This exploratory study proceeds in two parts: I first analyze Trump's charisma-claiming practices across genres and address Twitter's functions as a charisma booster. In a second step, I approach the online community (Herring 2004) r/The_Donald as a charismatic community (Weber 1968) and analyze how its members engage in communal practices.

3 As of February 2017, r/The_Donald ranked fourth in post numbers out of all subreddits with ca. 140,000 existing threads.

3 Data and method

Linguistic research is at the early stages of exploring and theorizing social media as discourse data. To exploit the data effectively, this study is rooted in the realm of corpus-assisted discourse studies and combines quantitative and qualitative methods. The amount of linguistic data that is produced online prompts a quantitative exploration to begin with a "general 'pattern map' of the data" (Baker *et al.* 2008: 294), to then focus on qualitative examination of concordances and keywords. A discourse analytical point of view on the relationality of charisma necessitates a serious consideration of the cultural, social, political and technological conditions under which Trump's charisma occurs. This includes the social and political contexts under which charisma is constructed, but also the awareness of the affordances that the respective platforms in particular provide. Social media as "technologies of entextualisation" (Jones 2009) impact the "meanings people can make in different situations, the kinds of actions they can perform, the kinds of relationships they can form, and the kinds of people they can be" (Jones *et al.* 2015: 4).

The compilation of the leader corpus (Donald Trump Corpus, DTC) took a conventional discourse-analytical approach by collecting multi-genre data. It is comprised of all speeches, written statements, televised presidential debates of the Republican Party, and tweets produced by Donald Trump (@realDonaldTrump) from June 16, 2015 (the day Trump announced his campaign) to election day, November 8, 2016. Retweets were identified and extracted but not included in the DTC.

The follower corpus (r/The_Donald corpus, TDRC) consists of a sample of the thread "DONALD J. TRUMP DECLARED THE WINNER". The sample contains ca. 7,000 comments and 85,000 words. The thread was selected because I expect potential charismatization strategies to be particularly dense at the peak point of the campaign on election day.

Both corpora were compiled manually. URLs were extracted, emojis were identified and remained in the corpus for concordancing with AntConc (Anthony 2019); they were, however, not coded to be included in keyword and other statistical analyses. The selection of reference corpora rests on a 'best fit approach' (Baker 2006). For the DTC analyses, multiple corpora were used, i.e., the Corpus of Contemporary American English, (COCA, Davies 2008), Global Web-based English (GloWbE, Davies 2013), and a corpus of presidential speeches (CoPS, Brown 2016). For the TDRC, COCA and GloWbE were used for the initial keyword analysis[4].

4 Trump's charismatic performance

4.1 Individual authority across genres

Since charisma is an interpersonal phenomenon that identifies itself in contrast to the existing social and political order, discursive strategies of positive self and negative other presentation (Wodak 2009) play a central role in the configuration of this relationship. Constructing the charismatic individual identity and uniting that identity with a collective community are at the core of charismatization. For Trump as a charismatic performer, I delve into the analysis by looking into how he talks about himself and positions himself in relation to his audience.

Most strikingly, the DTC shows a high saliency for the first-person pronoun 'I' (LL=1301.91), which seems unusual for democratic discourse, in which politicians often strive to construct solidarity through the use of inclusive 'we' (de Fina 1995). Inclusive 'we' fulfills the "double assumption of authority and communality" (Pennycook 1994: 176), and can create group identities, a sense of relatability, solidarity or kinship while claiming authority to speak on behalf of a community. This pronominal pattern is also visible in the DTC, where this collectivity is somewhat warped by explicitly focusing on the 'I'. The pronoun is distributed densely and evenly across speeches, tweets

4 Relative frequencies and keyness values will be given for DTC/COCA, TDRC/GloWbE unless noted otherwise. Relative frequencies FN are per 10,000 words.

and debates, but it only occurs in 127 instances in written statements. A closer inspection of the distribution in speeches, compared with the CoPS, shows the consistency of this finding (LL=1598.19), despite a slightly lower keyness value. In 18.78 % of all instances, 'I' co-occurs with 'am' or 'm', of which 46.09 % of instances are progressive constructions, mostly indicating policy-promises. See the concordances for 'I'm' in (1):

(1) I'm going to bring millions of new jobs back
I'm going to renegotiate NAFTA
I'm going to repeal and replace Obamacare
I'm going to save your 2nd amendment

Instilling faith in a better future through campaign pledges may be crucial for charismatic attachment between leader and followers (Shamir *et al.* 1993: 583), but it is also a common feature of political campaign discourse. With regard to charismatizing strategies, 'I' + copular 'be' constructions which function as declarations (Searle 2008) are particularly insightful, for which the DTC shows a prevalence of nomination strategies (Reisigl/Wodak 2016). Trump labels himself *a negotiator, a free-trader, a self-funder, a unifier, a truth-teller, a big defender of the 2nd Amendment, a job creator*. These nominals have the potential to validity claims irrespective of situational context; they "make something the case by representing it as being the case" (Searle 2008: 451). The aim of nominalization here is thus to claim absolute qualities that serve the construction of a stable leader character.

On the level of extraordinariness, Trump touches on discourses of an American individualist ethos (Huntington 2004) by using predication strategies (Reisigl/Wodak 2016). Exploiting his outsider status, he inserts an implicature that juxtaposes him with the *establishment* (LL=180.78) and the 'rigged' *system* (LL=163.53). In a 'me' + 'you' vs. 'them' strategy, he triggers the stereotype of corrupt politicians (Leigh 2002; Arendt/Marquart 2015) in order to dissociate himself personally. In the DTC, *politicians* (LL= 409.88) clusters with *the, our, these,* and the adjectives *corrupt, incompetent, typical, phony, failed, crooked*. He thus presupposes a generalized view of politicians as a morally corrupt group that is incapable of performing their duty to execute the will of the people: "the American people, frankly, are the victims of this rigged and corrupt system in every way". The ingroup marker *our* and the deictic expression *these* indicate solidarity between Trump and the people and at the same time set a demarcation between 'Us' and 'Them'. Trump thus taps into the growing distrust of American citizens in the government and political disenchantment. He explicitly dissociates himself from this group:

(2) I'm an outsider. I want to be an outsider.
I'm not a politician fighting, I'm me.
I'm not a politician and have never wanted to be a politician
I'm not a politician, proudly

In the context of the politician stereotype as inauthentic, incompetent and insincere, the concordance lines in (2) exemplify how Trump is constructed as authentic, epitomized by his statement "I'm not a politician fighting, I'm me". In a sea of corrupt and inauthentic politicians, Trump sets himself apart as a unique individual, "the only one who can fix it". In Weberian terms, he is extraordinary against the ordinary system of untrustworthy politicians.

The image of the politician functions as a meaningful cultural frame (Smith 2000) against which Trump's charismatic claim can be measured. He "gives discursive expression to" (Bourdieu 1987: 130) already existing feelings such as anger, disappointment, distrust of an audience eager to find a savior. By "model[ing] that anger through speech, [...] charismatic leaders evoke and focus emotion" (Wasielewski 1985: 212). Trump appears as an outside player on the political field, as an "isolated individual, a man without a past, lacking any authority other than himself" (Bourdieu 1987:130) and thus lays the foundation for being perceived and validated as charismatic.

4.2 Cultural authentication

Authenticity is the trust-generating 'root construct' (Avolio/Gardner 2005) underlying legitimate political authority. Trump claims cultural authenticity and gives cultural contours to his charisma-claiming strategies by weaving national symbols into his texts. Because charisma becomes effective through the cultural and symbolic context in which it is communicated (Lenze 2002), the specific cultural resources employed for charismatization are important. Accordingly, intertextual links as a means to "[insert] history (society) into a text and [...] this text into history" (Kristeva 1986: 39) are a strategy for cultural anchoring. The most prominent connection is in his references to Ronald Reagan. The first reference is made explicit by setting the Reagan area as a temporal point of reference for his planned policies, e.g., *the largest effort at rebuilding our military since Ronald Reagan*; *the biggest tax cut since Ronald Reagan.* The second, most impactful reference to Reagan is realized implicitly in Trump's campaign slogan 'Make America Great Again', which he adopted from Reagan's 1980 presidential campaign, and altered on the paradigmatic and syntagmatic axes (e.g., *we're going to make America safe again; we're going to make our country love again; we *re going to make our economy strong again*).

Ronald Reagan's presidency has shaped both the identity of the Republican Party and American self-conception. Republicans "see in Reagan's confident, optimistic presence and leadership a handy symbol for, perhaps also a source of, a renewal of national purpose and self-belief" (Hudson/Davies 2008: 1), which has made him an icon of patriotism, American optimism and economic growth. Trump thus establishes a connection to Reagan, tapping into the nostalgia of the Reagan Revolution. At the same time, Reagan's personal image as "personally authentic, sincere, and extremely likeable" (Hudson/Davies 2008: 10) is crucial. Trump's intertextual link to Reagan is culturally meaningful because it evokes the similar vision of a future Golden American Age like that of Reagan 35 years before him, and with Reagan as the political benchmark of the GOP, Trump offers a projection surface to a susceptible audience's hopes for their ideal America.

The link between cultural authenticity and the vision of a better future is further established implicitly and marked adverbially and morphologically through *again* and *back (we're going to be so proud of our country again; Government is going to start working for you again*; *the promise to give our government back to the people), and in the* prefix *re-* (*revitalize America, American Greatness will return, recapture our destiny, rebuild our military, restore honesty)*. Claiming authentic cultural belonging

> draws a contrast both internally between a present reality and some imagined or lost original or ideal [...], and externally, between the upholders of this ideal and the inauthenticity of those whose beliefs or practices appear to deviate from it or threaten it. (Gill 2014: 329)

Imaginaries of what the nation should and could be embody conservative and traditional values. To conservatives, the socially liberal value shift associated with the Obama administration presents a threat to the conservative value system, which triggers a 'cultural backlash' among conservatives (Norris/Inglehart 2019). Trump draws on these anxieties and appeals to traditional values as the true American values, 'Greatness', 'honesty', the 'American Dream', their 'destiny'. These values are a claim to institutionalized forms of charisma (Sable 2018) and can thus be utilized as a legitimation strategy of cultural authenticity.

4.2.1 Tweeting charisma

From the point of view of charismatization, particularly the distribution of the message is an essential aspect because it disrupts conventional flows of information. Trump's unprecedented use of Twitter is thus extraordinary in the Weberian sense (cf. Weber 1968). The day he announced his presidential campaign on Twitter, he entered the political arena as an outsider, businessman and entertainer, but he also chose a genre that lies outside the "socially ratified way[s] of using language in connection with a particular type of social activity" (Fairclough 1995: 14). In other words, using Twitter in the way he has been doing presents a breach with established norms of how and by what means to engage in political discourse. By exploiting the digital media environment (Williams/Delli Carpini 2004: 1212), and by (strategically) subverting other (linguistic) norms of political conduct, he disrupted political structure (Wagner-Pacifici/Tavory 2017; cf. Williams/Delli Carpini 2004) and set the foundation for charismatization on Twitter.

Trump utilizes the participatory design of Twitter to address other users directly or to incorporate their messages in his own by retweeting. Twitter allows heteroglossia (Zappavigna 2011: 790; cf. Bakhtin 1981) that traditional, non-digital modes of communication in political discourse do not. A comprehensive study by the Pew Research Center in 2016 found that Trump retweeted citizens more often during

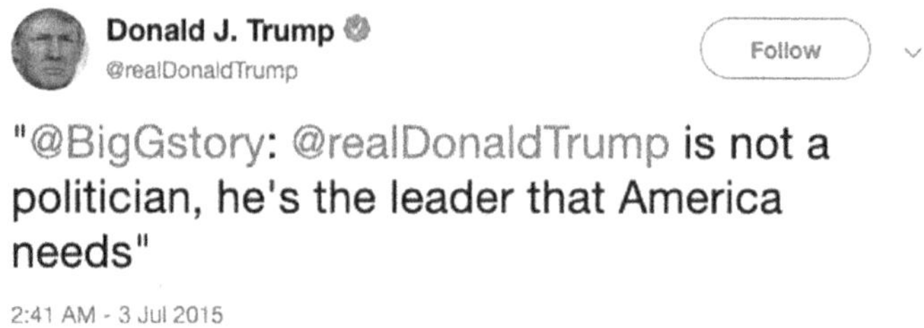

Fig. 1: Trump retweets a supporter.

the campaign than Clinton and Sanders, who mainly retweeted news media[5]. For the time span of DTC compilation, there were 5,154 original tweets by Donald Trump and 2,648 retweets; i.e., 33.94 % of all tweets produced during the campaign were retweets, such as Fig. 1.

Donald Trump and the user may not engage in dialogue; yet, engagement on Twitter is still significant. The retweet in this case serves multiple purposes: first, the user's claim that Trump is "the leader that America needs" serves to justify Trump's candidacy by popular demand; secondly, the user is seen by Donald Trump, and his or her support personally validated in turn; thirdly, because retweeting is publicly visible, both acts of justification and validation exude to other followers. Directly incorporating citizen's voices is an authentic way to establish common ground with followers, and thus highlights the immense potential to create a personal bond beyond spatial boundaries.

A second key practice is the use of hashtags, which occur frequently in the DTC. The majority relates to conventional practices of voter mobilization, e.g., #voteTrump or #TrumpPence. These types of hashtags allow organization online because users interested in the campaign may find all tweets linked through them, forming a loosely coherent community of shared interest. However, the practice of hashtagging is utilized beyond the purpose of discourse organization. Hashtags

5 78 % of Trump's retweets were from citizens, 18 % from news media, 2 % from celebrities, 2 % from non-governmental institutions. None of Clinton's retweets and 2 % of Sanders's were from citizens. For Clinton the largest share at 80 % were retweets from her own campaign staff; Sanders retweeted news media most frequently (66 %) (Pew Research Center 2016: 51).

present in the DTC include #MakeAmericaGreatAgain, #MAGA, #DrainTheSwamp, #ImWithYou, #BigLeagueTruth, #AmericaFirst, #ObamacareFail, #LightWeightSenatorMarcoRubio.

The campaign slogan 'Make America Great Again' becomes attached with values through the continuous use throughout the campaign by Donald Trump and his supporters. The use of the campaign slogan as a hashtag establishes an intermedial link between different genres, fusing together Trump's message across genres. Hashtagging tweets is an abridged expression of Trump's future vision that he simultaneously crafts in other texts. The hashtag is thus charged with the values behind Trump's vision of America. Therefore, hashtags are evaluative tools that mark affiliation. Initially Trump indicates affiliation with his followers who can then adopt the same hashtags to form a community of shared values. Hashtags are thus cohesive ties, in that they structure discourse according to topic of interest (Schubert 2017), which renders discourse searchable, and as 'interpersonal punctuation' (Knox 2009: 162) which enables social organization or 'ambient affiliation' (Zappavigna 2011: 788).

Finally, hashtags are closely connected to nominations (Reisigl/Wodak 2016) that complement the discourse strategy of negative other presentation. The hashtag #CrookedHillary occurs 42 times in the pre-election tweets (F_N=3.96), while the phrase 'Crooked Hillary' appears 37 times in the other DTC subcorpora (F_N=1.24). The expression is thus used over 3 times more frequently in tweets than in the other genres combined. #CrookedHillary is exemplary of how nominations work crossmedially and intertextually. Take for instance the tweet displayed in Fig. 2.

The tweet contains an embedded video of Donald Trump speaking about the investigations into Hillary Clinton's leaked emails. Clinton comes to confirm and embody the negative stereotype of the corrupt politicians that Trump has built over the course of the campaign, and even epitomizes it. The combination with the #DrainTheSwamp highlights this connection further. The capitalization of 'CRIMINAL' sets emphatic stress, but may also heighten affect (Heath 2018), and can be interpreted as anger or aggression to amplify the vigor Trump aims to instill in his followers. Clinton thus is scapegoated for the country "going in the wrong direction". The generalized view of politicians is

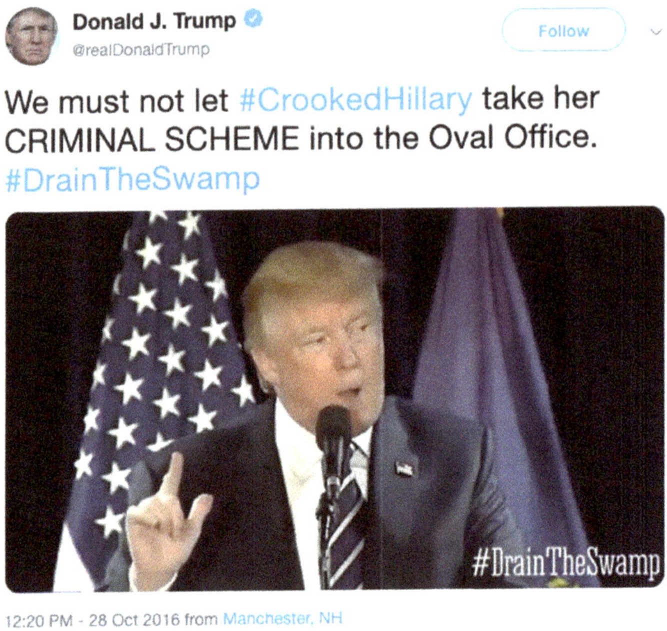

Fig. 2: Multimodal tweet.

fueled by Trump's slogan-like naming strategies and takes particular effect on Twitter because hashtags function as a virtual signpost and allow users to connect through it.

5 The charismatic community on r/The_Donald

Reddit is organized in a non-linear way, which means that threads and comments that receive the most upvotes appear on top of the page. Answers to comments are posted directly below and allow a potentially infinite organization of the post. Redditors[6] can post text but also

6 Redditors is the term used for users of Reddit.

frequently link to external content. For example, in the sample thread the post TEARS OF JOY links to an image of Pepe the Frog (Fig. 3). This adds another semiotic dimension of meaning to the post. The high level of multimodality across media is a unique feature of Reddit and characterizes its multifacetedness and the creative potential for users to express themselves. As a corpus-assisted study of discourse, however, the present analysis addresses linguistic expression on Reddit and leaves systematic multimodal analysis for future research.

Speaking of Reddit as one heterogeneous community would misdirect research, as others have already pointed out (Massanari 2015). Rather, the subreddits form microcosms with their own linguistic and social conventions, vocabulary and social practices. In other words, every subreddit potentially forms a virtual community (Herring 2004).

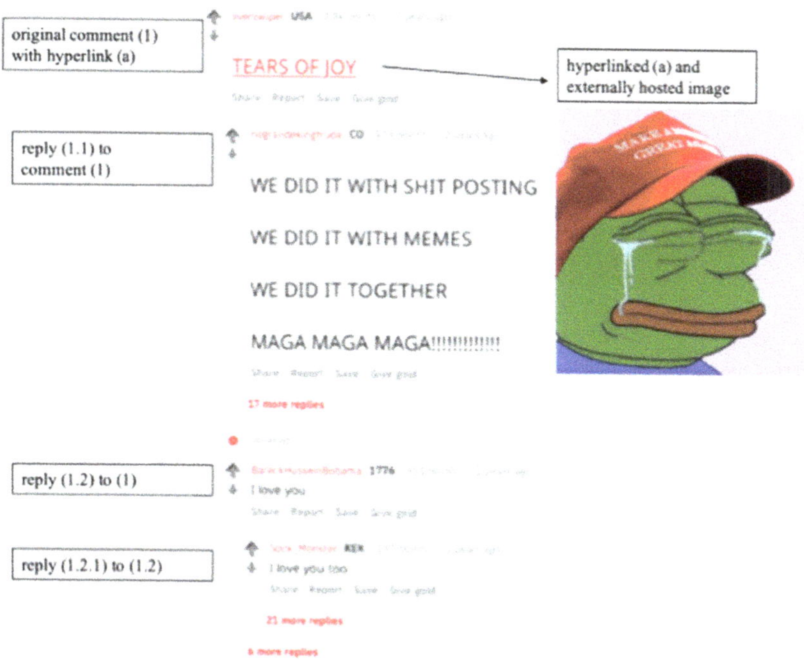

Fig. 3: Organization of a Reddit thread with externally hosted image, example from the analyzed thread.

Tab. 1: Discourse behaviors indicating virtual community (Herring 2004: 19).

structure	jargon, references to group, in-group/out- group language
meaning	exchange of knowledge, negotiation of meaning
interaction	reciprocity, extended (in–depth) threads, core participants
social behavior	solidarity, conflict management, norms of appropriateness
participation	frequent, regular, self-sustaining activity over time

However, this "does not negate the importance of understanding how larger cultural mores shape the space" (Massanari 2015: 14). According to Herring (2004), an online community is defined by the parameters structure, meaning, interaction, and social behavior (Tab. 1). Participation and interaction are non-linguistic parameters, which apply to r/The_Donald as a highly active, continuously growing forum. The analysis will thus focus on structure, meaning and social behavior to analyze community-building practices on the subreddit and their relation to the construction of Trump's charisma. Their discourse behavior must be interpreted against current political events and in relation to the semiotic affordances of the platform itself. The issues addressed in the following sections are thus concerned with how the Redditors on r/ The_Donald experience Donald Trump's election, what shared discursive practices they engage in to negotiate this collective experience, and how this communal activity contributes to the construction of Trump's charisma.

5.1 Indexing membership on r/The_DonaldCorpus

The most striking feature of the TDRC is the idiosyncratic vocabulary. With regard to the formation of a charismatic community, terms with which members reference themselves, their practices, and terms used to label opponents deserve particular attention. The best known label by which members address each other is *centipede*, sometimes abbreviated *pede*, or blended to indicate individual local and national belonging like *Ameripede* and *Floridapede*. Other terms include *deplorables, nimble navigators, autists*. The positive value as an ingroup marker only becomes explicit when seen in context, where it is used with other kinship markers (e.g., folks, brothers and sisters, fam):

(3) I feel great love for every centipede!
Thank you all, my centipede brothers and sisters.
WE HAVE THE BEST AUTISTS DONT WE FOLKS

A second, related category covers conventionally pejorative terms with verbs and adjectives of positive evaluation, e.g.

(4) I love all of you deplorable bastards!
MAGA YOU MAGNIFICENT MOTHERFUCKERS

Particularly for the former, the pragmatic meaning is entirely obscured to non-members. Given the publicness of the subreddit, there are multiple audiences for which the use of these terms has different functions. They are used only among those who associate themselves with r/The_Donald, wish to express group solidarity, and aim to create affiliation among users. At the same time, these terms are characterized by irony, sarcasm and playfulness. For instance, *deplorables* is intertextually linked to Hillary Clinton's description of Trump supporters as 'basket of deplorables'. Redditors have claimed the term and imbued it with positive meaning. By doing so, they employ a strategy of self-empowerment, making themselves invulnerable and challenging the opposing power, and inscribing their shared history. The term *centipede* originates in a video of a centipede killing a tarantula. In this way, a multimodal metaphor is constructed which stands for the power of the collective movement, and their unexpected force as underdogs. The terms here mark high levels of affectedness and are used in combination with a range of linguistic and other semiotic markers of high positive affect, e.g., *love*, LL=513.58, often with intensifier *fucking*, and adjectives like *magnificent, beautiful, deplorable, glorious*, capitalization, and emojis. Terms of address exemplify the highly codified use of "language within which their core concepts [are] embedded" (Wendling 2018: 103), and whose opaque multi-semiotic meaning system separates insiders from outsiders, supporters from enemies. The frequency of the terms used as well as the creation of a glossary on the frontpage of r/The_Donald demonstrates how their shared jargon (Herring 2004) has become part of the meaning system of the community. At the same time, these linguistic affiliation tactics are characterized by a high degree of emotion.

5.2 Ingroup and outgroup

r/The_Donald shows a high level of self-awareness, which in the TDRC is marked by the frequent use of the deictic markers *here* and *this* in combination with nouns that indicate different frames of reference for community boundaries. The subreddit is structured and categorized in relation to different dimensions of group membership: the subreddit (*this thread*, *proud to be here*), the platform (*this sub, this community, here at The_Donald*), and their social purpose (*this train*[7], *this movement*). The most significant instances refer to the role members attribute to themselves as a community in Trump's election, e.g.,

(5) This sub helped alter history, elected a president.
I strongly believe the meme magic from here had a big effect
PURE WEAPONISED AUTISM! MEME MAGIC WINS!
we shitposted a man into office soldiers

Practices of shitposting ("posting extreme content (or extreme amounts of it) in an attempt to derail a discussion" (Wendling 2018: 94)), 'meme magic' (the belief that shitposting and the creation of memes had significant influence on the election outcome), and autism (an obsessive trolling tactic), are referenced directly and frequently. This suggests that the Trump's 'online rally' consciously and purposefully engaged in these practices with the goal to cause disruption. From a community-oriented perspective, group membership seems to be graded; the virtual community is seen by its members as the core of a much broader *movement* that is also active offline. This means that while Trump supporters who are not Redditors are acknowledged as members of community of interest and value, they are not part of the core community on the virtual plane.

7 *train* here is a reference to the Trump Train, a metaphorical label for Trump supporters.

The metacommentary on such practices is meaningful because it suggests that the community defines itself through the collective engagement in these practices, but they are always targeted at an imagined or real outgroup. Community building relies on positive emotional relationships, but users on r/The_Donald explicitly identify themselves in opposition to their shared enemies. This is reflected in the word *fuck* (LL=1203.57; F_N=25.83) in the TDRC that expresses a high degree of negative affect, anger and hostility. In the corpus *fuck* collocates with *biased, parties, spez*[8], *SJWs* (social justice warriors), *cucks, them, media, establishment, Clinton, Hillary*. In a strategy parallel to Trump's, generalizations are constructed using the definite article *the*, e.g., *fuck the billionaires, fuck the biased media, fuck the parties*. In a move similar to Trump, users employ creative naming strategies. Hillary Clinton is the most notable example, who is labelled, for instance, *killary, hilliary, hitlery, Hildebe*st, hillbot*. Although they are low-frequency items, these word-formations are a crucial part of r/The_Donald's discourse as users encode in them meanings central to their community. Clinton is constructed as the absolute enemy, linking her to lying and killing, comparing her to Hitler, and likening her to a heartless, inauthentic robot and an animal. The aim is to dehumanize and ridicule her. The ironic playfulness is part of the linguistic encoding of practices on r/The_Donald and can be viewed as an incentive to be as creative as possible in creating new nicknames. The creativity and group appreciation of stark humor is both another element of social cohesion (Zappavigna 2012), and an additional vehicle to perpetuate hostile discourse patterns. The practices and naming strategy are symptomatic of the anger, distrust and contempt Trump supporters feel and are indexical of their ideological underpinnings. It is these sentiments that Trump can draw on to build his charismatic performance.

8 Spez is the username of Reddit CEO Steve Huffman, who altered Reddit's algorithm so that r/The_Donald would not appear on its front page where trending topics and subreddits usually appear. This sparked a feud between spez and r/The_Donald (Lagorio-Chafkin 2018).

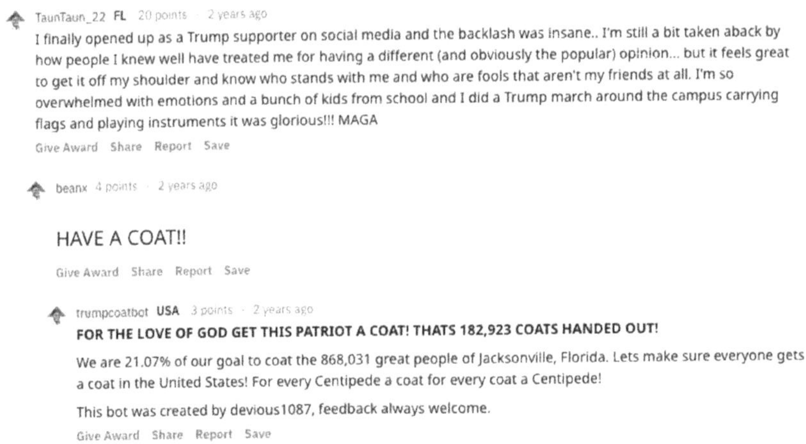

Fig. 4: Interaction with trumpcoatbot.

5.3 r/The_Donald bots

The use of bots on r/The_Donald is a striking example of how Reddit's opportunity structure allows users to interact in ways that add further layers of group-specific meaning. These bots differ from the social bots that Reddit identified and removed on suspicion of electoral interference (Huffman 2017) because they are explicitly identified as bots and are rather a gamified mechanism that incentivizes users to be active on r/The_Donald. One example is trumpcoatbot (Fig. 4). A trigger phrase (e.g., 'grab a coat') causes an automatic response from the bot in which a virtual 'coat' is handed out and the number of coats is tracked. The internal glossary notes:

> Coats – – A Bernie supporter crashed a Trump rally in the winter and Trump made a joke, ""take his coat and we'll mail it back," like he was going to throw the protester out in the cold. If you're new to the subreddit and become a Trump supporter, you're welcome to have a coat. If you're a Bernie Cuck or Hillshill however, we will be confiscating your coat.

Usually, users do not hand out coats to themselves, but users trigger the bot to pay respects to a new or particularly honorable member. A coat indicates acceptance into the community. Even though the bot is overtly a non-human interactant, the interaction is nevertheless social because it is contingent on the social relationship between Redditors. Trump-coatbot was created by a user in order to encode a previously existing meaning, which is to be expressed in a playful manner. The repeated interaction between bots and users is a routine action that takes shape as an acceptance ritual. Bots are thus meaning-making devices which help perpetuate and inscribe meaning within the community.

6 Discussion and conclusions

The construction of charisma is dependent on the reciprocal relationship between collective validation and leader performance. The analyses have presented a web of interrelated discourse phenomena that take effect because social media offer opportunity structures for charismatic self-performance and the formation of a charismatic community. Given that both charisma and the specific social media platforms, particularly Reddit, are under-researched in discourse studies, this chapter took an exploratory approach, and my findings should thus be interpreted with certain limitations in mind. The toolkit of discourse studies has been helpful for an initial exploration of goal-oriented discursive behavior on the respective platforms. Such conventional discourse studies approaches and their development into computer-mediated discourse analysis (Herring 2004) are fruitful for understanding micro-level discursive practices, but they must draw on insights from digital ethnography (Androutsopulos 2008; Massanari 2017; Wendling 2018) to understand how such a community is organized. A qualitatively-oriented approach can cater only to a portion of the demands of the study of social media discourse. Social media data are inevitably big data, and linguistic research must continue to find ways to address size, non-linear organization and multimodality.

While the charismatic performance and the formation of community were analyzed separately, the social-digital environment in which the relationship players act demonstrates how these two elements of charismatization form counterparts to each other. Twitter affords set functions regarding discourse distribution, audience affiliation, and the 'affective contouring' of discourse (cf. Dean 2018), which are at the heart of Trump's charismatic performance that is initially carried out in conventional genres. Trump's charismatic performance shows discursive patterns that resemble those of contemporary European populists (Wodak 2017). The 'us' vs. 'them' theme factors in significantly: Trump employs a populist style to frame his mission as an effort to protect the people from the corrupt establishment. In this scenario, he positions himself at the center, setting a spotlight on his individual power to solve the current problems of the nation, as a representative of authentic American values. There is a certain ambiguity at play, as Trump presents himself as both 'one of the people', but also as an authoritative individual. The crucial element for successful charismatic performance lies in the connection he can forge with his audience. Traditional genres offer him limited opportunities, but the dialogic design of Twitter and the 'authentic feel' of immediacy extend his sphere of action significantly and disrupt the flow of everyday political discourse. Personal connections via retweets and the shareability of political slogans are potential vehicles for voter mobilization and creating an emotional connection to his followers.

In Weber's original conception, a charismatic community is defined as an "organized group subject to charismatic authority [...]. It is based on an emotional form of communal relationship." (Weber 1968: 243) Reddit allows Trump supporters to organize virtually and use the platform to negotiate their group identity and engage in goal-oriented behavior aligned around support for Trump's election. The analysis of r/The_Donald as a charismatic community accounts only for one thread, yet at a significant point in time. r/The_Donald is a tight-knight virtual community (Herring 2004) that creates cohesion through a shared jargon and mutual engagement in sustained platform-specific practices. The euphoric experience of Trump's election prompts a high degree of positive affect and expressions of group affiliation. It has previously been suggested that followers have collective agency independent of their leader and that they "have different domains of agency" (Junker 2014: 419). Discursive idiosyncrasies on r/The_Donald are characterized by crass humor, encoding of their shared history as 'deplorables' in their collective practices. Strategic trolling and shitposting, as referenced in the thread, draw attention of a broader audience to the virtual community; the fringe medium Reddit is an extraordinary phenomenon in the context of civil discursive practice as it forms its own rules and is mysterious to those outside it. The virtual community may thus adopt a certain charisma itself, shaping the public perception of Donald Trump as a popular, disruptive underdog figure in the political field.

The charismatic effect is realized through the intermedial connection between the initial independent actions of community and leader. Followers give utterance to their feelings in a creative way and simultaneously construct powerful representations of 'the establishment' and 'the left'. On Reddit, these representations take shape and are cultivated linguistically, while other modes extend their meaning potential. Content on Reddit is publicly available and shareable on other social media and mainstream outlets. In this way, a marginal group of Trump supporters becomes visible, and the disruptive discourses of both Trump and r/The_Donald Redditors enter mainstream media discourses. The aim of both discursive actors is to cause provocation and disruption in their promotion of Trump, and their practices thus implicitly relate to each other. Social media facilitate charismatization in multiple ways: 1) they bridge physical distance, allowing people to organize; 2) followers can emotionally bond with each other; 3) followers experience validation by their prospective leader; 4) disruptive discourses take shape and become disseminated easily and visibly.

What we need to understand as researchers and as citizens is that social media do not create new phenomena and social media do not 'merely' influence democratic participation. We should view "socially mediated cultural production and exchange not as some frivolous activity on the margins of politics, but as increasingly central to how large numbers of predominantly young citizens experience politics" (Dean 2018: 2). Norms can be challenged and eventually changed as they are linked to the "digital strategies that rely on the specific norms and affordances of digital platforms" (Baldwin-Philippi 2019: 379). The way the lines are blurred between charismatizing activity online, political action offline, and the cultural, social and political backdrop against which these processes occur prompts us once more to dismiss the idea of "digital dualism" (Jurgenson 2012: 83) and acknowledge that social media have become a defining characteristic of the political and social sphere itself.

References

Alba, Davey 2016. Welcome to the Bizarro World of Trump Supporters on Reddit. *WIRED*, 27 July. <https://www.wired.com/2016/07/welcome-bizarro-world-trump-supporters-reddit/>

Alexa 2019. Reddit.Com Traffic Statistics. <https://www.alexa.com/siteinfo/reddit.com>

Androutsopoulos, Jannis 2008. Potentials and Limitations of Discourse-Centred Online Ethnography. *Language@Internet* 5. <https://www.languageatinternet.org/articles/2008/1610>

Anthony, Laurence 2019. *AntConc* (Version 3.5.8) [Computer Software]. Tokyo, Japan: Waseda University. Available online at <http://www.laurenceanthony.net/software>

Arendt, Florian / Marquart, Franziska 2015. Corrupt Politicians? Media Priming Effects on Overtly Expressed Stereotypes toward Politicians. *Communications* 40/2, 185-197.

Avolio, Bruce J. / Gardner, William L. 2005. Authentic Leadership Development: Getting to the Root of Positive Forms of Leadership. *The Leadership Quarterly* 16/3, 315-338.

Baker, Paul 2006. *Using Corpora in Discourse Analysis*. London: Continuum.

Baker, Paul / Gabrielatos, Costas / KhosraviNik, Majid / Krzyżanowski, Michał / McEnery, Tony McEnery / Wodak, Ruth 2008. A Useful Methodological Synergy? Combining Critical Discourse Analysis and Corpus Linguistics to Examine Discourses of Refugees and Asylum Seekers in the UK Press. *Discourse & Society* 19/3, 273-306.

Bakhtin, Mikhail 1981. *The Dialogic Imagination*. Austin/London: University of Texas Press.

Baldwin-Philippi, Jessica 2019. The Technological Performance of Populism. *New Media & Society* 21/2, 376-397.

Bligh, Michelle C. / Kohles, Jeffrey C. 2009. The Enduring Allure of Charisma: How Barack Obama Won the Historic 2008 Presidential Election. *The Leadership Quarterly* 20/3, 483-492.

Bourdieu, Pierre 1987. Legitimation and Structured Interests in Weber's Theory of Religion. In Whimster, Sam / Lash, Scott (eds) *Max Weber, Rationality and Modernity* London : Allen & Unwin, 119-136.

Brown, David W. 2016. Corpus of Presidential Speeches. Available online at <http://www.thegrammarlab.com>

Couch, Carl J. 1989. From Hell to Utopia and Back to Hell: Charismatic Relationships. *Symbolic Interaction* 12/2, 265-279.

Davies, Mark 2008–. The Corpus of Contemporary American English: 520 million words, 1990–present. Available online at <http://corpus.byu.edu/coca/>

Davies, Mark 2013. Corpus of Global Web-Based English: 1.9 billion words from speakers in 20 countries (GloWbE). Available online at <https://www.english-corpora.org/glowbe/>

De Fina, Anna 1995. Pronominal Choice, Identity, and Solidarity in Political Discourse. *Text - Interdisciplinary Journal for the Study of Discourse* 15/3, 379-410.

Dean, Jonathan 2018. Sorted for Memes and Gifs: Visual Media and Everyday Digital Politics. *Political Studies Review*, October.

Engesser, Sven / Ernst, Nicole / Esser, Frank / Büchel, Florin 2017. Populism and Social Media: How Politicians Spread a Fragmented Ideology. *Information, Communication & Society* 20/8, 1109-1126.

Fairclough, Norman 1995. *Critical Discourse Analysis: The Critical Study of Language*. London: Longman.

Fairclough, Norman / Mulderrig, Jane / Wodak, Ruth 2011. Critical Discourse Analysis. In van Dijk, Teun A. (ed.) *Discourse Studies: A Multidisciplinary Introduction*. London: SAGE, 357-378.

Fuchs, Christian 2017. Donald Trump: A Critical Theory-Perspective on Authoritarian Capitalism. *TripleC: Communication, Capitalism & Critique. Open Access Journal for a Global Sustainable Information Society* 15/1, 1-72.

Gainous, Jason / Wagner, Kevin M. 2013. *Tweeting to Power: The Social Media Revolution in American Politics*. Oxford University Press.

Geertz, Clifford [3]2001. *Local Knowledge: Further Essays in Interpretive Anthropology*. New York: Basic Books.

Gill, Martin 2014. 'Real Communities', Rhetorical Borders: Authenticating British Identity in Political Discourse and Online Debate. In Lacoste, Véronique / Leimgruber, Jakob R. E. / Breyer, Thiemo (eds) *Indexing Authenticity: Sociolinguistic Perspectives*. Berlin: De Gruyte, 324-342

Glassman, Ronald M. 1986. Legitimacy and Manufactured Charisma. In Glassman, Ronald / Swatos, William H. (eds) *Charisma, History, and Social Structure*. New York: Greenwood Press, 115-128.

Häusermann, Jürg (ed.) 2001. *Inszeniertes Charisma: Medien Und Persönlichkeit*. Tübingen: M. Niemeyer.

Heath, Maria 2018. Orthography in Social Media: Pragmatic and Prosodic Interpretations of Caps Lock. *Proceedings of the Linguistic Society of America* 3/1, 1-13.

Herring, Susan 2004. Computer-Mediated Discourse Analysis. In Barab, Sasha / Kling, Rob / Gray, James H. (eds) *Designing for Virtual Communities in the Service of Learning*. Cambridge: Cambridge University Press, 338-376.

Hochschild, Arlie Russell 2016. The Ecstatic Edge of Politics: Sociology and Donald Trump. *Contemporary Sociology: A Journal of Reviews* 45/6, 683-689.

Hudson, Cheryl / Davies, Gareth 2008. *Ronald Reagan and the 1980s Perceptions, Policies, Legacies*. Basingstoke: Palgrave Macmillan.

Huffman, Steve 2017. Reddit's 2017 Transparency Report and Suspect Account Findings. <https://www.reddit.com/r/announcements/comments/8bb85p/>

Huntington, Samuel P. 2004. *Who Are We? The Challenges to America's National Identity*. New York: Simon & Schuster.

Jones, Rodney H. 2009. Dancing, Skating and Sex: Action and Text in the Digital Age. *Journal of Applied Linguistics and Professional Practice* 6/3, 283-302.

Jones, Rodney H. / Chik, Alice / Hafner, Christoph A. 2015. Introduction: Discourse Analysis and Digital Practices. In Jones, Rodney H. / Chik, Alice / Hafner, Christoph A. (eds) *Discourse and Digital*

Practices: Doing Discourse Analysis in the Digital Age. London: Routledge, 1-17.

Joosse, Paul 2014. Becoming a God: Max Weber and the Social Construction of Charisma. *Journal of Classical Sociology* 14/3, 266-283.

Joosse, Paul 2018. Countering Trump: Toward a Theory of Charismatic Counter-Roles. *Social Forces* 97/2, 921-944.

Junker, A. 2014. Follower Agency and Charismatic Mobilization in Falun Gong. *Sociology of Religion* 75/3, 418-441.

Jurgenson, Nathan 2012. When Atoms Meet Bits: Social Media, the Mobile Web and Augmented Revolution. *Future Internet* 4/1, 83-91.

KhosraviNik, Majid 2017. Right Wing Populism in the West: Social Media Discourse and Echo Chambers. *Insight Turkey* 19/3, 53-68.

KhosraviNik, Majid 2018. Social Media Techno-Discursive Design, Affective Communication and Contemporary Politics. *Fudan Journal of the Humanities and Social Sciences* 11/4, 427-442.

Knox, John S. 2009. Punctuating the Home Page: Image as Language in an Online Newspaper. *Discourse & Communication* 3/2, 145-172.

Kristeva, Julia 1986. Word, Dialogue and Novel. In Moi, Toril (ed.) *The Kristeva Reader*. Oxford: Blackwell, 34-61.

Lagorio-Chafkin, Christine 2018. *We Are the Nerds: The Birth and Tumultuous Life of Reddit, the Internet's Culture Laboratory*. New York: Hachette Books.

Leigh, Andrew 2002. Explaining Distrust: Popular Attitudes towards Politicians in Australia and the United States. In Leigh, Andrew / Burchell, David (eds) *The Prince's New Clothes: Why Do Australians Dislike Their Politicians?* Sydney: University of New South Wales Press, 47-61.

Lenze, Malte 2002. *Postmodernes Charisma. Marken und Stars statt Religion und Vernunft*. Wiesbaden: Deutscher Universitätsverlag.

Massanari, Adrienne Lynne 2015. *Participatory Culture, Community, and Play: Learning from Reddit*. New York: Peter Lang.

Massanari, Adrienne Lynne 2017. #Gamergate and the Fappening: How Reddit's Algorithm, Governance and Culture Support Toxic Technocultures. *New Media & Society* 19/3, 329-346.

Meyrowitz, Joshua 1985. *No Sense of Place: The Impact of Electronic Media on Social Behavior*. New York: Oxford University Press.

Norris, Pippa / Inglehart, Ronald 2019. *Cultural Backlash: Trump, Brexit, and the Rise of Authoritarian-Populism*. New York: Cambridge University Press.

Pennycook, Alastair 1994. The Politics of Pronouns. *ELT Journal* 48/2, 173-178.

Pew Research Center. July 2016. Election 2016: Campaigns as a Direct Source of News.

Rauer, Valentin 2009. Magie der Performanz. Theoretische Anschlüsse an das Charisma-Konzept. In Gotzen, Daniel / Rychterová, Pavlína / Seit, Stefan / Veit, Raphaela (eds) *Das Charisma: Funktionen und symbolische Repräsentationen*. Berlin: Akademie-Verlag, 155-171.

Reisigl, Martin / Wodak, Ruth 2016. The Discourse-Historical Approach (DHA). In Wodak, Ruth / Meyer, Michael (eds) *Methods of Critical Discourse Studies*, 3rd ed. London: SAGE, 23-61.

Sable, Marc Benjamin 2018. Charisma, Value and Political Vocation: Max Weber on the 2016 Us Election. In Torres, Angel Jaramillo / Sable, Marc Benjamin (eds) *Trump and Political Philosophy*. Cham: Springer International Publishing, 255-274.

Sankin, Aaron 2016. Reddit Explodes after Trump Posts Pregame Debate Message. *The Daily Dot*, 2016. <https://www.dailydot.com/unclick/trump-third-debate-reddit-post/>.

Sarlin, Benjy 2016. How an Army of Pro-Donald Trump Trolls Are Taking over Reddit, April 14. <http://www.msnbc.com/msnbc/how-donald-trumps-army-trolls-took-over-reddit>.

Schreckinger, Ben 2017. World War Meme. How a Group of Anonymous Keyboard Commandos Conquered the Internet for Donald Trump –and Plans to Deliver Europe to the Far Right. *Politico. Org*, April. <https://www.politico.com/magazine/story/2017/03/memes-4chan-trump-supporters-trolls-internet-214856>

Schubert, Christoph 2017. Discourse and Cohesion. In Hoffman, Christian / Bublitz, Wolfram (eds) *Pragmatics of Social Media*. Berlin, Boston: De Gruyter, 317-344.

Searle, John R. 2008. *The Construction of Social Reality*. New York: Free Press.

Shamir, Boas / Arthur, Michael B. / House, Robert J. 1993. The Rhetoric of Charismatic Leadership: A Theoretical Extension, a Case Study, and Implications for Research. *The Leadership Quarterly* 5/1, 25-42.

Smith, Philip 2000. Culture and Charisma: Outline of a Theory. *Acta Sociologica* 43/2, 101-111.

Topinka, Robert J. 2018. Politically Incorrect Participatory Media: Racist Nationalism on R/Imgoingtohellforthis. *New Media & Society* 20/5, 2050-2069.

Turner, Fred 2018. Trump on Twitter. In Boczkowski, Pablo J. / Papacharissi, Zizi (eds) *Trump and the Media*. Cambridge, MA: The MIT Press, 143-149.

Unger, Johann W. /Wodak, Ruth / KhosraviNik, Majid 2016. Critical Discourse Studies and Social Media Data. In Silverman, David (ed.) *Qualitative Research*, 4th ed. Los Angeles: SAGE, 277-293.

Wagner-Pacifici, Robin, / Tavory, Iddo 2017. Politics as a Vacation. *American Journal of Cultural Sociology* 5/3, 307-321.

Wasielewski, Patricia L. 1985. The Emotional Basis of Charisma. *Symbolic Interaction* 8/2, 207-222.

Weber, Max 1958. Three Types of Legitimate Rule. Translated by Hans Gerth. *Berkeley Publications in Society and Institutions* 1.

Weber, Max 1968. *Economy and Society: An Outline of Interpretive Sociology*. Edited by Guenther Roth and Claus Wittich. Berkeley: University of California Press.

Wendling, Mike 2018. *Alt-Right: From 4chan to the White House*. London: Pluto Press.

Williams, Bruce A. / Delli Carpini, Michael X. 2004. Monica and Bill All the Time and Everywhere: The Collapse of Gatekeeping and Agenda Setting in the New Media Environment. *American Behavioral Scientist* 47/9, 1208-1230.

Wodak, Ruth 2009. *The Discourse of Politics in Action: Politics as Usual*. Basingstoke: Palgrave Macmillan.

Wodak, Ruth 2017. The 'Establishment', the 'Elites', and the 'People': Who's Who? *Journal of Language and Politics* 16/4, 551-565.

Zappavigna, Michele 2011. Ambient Affiliation: A Linguistic Perspective on Twitter. *New Media & Society* 13/5, 788-806.

Zappavigna, Michele 2012. *The Discourse of Twitter and Social Media*. London: Continuum.

Muhammad A. Badarneh

"You are not one of us!": Online responses to the premier's populist discourse in Jordan

1 Introduction

Populism has been a staple element in the contemporary political discourse of Arab regimes. Populist discourse has been exploited by Arab leaders, and their deputies and prime ministers, with the main goal of showing proximity to the populace and signalling identification with their goals and aspirations. Such populist discourse has been characterized by a calculated choice of words and expressions aimed at creating a rhetoric that emphasizes the 'greatness' of the people and justifies all policies and actions as carried out in the name of and for the sake of the people. McMillan (2016: 167) emphasizes that, in addition to "patronage", populism has been a form of "soft power" exploited by Arab leaders, whether kings or colonels, to "back up the narratives they have developed to legitimize their authority and to bridge the gap between the rulers and ruled".

Classical Arab populism, epitomized by Egypt's populist leader Nasser who "saw himself as the saviour of his people and the protector of the poor" (Dorraj 2017: 296), focused on opposition to "the old oligarchy associated with colonialism" (Ayubi 1995: 197–201), strived to "appeal to many groups (medium-sized landholders, landless labourers, bureaucrats, industrial workers, students)" (Abdel-Khalek and Tignor 1982, cited in Podeh/Winckler 2004: 5), and used "fiery anti-imperialist rhetoric (especially against Israel) [that] resonated with all sections of society" (McMillan 2016: 174). This classical form of Arab populism was pan-Arab, anti-imperialist, and anti-Western, claiming to struggle against Western imperialism and capitalism (Podeh/Winckler 2004).

In addition to Egypt, this classical form of populism also appeared in Algeria and Libya (Dorraj 2017: 298–301).

Since the Middle East has become more deeply integrated in the global capitalist economy, the idea of economic nationalism, while rhetorically alive, has become obsolete (Dorraj 2017: 292). Thus, classical notions of Arab populism have been largely supplanted by populism prompted by citizens who have "come to see themselves not simply as neglected, but actually abused by dishonest, hypocritical, and self-regarding governments", which culminated in the uprisings of the Arab Spring that "reflected the unusual depth of disillusion and despair in the region" (Anderson 2018: 483, 479). Rather than being driven by "ideological consistency", a "formidable prod" to popular rebellion was the suspicion that a better life "was slipping away as a corrupt elite grows fat" (Anderson 2018: 483–484).

With the triumph of the counter-revolutions and the end of the Arab Spring, local context-specific forms of populism in the Arab world have emerged. For example, in the semi-democratic countries of Iraq and Lebanon, controversial populist figures performed far better than expected in the parliamentary elections in 2018. In both countries, the winners were former militia leaders, Muslim Shiite in the first, and right-wing Christian in the second. As reported by Mansour and Khatib (2018), these elections signalled citizen disillusionment with the political process and discontent with the status quo and elite politics. What is interesting is that both leaders were part of this very club of elites, but nonetheless publicly criticized it for several years, and thus both appealed to the people and against their establishment colleagues, serving as markers of the emerging populism in the region (Mansour/Khatib 2018).

Another, yet different, form of populism has been taking shape in conservative countries like Saudi Arabia. According to Al-Rasheed (2018), slogans like *al-saoudiyya al-uẓma* 'Great Saudi Arabia' have been flourishing, and Saudis have been portrayed as resembling their own geography, particularly their famous mountains in their erect and imposing aura. As Al-Rasheed (2018) argues, this form of populist discourse is designed to shift the old focus on the holiness of sacred geography in order to generate a different kind of patriotism, detached from old religious legitimacy and sentiments.

In Jordan, which is the focus of this study, populism is used in a rather different fashion. Jordan has long been acknowledged as a stable country in a volatile region, a state that seeks peace and moderate ideologies, and allows for the cultivation of populist belonging (Massad 2001; Lynch 2002). Populism, or *aš-ša'bawiyyah* in Arabic, is typically used in Jordanian politics to refer to making statements, deploying discourses, or supporting measures and actions with the sole aim of satisfying and pleasing the people, such as opposing price or tax increases, or criticizing the government's performance. Whether used by the government, members of parliament, or the opposition, populist discourse in Jordan has often revolved around doing what the people want or 'like to hear', such as keeping the food subsidy intact, as discursively symbolized by 'bread' (see Martínez 2018), or taking decisions that are popularly appealing, such as the issuing of pardons for prisoners. Thus, populism in Jordanian politics can be viewed as predominantly "opportunistic", aimed at "(quickly) pleasing the people/voters – and so 'buying' their support" (Mudde 2004: 542). This negative and pejorative signification of populism in Jordanian politics was clearly communicated by King Abdullah of Jordan in 2013 when he stated that "those [MPs] who serve personal or private interests, or who act on the basis of short-term or *populist* considerations that are not in the nation's long-term interests, fail the people who elected them and [fail] all Jordanians" (my emphasis).[1] It is this meaning that will be shown to be exploited and deployed in the Jordanian premier's 'populist' claims analysed in this article. This variation in the use and understanding of populism in the Arab and Middle Eastern context in general, and the Jordanian context in particular, suggests the need for an emic rather than etic approach for the analysis of populist discourse in Arab and Middle East politics (Hamoa *et al.* 2018).

Following Nikisianis *et al.* (2019), the present article adopts the POPULISMUS research project's rigorous yet flexible method of identifying populist discourses. It argues in favour of a 'minimal

1 <https://kingabdullah.jo/en/discussion-papers/each-playing-our-part-new-democracy> (Accessed 20 November 2018).

criteria' approach, given the complicated phenomenon of populism. In particular, populist discourses should include (1) prominent references to 'the people' (or equivalent signifiers, e.g., the 'underdog') and to the 'popular will' and the need to truly represent it, and (2) an antagonistic perception of the sociopolitical terrain as divided between 'the people'/the underdog and 'the elites'/the establishment (POPULISMUS Background Paper 2015, cited in Nikisianis *et al.* 2019: 269).

The present article is specifically concerned with the analysis of public reactions toward a statement made by the then Jordanian prime minister, the veteran Abdullah Ensour, which was perceived as an attempt to deploy populism as a strategy to gain support for his economic policy. These public reactions were made through online news website commenting platforms and the social media and displayed a great deal of impoliteness and incivility toward the premier. This can be situated within the widespread and common presence of incivility in current online political commentary and online political expressions by members of the mass public (Coe *et al.* 2014; Gervais 2015). The analysis is informed by theorizing of populist discourse and the extant literature on populism. The chapter begins by providing the context and analysis for the populist statement that provoked public negative responses, and then proceeds to analyse the linguistic and discursive aspects of these responses.

The chapter aims to show the discursive features of public online attacks on the prime minister and his policy, and how public reactions to his populist statement are situated and performed within a specific (here Middle Eastern) socio-cultural and political communicative context. As will be seen, these public reactions constitute in themselves populist arguments and discourse, especially as regards the government's corruption, which is seen as an issue that lies at the foundation of any basic populist argument, the "pure people" against the "corrupt elite" (Mudde 2004). A populace-elite distinction was pronounced in the readers' online comments discussed below, which collectively show that "citizens do not feel their interests are being properly represented and many see politicians as self-serving, deceptive, and corrupt" (Salgado 2018).

2 Background

On 6 December 2015, the then prime minister of Jordan, Abdullah Ensour, delivered a speech in the parliament. The main aim of that speech was to justify and defend a wave of price hikes in the face of a disgruntled and disaffected public opinion. In the course of this speech, he tried to mobilize populist discourse to achieve that goal. Addressing members of the Jordanian parliament, and, by extension, the general public, Ensour said:

> أنا أتوجع مثلكم وابن ناس منكم ومن أفقر أي واحد منكم ولم آتي لكي اطعم الأغنياء من الفقراء، وإنما أتيت لكي أقوم باصلاح.
>
> I am suffering like you. I am one of the people, like you. I am like the poorest one of you, just like anyone of you. I have not come here to feed the rich [by taking] from the poor. I have only come to do reforms.

Ever since his appointment as a prime minister, Ensour has been widely perceived in Jordan as an establishment politician par excellence, but in addressing the Jordanian people, he chose to rebrand himself as an ordinary Jordanian and a defender of ordinary Jordanians' interests. In this statement, the premier is adopting a stance in which he claims to share the people's sufferings and thus attempting to narrow the growing divide between the people and the government as a result of his tough economic measures. Through this statement, the premier is trying to capitalize on Jordanian citizens' discontent by portraying himself to be equally suffering, thus portraying himself as having an anti-elitist and anti-establishment ideology that is essentially people-centred and moralistic (Mudde 2004). In doing so, the prime minister is reflexively vilifying the system that is oppressing the good and pure people through price and tax increases.

In the statement above, the premier deployed a feature of populist discourse as a "political style essentially displaying proximity of the people, while at the same time taking an anti-establishment stance" (Jagers/Walgrave 2007: 319). However, as Ekström *et al.* (2018) argue, "claiming the centrality of style is not to suggest that populism is nothing but style"; rather, it is "a truly contested concept". Acknowledging the various definitions that underlie different theoretical perspectives and the multidimensional characteristics of populism, Ekström *et al.* (2018: 2) perceive populism as:

> both a political discourse, or 'thin-centred ideology', representing politics and society as structured by a fundamental antagonistic relationship between 'the elite' and 'the people' and the performance of anti-establishment stances and identities, *and* claims to being one of 'the people', in which the dynamic processes of styling are absolutely central (original emphasis).

In his statement above, the premier is exactly involved in such a performance of populist stances and identities by claiming to be 'one of the people'. He is seeking to create a persona for himself as a populist and emphasize this persona through specific language. The premier presents himself as someone who wants to appeal to 'non-elite Jordanians', deploying language that indexes the characteristics and qualities associated with ordinary Jordanians, namely, suffering and poverty, thus displaying implicit antagonism toward the rich and powerful. The association with a non-elite Jordanian social identity is seen as being communicated basically through the use of "I am suffering like you", "I am one of the people, like you", and "I am as poor as any one of you". The use of the colloquial popular expression *ibn nās miθlkum* [one of the people, like you] is particularly indexical as it communicates a 'folksy' persona of a prime minister and indexes his identification with simple everyday Jordanians.

Abdullah Ensour had been regarded as a prominent opposition figure before he was named by the King as Jordan's prime minster in 2012. Thus, it seems that this populist statement he made as a prime minister was a vestige of his populist rhetoric as an opposition figure, which suggests that entry into government did not bring a clear moderation of populist discourse as might be expected (Bobba/McDonnell 2016: 282). Moreover, taking into consideration that as a premier he was popularly viewed as someone belonging to the 'establishment' and the 'elite', Ensour created through this populist language the context for "an efficient appropriation of an outsider, and anti-establishment, identity" by distancing himself from the discursive norms of being a premier, which would allow him to "claim social capital as he performs being an outsider" and "enact a populist discourse" (Ekström *et al.* 2018).

In the specific case of Jordan, the people have been disenchanted with the 1998—2008 'privatization program' through which the Jordanian government privatized fourteen state-owned enterprises in telecommunications, electricity, air transport, mining and other sectors, which are "often associated with classical populist economic models" (Dorraj 2017: 292). This privatization program was hailed at the time as transformative for Jordanian economy, but it "failed to find long-lasting solutions to major social and economic challenges facing the country" and was attacked as "tantamount to selling the country's strategic assets to foreigners" (Alissa 2007). Therefore, the populist statement above can be situated within the larger context of the government's discourse designed to appease a general public that is increasingly impacted by "social marginalization, precarious existence and disenchantment with the broken promises of liberal modernity" (Hadiz/Chryssogelos 2017: 399).

The political scene in Jordan has always been characterized by a classical distrust of governments by the citizenry. This distrust has manifested itself in implicit or explicit accusations of corruption and nepotism, which have been inextricably linked to identity politics in the country (Ryan 2012). Along with this distrust comes the public dissatisfaction with the continuing austerity measures and severe economic hardships without major political changes and accountability. The script of events has usually developed along regularly recurring lines: public protests over price or tax increases, the king dismissing the government, freezing the increases, naming a new prime minister, and asking for fresh reforms (Khouri 2018). At the zenith of the tumultuous 'Arab Spring' in 2012, and with a deteriorating economy, Abdullah Ensour was named the country's new premier. Coming at a time of political crisis, both locally and regionally, coupled with economic problems, Ensour attempted to portray himself as a saviour and a national hero. Some critics even accused him of trying to project a populist image comparable to the iconic populist image of the late Jordanian Prime Minister Wasfi El-Tal who is popularly credited with saving the country during the 1970 civil war in Jordan, informally known as Black September, when he fought and defeated the Palestinian guerrillas who tried to overthrow the monarchy. Wasfi El-Tal is described as "a man of genuinely national stature" and "an outstanding statesman" whose "political legacy is a focus of competition among those lesser men who would claim him as the patron saint of their political movements" (Robins 2004: 106-–107). Populist statements made by El-Tal in the last century are still invoked by Jordanians when commenting on problems facing the country today (see e.g. Badarneh/Migdadi 2018: 101).

Ensour's premiership, which ended in 2016, was characterized by notable increases in taxes and prices. As a result, there was popular anger that led to the eruption of large protests in Jordan. The general public was especially provoked by Ensour's move to raise cooking and heating gas prices, as well as imposing new taxes, which resulted in a wave of activism and protest. In this chaotic context, Ensour addressed the parliament to alleviate public discontent over his price and tax increases. In his famous statement above, he invoked a form of populist discourse by claiming to be one of 'the people' and hence deploying an inclusive language when addressing Jordanian people's grievances about prices and taxes. His populist statement above sought to exploit "the potency of an inclusive populist discourse in expressing societal grievances by means of constructing a popular identity that resonates with diverse constituencies" (Aslanidis 2018: 1260) of the Jordanian people. However, Ensour's employment of populist claims backfired and turned out to be futile as his statement did not resonate with ordinary Jordanians, as demonstrated by the extremely negative reactions and responses to his rhetoric.

3 Data and methodology

The data for this study are based on a total of 77 online reader comments posted in response to the premier's populist statement above. The online comments were posted on the reader commenting platforms of two prominent Jordanian online news websites: *Ammon*, which received 41 comments, and *Assawsana*, which received 36 comments. The first news site, *Ammon News* (<www.ammonnews.net>), launched in 2006, is the first online newspaper of Jordan, with both Arabic and English language websites, and is referred to as the most popular website in the country. The second news website, *Assawsana* 'The Iris' (<www.assawsana.com>), is an independent news website. Both are pure-player news sites, i.e., news sites that operate only online, which were found to be preferred by Jordanians over print newspapers with online versions (Sweis/Baslan 2013). The comments and responses analysed in this paper have been anonymized.

All these online comments and responses were characterized by incivility and impoliteness toward the premier as a means of collectively challenging the very populist appeal which he attempted to deploy. Specifically, these comments attacked the premier's 'face', that is, "the positive social value [he] effectively claims for himself" (Goffman 1967: 5) and his "public self-image" (Brown/Levinson 1987: 61) as a political figure. The impolite and aggressive nature of the comments to be discussed stems from being used strategically by respondents to "communicate disagreements" or "to discredit ideological opponents", where the use of such impoliteness is "linked to the respondent's identification of him/herself with a group and its ideological position" (Upadhyay 2010: 105). In the present case, this refers to the online commenters' identification of themselves as members of the downtrodden people who are subjected to injustices by those elites in the government. The significance of these online responses derives largely from displaying popular impolite behaviour toward the 'elite' in "forms of public debates" and "in front of a large audience" (Neurauter-Kessels 2011: 187).

3.1 Challenging the premier's populism

The analysis of the responses to the prime minister's populist statement showed that it was not well received, as commenters collectively challenged his populist message of being 'one of the people'. In doing so, the commenters deployed aggressive and impolite language to respond to his statement. The great majority of the comments constituted personal attacks on the prime minister himself rather than on his economic measures *per se*, as in the following two comments:[2]

(1) 6/12/2015 (<www.assawsana.com>)
You are neither one of us nor are we like you. You deceived us when you were a member of parliament standing fiercely against any decision impacting the citizens. We've discovered now that you were just furthering your own interests.

(2) 7/12/2015 (<www.ammonnews.net>)
Your (monthly) salary is (JD) four thousands two hundred. The salary of your son who is an ambassador is (JD) ten thousand. Your (car) gas is free. Your house is free. Yet you say you are poor. May God exact revenge on you! What should we, the people, say! Half of our salary goes to the bank as an apartment mortgage; a junky Kia is mortgaged up to the bank; we pay for the nursery; and this is to say nothing about the bills, and all of this is (only) for a salary of (JD) 400.[3]

The two comments above clearly challenge the premier's discourse by drawing a clear boundary between the premier (as the elite) and the ordinary citizen (as the populace). In text (1) the commenter dismisses the premier's populist claim of being 'one of the people' and equally implies that the Jordanian people wants nothing to do with the premier, an allusion to the fact that the premier in Jordan is appointed, not elected. The populist appeal made by the premier is undermined as the commenter accuses the premier of performing false populism when he was an MP who claimed to share the people's suffering and champion the people against the elitist government. The commenter explicitly states that the premier was only serving his own interests through pretending to defend the people's interests against the government's economic policies. This statement thus uses the premier's own populist statement and undermines it by evoking the premier's past political performance as a member of parliament. Accordingly, the premier is depicted as a politician who exploited the electorate in the pursuit of his own interests by claiming to represent simple ordinary people. This comment in itself

2 All translations are the author's unless otherwise indicated.
3 One Jordanian dinar is equal to USD 1.41 at the time of writing.

constitutes populist rhetoric "based on the claim that politicians do not adequately represent the electorate" (Bonikowski/Gidron 2016: 1601).

The comment in (2) vividly illustrates "the social distance between common people and the elites, with the latter portrayed as out of touch and disconnected from the everyday problems of the former" (Bonikowski/Gidron 2016: 1596). The thrust of this comment is the financial status and monthly income of the premier and his family compared to the meagre monthly income of ordinary citizens, which is deployed as a strategy for undermining and discrediting the premier's narrative of being 'like the people'. The comment challenges the premier's populist statement by showing the unbridgeable gap between the premier, as the 'elite', and the reader, as the 'common people'. This gap manifested itself in the stark difference between the premier's salary, which in local terms is strikingly high, and the commenter's salary, which is minute in comparison. In addition, the commenter lists the privileges that the premier is given, such as free housing and free car petrol, combined with the high-paying diplomatic position that his son was awarded, which is antithetical to the frail economy of the country. After denouncing the premier's statement 'I'm poor' and calling for divine punishment to befall the premier, the commenter draws an opposite picture of the economically grim situation lived by ordinary citizens by listing the needs that the citizen has to meet with a paltry salary, notably bank mortgages and monthly bills like the electric bill. The rhetorical question 'What should we, the people, say?!' posed by the commenter clearly serves to underline the huge gap between the elite and the people, and thus undermines the premier's claim that he is 'poor' and 'suffering'. Thus, the premier's populism is countered by an anti-government populist discourse whose visibility has been amplified by the availability of online news platforms. This comment further involves the construction of an antagonistic relationship between the elite government and the suffering populace. The discursive construction of these two antagonistic forces serves to undermine the populist identity that the premier was seeking to construct for himself, that is, as a social actor who shares with the people the same problems and worries, thus justifying his policies and measures to the people. The comment thus displays an "antagonistic division of the discursive space" (Hartz 2018: 227) between the premier and the people, projecting the premier as an 'antagonistic other' (Hartz

2018) rather than as someone who comes from and identify with the Jordanian people.

Reference to well-known multi-million corruption cases in Jordan was another strategy deployed by online commenters to challenge the populist claims of the premier. As corruption lies at the foundation of any basic populist argument, whereby the "pure people" are set against the "corrupt elite" (Mudde 2004), the premier's claim of 'being one of the people' is attacked through challenging him to address the 'corruption of the elite', as in the following anonymous comment:

(3) 06/12/2015 (<www.assawsana.com>)
Instead of imposing taxes on the poor, go bring back Umniah and have Al-Kurdi and Shaheen extradited – and the list goes on.

As in other societies, corruption is one of the 'chronic pathologies' of Jordanian society and economy, where, like other Arab societies, "monopolization of power by a small elite has led to a trickledown culture of corruption that has leaked into all aspects of public life" (McMillan 2016: 171). The commenter explicitly refers to three high-profile corruption cases in Jordan that were exposed by the authorities, but the culprits have not been brought to justice. The elite-populace opposition in these corruption cases can be appreciated if we consider the actors involved. The first case concerns the underhand sale of the national telecommunication company *Umniah*. According to critics, the government had sold its shares in the company at a 'shamefully low price' to an investor before it was sold on to a Bahraini telecommunications company for the much higher price of $415 million. While the commenter does not mention this for obvious reasons, the investor accused of being the main beneficiary in this sale was rumoured to be connected to the highest echelons of the political establishment. The second case, known as Al-Kurdi case, refers to the role of the mogul Walid Al-Kurdi, who was equally connected to the upper echelons of the political system, in the multi-million corruption case of the Jordan Phosphate Mines Company, of which Al-Kurdi was the CEO. Al-Kurdi was found guilty of illegally profiting from his position and was sentenced in absentia to 37 years in prison and over $400 million in fines. The third, equally highly publicized, case refers to the business mogul Khaled Shaheen, a government contractor of choice and one of the country's wealthiest businessmen, who was involved in a corruption scandal that rocked Jordan's political establishment at the time. The commenter's use of 'and the list goes on' suggests that these are just examples of many other corruption cases of the elite that the government has failed to address.

Reference to these high-profile corruption cases is deployed by the commenter by way of countering the populist claims of the premier. As the elite, principally the government and businessmen associated with it, are directly or indirectly involved in these corruption cases, the premier's claim to be one of the people and sharing their economic hardship becomes highly untenable and far-fetched. The commenter suggests that these multi-million corruption cases stand in sharp contrast with the government's imposition of more taxes on the already impoverished Jordanian lower and middle classes. By being part of the establishment in which this very corruption takes place, the premier is positioned by the commenter as a member of the corrupt elite that oppress the 'downtrodden' and 'pure' people. As one of the strong claims of populism is fighting corruption and establishing moral opposition between a corrupt elite and a virtuous populace, the commenter's adducing of these high-profile corruption cases radically undermines and challenges the premier who paradoxically advocates populist rhetoric, while simultaneously being a member of what the commenter perceives as a corrupt elite and establishment. The commenter thus combines both anti-corruption and anti-elite rhetoric, considering them two sides of the same coin. Such online comments thus "rhetorically emphasize the shortcomings of the political system", both "by pointing out the aloofness of its political elite" and "by pointing out its corrupt character", which are two principal features of populism (Jagers/Walgrave 2007; Rooduijn/Pauwels 2011; Polk *et al.* 2017: 2).

3.2 Mocking the premier's populism

In addition to projecting anti-elite and anti-corruption positions, rejection of the premier's populist rhetoric was conveyed by ridiculing and mocking such rhetoric. The deployment of this uncivil discourse toward Jordanian political institutions means that ordinary Jordanians, by exploiting online reader comment platforms, adopted their own populist rhetoric that is essentially concerned with proclaiming the evilness of the corrupt elite and portraying them as oppressing the good and pure people, and projecting “a set of attitudes and markers which all position ‘the common people’ against ‘the Establishment’” (Das 2018: 78). Unlike the commenters above who presented some evidence or facts to support their positions, the commenters who resorted to incivility used no arguments or facts to reinforce their views (see Coe *et al.* 2014). Consider the following anonymous comments:

(4) 7/12/2015 (<www.assawsana.com>)
Next Friday we will all gather in front of the Fourth Circle and announce the beginning of a big donation campaign for the poor of the Fourth Circle so as to bring joy to them and ease their pain and poverty.

(5) 7/12/2015 (<www.ammonnews.net>)
I hereby announce making a deduction of the amount of JD 0.25 of my daughter’s allowance and donating it to the poor servant Abu Zuhair.

(6) 7/12/2015 (<www.ammonnews.net>)
“I haven’t come to feed the rich from the money of the poor”. For a moment I thought the speaker was the caliph Umar Ibn Al-Khattab.

In these three examples, the commenters mock and ridicule the premier’s populist claims of ‘being one of the people and suffering from poverty’. In example (4), the commenter sarcastically proposes commencing a donation campaign for the premier and his cabinet, metonymically referred to as the ‘Fourth Circle’, which is the name of the traffic circle at which the Jordanian government headquarters is located. As the sarcastic goal of the campaign is to ‘bring joy to those in the government and ease their pain and poverty’, the commenter mockingly equates the elites with ordinary citizens, sarcastically collapsing the boundaries between the rich society elites and the impoverished populace. This constitutes a mockingly grotesque reversal of the Manichean populist view of society where corrupt and exploitative elites are disrespectful of the real interests and needs of the people (e.g. Akkerman *et al.* 2014). The same grotesque mocking of the premier and his populist rhetoric can be seen in (5). In this comment, the reader solemnly declares that he has decided to deduct a very trivial amount of money from his schoolgirl daughter's pocket allowance and donate it to the premier. The premier is referred to here by his byname *Abu Zuhair* 'Father of Zuhair', which in this context sarcastically follows a sociocultural naming practice in Jordanian, and Arab, society, whereby a person is commonly referred to as 'father of + name of first son' when this person is married and has a male child. As this referring expression can only be used among intimates, equals, or with familiar addressees, its use by an ordinary citizen to refer to the premier, who is of course much more powerful and has a higher status, deictically communicates the relegation of the premier to the realm of the common. Furthermore, the sarcastic portrayal of the premier as someone who needs charity, along with the symbolically trifling sum of donation that is offered and its source, i.e. out of a little girl's pocket money, serves to further mock the premier's attempt to project himself into the real everyday vortex of people's deprivation.

Finally, the commenter in (6) makes an ironic resemblance between the Jordanian premier and the renowned Muslim caliph Umar Ibn Al-Khattab. Ibn Al-Khattab is known in Islamic history as a strong ruler who was stern toward offenders, an ascetic to the point of harshness, universally respected for his justice and authority, and his role in decisively shaping the early Islamic community is widely acknowledged (Afsaruddin 2018). Furthermore, he is "regarded as the prototype for sound political governance and economic administration" (Andersson 2013: 4). The commenter's use of the direct quoted speech "I haven't come to feed the rich [by taking] from the money of the poor" prior to making this ironic resemblance serves to display distance between self and other and to distinguish the commenter's voice from the quoted voice (Bauman 1986). This invoking of ironic resemblance of the premier, popularly regarded as a symbol of 'economic oppression', to a figure taken as a paragon of justice in Arabo-Islamic history, further serves to communicate utmost incredulity in the premier's statement of being one of the people. The historically acknowledged asceticism and austerity of the caliph is implicitly contrasted with the privileges and prerogatives that the premier, and his family, has continuously received from the state, as explicitly referred to in example (2) above.

4 Conclusion

In this chapter, I analysed online responses of Jordanians on local news websites toward the populist rhetoric deployed by former Prime Minister Abdullah Ensour and showed how online commenters rejected this rhetoric while performing their own populist positions through online media. These commenters used the language of populist rhetoric to launch both anti-elite and anti-corruption attacks in the performance of support for the ordinary citizens burdened by price hikes and taxes, vilifying the premier and his government and publicly challenging and ridiculing the premier's attempted populism. The article particularly shows online commenters' mobilization of mockery and ridicule to counter the premier's populist rhetoric by way of rejecting his claims of "being one of the people and sharing their suffering".

These responses and reactions in the Jordanian context feed into and out of an environment of disdain for government officials and their discourse in Jordan. There was lay mobilization of long-standing anti-elite and anti-corruption discourse in the public performance of countering, rejecting and ridiculing government's populist claims. The online comments displayed one of the classic markers of populist rhetoric, namely, deploying a discourse that is designed to portray 'the establishment' (the government, most politicians, and venal businessmen associated with them) as self-serving and corrupt, thus becoming the 'out-group', while 'ordinary' people are portrayed as the wronged and vulnerable 'in-group' whose rights and interests are being transgressed by the elites (Das 2018).

While the populism deployed by the premier was characterized by its "emotional and moral appeal to the people" with "the articulation and embodiment of an anti-establishment political style" (Ekström/Morton 2017: 290), the essence of populism expressed by the commenters in their online discourse was based on the construction of a central opposition between the ordinary people and culprit government (Taggart 2000). In contrast with other societies, this construction can be described as predominantly moral and socioeconomic rather than ideological. These responses further help us understand "the fragmented ways in which populist ideas are communicated by citizens on the receiver side" (Hameleers 2018: 2172).

Comparable to the Israeli context (Hamoa *et al.* 2018), social and political actors in Jordan "add a moral-evaluative layer" to the conceptualization of 'populism', associating it with opportunism and duplicity, as can be seen in example (1), and thus making populist discourse "a highly flexible and multi-functional positioning resource" for self- and other-positioning (Hamoa *et al.* 2018). In the public reactions examined above, ordinary Jordanians created a moral opposition between themselves and the government, perceiving the latter as representing "the elites whose interests are perceived as inherently contrary to those of the populace" (Bonikowski/Gidron 2016: 1596). This shows that the commenters' "interpretation frames" (Hameleers 2018: 2172) were antagonistic to the premier's discourse. In the present context, the specific elites targeted by Jordanians' anti-elite rhetoric were the prime minister and his son, both accused of working to serve their special interests in order to increase their own political and economic power. These public reactions to populist discourse by the premier collectively emphasize "the social distance between common people and the elites, with the latter portrayed as out of touch and disconnected from the everyday problems of the former" (Bonikowski and Gidron 2016: 1596). These online comments discursively demonstrate how society is, effectively, separated between hardworking ordinary citizens and corrupt elites that do not represent ordinary citizens, who are excluded from political decision making (Laclau 2005).

References

Abdel-Khalek, Gouda / Tignor, Robert (eds) 1982. *The Political Economy of Income Distribution in Egypt*. New York: Holmes and Meier.

Afsaruddin, Asma 2018. 'Umar I: Muslim Caliph. *The Encyclopædia Britannica*. <https://www.britannica.com/biography/Umar-I>

Akkerman, Agnes / Mudde, Cas / Zaslove, Andrej 2014. How Populist Are the People? Measuring Populist Attitudes in Voters. *Comparative Political Studies* 47/9, 1324-1353.

Alissa, Sufyan 2007. *Rethinking Economic Reform in Jordan: Confronting Socioeconomic Realities*. Carnegie Papers, Number 4. <https://carnegie-mec.org/2007/07/31/rethinking-economic-reform-in-jordan-confronting-socioeconomic-realities-pub-19465>

Al-Rasheed, Madawi 2018. The Myth of the Benign Arab Monarchy Is Dead. *Middle East Eye*, 2 November. <https://www.middleeasteye.net/>

Anderson, Lisa 2018. Bread, Dignity and Social Justice: Populism in the Arab World. *Philosophy and Social Criticism* 44/4, 478-490.

Andersson, Tobias 2013. *Governance and Economics in Early Islamic Historiography*. M.A. Dissertation, University of Gävle, Sweden.

Aslanidis, Paris 2018. Measuring Populist Discourse with Semantic Text Analysis: An Application on Grassroots Populist Mobilization. *Quality and Quantity* 52, 1241-1263.

Ayubi, Nazih 1995. *Over-stating the Arab State: Politics and Society in the Middle East*. London: I. B. Tauris.

Badarneh, Muhammad A. / Migdadi, Fathi 2018. Acts of Positioning in Online Reader Comments on Jordanian News Websites. *Language & Communication* 58, 93-106.

Bauman, Richard 1986. *Story, Performance, and Event*. Cambridge: Cambridge University Press.

Bobba, Giuliano / McDonnell, Duncan 2016. Different Types of Right-Wing Populist Discourse in Government and Opposition: The Case of Italy. *South European Society and Politics* 21/3, 281-299.

Bonikowski, Bart / Gidron, Noam 2016. The Populist Style in American Politics: Presidential Campaign Discourse, 1952–1996. *Social Forces* 94/4, 1593-1621.

Brown, Penelope / Levinson, Stephen 1987. *Politeness: Some Universals in Language Usage*. Cambridge: Cambridge University Press.

Coe, Kevin / Kenski, Kate / Rains, Stephen 2014. Online and Uncivil? Patterns and Determinants of Incivility in Newspaper Website Comments. *Journal of Communication* 64, 658-679.

Das, Ranjana 2018. Populist Discourse on a British Social Media Patient-Support Community: The Case of the Charlie Gard Support Campaign on Facebook. *Discourse, Context & Media* 24, 76-84.

Dorraj, Manochehr 2017. Populism and Corporatism in the Middle East and North Africa: A Comparative Analysis. *Chinese Political Science Review* 2/3, 288-313.

Ekström, Mats / Morton, Andrew 2017. The Performances of Right-Wing Populism: Populist Discourse, Embodied Styles and Forms of News Reporting. In Ekström, Mats / Firmstone, Julie (eds) *The Mediated Politics of Europe: A Comparative Study of Discourse*. Basingstoke: Palgrave Macmillan, 289-316.

Ekström, Mats / Patrona, Marianna / Thornborrow, Joanna 2018. Right-Wing Populism and the Dynamics of Style: A Discourse-Analytic Perspective on Mediated Political Performances. *Palgrave Communications* 4/1, 83.

Gervais, Bryan 2015. Incivility Online: Affective and Behavioral Reactions to Uncivil Political Posts in a Web-Based Experiment. *Journal of Information Technology & Politics* 12/2, 167-185.

Goffman, Erving 1967. *Interaction Rituals: Essays on Face-to-Face Behavior*. New York: Anchor.

Hadiz, Vedi / Chryssogelos, Angelos 2017. Populism in World Politics: A Comparative Cross-Regional Perspective. *International Political Science Review* 38/4, 399-411.

Hameleers, Michael 2018. A Typology of Populism: Toward a Revised Theoretical Framework on the Sender Side and Receiver Side of Communication. *International Journal of Communication* 12, 2171-2190.

Hamoa, Michal / Kampf, Zohar / Weiss-Yaniv, Naama In Press. Populism as a Keyword and as a Meta-Discursive Resource for Positioning in Mediated Political Discourse. *Discourse, Context & Media*.

Hartz, Ronald 2018. 'The People' and Its Antagonistic Other: The Populist Right-Wing Movement Pegida in Germany. In T. Marttila (ed.) *Discourse, Culture and Organization: Inquiries into Relational Structures of Power*. Basingstoke: Palgrave Macmillan, 223-244.

Jagers, Jan / Walgrave, Stefaan 2007. Populism as Political Communication Style: An Empirical Study of Political Parties' Discourse in Belgium. *European Journal of Political Research* 46/3, 319-345.

Khouri, Rami 2018. Jordan Faces Its Historical Reckoning. <https://www.aljazeera.com/indepth/opinion/jordan-faces-historical-reckoning-180724114133597.html>

Laclau, Ernesto 2005. *On Populist Reason*. London: Verso

Lynch, Mare 2002. Jordan's Identity and Interests. In Telhami, Shibley / Barnett, Michael (eds) *Identity and Foreign Policy in the Middle East*. New York: Cornell University Press, 26-57.

Mansour, Renad / Khatib, Lina 2018. An Emerging Populism Is Sweeping the Middle East. *The Washington Post*, July 11.

Martínez, José Ciro 2018. Leavened Apprehensions: Bread Subsidies and Moral Economies in Hashemite Jordan. *International Journal of Middle East Studies* 50, 173-193.

Massad, Joseph 2001. *Colonial Effects: The Making of National Identity in Jordan*. New York: Columbia University Press.

McMillan, M. E. 2016. *From the First World War to the Arab Spring: What's Really Going On in the Middle East?* New York: Palgrave Macmillan.

Mudde, Cas 2004. The Populist Zeitgeist. *Government and Opposition* 39/3, 541-563.

Neurauter-Kessels, Manuela 2011. Im/Polite Reader Responses on British Online News Sites. *Journal of Politeness Research* 7, 187-214.

Nikisianis, Nikos / Siomos, Thomas / Stavrakakis, Yannis / Dimitroulia, Titika / Markou, Grigoris 2019. Populism Versus Anti-Populism in the Greek Press: Post-Structuralist Discourse Theory Meets Corpus Linguistics. In Marttila, T. (ed.) *Discourse, Culture and Organization Inquiries into Relational Structures of Power*. Basingstoke: Palgrave Macmillan, 267-295.

Podeh, Elie / Winckler, Onn 2004. Introduction: Nasserism as a Form of Populism. In Podeh, Elie / Winckler, Onn (eds) *Rethinking Nasserism: Revolution and Historical Memory in Modern Egypt*. Gainesville, FL: University Press of Florida, 1-42.

Polk, Jonathan / Rovny, Jan / Bakker, Ryan / Edwards, Erica / Hooghe, Liesbet / Jolly, Seth / Koedam, Jelle / Kostelka, Filip / Marks, Gary / Schumacher, Gijs / Steenbergen, Marco / Vachudova, Milada / Zilovic, Marko 2017. Explaining the Salience of Anti-Elitism and Reducing Political Corruption for Political Parties in Europe with the 2014 Chapel Hill Expert Survey Data. *Research and Politics*. January–March, 1-9.

Robins, Philip 2004. *A History of Jordan*. Cambridge: Cambridge University Press.

Rooduijn, Matthijs / Pauwels, Teun 2011. Measuring Populism: Comparing Two Methods of Content Analysis. *West European Politics* 34/6, 1272-1283.

Ryan, Curtis R. 2012. Identity and Corruption in Jordanian Politics. <https://foreignpolicy.com/2012/02/09/identity-and-corruption-in-jordanian-politics/>

Salgado, Susana 2018. Where's Populism? Online Media and the Diffusion of Populist Discourses and Styles in Portugal. *European Political Science*. <https://doi.org/10.1057/s41304-017-0137-4>

Sweis, Rana F. / Baslan, Dina 2013. *Mapping Digital Media: Jordan*. London: Open Society Foundations.

Taggart, Paul 2000. *Populism*. Buckingham: Open University Press.

Upadhyay, Shiv R. 2010. Identity and Impoliteness in Computer-Mediated Reader Responses. *Journal of Politeness Research* 6/1, 105-127.

Ruth Breeze

"Happy to be insulted": Offensive language in online discussions of UK radical politics

1 Introduction

One of the main claims made for online discussion boards is that the anonymity they offer gives people licence to express themselves in strong, even insulting terms that they would not use in face to face settings. What is less clear, however, is the social function of such uninhibited exchanges and how they fit into the bigger picture (Upadhyay 2010). It is a commonplace in social psychology that human beings derive much of their identity and self-worth from the groups to which they belong. Our desire to achieve and maintain positive feelings about our own social identity often finds expression in favouring the in-group and denigrating the out-group (Tajfel 1982). Evidence from non-online settings suggests that certain types of insult, such as intergroup identity insults, may actually be perceived by users to have a positive effect in building in-group solidarity (Branscombe/Wann 1994; Grant/Brown 1995). However, it is fair to assume that the dynamics of online insulting is likely to be different from face-to-face confrontation. The use of insults and aggressive language in many social settings may generate negative affect, humiliation and embitterment, or even trigger physical violence, but it is clear that the risk attached to verbal attacks is greatly reduced in online settings, which propitiate the airing of extreme views and the adoption of aggressive stances.

An excellent scenario for exploring this issue is in online discussions of radical politics. These are often characterised by the rapid escalation of conflict and the use of face-aggravating or even overtly threatening language (Hopkinson 2013). As online debates on social and political issues develop, they often become polarised (Yardi/Boyd

2010), and may push back previous consensual limits, leading to an increasing public use of uncivil political expressions and behaviours (Krzyżanowski/Ledin 2017). However, it is noteworthy that such exchanges are also often tinged with humour. There is certainly evidence to suggest that the "frame" through which people understand the ostensibly hostile interactions on online political comments pages is at least partly humorous (Dynel 2011: 221), and that many participants derive satisfaction from such proceedings. To investigate the dynamics of insulting on online comments pages further, empirical studies are needed focusing on what kinds of insult are used, how people react to them, and how the interactions fit into larger discursive patterns.

This chapter explores the dynamics of insulting language in two online discussions of an incident involving the controversial leader of the right-wing populist United Kingdom Independence Party (UKIP) in the context of the 2017 Stoke-on-Trent by-election. This election came in the wake of the Brexit referendum victory, was fought in a predominantly working class, traditionally Labour constituency, and was predominantly framed in the media as a two-way fight between UKIP and Labour (see Cobain 2017; Gill 2017). Regarding methodology, like previous authors (i.e. Perelmutter 2013), I take a genre approach to the notion of impoliteness (cf. Lorenzo-Dus *et al.* 2011), which consists in considering (im)politeness phenomena, in this case, insults, as they emerge and are constituted in conversation within recurring interactional patterns or "genres" recognizable to participants. By adopting this genre approach, I aim to illustrate how insults serve specific sociability functions within a genre understood by participants, and thereby to extend our understanding of radical political interactions in online media.

2 Theoretical framework

Since the aim of this chapter is to investigate the dynamics of insults in online comments pages, this section provides a very brief explanation concerning the nature and uses of insults, followed by a concise overview of the way that the affordances of online media are thought to influence the interactions within which they occur.

2.1 Insults

One standard definition of an insult is that it is an utterance that speakers use in order to cause open offence to the addressee (Goffman 1967), and in general, it is true that insults can usually be recognised by participants (by the target of the insult, or sometimes by onlookers) as at least potentially offensive. However, this definition is inadequate in a number of ways. First, concerning the definition by purpose, the intention to cause offence is clearly not present in all the examples encountered in everyday life, and the actual function of insults varies across different social contexts. Elements identifiable as "insults" by participants may actually have other functions, such as to build in-group solidarity, or even to give praise. Second, insults are easily blurred with other categories within the superordinate class of impoliteness (Culpeper 2011): insults exist in parallel - and very often overlap - with categories such as slurs, taboo words or expletives, swearing, and even humour (Dynel 2015), and it is not easy to draw clear a clear boundary line around the category of insult on its own.

Against this background and for my present purposes, I here adopt the view that insults are offensive utterances that are recognisable as such within the context and constraints of a specific speech event (Mateo/Yus 2013). Even where paralinguistic evidence is scarce, as on online comments pages, it is possible for participants (and observers) in speech events to identify utterances as insults. From the contributions immediately around them, we can form a reasonable hypothesis as to the speaker's intention, and the recorded reactions can help us to test our intuition. Our task is facilitated by the fact that most uses of insults reflect conventionalised patterns. Even the more innovative insults produced in an interaction between speakers tend to contain conventional elements (slurs, taboo words, directly or indirectly disrespectful references to the target, etc.), and can be easily recognised within the immediate communicative context.

Moreover, since our interest is in the dynamics of insulting, rather than in close analysis of individual instances, my focus will be on the main patterns of interaction found, and in the way the two main discernible groups involved in these exchanges behave towards out-group and in-group members.

2.2 Media effects

Online media are thought to have led to new developments in the way people interact in many areas of public life, and the political sphere is no exception to this (Schulz 2014). There is already a vast literature concerning the way different genres and discourses have been influenced by the move to online formats, dealing with issues such as the transition to more informal, even oral-conversational styles of communication, genre hybridisation, increasing interplay of multimodal affordances, and the emergence of looser and more spontaneous types of organisation (Campagna *et al.* 2013; Sergeant/Tagg 2014). Two of the aspects that have previously been discussed are particularly relevant to our present context. First, online participative media show evidence of a trend to disinhibition in the absence of immediate control or feedback, giving rise to a relaxation of restrictions, formalities, politeness conventions, and so on. Second, online media provide the opportunity for new forms of social display, since they allow people to exhibit aspects of their lives and personalities to large audiences, or even to assume new identities online. Even though these aspects could be regarded as mutually contradictory – disinhibition suggests that people are not paying attention to the possible impact of their actions, while display suggests that they are actually seeking maximum attention – they appear to coexist in online media, contributing to its particular dynamics.

One key factor in understanding how the new media system works is concerns the role of groups and social identities (Breeze forthcoming). The materiality of social media deeply affects identity building in various ways. First, it amplifies the "interactive and shared" elements of collective identity (Melucci 1996). Second, it sets in motion a politics of visibility characterized by individuality, performance and juxtaposition

(Milan 2015). To this, we can add a further product of display and disinhibition, that is, it also offers enhanced opportunities for staging social conflict, in a way that is both exciting and enjoyable (Hopkinson 2013). In what follows, I explore how insults evidence disinhibition and display, and examine how these aspects are orchestrated in terms of group allegiances and antagonisms. This analysis is intended to elucidate the way that offensive exchanges are organised and delivered, and thus to shed light on the nature of political skirmishes in online comments boards.

3 Empirical study: Insults in online comments forums

3.1 Corpus and methodology

This paper focuses on the reader comments published in two online British newspapers in response to articles about an incident involving Paul Nuttall, then head of the United Kingdom Independence Party (UKIP), during the 2017 by-election campaign in Stoke-on-Trent. The comments were published in: the *Independent*, with 440 comments (around 14,500 words), and the *Mail Online*, with 867 comments (approximately 22,000 words). These comment pages were chosen because they are entirely open access, that is, no registration is necessary to read or contribute. The *Independent* is an online-only newspaper, generally regarded as being in the political centre, while the *Mail Online* is an online version of a right-wing middle-market tabloid (Bingham/Conboy 2015). The comments in the *Independent* responded to an article that criticised Nuttall, while those in the *Mail* were prompted by a news story that dramatized Nuttall's confession and presented his election promises. Newspapers' online reader forums offer analysts a privileged window onto the ongoing enactment of these processes, but the fragmentary nature of contributions and the chaotic ordering of interactions mean that the material they offer is at best frustrating (Arendholtz 2013). To address this problem, I follow Unger *et al.* (2016) in using a case study approach to research discourse in media forums, taking account of contextual factors and patterns of interaction.

3.2 Results and discussion

If we look at the insults found in these comments, according to their primary social function identified from the context, we find two distinct macro-functions: to attack the out-group and foster solidarity within the in-group. But we should note that one insult may have more than one function, in a given context, and different participants may pick up on different roles, leading to complex interactions. However, in most cases, given the context of the utterance, it is possible for the analyst to determine what the primary role of the insult is, and to determine the patterns into which it fits. In what follows, we look first at the performance of antagonism towards the out-group, and then at the display of in-group affirmation and peer solidarity. After this, we will briefly consider combined effects, and examine some salient features of the dynamics of interaction.

3.2.1 Asserting identities through antagonism

The threads identified form recurring patterns within the comments pages, many of which take the form of skirmishes between supporters of UKIP and Labour, or between participants identified as representing some aspect of these parties and their policies. Antagonism finds the most obvious expression in slurs and taboo language, but is also present in ideologically charged insults. Moreover, political antagonism is often interspersed with overtly personal antagonism (explicit attacks on people's intelligence, appearance, maturity, etc.). In what follows, these categories will each be examined in turn.

3.2.1.1 Political slurs

Most of the slurs found here are primarily aimed at political parties or movements, their leaders and sympathisers. Such slurs act as labels that both identify and denigrate the adversary, but in themselves they are devoid of political content (i.e. they do not have any particular propositional meaning). In these comments pages, the adversary is usually UKIP or Labour, and the common slurs found either involve reference to the party's political position, or offensive wordplay on its name. Thus directed against UKIP we find frequent use of variants on "kippers", "kipperfilth", or "uKKKip" and "KKKippers", which make vague allusion to the Ku Klux Klan. The other familiar type of slur is directed at representatives of the right wing in politics generally, such as "fascist", "fascist scum", "nazi", "alt-right", "right wing dirt", "far right dirt", etc. This type of insult is also used to classify what the members of this party say or (allegedly) think, so we find combinations like "far-right gibberish", or "the kipper dream". Against the left, we find frequent use of the derogatory label "lefty": "lefties", "idealist lefties", "sad little lefty". Concerning their ideas, we find insulting generalisations, such as "lefty claptrap", or derogatory references, like "the little Marxist" (a reference to party leader Corbyn). Other slurs, which brand the left as "elitist", or merge them with those who oppose Brexit ("Remoaners", "Remainders"), have more substantial ideological content, and will be discussed below.

3.2.1.2 Ideologically charged insults

Notably, throughout the two comments pages, the same types of attack on and by the two parties and their supporters recur with considerable frequency. However, the patterns of actual content are not exactly the same for both sides. Both sides accuse the other of lying, being out of touch, and being insufficiently masculine. However, only UKIP are accused of being racists, being stupid or uneducated, and living in the past. Only Labour supporters are accused of being intolerant, immature, unpatriotic or un-British, and belonging to a social elite. Attitudes to immigration can be seen to motivate some of the attacks: thus UKIP, who are anti-immigrant, are characterised as "racist" and "living in the past", whereas Labour are represented as unpatriotic, un-British, and pro-Sharia. In an interesting twist on this, Labour voters are accused of "intolerance", an epithet usually more associated with jibes against the far right. The typical insults directed against UKIP and Labour and those who support them are displayed in Tab. 1.

A huge number of attacks directed at UKIP include some allusions to racism. The adjective "racist" is often appended to lists of attributes used in this context, sometimes in diatribes which vent anger and contempt:

(1) The last refuge for liars, racists, pondlife scum and bottom-feeding fascists.

Sometimes in sarcastic retorts:

(2) Oh, because the racists that UKIP attracts are such a bunch of good eggs and jolly nice people.

By contrast, a fair proportion of the insults directed against Labour (or anti-UKIP) participants seem to be directed against their supposed pro-immigrant stance: the "left luvvies hug a burqa brigade". It is fair to say that migration and racism provide the main discursive dividing line that runs through these discussion boards. Participants operate according to the underlying logic that UKIP are racists, or that people who support the left are in favour of migration, and these leitmotivs recur with great consistency, often in circumstances where the discussion seemed ostensibly to revolve around other issues.

Tab. 1: Focus of attacks against UKIP and Labour.

Against UKIP	Against Labour
• Racists	• Intolerant
• Old/living in the past	• Immature/students
• Thick/mad	• Associated with a social elite/establishment
• Strange clothes	• Snobbish
• Self-destructive	• Not patriots
• Deluded	• Pro-Sharia
• No sense of humour	• Not British
• No education	• Liars
• Liars	• Out of touch
• Out of touch	• Not masculine
• Not masculine	

However, there are also many insults directed against political/ideological groups that are simply derogatory, many of which emerge out of the cut and thrust of interaction. In the following example, the first comment has a (slightly) substantive element (the far right are "not entertaining", which might be a way of conveying the point that the far right is a serious problem), while the second simply takes up the simile used and uses it as an insult to retaliate.

(3) **Comment:** The far right are about as entertaining as haemorroids [sic].
Response: The left are hemorrhoids [sic].

3.2.1.3 Personal insults

Beyond slurs and politically framed insults, antagonistic performances also include derogatory comments aimed at specific people in the out-group (references to the adversary's appearance, intelligence, ethical standards, etc.). In the course of an exchange where one commentator has published a comment that contains some errors of expression, and a responder has objected to these, we find the following interchange of insults, in which the first accuses the second of poor comprehension skills, and the latter accuses the former of illiteracy and stupidity:

(4) **Comment.** It was perfectly legible. I think your comprehension skills may need a little brushing up.
Response. No, it was the ramblings of an angry, illiterate fool.

The following separate examples nicely illustrate the way the different participants use language to conjure up an insulting picture of the other side, activating stereotypes about the out-group (UKIP supporters are neo-fascists, while those who oppose Brexit are doom-mongers):

(5) I can picture you in shaved head and boots.
(6) all the Remainders blubbing about doom.

However, it is also fair to note that many personal attacks are humorously framed. Consider the following example, in which the first comment delivers hyperbolic praise in a sarcastic way, making his/her intent clear by the final word. The response picks up the force of this and quotes it in the response, holding it up to ridicule, and then adding a final coda that again clarifies the communicative intent (to be insulting), but also contributes humour.

(7) **Comment.** What a devastating riposte (sic). What a fabulous wordsmith you are! Tw4t!
Response. "What a fabulous wordsmith you are! Tw4t!" What a devastating riposte! (sic) Lesser gherkin of lesser cucumbers!

Such attacks are often rich in humorous wordplay, including the coining of new lexical items:

(8) **Comment:** At least fish and chips lovers will vote for him.
Response: Fishandchipocrites.

In the case of comments pages, humorous insults directed at political opponents might well have a particular group-strengthening effect, since to ridicule one's opponent fosters a sense of superiority among the in-group (Dynel 2013). Several of the exchanges found in these boards show different commentators competing both to provide humorous comments and mock the other side's attempts at humour.

3.2.1.4 Combining the personal and the political

Notably, in the exchanges found on these boards there is a strong tendency to counter political comments with personal comments, and vice versa. In the first case below, what is evidently an insulting reference to the quality of the previous user's comments is countered by an insulting comment on Tony Blair aimed as a jibe against Labour. The cohesion here can be found in the grammatical structure (comparative, followed by an augmentative comparative, is a common adjacency pair in conversation (compare Dressler/Barbaresi 1994: 509)), even though the actual content seems to have only the most tenuous connection:

(9) **Comment.** As usual more rubbish from Scottish kitten
Response. And even bigger whoppers from B'lair supporting his masters in the EU.

Humour is also a recurring feature of personal/political exchanges. The final excerpt here points to the way a political attack on the UKIP leader is countered by a personal attack on the writer, but this time with a humorous twist at the end ("Nice!").

(10) **Comment:** It's a fact that Nuttall lied about Hillsboro', about playing for Tranmere, about having a PhD
Response: I like the way you banter abuse around like a five year old bully boy. Nice!

3.2.2 Self and in-group affirmation

One aspect of some of the extracts discussed above is the way that attacks on an out-group are often perceived very positively by members of the in-group. In this section, we shall look in more detail at the way participants affirm their own identity, and that of their chosen political affiliation, by celebrating their skirmishes with the out-group, by performing online solidarity, and by engaging other societal discourses.

3.2.2.1 Affirming self and group identity

The use of insults against out-groups in boosting the self-esteem of the in-group has previous been noted in online discussions (Korostelina 2014). Insulting the other side is a component here in comments that seek to affirm the writer's own identity, and by implication, the identity of the side he/she supports. It is important to note that this type of insulting appears to be an enjoyable activity: the idea that participating in heated online exchanges is a form of entertainment is explicitly signalled more than once. The following example is revealing in this sense, in that it explains that "attacking UKIP" is a pastime, but does so in the first person plural ("we"), which suggests that attacks on political antagonists are perceived as a participative group activity:

(11) We're not desperate - just whiling away the hours. It's not much of a challenge - attacking UKIP is easier than shooting fish in a barrel.

Although this social bonding aspect is perhaps implicit in many of the examples, it is sometimes displayed quite explicitly. In the following exchange, each participant uses the discussion as an opportunity to justify his/her own political allegiance through insults directed at a social group or groups framed as rivals. Thus the first commentator explains his/her rejection of UKIP as "full of ex-Tories without a clue", and describes his/her disenchantment with the Conservative party in terms of a conversion experience ("seen the light"). The responder counters this by accusing the first writer of being "a kid" and "a leftie through and through", adding the denigrating, mock-sympathetic "poor little mite", and then boosting UKIP sympathisers through an extraordinary upbeat declaration delivered entirely in capitals.

(12) **Comment:** I been a tory all my life. Seen the light after I voted Cameron & co now never again and I would never vote UKIP either full of ex Tories without a clue
Response: Read this kid's previous comments, a leftie through and through, poor little mite! PROUD TO SUPPORT DEMOCRACY, HAPPY WITH THE BREXIT RESULT, THRILLED TO BE A KIPPER MAKING A DIFFERENCE!

Another interesting feature that relates to self-affirmation is materialised in the way that people react to insults received. Many comments by out-group representatives are ignored, others are dismissed in insulting terms ("idiotic piffle", "nurse!"), while others are countered. However, importantly for the discussion of self-affirmation, some are received with pleasure. In the following brief skirmish, names are provided for greater clarity:

(13) **Tim:** Mouton = moron
Mouton: Given your cock-eyed views on any other subject I'm happy with that assessment from you Tim, not even nice but very dim.

In this case, the writer proclaims that he/she is happy to receive the insult. The idea that someone is happy to receive a face attack has rather complex implications: it seems that in this polarised context, being insulted by the other side is understood positively as a cause for pride.

3.2.2.2 Building in-group solidarity

In this polarised setting, solidarity is only envisaged within the distinct political groups, not between them, and so identity signals play an important role in enabling participants to identify each other. Previous researchers have drawn attention to the new ways in which people are signalling identities and building alliances in online media (Milan 2015). Many of the pro-UKIP participants here enter the forum with an identity that draws attention to their political affiliation. In symbolic terms, UKIP supporters tend to brandish symbols, names and images that can be characterised as epitomising banal nationalism (Billig 1995): flags, slogans, images that recall military history. Labour supporters are generally less overtly identifiable. Such politicised identities are first launched, and then further performed through a variety of discursive moves (Breeze 2019). The UKIP supporters present here generally perform identities related to what they term "patriotism", underdog/victim status, working class allegiance and class resentment, anti-immigration stances, and masculinity. Labour supporters perform identities related to underdog/victim status, working class and northern identity, and associated with anti-racist stances (see section below on "other allegiances"). During the exchanges, commenters pick up on identity aspects signalled by others, and indicate their reactions in a positive or negative way.

One of the most obvious ways that commentators build solidarity is by expressing agreement with each other, picking up on the derogatory comments uttered by contributors on their own side, and expanding on the same idea further. In the following example, the first commentator gives a negative assessment of Nuttall, and the second contributor explicitly expresses agreement and elaborates on the first commentator's evaluation:

(14) **Comment:** He's never funny. He's known for it.
Response: I agree with you, dear "Tim". Paul Nutcase has a "never funny", seriously damaged mind. We should feel sorry for him.

Importantly, we can perceive in many of these a dynamics of augmentation. One comment is countered by another, in a cycle of escalation:

(15) **Comment:** If he didn't post it himself, are you seriously suggesting he was not aware/didn't read the post on his own website?
Response: Well, there are two options here: either he's deliberately dishonest or Nuttall is so spectacularly incompetent he's never bothered to check over his own website. He doesn't come out of it well in either case

The group bonding function here is evidently important, and it is significant that the participants themselves show metadiscursive awareness on this point. In the following separate comments, the writer explains a metadiscursive theory about comments made by "the left" and the deviant readings that "the electorate" will place upon this:

(16) when the left labels Nuttall as a racist/thicko/nutcase for his views on immigration then it indirectly insuts all those that share immigration concerns i.e. the majority of the electorate.
(17) The left labels the opposition 'fascists' but the electorate see through the smears and reject the intolerant and rude left.

In fact, part of the discursive game seems to consist of accusing each other of insulting and using this to delegitimise the other's arguments:

(18) **Comment:** The problem is that insulting is the left's only tactic for trying to win an election. It reinforces the image of the left as an angry crybaby that screams 'racist!' (as you just did) just because people have immigration concerns. When the left labels Nuttall as a racist/thicko/nutcase for his views on immigration then it indirectly insults all those that share immigration concerns i.e. the majority of the electorate! It isn't an election winning tactic but it makes you guys feel good so you self-indulge and push the electorate away. Hysterical self-destruction.
Response: Huh. . .that coming from the guy who's suggesting mental illness all round. . . . . .how very kipperfilth. . . . . .the amoral octogenarian tw4ts.

3.2.2.3 Drawing on other allegiances for group bonding

One of the frequent ways that group bonding is discursively enacted and enhanced is by roping in other allegiances and identities to create a sense that the in-group is part of a wider social community. Such online performances of "a networked self" have been observed elsewhere in studies of politics in social media (Cheng Leidig 2019, 88), and may be important in building community, creating political awareness and even gaining operativity (Nadeem, this volume). Prominent among these are deeply entrenched class allegiances, which in Britain are embedded in regional identities and prejudices (Evans/Mellon 2015). The north/south divide thus merges with a working/middle class divide, activating prejudices such as "effete southerners" versus "northern hooligans". For example, it is interesting to notice how northern and southern identities are mobilised in this exchange, in which the anti-UKIP commentator leads by attacking UKIP's claim to represent the working class north, and drawing on – but then refuting – the view of northerners as uneducated. The response counters this view of northerners by presenting southerners as "idiots in the home counties":

(19) **Comment:** From "Wooster" to "Bovver Boy", yes this party really speaks for the "working class". Nuttall the right wing mug, taking the north as mugs, very surprised people up there are being taken in by him
Response: Unfortunately they are - the same as the idiots in the home counties who believed the Tory's (sic) would enrich their lives (& wealth) - look how well THAT worked out!

Another popular discourse in British social life concerns the "Hampstead intellectual" who indulges in radical chic but has little commitment to (or sympathy with) the "real" working class. The following extract exploits this dynamics to ironic effect:

(20) **Comment:** I see you've all found your rhetorical level, aping this primate penned piece. Perhaps you could invite the "author" over to one of your "working class" themed partner swapping parties in Hampsread (sic); now that your kipper crippling cris-de-coeurs are the voices of the proles?

Central to all of this is the discursive battle between UKIP and Labour supporters over the claim to represent the working class. Ford and Goodwin (2014) present a strong argument that UKIP's support "is heavily concentrated among older blue-collar workers (...) groups who have been 'left behind' by the economic and social transformations of Britain in recent decades" (Ford/Goodwin 2014: 270). Even though, as Evans and Mellon (2015) point out, this interpretation lumps together two rather disparate groups with traditionally divergent political leanings (the working class as such and the self-employed), it is still useful for our present analysis. A discursive attack on the chattering classes is likely to appeal strongly both to industrial workers and to the low-earning self-employed, and the importance of these pre-existing social fault lines is such that it is hardly surprising that UKIP voters should choose to exploit them to gain support among the lower earning sectors of society for their party.

3.2.3 Combined effects

What is particularly interesting in these exchanges is the way the two sides line up, with different participants joining the fray to push the stock arguments further. The next excerpt shows how participants bring the key issue of immigration continually back into the debate, with three separate participants siding against "Standard" to make a hefty defence of immigration:

(21) **Standard:** A pounce from a lefty with nothing to bring to the table. Oh I know, a dummy with even less in that head.
Alancccccc: it's not about hugging a muslim, it's about realising that blaming immigrants for our problems is the oldest trick in the book.
If immigration is causing stagnating wages, unemployment, low wages, job insecurity, problems for health care etc how come the 1930's wasn't Nirvana for the English working class?
Standard: Population explosion.
Troll Hunter: immigration will not change. you will still be here spouting sh\te in years to come, but life will go on regardless. we are a nation of immigrants, yourself included.
St. Guine: And the kipper band keeps playing that old hackneyed tune "And we'll all lie together, cos then no-one will get caught." Only works in your own warped little world I'm afraid — the rest of the world sees you kippers and the ugliness you peddle. Alt-right, alt-fact, all-lies, all-con

The insults in this exchange would require extensive detailed analysis, but to summarise briefly, we can see that Standard accuses the left of having nothing to contribute (to political debates on immigration), and of stupidity in general. "Alancccccc" counters this by picking up on "hugging a muslim", a stereotypical jibe used by right-wingers to ridicule pro-immigration stances, and then debunking the idea behind this jibe by accusing people who blame immigration of using "the oldest trick in the book", that is, of deceit. He then backs this up with some more substantive arguments and ends with a rhetorical question. Standard counters this by answering the question in a rather oblique way. But then Troll Hunter dives in on Alancccccc's side immediately with an insult aimed at Standard ("spouting sh\te") and a positive assertion that everyone is an immigrant, with a special dig at Standard ("yourself included"). The culmination (and end of this particular exchange) is then delivered by "St. Guine", who delivers a highly insulting diatribe against UKIP, the gist of which is that they are out of date and living in a world of their own in which lies and racist views are the order of the day. What is interesting, perhaps, is the way that three different participants leap into the battle to attack "Standard", building on each other's arguments and topping each other's insults, until a kind of climax is reached ("Alt-right, alt-fact, all-lies, all-con") and this particular exchange is accepted as being over.

4 Concluding remarks: media effects and political polarisation

It is clear that the use of insulting language is ubiquitous in these online discussions of populist politics, and that these participants take great pleasure in such exchanges. There is evident enjoyment of the cut and thrust of verbal duelling, as well as plentiful humorous material. Several aspects of the foregoing discussion are evidently worth exploring further.

The notion of verbal skirmishing – whether ritualised or heartfelt – plays a significant role here, since these pages serve as a place for airing and countering extreme views, venting ire and airing frustrations (Perelmutter 2013). The online platform seems to be peculiarly appropriate for expressing extreme views in complete safety, without the inhibiting influence of social conventions or any risk of physical threats should matters escalate. If the participants were in physical proximity to each other, this would be potentially much more dangerous. But in this protected environment, people can let off steam and indulge in ostentatious display of controversial views. In this context, the particular affordances of the online platform need to be considered carefully. Elsewhere, online anonymity has been found to encourage more uncivil comments and more aggressive stances, and has been shown to encourage disinhibition (Suler 2004). Exposure to like-minded incivility has been found to prompt readers to be more likely to use uncivil language themselves (Gervais 2015). Moreover, online conflict is also thought to further group polarisation, boosting the tendency of like-minded individuals to become more extreme after interacting online (Christopherson 2007). For example, uncivil online text discussion after a video news story prompted subjects to perceive greater political polarization surrounding the issue (Hwang *et al.* 2014). The present study adds to these previous findings concerning impoliteness in online forums by showing its role in building solidarity, both through verbal displays of aggression against the out-group, and by enabling participants to forge strong bonds with other members of the in-group. On this basis, we might surmise that online discussions such as these might contribute substantially to the formation of extreme political views and the polarisation of the political scene.

With this in mind, it is interesting to consider parallels to the type of uninhibited verbal conflict found here. The phenomenon of online incivility can be related primarily to the concept of "flaming", a co-constructed behaviour in online media consisting of strings of utterances in which one impolite utterance is followed by another and maybe even more, often in a process of escalation (Arendholtz 2013). However, it is also worth considering certain resemblances to other situations where verbal sparring is enjoyable, namely certain types of comedy show, or parliamentary debates (Mollin 2018). We might also think of phenomena like football crowds (Crowley 2007), where fans indulge in use of formulaic insults and rude chants directed at rival groups in order to perform a common bond and identity. There is a genuine possibility that various public "conflict" genres may be influencing each other, as people enact a blend of comic display and angry posturing fuelled by ideological commitment and social prejudice. Just as in Kienpointner's account of inter-group rudeness (1997: 276), what we find here seems a) competitive, b) enjoyable, and c) in some way cooperative. Participants vie with each other, take pleasure in verbal aggression, and build on each other's contributions in an ordered, coherent manner. Culpeper has called this kind of phenomenon a "societal safety valve" (2017: 329), a venue where people can be impolite with impunity, often competing and trying to top each other's insults. In the present study, too, in terms of degree, the sequences tend to have a dynamics of escalation, sometimes reaching a highly vehement climax. Again, this internal dynamics is not conducive to moderation and tends to foment polarisation.

Although humour is obviously pervasive in these online settings, its role has less often been considered in the context of verbal conflict. It is clear that insults delivered online like those seen here often have an amusing quality, containing word play, colourful comparisons and other devices that make them entertaining. The element of competition is also present here, as comment writers scorn or cap each other's jokes. However, we should note that the presence of humour is polyvalent, since it sometimes mitigates the force of the attack by lightening the atmosphere, and sometimes appears to intensify the onslaught. The potential self-affirmatory effects of out-group insults on the in-group, mentioned above, might partly explain the presence of this ludic element. Another possibility is that many people may actually derive enjoyment – and amusement – from conflict itself, at the safe distance of the computer screen. Humour is an important ingredient in this experience, since it both raises and relieves tensions.

Perhaps more interestingly from a political perspective, we have also seen that the insulting sequences here are interwoven with references to familiar topoi in British culture, such as social class (particularly claiming working class identity), patriotism versus racism/fascism, and masculinities, as well as to personal qualities such as intelligence/stupidity or appearance. Group identities play a major role in social conflicts (Breeze forthcoming), and are reinforced by the deployment of stereotypes and slurs. It is interesting to speculate that broader polarising forces are at work behind the scenes: we see that agents take up one of a number of socially available stances, and then they seem to be forced by the polarity of this speech event into increasingly extreme subject positions. This is doubtless a psychological effect of the strong group identities that are constantly being reinforced (e.g. by insults). Offensive language propels people into particular subject positions, as participants establish and enact identity in relation to chains of socially available signifiers. In a polarised interaction, agents are effectively offered the opportunity to take up one of a limited number of available stances, and here, it is patent that the polarity available invites people to place themselves in increasingly extreme subject positions. In this particular case there is evidence to consider that in this struggle over social and political subject positions, agency can be conceptualized as a function of the discourse: "it is the discourse which constitutes the subject position of the social agent, and not, therefore, the social agent which is the origin of discourse" (Laclau/Mouffe 1985: 82). More reflection is needed on the long-term effects of polarising online discourses such as those discussed in this chapter.

Acknowledgements

The author wishes to acknowledge the support of the GradUN project, Instituto Cultura y Sociedad, University of Navarra, and the Spanish Ministry of Economy and Competitiveness (MINECO), for the funding received through the research project: *Imagining the people in the new politics*, Ref. FFI2015-65252-R.

References

Arendholtz, Jenny 2013. *(In)appropriate Online Behaviour: A Pragmatic Analysis of Message Board Relations*. Amsterdam: John Benjamins.

Billig, Michael 1995. *Banal Nationalism*. London: Sage.

Bingham, Adrian / Conboy, Mark 2015. *Tabloid Century: The Popular Press in Britain, 1896 to the Present*. Oxford: Oxford University Press.

Branscombe, Nyla / Wann, Daniel 1994. Collective Self-Esteem Consequences of Outgroup Derogation When a Valued Social Identity Is on Trial. *European Journal of Social Psychology* 2, 641-657.

Breeze, Ruth 2019. Fixing Points on a Shifting Landscape: Truth, Lies and Politics in Two Reader Comments Pages. *Journal of Language and Politics* 18/1, 1-20.

Breeze, Ruth Forthcoming. Reinforcing Right-Wing Political Identities on Reader Comments Pages. *Pragmatics and Society*.

Campagna, Sandra / Garzone, Giuliana / Ilie, Cornelia / Rowley-Jolivet, Elizabeth 2013. *Evolving Genres in Web-Mediated Communication*. Bern: Peter Lang.

Cheng Leidig, Eviane 2019. Immigrant, Nationalist and Proud: A Twitter Analysis of Indian Diaspora Supporters of Brexit and Trump. *Media and Communication* 7/1, 78-89.

Christopherson, Kimberly 2007. The Positive and Negative Implications of Anonymity in Internet Social Interactions: "On the Internet, Nobody Knows You're a Dog". *Computers in Human Behavior* 23, 3038-3056.

Cobain, Ian 2017. Ukip Leader Paul Nuttall Denies Lying about Being at Hillsborough Disaster". *The Guardian*, 10 February.

Crowley, Tony 2007. When Saturday Comes: The Boundaries of Football Rudeness. In Gorji, Mina (ed.) *Rude Britannia*. London: Routledge, 115–126.

Culpeper, Jonathan 2011. *Impoliteness: Using Language to Cause Offence*. Cambridge: Cambridge University Press.

Culpeper, Jonathan / Haugh, Michael / Sinkeviciute, Valeria 2017. (Im) politeness and Mixed Messages. *Palgrave Handbook of Linguistic Impoliteness*. London: Palgrave Macmillan, 323-356.

Dressler, Wolfgang / Barbaresi, Lavinia 1994. *Morphopragmatics*. Berlin: De Gruyter.

Dynel, Marta 2011. Towards Determining the Status of Humorous Framing in Conversation. In Dynel, Marta (ed.) *The Pragmatics of Humour across Discourse Domains*. Amsterdam: John Benjamins, 217-242.

Dynel, Marta 2013. Impoliteness as Disaffiliative Humour in Film Talk. In Dynel, Marta (ed.) *Developments in Linguistic Humour Theory*. Amsterdam: JohnBenjamins, 105-144.

Dynel, Marta 2015. The Landscape of Impoliteness Research. *Journal of Politeness Research* 11, 329–354.

Evans, Geoffrey / Mellon, Jonathan 2015. Working Class Votes and Conservative Losses: Solving the Ukip Puzzle. *Parliamentary Affairs* 60/2, 1-16.

Ford, Robert / Goodwin, Matthew 2014. *Revolt on the Right: Explaining Support for the Radical Right in Britain*. London: Routledge

Gervais, Bryan 2015 Incivility Online: Affective and Behavioral Reactions to Uncivil Political Posts in a Web-Based Experiment. *Journal of Information Technology & Politics* 12, 167-185.

Gill, Martha 2017. Tories Write off Stoke-on-Trent Central by-Election, Party Sources Say. *The Huffington Post*. 23 January 2017.

Goffman, Erwin 1967. *Interaction Ritual: Essays on Face-to-Face Behavior*. New York: Anchor Books.

Grant, Peter / Brown, Rupert 1995. From Ethnocentrism to Collective Protest: Responses to Relative Deprivation and Threats to Social Identity. *Social Psychology Quarterly* 25, 195-211.

Hopkinson, Christopher 2013. Trolling in Online Discussions: From Provocation to Community Building. *Brno Studies in English* 39/1, 6-25.

Hwang, Hyunseo / Kim, Youngju / Huh, Catherine 2014. Seeing Is Believing: Effects of Uncivil Online Debate on Political Polarization and Expectations of Deliberation. *Journal of Broadcasting & Electronic Media* 58, 621-633.

Kienpointner, Manfred 1997. Varieties of Rudeness. Types and Functions of Impolite Utterances. *Functions of Language* 4/2, 251-287.

Korostelina, Karina 2014. Intergroup Identity Insults: A Social Identity Theory Perspective. *Identity: An International Journal of Theory and Research* 14, 214-229.

Krzyżanowski, Michał / Ledin, Per 2017. Uncivility on the Web: Populism in/and the Borderline Discourses of Exclusion. *Journal of Language and Politics* 16/4, 566-581.

Laclau, Ernesto / Mouffe, Chantal 1985. *Hegemony and Socialist Strategy*. London: Verso.

Lorenzo-Dus, Nuria / Garcés-Conejos Blitvich, Pilar / Bou-Franch, Patricia 2011. On-Line Polylogues and Impoliteness: The Case of Postings Sent in Response to the Obama Reggaeton Youtube Video. *Journal of Pragmatics* 43, 2578-2593.

Mateo, José / Yus, Francisco 2013. Towards a Cross-Cultural Pragmatic Taxonomy of Insults. *Journal of Language Aggression and Conflict* 1/1, 87-114.

Melucci, Alberto 1996. *Challenging Codes: Collective Action in the Information Age*. Cambridge: Cambridge University Press.

Milan, Stefania 2015. From Social Movements to Cloud Protesting. The Evolution of Collective Identity. *Information, Communication and Society* 18/8, 887-900.

Mollin, Sandra 2018. The Use of Face-Threatening Acts in the Construction of in- and Out-Group Identities in British Parliamentary Debates. In Bös, Birte / Kleinke, Sonja / Mollin, Sandra / Hernández, Nuria (eds) *The Discursive Construction of Identities On and*

Offline. Personal – Group – Collective. Amsterdam: John Benjamins.
Perelmutter, Renee 2013. Klassika Zhanra: The Flamewar as a Genre in the Russian Blogosphere. *Journal of Pragmatics* 45/1, 74-89.
Schulz, Winifred 2014. Mediatization and New Media. In Esser, Franz / Strömback,Jesper (eds) *Mediatization of Politics. Understanding the Transformation of Western Democracies*, Basingstoke: Palgrave Macmillan, 57-73.
Sergeant, John / Tagg, Caroline 2014. *The Language of Social Media: Identity and Community on the Internet*. Cham: Springer.
Suler, John 2004. The Online Disinhibition Effect. *Cyberpsychology & Behavior* 7, 321-326.
Tajfel, Henri 1982. Social Psychology of Intergroup Relations. *Annual Review of Psychology* 33, 1-39.
Unger, Johann / Wodak, Ruth / KhosraviNik, Majid 2016. Critical Discourse Studies and Social Media Data. In Silverman, David (ed.) *Qualitative Research*. London: Sage, 227-293.
Upadhyay, Shiv 2010. Identity and Impoliteness in Computer-Mediated Reader Responses. *Journal of Politeness Research* 6, 105-127.
Yardi, Sarita / Boyd, Danah 2010. Dynamic Debates. An Analysis of Group Polarization over Time on Twitter. *Bulletin of Science, Technology & Society* 30/5, 316-327.

Nahla Nadeem

Politicizing collective identities: Online news commentaries in the Arab Spring

1 Introduction

Contemporary research on collective identity and social movement theory has identified the multiple psychosocial factors that led to the wave of Revolutions in North Africa and the Middle East (ME) popularly known as the Arab Spring. Many studies have stressed the role of information technology, particularly the Al Jazeera website (AJN) and social media, which facilitated the airing of shared grievances and the sharing of emotional reactions to the tragic events that took place at the time, especially the suicide of Bouazizi in Tunisia. According to some authors, these phenomena were accompanied by a rise in efficacy beliefs and a new assertion of social identities among Arab citizens. Howard and Hussain (2013: 3) state:

> Social protests in the Arab World have spread across North Africa and the Middle East, largely because digital media allowed communities to realize that they shared grievances and because they nurtured transportable strategies for mobilizing against dictators.

During the Arab Spring, the AJN website emerged as a particularly important communication platform that played a key role in allowing various segments of Arab society to access free and uncensored information, and more importantly to compete in the production of information, narratives and frames that helped to recreate and politicize collective identities in the ME region. It provided an alternative communication path through which "social relations are constituted and practiced", and thus, "made possible the articulation of a social order different from and often opposed to the dominant" (Hamilton 2000: 362).

1.1 Online news commentaries as a tool for politicizing collective identities

The Arab spring clearly signalled major shifts in collective identity narrative. There is no doubt that profound transformations in collective identity in the region are linked to the widespread of online news and social media prior to the Arab Spring. The key role of technological innovations in creating and politicizing collective identities and collective action in general is well discussed in the literature (Castells 2001; Downey/Fenton 2003; Garrett 2006; Howard *et al.* 2011; Ben Moussa 2013; Nadeem 2014). Garrett identifies three types of mechanism linking the technology to collective identity and social movements, namely "reduction of participation costs, promotion of collective identity, and creation of community" (2006: 204) (quoted in Ben Mousssa 2013: 56).

Similarly, the commentary option on AJN articles provided an extra space for expression, where readers could negotiate different point of views, ways to participate in the events, aspirations, and expectations about the turn of events. As these news commentaries accumulated day by day, more voices started accumulating, discussing and expressing consensus or debate around the articles published. Whether and how news commentaries can provide linguistic evidence of the emergence of the commentators' politicized collective identity (PCI)[1] and

---

1 Abbreviations and definitions of terms:

Politicized collective identity (PCI). According to Simon and Klandermans (2001: 319), politicized collective identity revolves around three conceptual triads. The first triad consists of collective identity, the struggle between groups for power, and the wider societal context. It is proposed that people evince politicized collective identity to the extent that they engage as self-conscious group members in a power struggle on behalf of their group knowing that it is the more inclusive societal context in which this struggle has to be fought out. Next, three antecedent stages leading to politicized collective identity are distinguished: awareness of shared grievances, adversarial attributions, and involvement of society at large.

Face attacks are defined as instantiations of offensive linguistic behaviour (acts of rudeness) in which socially accepted norms of behaviour are violated. In the data, they reflect the posters' politicized collective identity as a form of social capital and are linguistically expressed.

the psycho-social dynamics that contribute to its emergence in online news commentaries need further research (Breeze 2019). In this study, I explore some of the linguistic manifestations of the social-psychological mechanisms that underlie the emergence of politicized collective narrative through the analysis of online commentaries on an article that was posted on AJN website prior to the Tunisian Revolution. The key question that needs to be investigated is the extent to which the commenters' language behaviour and discursive display of identity can provide empirical evidence on the emergence of politicized collective identity in this setting.

1.2 Research questions and methods of analysis

The core question in this study is how the emergence of the posters' PCI operates linguistically. It mainly explores the linguistic manifestations of the consensualization and debate over who the posters considered their allies or enemies through the discursive display of the posters' identity and the analysis of the posters' face attacks (FAs) and solidarity acts (SAs) in the data. The study adopts a multi-disciplinary approach. The psychosocial factors that potentially lead to the emergence of PCI and the analytical framework adopted are based on insights from several fields of study: social identity, social movement theories, pragmatics studies of politeness and discourse analysis. In the analysis, the researcher adopts a mixture of quantitative and qualitative methods to address three key questions:

1) What is politicized collective identity? How does it operate via digital media networks during the Arab Spring?
2) What are the linguistic manifestations of the psychosocial factors that lead to the emergence of the poster's PCI in the data?
3) What are the implications for digital media, social identity, social movement and sociolinguistic theories?

To analyse and evaluate the linguistic evidence for the emergence of PCI in the data, the following variables will specifically be considered:

1) The discursive display of the posters' identity will be measured through percentages of the posters' nationalities as well as the manipulation of other identity display markers that bind them together as a social group.
2) To measure the role of networking in the consensualization and debate over who the posters considered their allies or enemies, the message content will be analysed by presenting the most representative topics in the data and the frequency percentage of each topic. The percentages will reveal the topics that they seem to agree about, especially the out-group entities that receive their attacks and the in-group entities that receive their empathy, support and praise.
3) To investigate the posters' shared grievances, especially their shared perception of social injustice and other shared feelings of anger and/or empathy, excerpts from the data are qualitatively analysed using a speech act and discourse analysis approach following Brown and Levinson's work (1987) and Leech's maxims of politeness (1983). The posters' performance of certain speech acts and their lexical choices are viewed as discursive resources to develop their PCI, e.g. insults, dispraise, accusations of theft and looting are used as FAs towards out-group entities (mainly Arab political regimes, heads of states and the opposition parties) while agreement, greetings, prayers, praise are SAs targeting in-group entities (mainly Tunisian protestors, Al Jazeera channel and other oppressed Arabs in other Arab countries). Finally, the implications for the sociolinguistic studies of PCI and social action movements will be discussed along with suggestions for future research.

Since the postings are all in Modern Standard Arabic (MSA), translations of the examples cited are provided by the researcher and added underneath the cited commentary. In what follows, I will give a brief summary of the article posted on AJN on which the posters comment, and a brief description of the computer mediated data used in the analysis. Section 2 briefly reviews the literature on what constitutes PCI and the psychosocial factors that lead to its emergence. It reviews the sociolinguistic aspects of politicized collective identity by making links between the emergence of the posters' PCI and its linguistic manifestations in the data. Section 3 includes the conclusion and suggestions for future research.

1.3 A brief note on the article and the data

The article on which the posters commented was written after the suicide incident involving the Tunisian Bouazizi, which was considered the initial

Nationality	Tunisians/ Tunisian immigrants	A mixture of Arab nationalities	Anonymous
Percentage of posters	38.37%	45.71%	15.92%

Tab. 1: Posters' nationalities as percentage.

spark that led to the Tunisian Revolution. The data used in the study are computer mediated commentaries posted on the article. They are asynchronous responses that represent the posters' opinion on the article or related issues, mainly, the corruption of Arab regimes and the prevailing social injustices in the Arab world and the key role of the AJN in covering the uprising news and exposing the corruption in other Arab countries.

The article and the commentaries were retrieved from Al-Jazeera website <http://www.aljazeera.net> just before the Tunisian Revolution broke out. There were 245 asynchronous postings on the article which were chosen to serve as a corpus of data from which the examples cited and examined are taken. Judging by the content of the postings and names used, the commentaries are written by Arabs from different Arab countries, as shown in Tab. 1. They are mostly written in Modern Standard Arabic, which facilitates communication among the Arab posters (except for few incidents of dialectal Arabic, especially Egyptian and Tunisian). The posters used mixed identity representations together with a mixture of face attacks (Brown/Levinson 1987) and solidarity acts. For this reason, their responses are considered appropriate data for analysing the sociolinguistic aspects of PCI through making links between the emergence of the posters' PCI and its linguistic manifestations, through the identity signals chosen and the speech acts performed by the posters.

2 The psychological predictors of the emergence of the posters' PCI and its discursive manifestations

Identity construction is generally viewed as a dynamic process that arises in the flow of events in the encounter. Different identity features are foregrounded in different contexts and social settings according to personal and social needs. Simon's (2004) Self-Aspect Model of Identity provides a useful tool to account for both individual and collective (social) identities. According to the model, individual identity results "whenever self-interpretation is based on a more comprehensive set or configuration of different, non-redundant self-aspects", and collective identity results "whenever self-interpretation is based primarily on a single self-aspect that one shares with other, but not all other, people in the relevant social context" (Simon 2004: 49–50). Foregrounding individual or collective aspects of identity depends on a number of psychosocial factors. For example, when social (collective) identity becomes salient in certain contexts or culture, "the similarity or interchangeability of oneself with other people sharing the same self-aspect moves into the psychological foreground", while other self-aspects become irrelevant; as a consequence, "perceived ingroup homogeneity" is promoted (Simon 2004: 49). In a nutshell, "collective identity signals that one is not alone but can count on the social support and solidarity of other in-group members so that, as a group, one is a much more efficacious social agent ('Together we are strong')" (Simon/Klandermans 2001: 321).

A sub-type of collective identity is what Simon and Klandermans (2001) call "politicized collective identity" (PCI). They note that when people become aware of shared grievances and understand that these grievances can be addressed by influencing other members of society, they will come to develop a form of identity that incorporates explicit motivations to engage in a struggle for power. In such case, they often present themselves as being representative or aligned with dominant, positively valued social categories such as "nations". Simon and Klandermans (2001) claim that PCI might lead unprivileged groups of people to perform social actions such as protesting or revolting against what they see as an oppressive power or authority. In this case, their communication and later action depends on this politicized collective identity through which they attain power as an "in-group".

Moreover, according to the social identity model of deindividuation effects (SIDE model), visual anonymity in online communication settings can also contribute to the evolution of the communicators' politicized collective identity (Spears/Lea 1992, 1994). When communicators cannot see each other, they are free to pick the signals they choose to display and very often "their only psychological connection is the knowledge that they belong to the same group; i.e., their self-concept shifts from a personal to a social identity" (what Spears and Lea (1992) called "depersonalization"). This depersonalization is manifested in the discursive strategies the posters' use to display their identity in computer-mediated communication.

2.1 The posters' display of their PCI: Uniting as an Arab nation

In the data, the posters used a mixture of strategies to reveal their identity: e.g. using name or a pseudonym, nationality or country of residence and an 'intro' statement. In case of anonymity, they simply use introductory statements that indicate the poster's standpoint on one of the topics discussed in the article (see sections 2.2 and 2.3). Of all the identity markers picked by the posters, nationality is observed to be the most prominent. As predicted by Simon and Klandermans (2001), it seems to function as a key parameter in creating a politicized collective identity in the data. In fact, most Arab nationalities are represented, but the highest percentage is Tunisians (29.98 %) and Tunisian immigrants (9.39 %). Using MSA is another important signal of the posters' collective identity, as it is the most widely used variety among educated Arabs. especially if they want to communicate across country boundaries.

The posters' foregrounding of their Arab nationality, using MSA and online interaction, provide support for the emerging PCI as defined by Simon and Klandermans (2001). The posters collaboratively interact as "an Arab nation" sharing common pain and goals, and this largely explains the FAs and the SAs performed (see section 2.3). It accounts for the alignment of "we" against the "oppressive powers" and their call for action and reform in the message content. The word "Arab" with its many derivations is significantly repeated and stressed in the data. It functions as a superordinate term under which all other Arab nationalities are subsumed. The posters also talk about "a new Arab generation", "Arab youth", "Arab future", "oppressive Arab regimes" and "an Arab nation". They culturally allude to Islamic slogans and verses that are shared and appreciated (e.g. prayers and verses of the Quran are cited within the posts). Their discourse also defines 'who are the allies' and 'who are the enemies'. It clearly matches what Simon and Klandermans (2001: 321) describe as a "politicized collective identity" where shared grievances and pain bring people to align together around a dominant, positively valued identity marker, as being 'part of a nation', in order to engage in a struggle against those who represent an oppressive power. The emergence of the posters' PCI also shows in the percentage of non-Tunisians criticizing and attacking the Tunisian government - 61.63 % of all respondents (including anonymous posters) compared to Tunisians, who account for only 38.37 %. The posters' collective identities emerge as they share their opinions and reach a consensus about their common suffering and aim, allowing them to override any local sensitivities or considerations (McGarty/Lala/Douglas 2011).

Anonymity (15.92 % of the posters) was equally effective in highlighting the shared grievances and emotional reactions to what were seen as unjust political, social and economic conditions. Whether this was out of fear or the desire to focus more on the message is unknown. The anonymous posters used introductory statements as identity signals instead (see section 2.3). McGarty *et al.* (2014: 729) maintain that the dynamics of PCI can be different from one socio-political context to another. They state that in the case of mass opposition movements trying to overthrow a national government, these opposition groups can be presented as being disloyal to the nation, which is why they tend to transcend their local identities and align with a bigger social identity, e.g. as an Arab nation, or as human rights activists. Other factors seem to contribute to the evolution of the posters' PCI and unite them together as a socio-political group, namely: a) the ability to create connective structures through the consensualization process of shared opinions and online networking, and b) the expression of shared grievances, aspirations and fears.

2.2 Creating connective structures through the consensualization process

Recent research has demonstrated that the politicizing process of collective identity can take on different forms. In the Arab Spring, Lim

(2013) described how online bloggers, Facebook and Twitter users created "connective structures that helped in disseminating and sharing information on or about Sidi Bouzid and/or the Tunisian uprising". She maintained (2013: 937) that these:

> connective structures also helped generate connective action that allows individuals who are familiar with everyday practices of social networking to contribute to concerted action through more personalized paths.

Their online contribution was "an act of personal expression or recognition or self-validation achieved by sharing ideas and actions" (Bennett/Segerberg 2012: 752–3).

Computer-mediated communication via the AJN website or social media certainly provided these posters with public space and allowed them to form a socio-political network away from the control of the government censorship and mainstream media. Ben Moussa (2013: 59) describes:

> the parallelism between the internet as a communication media and social movements as 'networks of networks', where rapport between nodes/members is built on non-hierarchical, non-linear and highly flexible structures.

These online networks often involve online groups and communities that do not necessarily have offline structures and presence, so they represent "networks of informal relationships between a multiplicity of individuals and organizations, who share a distinctive collective identity, and mobilize resources on conflictual issues" (Diani 2000: 387, quoted in Ben Moussa 2013: 59).

2.3 *Evidence of the consensualization and debate process*

The data also provide evidence that online news commentaries on the AJN website managed to create online connective structures across the AW that allowed the posters to share their opinions on the political events, their aspirations and fears. The posters' identity represents different Arab nationalities and Arab immigrants who not only follow the news but contribute with their opinion on the article and political events in general. Their opinion was not limited to the local events in Tunisia or the topic of the article but extended to cover other shared grievances that they felt were of great concern to all Arabs at the time. Being able to participate from a distance, the majority of the commentaries show the consensual public dissent against the Tunisian government, Ben Ali and his family (particularly his wife and in-laws) and other Arab regimes. To examine how the consensualization process of shared opinions and/or debate contributes to the emergence of PCI, Tab. 2 shows the most recurrent topics in the posts, organized according to the order of frequency and percentage of mention:

As shown in the table, the most frequently recurring topic, found in 50 % of the posts, is the consensual public dissent against the Tunisian government, Ben Ali, Arab regimes, the opposition and mainstream media. The political corruption and social injustices are generally considered the root cause of Bouazizi's self-immolation, and are described as shared in most Arab countries. This was the topic that showed by far the maximum amount of consensus. The posters, who belong to different parts of the Arab world, all made fierce and fearless attacks against Ben Ali's regime and other heads of states (see section 2.3).

Next in frequency and degree of consensus is the key role of the AJN website in covering the news of the uprising and exposing the corruption in the Arab world. About 43 % of the posts include messages conveying heartfelt support for the AJN's spirited coverage and its key role in getting the voices of the street protesters in Sidi Bouzid and other parts of the Arab world heard. AJN was described as a long-awaited media alternative that Arabs badly needed to expose the state of corruption and articulate their aspirations, fears and concerns. It was often described by the posters as "Arab WikiLeaks". AJN's broadcasting of the protests is also contrasted with the censored, controlled and repressive mainstream media in 11 % of the posts. The posters almost considered AJN part of the socio-political network itself since it encouraged user-generated content to help track events as they unfolded in Sidi Bouzid (Russell 2011: 1).

Another area of consensus is found in the recurring messages of solidarity, prayers and faith in the protestors' social and political reform actions. These messages are found in 32 % of the posts and often encourage other Arab countries to rise and revolt so they can

Order of frequency	Recurring topics	Number of posts	Percentage of the frequency of mention
1-	The state of political and social corruption in Tunisia and other Arab states.	123	50%
2-	The key role of AJN's news coverage in exposing the tragic events in Tunisia & the Arab World	106	43%
3-	Showing Support, love and offering prayers to the Tunisian people, the protestors & Arab youth	79	32%
4-	Call for continuous action till Ben Ali's fall and urging other Arab countries to revolt.	59	24%
5-	Harsh criticism of the government, the parliament and opposition as sycophants of the regime.	31	12%
6-	AJN's news coverage versus mainstream media & other western media resources	27	11%
7-	Reporting offline events (e.g. tragic events of repression, torture and of the brutality of the police in Tunisia and other countries).	18	7%
8-	Miscellaneous topics range from expressing disagreement with the above opinions (e.g. supporting Ben Ali's regime, to attacking Bouazizi' s self-immolation, AJN's double measures in covering the news in the Arab World, and a call for the Islamization of the uprising.	38	15%

Tab. 2: Recurring topics: percentage and frequency.

bring about social and political reform; 12 % of the posts also contain harsh criticism of the official opposition, describing them as sycophants who will do anything to benefit from the current state of corruption. Seven percent of the posts include the posters' reporting of events (e.g. tragic personal stories of repression and torture, exposing the corruption of the ruling family, sharing news stories about the uprising in Sidi Bouzid, other Tunisian cities and the brutality of the police). Other miscellaneous topics are of much lower frequency, e.g. posts by Ben Ali's regime supporters, posts that describe the economic situation in Tunisia as much better than other Arab countries, pleas to the Tunisian police and the army to side with the protestors, a call for the Islamization of the uprising in Tunisia and across the Arab world, predicting the fall of the Tunisian regime and other Arab regimes, commenting on the situation in Gaza and the conspiracy of the Arab States or commenting on another post in the thread. Such topics appear in 15 % of the posts, and they are debatable as they do not represent the general trend.

Bearing in mind that the article and commentaries are mainly written in response to Al-Jazeera's coverage of the uprising that took place in Tunisia, the attacks made against other Arab countries and heads of states is relatively big. Although the postings mainly tackle the posters' evaluation of the official reaction to Al-Jazeera's coverage of the protests in Tunisia after Bouazizi's suicide, they seize the chance to share uncensored dissenting opinions, common pain and sufferings. The messages show general consensus on what they perceive as common injustices and corruption in the Arab world. There are cases of minor disagreements among contributors on the miscellaneous topics; yet, they do not reflect major differences in opinion regarding entities generally seen as oppressive powers that need to be attacked. Apart from this, the posters mainly seem to differ in their attitude towards Al-Jazeera's role and its political agenda. However, they generally tend to praise rather than attack: 34.29 % of the data include praise of AJN whilst only 6.12 % represent attacks against its political agenda, accusing it of biased and unbalanced coverage.

Online news commentaries thus allowed the posters to create virtual connective structures and transcend geographical and political boundaries to share their opinions within a group, and act as social agents who are determined to bring about political and social change. The public space provided where they share, discuss, debate and consensualize their opinions over topics that are of major concern to them helped them achieve a shared sense of "who we are" and "how we should act". McGarty *et al.* (2009, 2011, 2014) have shown how this constitutes the foundation for politicizing collective identities that can ultimately lead to social action.

2.4 Expressions of shared grievances and emotional reactions to unjust political and social conditions

A third key factor in the politicizing process of the posters' collective identity is the expression of shared grievances, aspirations and fears. Through sharing their opinions and reaching a reasonable degree of consensus over the unjust conditions and the need for change, they develop a shared sense of "we" versus the oppressors "them". According to Smith, Thomas and McGarty (2015) (quoted in Alberici/Milesi 2015: 45):

> when people encounter a conflict between how things are and how they should be, they are more inclined to express their ideas and opinions. Expressing and exchanging an understanding of social reality thus enables individuals to convert personal subjective perceptions into socially validated norms and identities.

Thus, consensus over shared grievances is shown to be a major factor in the emergence of politicized collective identity in online political discussions.

The consensus over shared grievances mainly involves agreement on the prevailing state of political corruption, social injustices, feelings of oppression, the uselessness of opposition parties, and the deteriorating economic situation. It also reflects a strong "we" against "them" narrative and strong emotional reactions in general (anger against the oppressors vs. sympathy and support for the protestors). The posts below show the harsh criticism and fierce attacks the posters made against the Tunisian government, the opposition and other Arab regimes. The speech acts used are: assertions of the prevailing state of corruption in the AW and blaming the opposition for not acting on behalf of the oppressed people -e.g.:

- (13) هذه هي أحزاب العار
- These (opposition) are parties of shame.
- (70) قذارة الانظمة العربية الناهبة لخيرات الشعوب
- Dirty Arab regimes that rob the countries' resources.
- (19) إنتهى زمن الخوف و الكذب و التدجيل
- Time for fear and fraud has ended.

Though there were no threads and little interaction between the posters, the messages mostly express the same sentiments of anger and empathy towards the same entities. They are emotionally charged; e.g., strong feelings of anger and resentment are expressed through the use of lexical items such as 'injustices', 'oppression', 'dirty Arab regimes', 'rob', 'shameful', and 'fraud', which are generally shared and agreed upon. On the other hand, allegiances are formed through emphasizing a shared identity aspect "being an Arab" (e.g. "an Arab in Chains" or "an Arab aspiring for freedom and dignity"), stressing shared pain and the need for change. Strong feelings of support and empathy are reflected in the SAs used (e.g. "pray for your brothers (and sisters) in Tunisia" and "greetings from Yemen to the heroes") and the subtle lexical choices used in the headings and content of many commentaries (e.g. the recurring use of terms of affiliation such as 'Arabs', 'brothers' and 'heroes' to describe the protestors in Tunisia). One poster described the patriotic protestors "as a new generation of Arab youth who call for change and reform" while others stress shared goals, common grievances and interests through sharing prayers, praise and greetings to Tunisians and other Arab citizens who aspire for change. In contrast to the curses, threats, insults and accusations targeting 'the enemies', terms of endearment and affiliation, consensus and praise are used with 'the allies'. There are also recurring calls for action and revolt: e.g. "Every free and honest Arab should revolt". Below is the translation of some of the SAs in the data:

- عـــربي مكبّـــــل
- An Arab in Chains
- عربي متلهف للحرية والكرامة
- An Arab aspiring for freedom and dignity
- العرب الجدد
  العرب الجدد هم فئة من الشباب المثقف الذي يسعى للإصلاح والتغيير، فتحية خاصة للشباب العرب
- The new Arabs
  The new Arabs are a group of cultured youth who aspire for change and reform. Special greetings to the new Arab youth!
- الجزيرة وكيليكس العرب
- Al-Jazeera- Arabs' WikiLeaks
- الثورة اتية على كل وطن عربي
- The revolution is coming in all Arab countries.
- ادعوا لإخوانكم في تونس
- Pray for your brothers (and sisters) in Tunisia.
- مصـــــــــر التي تغبط شعب تونس
- Egypt feels happy for all Tunisians
- تحيه من اليمن للأبطال
- Greetings from Yemen to the heroes

Very often, the same posting includes tokens of FAs and SAs. The strategies used in giving praise and showing solidarity and the target recipients are: praise and thanks to AJN for exposing the corruption, showing empathy and solidarity to the Tunisians and other Arabs who share similar economic and political conditions. The commentary below is an example of the common strategies used to show solidarity in a collective sense:

- يمنى مغترب
  بلاد الغربة
  كان الله معكم مؤيدًا ونصيرًا. ونشكر الجزيرة على تغطيتها للأحداث كما هي. ليست تونس من تجب عليها الانتفاضة فأجزم أن في الدول العربية الظلم الكثير.
- A Yemeni- Away from my homeland
  May God be with you and support you (Tunisians). Thanks to Al-Jazeera for its accurate coverage of the events. Tunisia is not the only Arab country that should revolt; surely other Arab countries suffer from a lot of injustices too. (Post 217)

Here, the social support and the shared perception of pain and oppression in all Arab countries give a sense of unity and hope. The feelings of solidarity and a common destiny are subtly invoked through the repeated use of the aligned 'we' and 'our brothers', besides the long list of Arab countries the poster provides to show that Arabs all over the Arab world share the same conditions of political corruption and the wish for change.

3 Conclusion and suggestions for future research

So far, I have aimed to explore the discursive manifestations of the different psycho-social processes involved in the development of PCI in online news commentaries, as shown in the data selected. Through the theoretical underpinnings of social identity, social action, and discourse analysis theories, the discussion tackled two key concepts: a) the psychosocial factors that underlie the politicizing process of collective identities prior to the Arab Spring, and b) their sociolinguistic manifestations in the light of the data. The data analysis provided empirical linguistic evidence of the emergence of the posters' PCI through a) uniting as an Arab nation, and b) creating virtual connective structures that enabled them to share their opinions and reach a shared sense of 'who they are' and a degree of consensus over who they considered to be their 'allies' or 'enemies'. Though the comments were written in response to the article published, the topics discussed tackled other shared socio-political concerns, aspirations and fears. Their emerging PCI also defined the in-group and out-group members and determined the direction of the FAs and SAs performed in the data. Postings typically included at least one type of FA (e.g. name-calling, insults, curses, accusations and threats) targeting what the posters defined as an out-group: "oppressive power/s that they needed to align against". This was usually mixed with the use of abusive language and direct insults aimed at governments and heads of state (e.g., حرامي، عصابة، خائن، سفلة) (bastards, gang, traitor, and thief) along with accusations of lying, looting and deliberate fraud. On the other hand, acts of solidarity were typically shown in the general agreement the posters shared of 'who the allies and the enemies are' and the call for action. This was reflected in the verbal strategies used (e.g. praise of Al-Jazeera's news coverage, sharing greetings, heart-felt prayers, praise of Arab citizens who wish for change and a show of empathy and solidarity to Tunisians and other Arabs who shared similar unjust conditions).

The analysis of online news commentaries on AJN website has indicated that a multidisciplinary approach can be extremely useful in gaining a deeper understanding of the concept of politicized collective identity in the socio-political context of the Arab Spring. The data analysis has also confirmed that collective identities and the psychosocial factors behind them are as dynamic and varied as the communities and the socio-political contexts that gave rise to these narratives. Thanks to digital media, new political movements are no longer a set of political processes "within either the polarized loci of 'politics' on the one hand, or 'people', or its representatives on the other", but rather can be located in "a continuum of practices which locate between 'politics' and the 'people'" (Krzyżanowski/Ledin 2017, cited in Breeze 2019: 3). New media also provide the protective shield of anonymity which allows these posters to attack the political regimes without the fear of retribution. The public space provided to develop a shared understanding of the political situation and the collaborative attacks against the oppressive regimes are, in fact, the building blocks of these collective identities (see Hopkinson 2013; Perelmutter 2013; Kelsey/Bennett 2014).

Multiple psychosocial factors can influence the extent to which people perceive social or political situations as unjust and collaborate to mobilize resources to bring about the aspired change. The larger the discrepancy between actual and ideal situations, the more strongly people will be motivated to act through various forms of resistance. In each case, pathways and collective identity narratives might be different. More empirical research is needed to understand the ever-changing and constantly emerging PCI narratives. For example, recent research on post Arab Spring narratives showed how the complex local dynamics led to different outcomes in Tunisia, Egypt, Yemen and Syria. Quoting SWP's Arab elite project, Heydemann (2016: 159) writes about the challenge of explaining post Arab Spring outcomes:

> The challenge is how to capture the dynamism of the uprisings and their effects without implying either that Arab states are moving in a linear if bumpy transition towards a visible if dimly perceived outcome or that the uprisings were a moment of sound and fury signifying relatively little. Their response to this challenge, in part, is to frame the uprisings as moments of transformation rather than transition. The distinction between these terms is important. The term transformation captures the notion of systemic change yet without implying directionality or some form of democratic teleology. It emphasizes the fluidity and unpredictability of transformational settings, a point the editors stress in their introduction.

More research is still needed to understand the post Arab Spring PCI narratives that emerged and led to these startlingly different outcomes in the region.

References

Alberici, Augusta / Milesi, Patrizia 2015. Online Discussion, Politicized Identity and Collective Action. *Group Processes & Intergroup Relations* 19/1, 43–59.

Ben Moussa, Mohamed 2013. From Arab Street to Social Movements: Re-theorizing Collective Action and the Role of Social Media in the Arab Spring. *Westminster Papers* 9/2, 45-68.

Bennett, Lance / Segerberg, Alexandra 2012. The Logic of Connective Action. *Information, Communication & Society* 15/5, 739-768.

Breeze, Ruth 2019. Fixing Points on a Shifting Landscape: Truth, Lies and Politics in Two Reader Comments Pages. *Journal of Language and Politics* 18/1, 1-20.

Brown, Penelope / Levinson, Stephen C. 1987. *Politeness. Some Universals in Language Usage*. Cambridge: Cambridge University Press.

Castells, Manuel 2001. *The Internet Galaxy: Reflections on the Internet, Business, and Society*. Oxford: Oxford University Press.

Diani, Mario 2000. Social Movement Networks Virtual and Real. *Information, Communication & Society* 3/3, 386-401.

Downey, John / Fenton, Natalie 2003. New Media, Counter Publicity and the Public Sphere. *New Media and Society* 5/2, 185-202.

Garrett, Kelly 2006. Protest in an Information Society: A Review of Literature on Social Movements and New Icts. *Information, Communication & Society* 9/2, 202-224.

Hamilton, James 2000. Alternative Media: Conceptual Difficulties, Critical Possibilities. *Journal of Communication Inquiry* 24/4, 357-378.

Heydemann, Steven 2016. Explaining the Arab Uprisings: Transformations in Comparative Perspective. *Mediterranean Politics* 21/1, 192-204. <http://dx.doi.org/10.1080/13629395.2015.1081450>

Hopkinson, Christopher 2013. Trolling in Online Discussions: From Provocation to Community Building. *Brno Studies in English* 39/1, 5-25.

Howard, Phil / Duffy, Aiden / Hussain, Muzammil / Mari, Will / Mazaid, Marwa 2011. Opening Closed Regimes: What Was the Role of Social Media During the Arab Spring? 17 (Project on Info. Tech. & Political Islam, Univ. of Wash., Working Paper No. 2011.1, 2011), <http://philhoward.org/opening-closed-regimes-what-was-the-role-of-social-media-during-the-arab-spring/>

Howard, Phil / Hussain, Muzammil 2013. *Democracy's Fourth Wave? Digital Media and the Arab Spring*. Oxford, UK: Oxford University Press. doi:10.1093/acprof:oso/9780199936953.001.0001

Kelsey, Darren / Bennett, Lucy 2014. Discipline and Resistance on Social Media. *Discourse, Context & Media* 3, 37-45.

Krzyżanowski, Michał / Ledin, Per 2017. Uncivility on the Web. *Journal of Language and Politics* 16/4, 566-581.

Leech, Geoffrey 1983. *Principles of Pragmatics*. London: Longman.

Lim, Merlyna 2013. Framing Bouazizi: 'White Lies', Hybrid Network, and Collective/Connective Action in the 2010–11 Tunisian Uprising. *Journalism* 14/7, 921-941.

McGarty, Craig / Lala, Girish / Douglas, Karen 2011. Opinion-Based Groups: (Racist) Talk and (Collective) Action on the Internet. In Birchmeier, Zachary / Dietz-Uhler, Beth / Stasser, Garold (eds) *Strategic Uses of Social Technology. An Interactive Perspective of Social Psychology*. Cambridge: Cambridge University Press, 145-171.

McGarty, Craig / Bliuc, Anna-Maria / Thomas, Emma / Bongiorno, Renate 2009. Collective Action as the Material Expression of Opinion-Based Group Membership. *Journal of Social Issues* 65/4, 839-857.

McGarty, Craig / Thomas, Emma / Lala, Girish / Smith, Laura / Bliuc, Anna.-Maria 2014. New Technologies, New Identities, and the Growth of Mass Opposition in the Arab Spring. *Political Psychology* 35, 725-740. doi:10.1111/pops.12060

Nadeem, Nahla 2014. The Emergence of Politicized Collective Identity in Online News Commentaries as a Form of Social Capital. In Hickey, Dona / Essid, Joseph (eds) *Identity and Leadership in Virtual Communities: Establishing Credibility and Influence*. Hershey, PA: IGI Global, 47-60.

Perelmutter, Renee 2013. Klassika Zhanra: The Flamewar as a Genre in the Russian Blogosphere. *Journal of Pragmatics* 45/1, 74-89.

Russell, Adrienne 2011. *Networked: A Contemporary History of News in Transition*. Cambridge: Polity Press.

Simon, Bernd 2004. *Identity in Modern Society: A Social Psychological Perspective*. Oxford: Blackwell.

Simon, Bernd / Klandermans, Bert 2001. Politicized Collective Identity: A Social Psychological Analysis. *American Psychologist* 56/4, 319-331.

Smith, Laura / Thomas, Emma / McGarty, Craig 2015. "We Must Be the Change We Want to See in the World": Integrating Norms and Identities through Social Interaction. *Political Psychology* 36, 543-557. doi:10.1111/pops.12180

Spears, Russell / Lea, Martin 1992. Social Influence and the Influence of the 'Social' in Computer-Mediated Communication. In Lea, Martin (ed.) *Contexts of Computer-Mediated Communication. Hemel Hempstead.* England: Harvester Wheatsheaf, 30-65.

Spears, Russell / Lea, Martin 1994. Panacea or Panopticon? The Hidden Power in Computer-Mediated Communication. *Communication Research* 21, 427-459. doi:10.1177/009365094021004001

Víctor A. Meléndez

Social networks and the construction of political culture: Where are we looking from?

1 Introduction

The emergence of social networks has transformed the social environment and, consequently, our way of living, our way of understanding reality and, certainly, our way of building it. In this sense, technological development brings elements such as speed and the notion of immediacy, which obviously affect how we interpret the social space. However, it is interesting to ask: where do we observe society from and, consequently, from what standpoint do we interpret it? For this reason, the objective of this chapter is, on the one hand, to present a theoretical model that facilitates observation from complexity and, on the other hand, to explain the relationship between social networks and political culture using Puerto Rico as an example.

In this sense, when addressing the issue of social networks and the construction of political culture, there is a set of questions that are essential. In the first place, it is necessary to ask what social networks are, what they are for and what they are used for. Secondly, it is useful to think about what political culture is, what its scope is, what its purpose is, and what its relationship with social networks is. From this basic questioning I intend to present the bases for a conceptual scheme that I have named the Social Interpretation Complex (SIC). The SIC is a scheme of theoretical organization that facilitates the ordering and understanding of social complexity based on questions addressing the links between the spheres of social interaction. To achieve this, I have used the fusion of three conceptual schemes explained by Fraser (2008), Morin (2011) and Bronfenbrenner (1979). I have selected these authors, given the approach traditionally applied by the social sciences, which has addressed the formal and procedural nature of political interaction and leaves aside the social foundation that contextualizes these exchanges. In addition, I understand that beyond analyzing the usefulness of networks to offer results in terms of electoral participation, or political mobilization, it would be beneficial to reflect on what social networks represent in the contemporary world and what they say about our society.

The nature and internal coherence of the SIC must first be explained in order to facilitate its use as a conceptual tool. The first step within this construction of social interpretation responds, to a large extent, to the political imaginary of Nancy Fraser (2008) who uses the triad politics, economy and culture to pursue her analysis on the fundamental requirements for enhancing social justice scenarios. From her point of observation, Fraser built up each sphere according to a need or social link. For example, the economic sphere addressed issues of distribution and redistribution of resources within the social complex. The political sphere observed elements of social representation and the individual-State relationship. Finally, the cultural aspect was linked to the recognition factor, which inevitably results in the fact that to generate spaces for social justice, it is essential to analyze the levels of economic distribution, political representation and identity construction linked to the cultural and social recognition of the people or groups involved.

However, within the SIC, this triad works as a malleable and adaptable base for the observed phenomenon. And, of course, it sets out from the premise that everything that affects the political sphere will necessarily impact the other two. That being the case, what affects the cultural and economic aspects, respectively, will have an impact on the rest of the model. It is a broad, binding and interconnected base that deals with the relationships and links between the different spheres of social interaction. Now, this binding nucleus, in order to maximize its scope and attention to complexity, incorporates the three basic principles of the complexity paradigm of Morin (2011). These are the dialogical, the recursive and the hologrammatic principle. What does this imply? That the interrelation between the political, economic and cultural spheres occurs in a context that admits contradiction, since the dialogic principle states that those concepts that are apparently contradictory are necessarily complementary. In this sense, contradiction does not represent a problem within this interpretive framework. Likewise, the cyclical and changing nature of phenomena is recognized in the principle of recursion which allows that the product of a certain relationship is, at the same time, the producer of that which has produced it. From this lens, the phenomenon observed not only admits the contradiction, but also values the transformation and recursive variability of the social process. This moves us inexorably to examine the relevance of the hologrammatic principle, which proposes a special relationship between generality and particularity when it recognizes that the part is in the whole and the whole is in the part. This statement makes the interconnection between culture, politics and economy even more tangible because they are all part of social ties that contradict and cooperate in unison.

So far, the relationships defined are of a horizontal nature, so to speak. They are established links between fields that seem to be different but contiguous. For this reason, I have incorporated the levels of social interaction devised by Bronfenbrenner (1979) in order to provide depth and height for the SIC. In his theory of the Ecology of Human development, the author distinguishes between different levels of social interaction; the microsystem, mesosystem, exosystem and macrosystem. In each of these, the individual interacts with people or groups that influence or condition (in some way) his/her development. From the perspective of the SIC, the categories are not constructed in the same sense as in Bronfenbrenner's model because we are not interested properly in his categorization of spaces, but rather in the recognition of the existence of interactional spheres that can go from the cellular level to international or even intergalactic relationships. Everything depends on the observed phenomenon and the scope that the researcher wants to grant to it.

The Social Interpretation Complex (SIC) (Fig. 1) is a conceptual tool that seeks to facilitate the recognition of relationships and interdisciplinary links. Its objective is not to apply a rationalizing order to the phenomenon studied but to recognize its scope. It does not seek to mold reality to a set of norms or theoretical notions, so its purpose is not to reduce or delimit a topic but rather the opposite. It seeks to find and, above all, recognize relationships to describe them in the most complex way possible, provided that the pertinent questions are asked. It is an

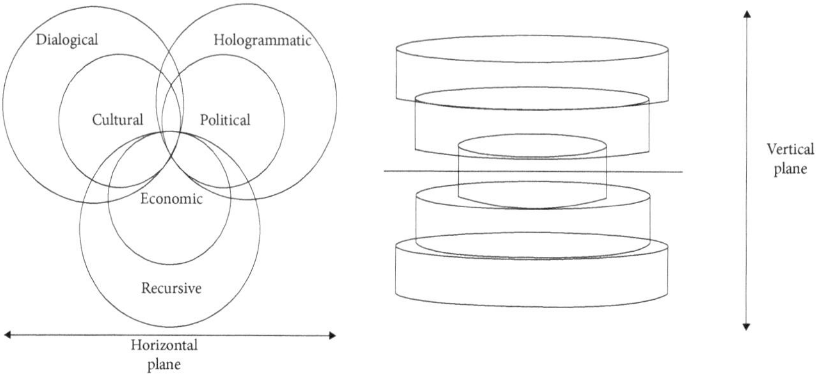

Fig. 1: Social Interpretation Complex (SIC) conceptual representation elaborated by the author.

ideal analysis model for research carried out in groups, or for interdisciplinary research teams.

In the following section a very general summary of the recent political history of Puerto Rico will be offered in order to create a context on which to build an analysis. The idea is to provide a basis that includes diverse bibliographical sources so that the reader can corroborate what is set out here and reinforce its structure of analysis.

2 The case of Puerto Rico

The Puerto Rican social reality is especially complicated because Puerto Rico is representative of the complexity and ambiguity of the contemporary era. Puerto Rico is a country that at the same time does not exist as such. It has a culture produced by centuries of domination but that still cannot be completely dominated or encapsulated. In the economic sphere, the country has been facing a recession since 2005 and in 2019 it faces substantial challenges to maintain a functioning government after the passage of Hurricane Maria in September 2017 and the creation of the Fiscal Control Board[1]. The FCB is an organism created by the Congress of the United States with authority to exercise powers comparable to those of the local government, thus forming a parallel government without democratic recognition whose purpose is to ensure the collection of a multi-million-dollar public debt of questionable constitutional legality[2].

However, in the face of this panorama of fiscal austerity, the underground economy and drug trafficking continue to sustain patterns of consumption incompatible with the reality facing the island. It should be noted that the country, according to the United States Census, has around 3,195,153 inhabitants. Of these, 40 % belong to the workforce and 36 % of them are employed, in jobs that belong mostly to the service sector, management and sales. This implies that the size of the welfare state is considerable, which generates specific behavioral patterns. To all of this we should add the urban organization, the influence of the American ghetto culture, the prominence of reggaeton and trap, and the systematic impoverishment of the educational system. All of this represents a difficult base on which to build scenarios of social justice. In this sense, all the information obtained through social networks comes from a socio-political and cultural background that sustains and molds it. Since the presence of mobile devices is growing and life is transmitted through social networks, they offer an accumulation of special information for the analysis of the sociopolitical reality of the country. For this reason, a brief historical[3] summary will be presented to facilitate the contextualization of the information that will be discussed further on.

In 1900, after the invasion of 1898, the United States passed the Foraker Law that established the colonial bases of its relationship with the unincorporated territory of Puerto Rico. Once the provisions that would regulate the territory and subject it to federal jurisdiction, or ownership were presented, in 1917 the US government approved the

1 For consultation of the law project visit: <https://www.congress.gov/114/crpt/hrpt602/CRPT-114hrpt602-pt1.pdf>

2 For more opinions, see Abreu (2017), NotiCel Suplemento (2017), Pérez Mendez (2019), Yera (2018).

3 For more detail view: Ayala and Bernabé (2011), Rivera (2007)

Jones Act. This law unilaterally granted US citizenship to every Puerto Rican born on the island and established the basis for the adoption of the presidential political system, similar to that of the United States, through the creation of the three branches of state power: legislative, executive and judicial. In 1950, the US Congress produced Law 600 that empowered the people of Puerto Rico to draft their own constitution, a constitution that maintains in force the territorial clauses of the Foraker law, the commercial and tariff restrictions of the Jones Act and the cloned ordering of the North American political institutions.

After the constitution of the Commonwealth of Puerto Rico was ratified in 1952 by the United States Congress, a series of nationalist riots and quarrels began in the country that led to acts of violence against institutions such as the Congress of the United States, and Blair House, which is the official presidential guest house in Washington DC. This facilitated the passage of the so-called Mordaza Law (Gagging Law), an ordinance that restricted expressions against the local and US government, which made possible the incarceration of many nationalist leaders in Puerto Rican and American prisons. In 1954, section 936[4] of the Internal Revenue Code of the United States was issued. This section facilitated the establishment of US companies, particularly financial, manufacturing and pharmaceutical companies, in Puerto Rico, thanks to incentives and tax exemptions. During this period, the Puerto Rican economy grew gradually until 1993 when section 936 was eliminated by President Bill Clinton. From this date, the deficiencies and limitations of the country's socioeconomic and political model became evident. It was precisely during the years 1993–2000, under the administration of Governor Pedro Rosselló, that the political culture took the shape that it exhibits today.

The imaginary of dependence on the United States, the need for a strong and restrictive paternalistic leadership, the lack of citizen participation beyond the electoral exercise, and dependence on the state apparatus of services are elements that characterize the Puerto Rican sociopolitical reality. At the same time, these aspects converge with broad levels of distrust towards public institutions, a product of years of

4 See Melendez (1994), Martínez Borrás (2014).

poor administration, added to a sustained discursive bombardment that highlights the benefits of privatization. This mistrust is linked to scales of values anchored in consumption and individual benefit, and leads to the society we can observe today. In what follows, some information will be offered about a concept that, in my opinion, conditions all the political debate in the country: statehood. This concept refers to the possibility of the incorporation of Puerto Rico in the federated union of the United States. The discourses on statehood present two trends that will be discussed in the next section.

3 Two currents of statehood: populist statehood and neoliberalist statehood

The imaginary of statehood is not a novel phenomenon in Puerto Rico, it rather responds to a historical tradition and to a line of thought constituted more than a century ago. However, for the purposes of this discussion we will focus on the notion of statehood from 1967, after the founding of the New Progressive Party (PNP), a party that advocates the annexation of Puerto Rico to the United States. Likewise, it is important to remember that this party arose in the twilight of the Bootstrap Operation[5] promoted by former Popular Democratic Party (PPD)[6] Governor Luis Muñoz Marín during the 1940s. This was a program of economic development that changed the way of life on the island completely, in just about twenty years. During the 1940s and 1960s, Puerto Rico went from being a largely rural and agricultural country to a highly industrialized urban country linked to the US economy and its

5 See Ayala. C y Bernabe, R. (2011), Democracy at Work (2018), Ruiz Toro (2013), Santana D. (1998).

6 The Popular Democratic Party is a center-right political party that advocates maintaining the island's status quo. It argues that the Commonwealth is a formula of government that allows to enjoy self-government and the benefits of a political-economic relationship with the United States. However, the party is divided between the traditionalist current and a (minimal) wing of sovereignty advocates.

model of production. In this sense, the depth of these changes naturally extended to all areas of life in society, which affected the political, economic and cultural spheres.

In 1968, after the decline in economic growth and the passage of two years of PPD administration, Luis A. Ferré, leader and founder of the PNP, came to power. This date marked the beginning of a new era of populism, because while the populism of the PPD went hand in hand with the slogan "bread, land and freedom" the message of the PNP was to emphasize a closer relationship with the United States. This even reached levels of considerable dependence, as expressed in the popular car stickers that read: "where would we be without it" in reference to the American flag. This new phase of populism occurred in a postwar social context characterized by a rapid process of cultural, economic and imminently political transformation. In this sense, the government of Luis A. Ferré introduced into the political plane what, in my opinion, is the most problematic idea within the Puerto Rican social imaginary, namely, the idea that Puerto Rico can be a state of the United States.

I have selected problematic as an adjective, not in terms of my acceptance or contempt for the idea of annexation, but because of the effect it has had as an element of civic disruption and alienation, which will be discussed later. On the other hand, the period of government by the PNP (1968–1972) was marked by the birth of different pro-independence groups that repudiated the presence of the United States on the island. These groups, some of a student or academic nature, unleashed protests and acts of violence against the State and the ROTC, better known as the USA's Army cadet program within the public university. These confrontations provoked great social tensions and internal divisions in the main political parties (PNP and PPD). As a consequence of this instability, the PPD returned to the governorship in 1972, although in 1976 the PNP took power again at the hands of Carlos Romero Barceló.

During this administrative period, from 1976 to 1984, two phenomena occurred that shaped the socio-political and economic development of the country. The first was the monumental increase in the flow of federal funds to the island through food stamps and other programs, which increased from 500 to 6000 million dollars during the 1970s and 1990s (Ayala/Bernabe: 2011). Secondly, the consolidation of the State as the country's main employer, which doubled its employing capacity during these years. From this period on, a social imaginary was built in which the government was seen as a paternalistic organism that "must solve the problems" of the people. At the same time, the federal government gained supporters because it was seen as a "organism for salvation" while the average citizen ignored the real causes of the cyclical recessions that affected the country, causes that reside in the legal scaffolding of the colonial reality affecting the political-economic spectrum, which results in a complex love-hate relationship in the cultural sphere.

Throughout these eight years a social reality was constructed from what we could call a kind of statehood populism. The population was subjected to a media bombardment that triggered psychological and emotional responses fueled by material and economic causes. During these years the dependent society was consolidated, or as it is known in Puerto Rico, "the Welfare society"[7], a situation that was aggravated during the recession of 1981–1983, which together with other political problems cost Romero Barceló his governorship at the hands of the PPD. However, in 1992 the PNP returned to power, this time with the impulse of Pedro Roselló. This period maintained the populist base as still dependent on the "attainable" imaginary of statehood, but was differentiated by its neoliberal orientation. This trend was consistent with the US agenda of the time and sought to demonize the public services that, during the period from 1976 to 1984, had proliferated massively with the party's encouragement.

This new political-economic orientation used the privatization of institutions as a management tool, arguing that a public sector as large as that of Puerto Rico hindered business development and impaired the competitive value of the island (Ayala/Bernabe 2011). Considering that the government's main strategy was to attract foreign investment, its economic policy was aimed, mainly, against trade unionism and worker's unions, which generated important clashes and social convulsions. This whirlwind change, characterized by health system reforms, the sale of the Puerto Rico Telephone Company, the fight against the United States Navy on the island municipality of Vieques, and two plebiscites (1993

7 *Sociedad del mantengo* in Spanish.

and 1998) in which statehood was defeated, eventually found its closure with serious accusations of corruption against the Roselló administration. This dynamic was normalized in future decades, in which even the federal government intervened through institutions such as the FBI to dismantle corruption schemes organized by both parties.

After Roselló's departure, the PPD occupied power until 2008 when the PNP returned with Luis Fortuño as governor. However, the policies of a neoliberal type did not stop during the PPD administration and, as of 2008, with Luis Fortuño, this approach was intensified. Under his administration, the so-called Law 7[8] or the *Special Law Declaring a State of Fiscal Emergency and Establishing an Integral Fiscal Stabilization Plan to Save the Credit of Puerto Rico* was approved. This bill consisted of a gesture of "good faith" toward the bondholders to whom Puerto Rico still owes over 70 billion dollars. This legislation facilitated the closure and consolidation of public institutions, which resulted in the dismissal of around 10,000 public employees and the reduction of services to citizens. To this is added the establishment of the Faith Base Offices, which clearly violate the separation of church and state, the hardening of prison sentences in most crimes, and the consideration of adultery, abortion and social protest as crimes.[9]

This mixture of tightening legal controls, increased religious fundamentalism, and economic insecurity generated a social pressure pump that exploded through the underground economy and drug trafficking. The year 2011 was the most violent in history, with 1,135 violent deaths in a country of 3.4 million inhabitants. From my point of view, this four-year period marked a precedent for Puerto Rico both politically and economically, but above all, culturally, that reshaped life on the island. The next four years led by the PPD under Alejandro García Padilla (2012–2016) evidenced the deep crisis that the party was going through and the scarce governmental capacity they have. To this was added the final thrust issued by the Supreme Court of the United States in 2016, where in its resolution of the case Puerto Rico vs. Sánchez

8 For more detail see Santiago (2016) y <http://www.lexjuris.com/lexlex/leyes2009/lexl2009007.htm>

9 See: <https://www.noticel.com/ahora/las-leyes-ms-controversiales-del-cuatrienio-fortuo/608032583>

Valle, it determined that the Commonwealth of Puerto Rico (ELA) does not have its own sovereignty and therefore the federal government is the competent institution to exercise powers over the island. This opinion belies the myth of ELA as an independent, self-sufficient and egalitarian government. Faced with this crisis of identity, the PNP returned to power in 2016, but this time under the leadership of Ricardo Rossello, son of ex-governor Pedro Roselló.

This administration still governs the country at the time of writing and has been mainly responsible for the recovery of the island after the passage of Hurricane Maria in September 2017, a catastrophic event that impacted a country with a poor political structure, a worse physical infrastructure and with an economy in default under the tutelage of President Trump. The base of statehood populism persists, in which Puerto Rico aspires to be a state through the application of formulas of economic austerity and policies that actually undermine the productive consolidation of the country and promote political models alien to self-determination.

4 Twitter and the Puerto Rican political culture

The previous section, in a very general way, sketched out a sociopolitical context on which the discussion below will be developed. In this section we will devote ourselves to reflect on the relationship between social networks, especially Twitter, and Puerto Rican political culture. In the first place, I consider it appropriate to point out that the political culture is necessarily the by-product of the broader relationships that shape the socio-cultural environment of a country. In other words, the way in which people relate to power, to politics, is closely related to how that society is organized or wired. It is necessary to understand what the scales of values are, what the different dynamics of socialization are, how language is constructed and, consequently, how the social imaginary is shaped to offer some sort of responsible explanation.

In this perspective, we must recognize the social function of Twitter within this sociocultural context. Of course, Twitter works as a channel for disseminating ideas, as a platform for diffusion and image creation, as a generator of public opinion or even as a scenario for personal battles. It is a virtual platform that, while generating new forms of socialization, also replicates behaviors that are very specific to each society. It is a space that gives a new dimension to the notion of public sphere[10] and in turn generates new problems of scope. Similarly, it should be noted that the use of Twitter in Puerto Rico is minimal[11], covering less than 10 % of the population, compared to Facebook. However, the use made by politicians of these platforms is generally informative, or related to public image management, so there are few major differences in the contents published in these two applications. Such social media data, at the same time, offers information about the behavior or culture of the citizenship because people are inclined to access social networks where they can restrict access to their own publications but, in turn, interact freely with public figures. This phenomenon is especially illustrative of the contradictions that are experienced within the Puerto Rican political culture, a culture that embraces privacy with respect to one's own image but investigates the privacy of the 'other'.

In this sense, University of Puerto Rico Professor Roberto Gándara Sánchez (2014) succinctly summarizes the generality of the political culture of the island in these lines:

> Broadly speaking, Puerto Rico is characterized by a broad participation, especially electoral, of all social sectors. At the same time, this massive participation occurs, ironically, in an institutional context over which Puerto Ricans show little confidence. For example, they support the regime of the political parties in which, simultaneously, they say they do not trust. However, the empirical evidence of the important role played by partisan loyalty in the public sphere suggests that the vote is more marked every day by the personal evaluation of the candidates and by

10 See authors as Dahlgren, Benker, Castells, Lewis, Papacharissi, Hilbert, Boulliane and Marcinkowski.

11 Considering that the approximate number of active Twitter accounts is around 300,000 in a country of 3.2 million inhabitants. <https://www.metro.pr/pr/sin-categoria/2013/03/25/aumenta-el-uso-de-twitter-en-puerto-rico.html>

considerations of family continuity and personal interests and links, than for the confidence in the parties.

From this approach, the personalist character of Puerto Rican culture and the value of family tradition and ideology stand out. Something related to this phenomenon can be found in Fig. 2:

In the first tweet published by Ricardo Rosselló, current governor of the country, he shows his son inside the executive's office and says: *Working with my little partner; he's messing around with everything*. This publication has multiple purposes from the symbolic, family, cultural and above all political point of view. First, the child's public exposure sends multiple messages to the public. On the one hand, it responds to an image of responsibility and family unity that is very important for the Puerto Rican. It is, in a certain way, the reaffirmation of Rosselló's commitment to the future of Puerto Rico, hand in hand with an image of sacrifice and surrender to the country. He shows his son in the public sphere and mixes him with other popular affairs, in an image implying trust in the 'people'. This is the stage set for a politician who is responsible for the future and lives without resting, without giving in, even sacrificing the most important thing: the family. But of

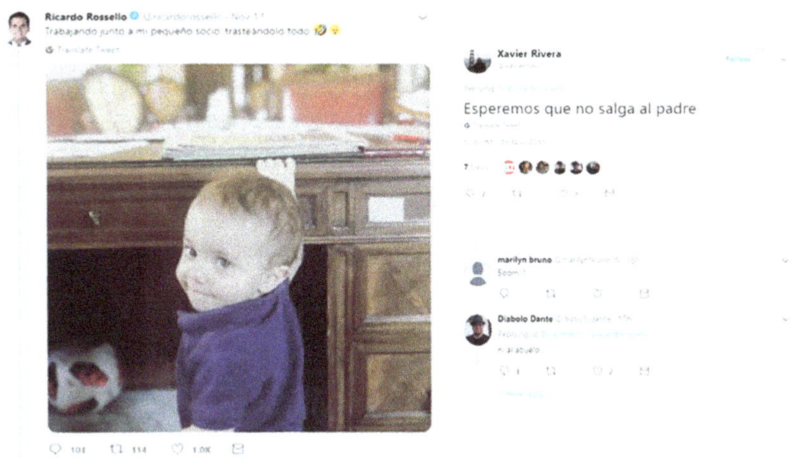

Fig. 2: Twitter interaction: Example of Puerto Rican political culture.

course, these are only some potential readings of the post in question. There is the possibility that he simply appreciated the tender image and decided to share it. The fact is that the intentionality behind this publication, in this world of immediacy and image, is increasingly uncertain. Because in the social reality of today, interests, notions and expectations converge regarding the value of information and privacy that are not always rational.

However, Xavier Rivera's comment, on the right, creates distances from any political or symbolic depth and is reduced to personal character: *Let's hope he does not grow up to be like his father*. This criticism is directed, mainly, towards the person of the governor. It would be possible to infer a negative evaluation of Rosselló's administrative work during the post-Maria crisis. Or maybe Rivera is a militant of the opposition party (PPD) and participates in the political polarization so common in the country. This bipartisan polarization is perpetuated through personal attacks and disqualifications, and its proponents are oblivious to political reasoning in any sociopolitical context.

Along the same lines, Diabolo Dante responds: *Nor to his grandfather*, making a clear personalist allusion to former Governor Pedro Roselló. This allows us to infer the distrust generated by this family after the corruption scandals that characterized that administration. In this sense, the criticisms made do not address the quality of political processes, assess the performance of parties or offer arguments or information. But rather they are reduced to a visceral and twisted attack. The political debate, after being reduced to personal criticism, gets depoliticized and loses any validity of thought for social construction. Then, the debate stops, and degenerates into a crossfire of nonsensical insults and absurd reasoning, producing social fractures that boost the political-partisan agendas that tend to affect most those who suffer the fracture. It represents the degradation from living in a political society to living in a "politicking"[12] society, a concept used in Puerto Rico to describe a policy lacking important meanings, depth or serious approaches.

Within the politicking, and thanks to the perceived mediocrity of the officials and other discourses produced throughout modern history,

---

12 *Politiquería* in Spanish

the citizenry has developed a profound distrust of public institutions, but at the same time exhibits a dependence on these figures of power and authority. This is a kind of symbiotic relationship that feeds on the deterioration of the economic situation, the crisis of governability and governance that the country is experiencing. It is a form of paternalism in which the country craves more power, authority or 'hard hand'[13] on the part of the rulers, but at the same time resents it. Something similar happened with the Fiscal Control Board, when a large part of the population endorsed its creation by the United States Congress, thinking that politicians would have to 'walk straight'[14]. But what they failed to interpret was that this political body is the representation of the deficiencies in matters of sovereignty and self-government that the country has. A large part of the public did not perceive the real and evident fact that Puerto Rico does not govern itself and that this, to a large extent, is the main cause of its economic and socio-political disaster. This, in a certain way, evidences a problem experienced by contemporary countries that have democracies without citizens (Camps 2010). This problem could be interpreted as a by-product of the labor society and the structure of education that has gradually generated an idea that the political is something distant, a matter for institutions and public officials, when in fact it is everyone's responsibility.

Within this spectrum, it is evident that to define the political culture of a country it is necessary to know its history. In the case of Puerto Rico, we observe a country that today does not manage to consolidate its sovereignty and its political leaders do not really pursue this goal either. This, to a large extent, is due to the lack of citizen maturity in the Kantian sense. Puerto Rico is a country that has been subjected to dependency regimes for more than 500 years and that today shows no signs of political maturity. This is in part because it has an educational system that fails miserably when it comes to providing tools

---

13 *Mano dura* in Spanish: It was a program oriented to the hardening of prison sentences and strengthening the police force in the country to fight crime under the administration of Pedro Rosselló. Little by little, the concept became a key element when referring to authoritarian processes or opinions. For example: "You have to have a hard hand", means not giving in, being implacable, firm, compliant.

14 *Caminar derechito* in Spanish. It means to behave properly.

in socio-political training and the development of critical thinking. In addition, the future of the country rests on a citizen's majority that delegates its civic responsibility to the institutions, that observes and values the politicians for their personal qualities, and that limits their participation in elections. This is also explained by Professor Gándara Sánchez (2014):

> [. . .] the electoral political participation is valued, there is very little confidence in the other forms of direct political participation that are common in other democratic countries, such as the right to petition, citizen (community) initiatives, the strike or the boycott. The authoritarian tradition experienced by Puerto Ricans since the Spanish Empire (and which was later privileged by the administrative institutions imposed by the United States) explains, in part, why they are interested in participating in the selection of its rulers (by vote), but not in challenging or questioning their authority once elected. It is thought that a good attribute of the rulers is, precisely, their ability to impose their authority on the political life (and institutions) of the country.

This reality is intertwined with the fact that US citizenship functions as an escape valve in the face of the crisis facing the country, since it facilitates mass migration[15] to the United States when living conditions deteriorate on the island. This phenomenon at present represents a problem for the future development of the country, and works as an incentive to deter citizens from overseeing the government's performance and working to build responsible and efficient public institutions.

On the other hand, it is evident that the colonial context alone is insufficient to explain the Puerto Rican political culture. In fact, these general provisions cannot even be considered as constituting the Puerto Rican political culture, because this hides in itself multiple realities, worldviews and symbolisms. Nonetheless, it offers distinctive patterns that are repeated in daily coexistence and are replicated in some way in social networks. Another aspect that stands out is, in the words of Gándara Sánchez, tolerance of injustice. In some way, social networks allow people to vent dissatisfaction in different situations, but this feeling does not usually transcend the virtual sphere into action. In this matter, social networks function as another type of escape valve that

---

15 See Duany (2002a; 2002b) and Sutter (2018).

offers a sense of belonging (Bauman 2007) and existence in the social environment. They help the citizenship to fulfill its basic need to 'feel heard'. It is the cultural dimension that Fraser (2008) spoke of when establishing recognition as an important value to promote social justice. On the other hand, this recognition of peers contrasts with the lack of political representation, both locally and in the United States, where important determinations do not depend on Puerto Rican political actors and citizen complaints persist in the digital sphere. This inevitably results in an economic/redistribution inequality, represented in the post Maria response, which demonstrates the asymmetric power bond that unites Puerto Rico to the United States.

5 Conclusions

As a result of the above, it is notable that the Puerto Rican virtual reality expresses the confluence between the political, economic and cultural spheres. The complexity exhibited within these three areas is maximized when we consider that different social phenomena feed off one another as they affect different spaces. These areas range from the psychological, the evaluative, the spiritual, the construction of power relations, the development of pedagogical structures, the relationship with the environment and with social organization among others. In the same way, we have observed a series of interactions of a vertical nature when relating individuals with diverse socio-economic and political backgrounds in an ocean of symbols and interpretations. All this, in my opinion, is a manifestation of the convergence between ideological systems, political actors, citizen agents, partisan agendas, cultural experiences, future expectations and limitations of the macrosocial system, interwoven in a cyclical process in which both individuals and institutions feed on their by-products. This leads the latter to many representative forms such as artistic, literary, musical and academic production and, of course, both private and public discursive construction.

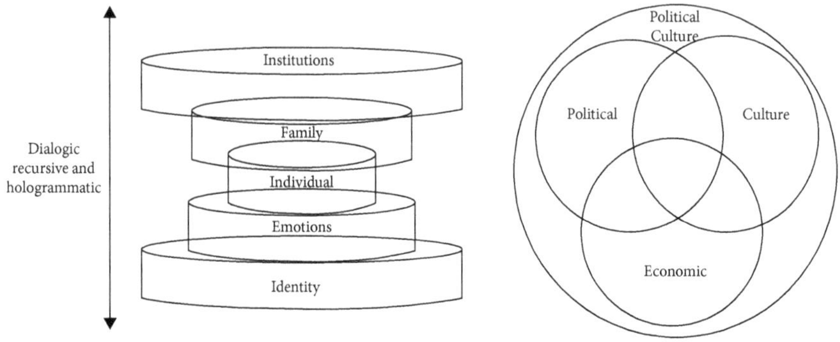

Fig. 3: Conceptual example of SIC application.

In this network of relationships we can understand how the Social Interpretation Complex (SIC) facilitates the deconstruction of a seemingly trivial scene and favors the inclusion of elements that are apparently absent in the analysis (Fig. 3). This allows us to navigate from the individual-personal perspective to the socio-political reality and the relationship between Puerto Rico and the United States, without forgetting the role of the local government as intermediary agent and producer of cultural discourses and symbols. In a certain sense, this prism offered by the SIC makes possible the detection of links between phenomena or elements that transversally move across the three spheres of the social environment. For the political, the economic and the cultural are everywhere, since the whole is in the part and the part in the whole. Thus, this transversality resides within each of the elements that make it up and it feeds on the recursiveness that is born from their interactions. However, it should be noted that the SIC is only a lens through which to interpret society and cannot explain the whole of it, since the ability to order the amalgam of relationships exhibited by the environment escapes the limits of the human mind's structure.

On the other hand, we must not forget the role of social networks within the social fabric. In this specific case, Twitter works as an arena in which debates, symbols and imaginary constructions converge. It is a very useful platform for creating images and manipulating public opinion. Although, obviously, it is used according to the cultural parameters of the recipient society, which allows the replication of patterns of socialization visible in everyday life. And in other cases, it allows the creation of unique dynamics of the network which also have an effect on everyday life's construction. It is the representation of the rapid development of the society of immediacy. It is the paradigm of the now, of the immediate, of the ephemeral, that at the same time generates information that can be reached and persists in databases, which allow its corroboration. The explosion of social networks has made possible the birth of a massive flow of information that, linked to the imaginary of post-truth and the presence of algorithms, presents serious challenges for the development of a critical political debate.

Nevertheless, this type of contradiction or phenomenon requires the work of interdisciplinary research teams, with approaches that address complexity and avoid building from rationalization. It is important to develop more group work of an inter- and transdisciplinary character that transcends the limits of the academic disciplines. In short, it is necessary to look with different eyes, with another understanding that focuses on the links, relationships and interconnectivity between actors, processes and flows, because the changes in media necessarily represent a change in social behavior and therefore a potential change in social structures and imaginaries.

References

Abreu, Luis F. 2017. No es legítimo pagar deuda ilegal. *El Nuevo Día*. 13 April. <https://www.elnuevodia.com/opinion/columnas/noeslegitimopagardeudailegal-columna-2310428/>

Ayala, Cesar / Bernabe, Rafael 2011. *Puerto Rico en el siglo americano: Su historia desde 1898*. San Juan, Puerto Rico: Ediciones Callejón.

Bauman, Zygmunt 2007. *Vida de Consumo*. Mexico: Fondo de Cultura Económica.

Bronfenbrenner, Urie 1979. *The Ecology of Human Development: Experiments by Nature and Design*. Cambridge, MA: Harvard University Press.

Camps, Victoria 2010. *Democracia sin ciudadanos: La construcción de la ciudadanía en las democracias liberales*. Barcelona: Trotta.

Democracy at Work 2018. *Puerto Rico Forward: Operation Bootstrap (Manos a la obra)* [Video file]. <https://www.youtube.com/watch?v=zsl0ePhtDso&vl=en>

Duany, Jorge 2002a. Nación, migración, identidad. *Revista Nueva Sociedad* 178/1, 56-69.

Duany, Jorge 2002b. Más allá de la válvula de escape: Tendencias recientes en la migración caribeña. *Nueva Sociedad* 127, 80-99.

Fraser, Nancy 2008. *Scales of Justice: Reimagining Political Space in a Globalizing World*. Cambridge, UK / Malden, MA: Polity.

Gándara, Roberto 2014. *La cultura política de Puerto Rico*. <https://enciclopediapr.org/encyclopedia/la-cultura-politica-de-puerto-rico/>

Martínez Borrás, José G. 2014. *Section 936*. <https://enciclopediapr.org/en/encyclopedia/section-936-of-the-internal-revenue-code/>

Melendez, Edwin / Blum, Jorge 1994. *The tax elasticity of Section 936 investment in Puerto Rico*. Boston: Mauricio Gaston Institute, University of Massachusetts. Mimeo. <http://economia.uprrp.edu/The%20Tax%20Elasticity%20of%20Section%20936%20Investment%20in%20Puerto%20Rico.pdf>

Morin, Edgar 2011. *Introducción al pensamiento complejo*. Barcelona: Gedisa.

NotiCel Suplemento 2017. *¿Por qué la deuda es ilegal?* <https://www.noticel.com/auspiciado/por-qu-la-deuda-es-ilegal/609408609>

Pérez Méndez, Osman 2019. *Si parte de la deuda es ilegal "no se va a pagar" dice Rosselló*. <https://www.primerahora.com/noticias/gobierno-politica/nota/sipartedeladeudaesilegalnosevaapagardicerossello-1321455/>

Rivera, Israel 2007. *Puerto Rico ante los retos del siglo XXI: Cambio económico, cultural y político en los inicios del nuevo siglo*. San Juan, Puerto Rico: Ediciones Nueva Aurora.

Ruiz Toro, Juan 2013. Puerto Rico's Operation Bootstrap. In Skidmore, Thomas E. / Smith, Peter H. / Green, James Naylor (eds) *Modern Latin America*, 8a ed. New York: Oxford University Press.

Santana, Deborah 1998. Puerto Rico's Operation Bootstrap: Colonial Roots of a Persistent Model for "Third World" Development. *Revista Geográfica* 124, 87-116. <http://www.jstor.org/stable/40992748>

Santiago, Carlos 2016. Diez años de crisis, flexibilidad laboral y medidas de austeridad en Puerto Rico. *Revista Jurídica de los derechos sociales* 6/1, 201-240.

Sutter, John D. / Hernández, Sergio 2018. *La guía visual del éxodo en Puerto Rico: ¿a dónde están llegando sus habitantes?* <https://cnnespanol.cnn.com/2018/S02/23/puerto-rico-exodo-huracan-maria-estados-unidos-datos-fema-inmigracion/>

Yera, A. 2018. *Puerto Rico: Expertos piden auditoría integral para evitar pagar la deuda* [Blog post]. <http://www.cadtm.org/Puerto-Rico-Expertos-piden-auditoria-integral-para-evitar-pagar-la-deuda>

Notes on Contributors

MARIA CRISTINA AIEZZA is Post-Doctoral Research Fellow and Lecturer in English Language and Translation at the University of Sannio, Benevento, Department of Law, Economics, Management and Quantitative Methods. She holds a PhD in English for Specific Purposes from the University of Naples Federico II, with a corpus-assisted study on the discourse of sustainability reports in emerging and industrialised countries. Her research interests include institutional and corporate discourse, legal discourse, political discourse, popularisation, news media discourse, advertising, user-generated discourse, web genres and social media. Her recent works have analysed the genre of online promotional coupons, TripAdvisor customer-generated reviews, the management of Volkswagen corporate scandal, marketing and political messages over Twitter, the UK and EU discourse on Brexit, media discourses about President Trump's policies, environmental discourse and online petitionary discourse. She is currently conducting a research project on "Institutional and corporate communication and new media", which investigates promotional discourse and image management in the web 2.0 era.

MIGUEL AYERBE LINARES studied German Philology at the Universities of Seville and Cologne. He has a PhD on Germanic historical and comparative Linguistics. He is currently teaching at the University of the Basque Country / Euskal Herriko Unibertsitatea in Vitoria-Gasteiz, Spain. His research interests are Old Germanic linguistics and literatures, lexical issues in translation from Old German, and Discourse Analysis, focusing on the discourse of populist parties as well as the language used by other political parties talking about populism and populist parties in German speaking countries. He has also analysed the use of "Volk" by political parties in German speaking countries in order to interpret the referential content of this word, in terms of who is being included and who is not.

MUHAMMAD A. BADARNEH is Professor of Linguistics in the Department of English Language and Linguistics at Jordan University of Science and Technology, Jordan. His research resides within the intersection of language, culture, religion, and interaction. His main research interests include pragmatics, discourse analysis, politeness and impoliteness, online communication, social semiotics, and genre. He has published papers on Arabic discourse and interaction in leading international scholarly journals such as *Journal of Pragmatics, Language & Communication, Folia Linguistica, Humor: International Journal of Humor Studies, Social Semiotics, Text & Talk,* and *Applied Linguistics*. He has forthcoming chapters in edited volumes on formulaicity, politeness, positioning and identity in Jordanian Arabic.

ADITI BHATIA is Associate Professor at the Hong Kong Polytechnic University. Her main interest is in the area of (critical) discourse analysis, with particular reference to the study of public discourses. Her research employs a novel multiperspective theoretical framework, that of 'discursive illusions', on which she has published in a number of international *journals, including the Journal of Pragmatics, Journal of Language and Politics, Text & Talk, World Englishes,* and *Discourse & Society*, and her monograph, *Discursive Illusions in Public Discourse: Theory and Practice* (Routledge, 2015). She is now engaged in further extending the concept of discursive illusions by investigating the discourses of Public Square Movements and Digital Professions.

RUTH BREEZE is Senior Lecturer in English at the University of Navarra, Spain, and combines teaching in the Schools of Education and Law with research as Co-Principal Investigator of the GradUN Research Group in the Institute for Culture and Society. Her most recent books are the monograph *Corporate Discourse* (Bloomsbury Academic, 2015) and the co-edited volumes *Interpersonality in Legal Genres* (Peter Lang, 2014), *Essential Competencies for English-Medium University Teaching* (Springer, 2016), *Power, Persuasion and Manipulation in Specialised Genres* (Peter Lang, 2017), and *Imagining the Peoples of Europe: Populist Discourses across the Political Spectrum* (John Benjamins, 2019). She teaches and supervises PhD candidates in the area of language education and public discourse, and she has published widely on specialised languages and discourse analysis. She was Co-Principal Investigator of the project "DEMOS: Imagining the people in the new politics" (MINECO, 2016-2018), and her recent (2019) articles include "Emotion in politics: Affective-discursive practices in UKIP and Labour" in *Discourse & Society*, "Positioning the people and its enemies: Populism and nationalism in AfD and UKIP" in *Javnost – the Public*, and "Fixing points on a shifting landscape: truth, lies and politics in two reader comments pages" in *Journal of Language and Politics.*

ANA M. FERNÁNDEZ VALLEJO is Associate Professor at the Department of Communication at School of Management Assistants (University of Navarra), where she teaches Spanish for Academic and Professional Communication. She is a member of the Institute for Culture and Society as internal collaborator in the Public Discourse Project (GradUN). Her research focus is the interdisciplinary study of academic and professional discourse, and her interests include topics such as discourse linguistics, pragmatics and corpus linguistics. She is currently engaged in projects dealing with language and emotion in professional and political settings through digital media, and CSR discourse in digital media.

SAQLAIN HASSAN is a PhD scholar at the Institute for Culture and Society at the University of Navarra, Spain. His research interests include the study of media discourse through corpus-assisted discourse methodologies. He obtained an MA in "Language and Mind: Linguistics and Cognitive Studies" from the University of Siena, Italy where he gained specialized knowledge in discourse studies. Currently, he is writing his PhD thesis on the topic "The representation of Afghani refugees in the press". Saqlain is an Afghani/Pathan by origin and a Pakistani national, born in the Khyber Pakhtunkhwa province of Pakistan. He speaks Pashto, Urdu, Hindi, English, Italian and Spanish.

VÍCTOR A. MELÉNDEZ has a bachelor's degree in Political Science from the University of Puerto Rico, Rio Piedras Campus. In 2009 he undertook postgraduate studies on the sociology of migrations at the Complutense University of Madrid. He then studied for an MA at the University of Granada in "Peace Culture, Conflict, Education and Human Rights". In 2012 he returned to Puerto Rico to teach political science and sociology at undergraduate level in various universities there. He is currently a PhD student at the University of Navarra in the "Government and Culture of Organisations" program, and his thesis focuses on the topic of social networks and the construction of political culture in Puerto Rico. In addition, he is a collaborating student of the Institute of Culture and Society at the University of Navarra in the Public Discourse project (GradUN).

NAHLA NADEEM is an Associate Professor of Applied Linguistics at King Abdul Aziz University, Saudi Arabia. She has an MA and PhD in applied linguistics from Cairo University. Her research interests are narrative studies, political media and communication studies. Her latest publication explores the various uses of rhetorical devices as multimodal conceptual blends in TED Talks.

ANTONELLA NAPOLITANO is Researcher in English Language and Translation at the University of Sannio, Benevento, Italy, in the Department of Law, Economics, Management and Quantitative Methods. Before working fulltime at university, she taught at high school for many years, being involved in numerous innovative linguistic projects. Recently, she has channelled her energies into enhancing the Language Centre at the University of Sannio, exploiting her past experience in the organisation and management of language courses for university students, including PhD students and Italian school teachers of English. Her research interests and publications have centred on the field of ESP theory and applications, focusing on advertising, legal, corporate and institutional (especially EU) discourse, identity-building and gender studies. Some of her recent studies focus on gender and advertising, online customer reviews, the Volkswagen environmental scandal, security discourse, populist discourse, and discourse on President Trump. She is currently conducting research on "Institutional and corporate communication and new media".

ANDREW S. ROSS is Lecturer in the School of Education and Social Work at the University of Sydney, Australia. His research interests are interdisciplinary and varied, but include critical discourse studies, political communication, discourses of new media and sociolinguistics. His work has been published such venues as *Communication and Sport, The Language Learning Journal, Journal of Language, Identity and Education, Discourse, Context and Media, Journal of Pragmatics* and *Language and Dialogue*. He is the co-editor of the volume *The Sociolinguistics of Hip-Hop as Critical Conscience: Dissatisfaction and Dissent* (Palgrave, 2018) and *Discourses of (De)Legitimization: Participatory Culture in Digital Contexts* (Routledge, 2018).

DANIELA ROVENȚA-FRUMUȘANI is Emeritus Professor at the University of Bucharest, Romania, in the Department of Cultural Anthropology and Communication, College of Journalism and Communication Sciences. She is director of the French Master's Program "Media, Development, Society" (in collaboration with Lyon University Lumiere); she is also a member of the Doctoral School of Communication and has directed 15 PhD theses in communication science (focused on advertising, gender studies, and discourse analysis). A specialist in semiotics, gender studies and discourse analysis, she has authored 6 books, over 100 studies and articles in the above mentioned fields, and coordinated and edited 5 publications (books and international journals). She is a member of the ISA-RC14 (Sociology of Communication) board, and since 2010, of the SFSIC (French Society of the Information and Communication Sciences), IPrA (International Pragmatic Association), of the team of AUF experts of Central and Eastern Europe, and of the scientific committees of *Recherches feministes, Communication, Essachess, French Journal for Media Research*.

ALINE SCHMIDT is currently a Researcher at the Heidelberg Center for American Studies and affiliated to the English Department at the University of Heidelberg. She is a member of the interdisciplinary Research Training Group "Authority and Trust in American Culture, Society, History and Politics" funded by the German Research Foundation (DFG). In her PhD project, she combines classical sociology and discourse studies to develop a framework to explore the discursive formation of charismatic movements online during the Trump Presidency. Her research interests lie mostly in the area of (critical) corpus assisted discourse studies with a particular focus on American political discourse and trustbuilding practices. Furthermore, she is interested in urban linguistics and multimodal placemaking.

ADRIANA ŞTEFĂNEL is Assistant Professor in the Faculty of Journalism and Communication Studies, University of Bucharest, Romania. She holds two BA diplomas, one in Economy (2001, Babeş-Bolyai University) and the other in Sociology (2004, University of Bucharest), an MA diploma in Marketing and Business Communication (2004, Academy of Economic Sciences) and a PhD in Sociology (2011, University of Bucharest). She is interested in communication studies, social representation theory, nationalism and populism as styles of political communication, the political imaginary, and discourse analysis. Since 2005, she has published more than 20 articles in peer reviewed journals, book chapters, and conference proceedings; she has participated in more than 30 international conferences. Her PhD thesis was published by a highly esteemed Romanian publishing house. In 2016 she co-edited *Political Communication and European Parliamentary Elections in Times of Crisis: Perspectives from Central and SouthEastern Europe* published by Palgrave MacMillan, London.

GIORGOS VENIZELOS is a PhD candidate at the Department of Political and Social Sciences at the Scuola Normale Superiore in Florence and a member of the Centre on Social Movement Studies (COSMOS). His current research focuses on populism in power, political discourse and collective identities. He holds a BA in Politics from the University of Essex and an MA in International Studies from Goldsmiths, University of London.

Linguistic Insights

Studies in Language and Communication

This series aims to promote specialist language studies in the fields of linguistic theory and applied linguistics, by publishing volumes that focus on specific aspects of language use in one or several languages and provide valuable insights into language and communication research. A cross-disciplinary approach is favoured and most European languages are accepted.

The series includes two types of books:

- Monographs – featuring in-depth studies on special aspects of language theory, language analysis or language teaching.
- Collected papers – assembling papers from workshops, conferences or symposia.

Each volume of the series is subjected to a double peer-reviewing process.

Vol. 1 Maurizio Gotti & Marina Dossena (eds)
Modality in Specialized Texts. Selected Papers of the 1st CERLIS Conference.
421 pages. 2001. ISBN 3-906767-10-8 · US-ISBN 0-8204-5340-4

Vol. 2 Giuseppina Cortese & Philip Riley (eds)
Domain-specific English. Textual Practices across Communities and Classrooms.
420 pages. 2002. ISBN 3-906768-98-8 · US-ISBN 0-8204-5884-8

Vol. 3 Maurizio Gotti, Dorothee Heller & Marina Dossena (eds)
Conflict and Negotiation in Specialized Texts. Selected Papers of the 2nd CERLIS Conference.
470 pages. 2002. ISBN 3-906769-12-7 · US-ISBN 0-8204-5887-2

Vol. 4 Maurizio Gotti, Marina Dossena, Richard Dury, Roberta Facchinetti & Maria Lima
Variation in Central Modals. A Repertoire of Forms and Types of Usage in Middle English and Early Modern English.
364 pages. 2002. ISBN 3-906769-84-4 · US-ISBN 0-8204-5898-8

Editorial address:

Prof. Maurizio Gotti Università di Bergamo, Dipartimento di Lingue, Letterature e Culture Straniere Piazza Rosate 2, 24129 Bergamo, Italy
Fax: +39 035 2052789, E-Mail: m.gotti@unibg.it

Vol. 5 Stefania Nuccorini (ed.)
Phrases and Phraseology. Data and Descriptions.
187 pages. 2002. ISBN 3-906770-08-7 · US-ISBN 0-8204-5933-X

Vol. 6 Vijay Bhatia, Christopher N. Candlin & Maurizio Gotti (eds)
Legal Discourse in Multilingual and Multicultural Contexts.
Arbitration Texts in Europe.
385 pages. 2003. ISBN 3-906770-85-0 · US-ISBN 0-8204-6254-3

Vol. 7 Marina Dossena & Charles Jones (eds)
Insights into Late Modern English. 2nd edition.
378 pages. 2003, 2007.
ISBN 978-3-03911-257-9 · US-ISBN 978-0-8204-8927-8

Vol. 8 Maurizio Gotti
Specialized Discourse. Linguistic Features and Changing Conventions.
351 pages. 2003, 2005.
ISBN 3-03910-606-6 · US-ISBN 0-8204-7000-7

Vol. 9 Alan Partington, John Morley & Louann Haarman (eds)
Corpora and Discourse.
420 pages. 2004. ISBN 3-03910-026-2 · US-ISBN 0-8204-6262-4

Vol. 10 Martina Möllering
The Acquisition of German Modal Particles. A Corpus-Based Approach.
290 pages. 2004. ISBN 3-03910-043-2 · US-ISBN 0-8204-6273-X

Vol. 11 David Hart (ed.)
English Modality in Context. Diachronic Perspectives.
261 pages. 2003. ISBN 3-03910-046-7 · US-ISBN 0-8204-6852-5

Vol. 12 Wendy Swanson
Modes of Co-reference as an Indicator of Genre.
430 pages. 2003. ISBN 3-03910-052-1 · US-ISBN 0-8204-6855-X

Vol. 13 Gina Poncini
Discursive Strategies in Multicultural Business Meetings.
2nd edition. 338 pages. 2004, 2007.
ISBN 978-3-03911-296-8 · US-ISBN 978-0-8204-8937-7

Vol. 14 Christopher N. Candlin & Maurizio Gotti (eds)
Intercultural Aspects of Specialized Communication.
2nd edition. 369 pages. 2004, 2007.
ISBN 978-3-03911-258-6 · US-ISBN 978-0-8204-8926-1

Vol. 15 Gabriella Del Lungo Camiciotti & Elena Tognini Bonelli (eds)
Academic Discourse. New Insights into Evaluation.
234 pages. 2004. ISBN 3-03910-353-9 · US-ISBN 0-8204-7016-3

Vol. 16 Marina Dossena & Roger Lass (eds)
Methods and Data in English Historical Dialectology.
405 pages. 2004. ISBN 3-03910-362-8 · US-ISBN 0-8204-7018-X

Vol. 17 Judy Noguchi
The Science Review Article. An Opportune Genre in
the Construction of Science.
274 pages. 2006. ISBN 3-03910-426-8 · US-ISBN 0-8204-7034-1

Vol. 18 Giuseppina Cortese & Anna Duszak (eds)
Identity, Community, Discourse. English in Intercultural Settings.
495 pages. 2005. ISBN 3-03910-632-5 · US-ISBN 0-8204-7163-1

Vol. 19 Anna Trosborg & Poul Erik Flyvholm Jørgensen (eds)
Business Discourse. Texts and Contexts.
250 pages. 2005. ISBN 3-03910-606-6 · US-ISBN 0-8204-7000-7

Vol. 20 Christopher Williams
Tradition and Change in Legal English. Verbal Constructions in Prescriptive Texts.
2nd revised edition. 216 pages. 2005, 2007. ISBN 978-3-03911-444-3.

Vol. 21 Katarzyna Dziubalska-Kolaczyk & Joanna Przedlacka (eds)
English Pronunciation Models: A Changing Scene.
2nd edition. 476 pages. 2005, 2008. ISBN 978-3-03911-682-9.

Vol. 22 Christián Abello-Contesse, Rubén Chacón-Beltrán, M. Dolores López-Jiménez & M. Mar Torreblanca-López (eds)
Age in L2 Acquisition and Teaching.
214 pages. 2006. ISBN 3-03910-668-6 · US-ISBN 0-8204-7174-7

Vol. 23 Vijay K. Bhatia, Maurizio Gotti, Jan Engberg & Dorothee Heller (eds)
Vagueness in Normative Texts.
474 pages. 2005. ISBN 3-03910-653-8 · US-ISBN 0-8204-7169-0

Vol. 24 Paul Gillaerts & Maurizio Gotti (eds)
Genre Variation in Business Letters. 2nd printing.
407 pages. 2008. ISBN 978-3-03911-681-2.

Vol. 25 Ana María Hornero, María José Luzón & Silvia Murillo (eds)
Corpus Linguistics. Applications for the Study of English.
2nd printing. 526 pages. 2006, 2008. ISBN 978-3-03911-726-0

Vol. 26 J. Lachlan Mackenzie & María de los Ángeles Gómez-González (eds)
Studies in Functional Discourse Grammar.
259 pages. 2005. ISBN 3-03910-696-1 · US-ISBN 0-8204-7558-0

Vol. 27 Debbie G. E. Ho
Classroom Talk. Exploring the Sociocultural Structure of Formal ESL Learning.
2nd edition. 254 pages. 2006, 2007. ISBN 978-3-03911-434-4

Vol. 28 Javier Pérez-Guerra, Dolores González-Álvarez, Jorge L. Bueno-Alonso & Esperanza Rama-Martínez (eds)
'Of Varying Language and Opposing Creed'. New Insights into Late Modern English.
455 pages. 2007. ISBN 978-3-03910-788-9

Vol. 29 Francesca Bargiela-Chiappini & Maurizio Gotti (eds)
Asian Business Discourse(s).
350 pages. 2005. ISBN 3-03910-804-2 · US-ISBN 0-8204-7574-2

Vol. 30 Nicholas Brownlees (ed.)
News Discourse in Early Modern Britain. Selected Papers of CHINED 2004.
300 pages. 2006. ISBN 3-03910-805-0 · US-ISBN 0-8204-8025-8

Vol. 31 Roberta Facchinetti & Matti Rissanen (eds)
Corpus-based Studies of Diachronic English.
300 pages. 2006. ISBN 3-03910-851-4 · US-ISBN 0-8204-8040-1

Vol. 32 Marina Dossena & Susan M. Fitzmaurice (eds)
Business and Official Correspondence. Historical Investigations.
209 pages. 2006. ISBN 3-03910-880-8 · US-ISBN 0-8204-8352-4

Vol. 33 Giuliana Garzone & Srikant Sarangi (eds)
Discourse, Ideology and Specialized Communication.
494 pages. 2007. ISBN 978-3-03910-888-6

Vol. 34 Giuliana Garzone & Cornelia Ilie (eds)
The Use of English in Institutional and Business Settings.
An Intercultural Perspective.
372 pages. 2007. ISBN 978-3-03910-889-3

Vol. 35 Vijay K. Bhatia & Maurizio Gotti (eds)
Explorations in Specialized Genres.
316 pages. 2006. ISBN 3-03910-995-2 · US-ISBN 0-8204-8372-9

Vol. 36 Heribert Picht (ed.)
Modern Approaches to Terminological Theories and Applications.
432 pages. 2006. ISBN 3-03911-156-6 · US-ISBN 0-8204-8380-X

Vol. 37 Anne Wagner & Sophie Cacciaguidi-Fahy (eds)
Legal Language and the Search for Clarity / Le langage juridique et la quête de clarté. Practice and Tools / Pratiques et instruments.
487 pages. 2006. ISBN 3-03911-169-8 · US-ISBN 0-8204-8388-5

Vol. 38 Juan Carlos Palmer-Silveira, Miguel F. Ruiz-Garrido & Inmaculada Fortanet-Gómez (eds)
Intercultural and International Business Communication.
Theory, Research and Teaching.
2nd edition. 343 pages. 2006, 2008. ISBN 978-3-03911-680-5

Vol. 39 Christiane Dalton-Puffer, Dieter Kastovsky, Nikolaus Ritt & Herbert Schendl (eds)
Syntax, Style and Grammatical Norms. English from 1500–2000.
250 pages. 2006. ISBN 3-03911-181-7 · US-ISBN 0-8204-8394-X

Vol. 40 Marina Dossena & Irma Taavitsainen (eds)
Diachronic Perspectives on Domain-Specific English.
280 pages. 2006. ISBN 3-03910-176-0 · US-ISBN 0-8204-8391-5

Vol. 41 John Flowerdew & Maurizio Gotti (eds)
Studies in Specialized Discourse.
293 pages. 2006. ISBN 3-03911-178-7

Vol. 42 Ken Hyland & Marina Bondi (eds)
Academic Discourse Across Disciplines.
320 pages. 2006. ISBN 3-03911-183-3 · US-ISBN 0-8204-8396-6

Vol. 43 Paul Gillaerts & Philip Shaw (eds)
The Map and the Landscape. Norms and Practices in Genre.
256 pages. 2006. ISBN 3-03911-182-5 · US-ISBN 0-8204-8395-4

Vol. 44 Maurizio Gotti & Davide Giannoni (eds)
New Trends in Specialized Discourse Analysis.
301 pages. 2006. ISBN 3-03911-184-1 · US-ISBN 0-8204-8381-8

Vol. 45 Maurizio Gotti & Françoise Salager-Meyer (eds)
Advances in Medical Discourse Analysis. Oral and Written Contexts.
492 pages. 2006. ISBN 3-03911-185-X · US-ISBN 0-8204-8382-6

Vol. 46 Maurizio Gotti & Susan Šarcević (eds)
Insights into Specialized Translation.
396 pages. 2006. ISBN 3-03911-186-8 · US-ISBN 0-8204-8383-4

Vol. 47 Khurshid Ahmad & Margaret Rogers (eds)
Evidence-based LSP. Translation, Text and Terminology.
584 pages. 2007. ISBN 978-3-03911-187-9

Vol. 48 Hao Sun & Dániel Z. Kádár (eds)
It's the Dragon's Turn. Chinese Institutional Discourses.
262 pages. 2008. ISBN 978-3-03911-175-6

Vol. 49 Cristina Suárez-Gómez
Relativization in Early English (950-1250). the Position of Relative Clauses.
149 pages. 2006. ISBN 3-03911-203-1 · US-ISBN 0-8204-8904-2

Vol. 50 Maria Vittoria Calvi & Luisa Chierichetti (eds)
Nuevas tendencias en el discurso de especialidad.
319 pages. 2006. ISBN 978-3-03911-261-6

Vol. 51 Mari Carmen Campoy & María José Luzón (eds)
Spoken Corpora in Applied Linguistics.
274 pages. 2008. ISBN 978-3-03911-275-3

Vol. 52 Konrad Ehlich & Dorothee Heller (Hrsg.)
Die Wissenschaft und ihre Sprachen.
323 pages. 2006. ISBN 978-3-03911-272-2

Vol. 53 Jingyu Zhang
The Semantic Salience Hierarchy Model. The L2 Acquisition of Psych Predicates
273 pages. 2007. ISBN 978-3-03911-300-2

Vol. 54 Norman Fairclough, Giuseppina Cortese & Patrizia Ardizzone (eds)
Discourse and Contemporary Social Change.
555 pages. 2007. ISBN 978-3-03911-276-0

Vol. 55 Jan Engberg, Marianne Grove Ditlevsen, Peter Kastberg & Martin Stegu (eds)
New Directions in LSP Teaching.
331 pages. 2007. ISBN 978-3-03911-433-7

Vol. 56 Dorothee Heller & Konrad Ehlich (Hrsg.)
Studien zur Rechtskommunikation.
322 pages. 2007. ISBN 978-3-03911-436-8

Vol. 57 Teruhiro Ishiguro & Kang-kwong Luke (eds)
Grammar in Cross-Linguistic Perspective.
The Syntax, Semantics, and Pragmatics of Japanese and Chinese.
304 pages. 2012. ISBN 978-3-03911-445-0

Vol. 58 Carmen Frehner
Email – SMS – MMS
294 pages. 2008. ISBN 978-3-03911-451-1

Vol. 59 Isabel Balteiro
The Directionality of Conversion in English. A Dia-Synchronic Study.
276 pages. 2007. ISBN 978-3-03911-241-8

Vol. 60 Maria Milagros Del Saz Rubio
English Discourse Markers of Reformulation.
237 pages. 2007. ISBN 978-3-03911-196-1

Vol. 61 Sally Burgess & Pedro Martín-Martín (eds)
English as an Additional Language in Research Publication and Communication.
259 pages. 2008. ISBN 978-3-03911-462-7

Vol. 62 Sandrine Onillon
Pratiques et représentations de l'écrit.
458 pages. 2008. ISBN 978-3-03911-464-1

Vol. 63 Hugo Bowles & Paul Seedhouse (eds)
Conversation Analysis and Language for Specific Purposes.
2nd edition. 337 pages. 2007, 2009. ISBN 978-3-0343-0045-2

Vol. 64 Vijay K. Bhatia, Christopher N. Candlin & Paola Evangelisti Allori (eds)
Language, Culture and the Law.
The Formulation of Legal Concepts across Systems and Cultures.
342 pages. 2008. ISBN 978-3-03911-470-2

Vol. 65 Jonathan Culpeper & Dániel Z. Kádár (eds)
Historical (Im)politeness.
300 pages. 2010. ISBN 978-3-03911-496-2

Vol. 66 Linda Lombardo (ed.)
Using Corpora to Learn about Language and Discourse.
237 pages. 2009. ISBN 978-3-03911-522-8

Vol. 67 Natsumi Wakamoto
Extroversion/Introversion in Foreign Language Learning.
Interactions with Learner Strategy Use.
159 pages. 2009. ISBN 978-3-03911-596-9

Vol. 68 Eva Alcón-Soler (ed.)
Learning How to Request in an Instructed Language Learning Context.
260 pages. 2008. ISBN 978-3-03911-601-0

Vol. 69 Domenico Pezzini
The Translation of Religious Texts in the Middle Ages.
428 pages. 2008. ISBN 978-3-03911-600-3

Vol. 70 Tomoko Tode
Effects of Frequency in Classroom Second Language Learning.
Quasi-experiment and stimulated-recall analysis.
195 pages. 2008. ISBN 978-3-03911-602-7

Vol. 71 Egor Tsedryk
Fusion symétrique et alternances ditransitives.
211 pages. 2009. ISBN 978-3-03911-609-6

Vol. 72 Cynthia J. Kellett Bidoli & Elana Ochse (eds)
English in International Deaf Communication.
444 pages. 2008. ISBN 978-3-03911-610-2

Vol. 73 Joan C. Beal, Carmela Nocera & Massimo Sturiale (eds)
Perspectives on Prescriptivism.
269 pages. 2008. ISBN 978-3-03911-632-4

Vol. 74 Carol Taylor Torsello, Katherine Ackerley & Erik Castello (eds)
Corpora for University Language Teachers.
308 pages. 2008. ISBN 978-3-03911-639-3

Vol. 75 María Luisa Pérez Cañado (ed.)
English Language Teaching in the European Credit Transfer System. Facing the Challenge.
251 pages. 2009. ISBN 978-3-03911-654-6

Vol. 76 Marina Dossena & Ingrid Tieken-Boon van Ostade (eds)
Studies in Late Modern English Correspondence. Methodology and Data.
291 pages. 2008. ISBN 978-3-03911-658-4

Vol. 77 Ingrid Tieken-Boon van Ostade & Wim van der Wurff (eds)
Current Issues in Late Modern English.
436 pages. 2009. ISBN 978-3-03911-660-7

Vol. 78 Marta Navarro Coy (ed.)
Practical Approaches to Foreign Language Teaching and Learning.
297 pages. 2009. ISBN 978-3-03911-661-4

Vol. 79 Qing Ma
Second Language Vocabulary Acquisition.
333 pages. 2009. ISBN 978-3-03911-666-9

Vol. 80 Martin Solly, Michelangelo Conoscenti & Sandra Campagna (eds)
Verbal/Visual Narrative Texts in Higher Education.
384 pages. 2008. ISBN 978-3-03911-672-0

Vol. 81 Meiko Matsumoto
From Simple Verbs to Periphrastic Expressions: The Historical Development of Composite Predicates, Phrasal Verbs, and Related Constructions in English.
235 pages. 2008. ISBN 978-3-03911-675-1

Vol. 82 Melinda Dooly
Doing Diversity. Teachers' Construction of Their Classroom Reality.
180 pages. 2009. ISBN 978-3-03911-687-4

Vol. 83 Victoria Guillén-Nieto, Carmen Marimón-Llorca & Chelo Vargas-Sierra (eds)
Intercultural Business Communication and Simulation and Gaming Methodology.
392 pages. 2009. ISBN 978-3-03911-688-1

Vol. 84 Maria Grazia Guido
English as a Lingua Franca in Cross-cultural Immigration Domains.
285 pages. 2008. ISBN 978-3-03911-689-8

Vol. 85 Erik Castello
Text Complexity and Reading Comprehension Tests.
352 pages. 2008. ISBN 978-3-03911-717-8

Vol. 86 Maria-Lluisa Gea-Valor, Isabel García-Izquierdo & Maria-José Esteve (eds)
Linguistic and Translation Studies in Scientific Communication.
317 pages. 2010. ISBN 978-3-0343-0069-8

Vol. 87 Carmen Navarro, Rosa Mª Rodríguez Abella, Francesca Dalle Pezze & Renzo Miotti (eds)
La comunicación especializada.
355 pages. 2008. ISBN 978-3-03911-733-8

Vol. 88 Kiriko Sato
The Development from Case-Forms to Prepositional Constructions in Old English Prose.
231 pages. 2009. ISBN 978-3-03911-763-5

Vol. 89 Dorothee Heller (Hrsg.)
Formulierungsmuster in deutscher und italienischer Fachkommunikation. Intra- und interlinguale Perspektiven.
315 pages. 2008. ISBN 978-3-03911-778-9

Vol. 90 Henning Bergenholtz, Sandro Nielsen & Sven Tarp (eds)
Lexicography at a Crossroads. Dictionaries and Encyclopedias Today, Lexicographical Tools Tomorrow.
372 pages. 2009. ISBN 978-3-03911-799-4

Vol. 91 Manouchehr Moshtagh Khorasani
The Development of Controversies. From the Early Modern Period to Online Discussion Forums.
317 pages. 2009. ISBN 978-3-3911-711-6

Vol. 92 María Luisa Carrió-Pastor (ed.)
Content and Language Integrated Learning. Cultural Diversity.
178 pages. 2009. ISBN 978-3-3911-818-2

Vol. 93 Roger Berry
Terminology in English Language Teaching. Nature and Use.
262 pages. 2010. ISBN 978-3-0343-0013-1

Vol. 94 Roberto Cagliero & Jennifer Jenkins (eds)
Discourses, Communities, and Global Englishes
240 pages. 2010. ISBN 978-3-0343-0012-4

Vol. 95 Facchinetti Roberta, Crystal David, Seidlhofer Barbara (eds)
From International to Local English – And Back Again.
268 pages. 2010. ISBN 978-3-0343-0011-7

Vol. 96 Cesare Gagliardi & Alan Maley (eds)
EIL, ELF, Global English. Teaching and Learning Issues
376 pages. 2010. ISBN 978-3-0343-0010-0

Vol. 97 Sylvie Hancil (ed.)
The Role of Prosody in Affective Speech.
403 pages. 2009. ISBN 978-3-03911-696-6

Vol. 98 Marina Dossena & Roger Lass (eds)
Studies in English and European Historical Dialectology.
257 pages. 2009. ISBN 978-3-0343-0024-7

Vol. 99 Christine Béal
Les interactions quotidiennes en français et en anglais. De l'approche comparative à l'analyse des situations interculturelles.
424 pages. 2010. ISBN 978-3-0343-0027-8

Vol. 100 Maurizio Gotti (ed.)
Commonality and Individuality in Academic Discourse.
398 pages. 2009. ISBN 978-3-0343-0023-0

Vol. 101 Javier E. Díaz Vera & Rosario Caballero (eds)
Textual Healing. Studies in Medieval English Medical, Scientific and Technical Texts.
213 pages. 2009. ISBN 978-3-03911-822-9

Vol. 102 Nuria Edo Marzá
The Specialised Lexicographical Approach. A Step further in Dictionary-making.
316 pages. 2009. ISBN 978-3-0343-0043-8

Vol. 103 Carlos Prado-Alonso, Lidia Gómez-García, Iria Pastor-Gómez &
David Tizón-Couto (eds)
New Trends and Methodologies in Applied English Language Research.
Diachronic, Diatopic and Contrastive Studies.
348 pages. 2009. ISBN 978-3-0343-0046-9

Vol. 104 Françoise Salager-Meyer & Beverly A. Lewin
Crossed Words. Criticism in Scholarly Writing?
371 pages. 2011. ISBN 978-3-0343-0049-0.

Vol. 105 Javier Ruano-García
Early Modern Northern English Lexis. A Literary Corpus-Based Study.
611 pages. 2010. ISBN 978-3-0343-0058-2

Vol. 106 Rafael Monroy-Casas
Systems for the Phonetic Transcription of English. Theory and Texts.
280 pages. 2011. ISBN 978-3-0343-0059-9

Vol. 107 Nicola T. Owtram
The Pragmatics of Academic Writing.
A Relevance Approach to the Analysis of Research Article Introductions.
311 pages. 2009. ISBN 978-3-0343-0060-5

Vol. 108 Yolanda Ruiz de Zarobe, Juan Manuel Sierra &
Francisco Gallardo del Puerto (eds)
Content and Foreign Language Integrated Learning.
Contributions to Multilingualism in European Contexts
343 pages. 2011. ISBN 978-3-0343-0074-2

Vol. 109 Ángeles Linde López & Rosalía Crespo Jiménez (eds)
Professional English in the European context. The EHEA challenge.
374 pages. 2010. ISBN 978-3-0343-0088-9

Vol. 110 Rosalía Rodríguez-Vázquez
The Rhythm of Speech, Verse and Vocal Music. A New Theory.
394 pages. 2010. ISBN 978-3-0343-0309-5

Vol. 111 Anastasios Tsangalidis & Roberta Facchinetti (eds)
Studies on English Modality. In Honour of Frank Palmer.
392 pages. 2009. ISBN 978-3-0343-0310-1

Vol. 112 Jing Huang
Autonomy, Agency and Identity in Foreign Language Learning and Teaching.
400 pages. 2013. ISBN 978-3-0343-0370-5

Vol. 113 Mihhail Lotman & Maria-Kristiina Lotman (eds)
Frontiers in Comparative Prosody. In memoriam: Mikhail Gasparov.
426 pages. 2011. ISBN 978-3-0343-0373-6

Vol. 114 Merja Kytö, John Scahill & Harumi Tanabe (eds)
Language Change and Variation from Old English to Late Modern English.
A Festschrift for Minoji Akimoto
422 pages. 2010. ISBN 978-3-0343-0372-9

Vol. 115 Giuliana Garzone & Paola Catenaccio (eds)
Identities across Media and Modes. Discursive Perspectives.
379 pages. 2009. ISBN 978-3-0343-0386-6

Vol. 116 Elena Landone
Los marcadores del discurso y cortesía verbal en español.
390 pages. 2010. ISBN 978-3-0343-0413-9

Vol. 117 Maurizio Gotti & Christopher Williams (eds)
Legal Discourse across Languages and Cultures.
339 pages. 2010. ISBN 978-3-0343-0425-2

Vol. 118 David Hirsh
Academic Vocabulary in Context.
217 pages. 2010. ISBN 978-3-0343-0426-9

Vol. 119 Yvonne Dröschel
Lingua Franca English. The Role of Simplification and Transfer.
358 pages. 2011. ISBN 978-3-0343-0432-0

Vol. 120 Tengku Sepora Tengku Mahadi, Helia Vaezian & Mahmoud Akbari
Corpora in Translation. A Practical Guide.
135 pages. 2010. ISBN 978-3-0343-0434-4

Vol. 121 Davide Simone Giannoni & Celina Frade (eds)
Researching Language and the Law. Textual Features and Translation Issues.
278 pages. 2010. ISBN 978-3-0343-0443-6

Vol. 122 Daniel Madrid & Stephen Hughes (eds)
Studies in Bilingual Education.
472 pages. 2011. ISBN 978-3-0343-0474-0

Vol. 123 Vijay K. Bhatia, Christopher N. Candlin & Maurizio Gotti (eds)
The Discourses of Dispute Resolution.
290 pages. 2010. ISBN 978-3-0343-0476-4

Vol. 124 Davide Simone Giannoni
Mapping Academic Values in the Disciplines. A Corpus-Based Approach.
288 pages. 2010. ISBN 978-3-0343-0488-7

Vol. 125 Giuliana Garzone & James Archibald (eds)
Discourse, Identities and Roles in Specialized Communication.
419 pages. 2010. ISBN 978-3-0343-0494-8

Vol. 126 Iria Pastor-Gómez
The Status and Development of N+N Sequences in
Contemporary English Noun Phrases.
216 pages. 2011. ISBN 978-3-0343-0534-1

Vol. 127 Carlos Prado-Alonso
Full-verb Inversion in Written and Spoken English.
261 pages. 2011. ISBN 978-3-0343-0535-8

Vol. 128 Tony Harris & María Moreno Jaén (eds)
Corpus Linguistics in Language Teaching.
214 pages. 2010. ISBN 978-3-0343-0524-2

Vol. 129 Tetsuji Oda & Hiroyuki Eto (eds)
Multiple Perspectives on English Philology and History of Linguistics.
A Festschrift for Shoichi Watanabe on his 80th Birthday.
378 pages. 2010. ISBN 978-3-0343-0480-1

Vol. 130 Luisa Chierichetti & Giovanni Garofalo (eds)
Lengua y Derecho. líneas de investigación interdisciplinaria.
283 pages. 2010. 978-3-0343-0463-4

Vol. 131 Paola Evangelisti Allori & Giuliana Garzone (eds)
Discourse, Identities and Genres in Corporate Communication.
Sponsorship, Advertising and Organizational Communication.
324 pages. 2011. 978-3-0343-0591-4

Vol. 132 Leyre Ruiz de Zarobe & Yolanda Ruiz de Zarobe (eds)
Speech Acts and Politeness across Languages and Cultures.
402 pages. 2012. 978-3-0343-0611-9

Vol. 133 Thomas Christiansen
Cohesion. A Discourse Perspective.
387 pages. 2011. 978-3-0343-0619-5

Vol. 134 Giuliana Garzone & Maurizio Gotti
Discourse, Communication and the Enterprise. Genres and Trends.
451 pages. 2011. ISBN 978-3-0343-0620-1

Vol. 135 Zsuzsa Hoffmann
Ways of the World's Words.
Language Contact in the Age of Globalization.
334 pages 2011. ISBN 978-3-0343-0673-7

Vol. 136 Cecilia Varcasia (ed.)
Becoming Multilingual.
Language Learning and Language Policy between Attitudes and Identities.
213 pages. 2011. ISBN 978-3-0343-0687-5

Vol. 137 Susy Macqueen
The Emergence of Patterns in Second Language Writing.
A Sociocognitive Exploration of Lexical Trails.
325 pages. 2012. ISBN 978-3-0343-1010-9

Vol. 138 Maria Vittoria Calvi & Giovanna Mapelli (eds)
La lengua del turismo. Géneros discursivos y terminología.
365 pages. 2011. ISBN 978-3-0343-1011-6

Vol. 139 Ken Lau
Learning to Become a Professional in a Textually-Mediated World.
A Text-Oriented Study of Placement Practices.
261 pages. 2012. ISBN 978-3-0343-1016-1

Vol. 140 Sandra Campagna, Giuliana Garzone, Cornelia Ilie & Elizabeth Rowley-Jolivet (eds)
Evolving Genres in Web-mediated Communication.
337 pages. 2012. ISBN 978-3-0343-1013-0

Vol. 141 Edith Esch & Martin Solly (eds)
The Sociolinguistics of Language Education in International Contexts.
263 pages. 2012. ISBN 978-3-0343-1009-3

Vol. 142 Forthcoming.

Vol. 143 David Tizón-Couto
Left Dislocation in English. A Functional-Discoursal Approach.
416 pages. 2012. ISBN 978-3-0343-1037-6

Vol. 144 Margrethe Petersen & Jan Engberg (eds)
Current Trends in LSP Research. Aims and Methods.
323 pages. 2011. ISBN 978-3-0343-1054-3

Vol. 145 David Tizón-Couto, Beatriz Tizón-Couto, Iria Pastor-Gómez & Paula Rodríguez-Puente (eds)
New Trends and Methodologies in Applied English Language Research II.
Studies in Language Variation, Meaning and Learning.
283 pages. 2012. ISBN 978-3-0343-1061-1

Vol. 146 Rita Salvi & Hiromasa Tanaka (eds)
Intercultural Interactions in Business and Management.
306 pages. 2011. ISBN 978-3-0343-1039-0

Vol. 147 Francesco Straniero Sergio & Caterina Falbo (eds)
Breaking Ground in Corpus-based Interpreting Studies.
254 pages. 2012. ISBN 978-3-0343-1071-0

Vol. 148 Forthcoming.

Vol. 149 Vijay K. Bhatia & Paola Evangelisti Allori (eds)
Discourse and Identity in the Professions. Legal, Corporate and Institutional Citizenship.
352 pages. 2011. ISBN 978-3-0343-1079-6

Vol. 150 Maurizio Gotti (ed.)
Academic Identity Traits. A Corpus-Based Investigation.
363 pages. 2012. ISBN 978-3-0343-1141-0

Vol. 151 Priscilla Heynderickx, Sylvain Dieltjens, Geert Jacobs, Paul Gillaerts & Elizabeth de Groot (eds)
The Language Factor in International Business.
New Perspectives on Research, Teaching and Practice.
320 pages. 2012. ISBN 978-3-0343-1090-1

Vol. 152 Paul Gillaerts, Elizabeth de Groot, Sylvain Dieltjens, Priscilla Heynderickx & Geert Jacobs (eds)
Researching Discourse in Business Genres. Cases and Corpora.
215 pages. 2012. ISBN 978-3-0343-1092-5

Vol. 153 Yongyan Zheng
Dynamic Vocabulary Development in a Foreign Language.
262 pages. 2012. ISBN 978-3-0343-1106-9

Vol. 154 Carmen Argondizzo (ed.)
Creativity and Innovation in Language Education.
357 pages. 2012. ISBN 978-3-0343-1080-2

Vol. 155 David Hirsh (ed.)
Current Perspectives in Second Language Vocabulary Research.
180 pages. 2012. ISBN 978-3-0343-1108-3

Vol. 156 Seiji Shinkawa
Unhistorical Gender Assignment in Lahamon's *Brut*. A Case Study of a Late Stage in the Development of Grammatical Gender toward its Ultimate Loss.
186 pages. 2012. ISBN 978-3-0343-1124-3

Vol. 157 Yeonkwon Jung
Basics of Organizational Writing: A Critical Reading Approach.
151 pages. 2014. ISBN 978-3-0343-1137-3.

Vol. 158 Bárbara Eizaga Rebollar (ed.)
Studies in Linguistics and Cognition.
301 pages. 2012. ISBN 978-3-0343-1138-0

Vol. 159 Giuliana Garzone, Paola Catenaccio, Chiara Degano (eds)
Genre Change in the Contemporary World. Short-term Diachronic Perspectives.
329 pages. 2012. ISBN 978-3-0343-1214-1

Vol. 160 Carol Berkenkotter, Vijay K. Bhatia & Maurizio Gotti (eds)
Insights into Academic Genres.
468 pages. 2012. ISBN 978-3-0343-1211-0

Vol. 161 Beatriz Tizón-Couto
Clausal Complements in Native and Learner Spoken English. A corpus-based study with Lindsei and Vicolse. 357 pages. 2013. ISBN 978-3-0343-1184-7

Vol. 162 Patrizia Anesa
Jury Trials and the Popularization of Legal Language. A Discourse Analytical Approach.
247 pages. 2012. ISBN 978-3-0343-1231-8

Vol. 163 David Hirsh
Endangered Languages, Knowledge Systems and Belief Systems.
153 pages. 2013. ISBN 978-3-0343-1232-5

Vol. 164 Eugenia Sainz (ed.)
De la estructura de la frase al tejido del discurso. Estudios contrastivos español/italiano.
305 pages. 2014. ISBN 978-3-0343-1253-0

Vol. 165 Julia Bamford, Franca Poppi & Davide Mazzi (eds)
Space, Place and the Discursive Construction of Identity.
367 pages. 2014. ISBN 978-3-0343-1249-3

Vol. 166 Rita Salvi & Janet Bowker (eds)
Space, Time and the Construction of Identity.
Discursive Indexicality in Cultural, Institutional and Professional Fields.
324 pages. 2013. ISBN 978-3-0343-1254-7

Vol. 167 Shunji Yamazaki & Robert Sigley (eds)
Approaching Language Variation through Corpora. A Festschrift in Honour of Toshio Saito.
421 pages. 2013. ISBN 978-3-0343-1264-6

Vol. 168 Franca Poppi
Global Interactions in English as a Lingua Franca. How written communication is changing under the influence of electronic media and new contexts of use.
249 pages. 2012. ISBN 978-3-0343-1276-9

Vol. 169 Miguel A. Aijón Oliva & María José Serrano
Style in syntax. Investigating variation in Spanish pronoun subjects.
239 pages. 2013. ISBN 978-3-0343-1244-8

Vol. 170 Inés Olza, Óscar Loureda & Manuel Casado-Velarde (eds)
Language Use in the Public Sphere. Methodological Perspectives and Empirical Applications
564 pages. 2014. ISBN 978-3-0343-1286-8

Vol. 171 Aleksandra Matulewska
Legilinguistic Translatology. A Parametric Approach to Legal Translation.
279 pages. 2013. ISBN 978-3-0343-1287-5

Vol. 172 Maurizio Gotti & Carmen Sancho Guinda (eds)
Narratives in Academic and Professional Genres.
513 pages. 2013. ISBN 978-3-0343-1371-1

Vol. 173 Madalina Chitez
Learner corpus profiles. The case of Romanian Learner English.
244 pages. 2014. ISBN 978-3-0343-1410-7

Vol. 174 Chihiro Inoue
Task Equivalence in Speaking Tests.
251 pages. 2013. ISBN 978-3-0343-1417-6

Vol. 175 Gabriel Quiroz & Pedro Patiño (eds.)
LSP in Colombia: advances and challenges.
339 pages. 2014. ISBN 978-3-0343-1434-3

Vol. 176 Catherine Resche
Economic Terms and Beyond: Capitalising on the Wealth of Notions.
How Researchers in Specialised Varieties of English Can Benefit from Focusing on Terms.
332 pages. 2013. ISBN 978-3-0343-1435-0

Vol. 177 Forthcoming.

Vol. 178 Cécile Desoutter & Caroline Mellet (dir.)
Le discours rapporté: approches linguistiques et perspectives didactiques.
270 pages. 2013. ISBN 978-3-0343-1292-9

Vol. 179 Ana Díaz-Negrillo & Francisco Javier Díaz-Pérez (eds)
Specialisation and Variation in Language Corpora.
341 pages. 2014. ISBN 978-3-0343-1316-2

Vol. 180 Pilar Alonso
A Multi-dimensional Approach to Discourse Coherence. From Standardness to Creativity.
247 pages. 2014. ISBN 978-3-0343-1325-4

Vol. 181 Alejandro Alcaraz-Sintes & Salvador Valera-Hernández (eds)
Diachrony and Synchrony in English Corpus Linguistics.
393 pages. 2014. ISBN 978-3-0343-1326-1

Vol. 182 Runhan Zhang
Investigating Linguistic Knowledge of a Second Language.
207 pages. 2015. ISBN 978-3-0343-1330-8

Vol. 183 Hajar Abdul Rahim & Shakila Abdul Manan (eds.)
English in Malaysia. Postcolonial and Beyond.
267 pages. 2014. ISBN 978-3-0343-1341-4

Vol. 184 Virginie Fasel Lauzon
Comprendre et apprendre dans l'interaction. Les séquences d'explication en classe
de français langue seconde.
292 pages. 2014. ISBN 978-3-0343-1451-0

Vol. 185 Forthcoming.

Vol. 186 Wei Ren
L2 Pragmatic Development in Study Abroad Contexts
256 pages. 2015. ISBN 978-3-0343-1358-2

Vol. 187 Marina Bondi & Rosa Lorés Sanz (eds)
Abstracts in Academic Discourse. Variation and Change.
361 pages. 2014. ISBN 978-3-0343-1483-1

Vol. 188 Giuditta Caliendo
Rethinking Community. Discourse, Identity and Citizenship in the European Union.
240 pages. 2017. ISBN 978-3-0343-1561-6

Vol. 189 Paola Evangelisti Allori (ed.)
Identities in and across Cultures.
315 pages. 2014. ISBN 978-3-0343-1458-9

Vol. 190 Erik Castello, Katherine Ackerley & Francesca Coccetta (eds).
Studies in Learner Corpus Linguistics. Research and Applications for Foreign Language Teaching and Assessment.
358 pages. 2015. ISBN 978-3-0343-1506-7

Vol. 191 Ruth Breeze, Maurizio Gotti & Carmen Sancho Guinda (eds)
Interpersonality in Legal Genres.
389 pages. 2014. ISBN 978-3-0343-1524-1

Vol. 192 Paola Evangelisti Allori, John Bateman & Vijay K. Bhatia (eds)
Evolution in Genre. Emergence, Variation, Multimodality.
364 pages. 2014. ISBN 978-3-0343-1533-3

Vol. 193 Jiyeon Kook
Agency in Arzt-Patient-Gesprächen. Zur interaktionistischen Konzeptualisierung von Agency
271 pages. 2015. ISBN 978-3-0343-1666-8

Vol. 194 Susana Nicolás Román & Juan José Torres Núñez (eds)
Drama and CLIL. A new challenge for the teaching approaches in bilingual education.
170 pages. 2015. ISBN 978-3-0343-1629-3

Vol. 195 Alessandra Molino & Serenella Zanotti (eds)
Observing Norm, Observing Usage. Lexis in Dictionaries and in the Media.
430 pages. 2015. ISBN 978-3-0343-1584-5

Vol. 196 Begoña Soneira
A Lexical Description of English for Architecture. A Corpus-based Approach.
267 pages. 2015. ISBN 978-3-0343-1602-6

Vol. 197 M Luisa Roca-Varela
False Friends in Learner Corpora. A corpus-based study of English false friends in the written and spoken production of Spanish learners.
348 pages. 2015. ISBN 978-3-0343-1620-0

Vol. 198 Rahma Al-Mahrooqi & Christopher Denman
Bridging the Gap between Education and Employment. English Language Instruction in EFL Contexts.
416 pages. 2015. ISBN 978-3-0343-1681-1

Vol. 199 Rita Salvi & Janet Bowker (eds)
The Dissemination of Contemporary Knowledge in English. Genres, discourse strategies and professional practices.
171 pages. 2015. ISBN 978-3-0343-1679-8

Vol. 200 Maurizio Gotti & Davide S. Giannoni (eds)
Corpus Analysis for Descriptive and Pedagogical Purposes. ESP Perspectives.
432 pages. 2014. ISBN 978-3-0343-1516-6

Vol. 201 Ida Ruffolo
The Perception of Nature in Travel Promotion Texts. A Corpus-based Discourse Analysis.
148 pages. 2015. ISBN 978-3-0343-1521-0

Vol. 202 Ives Trevian
English suffixes. Stress-assignment properties, productivity, selection and combinatorial processes.
471 pages. 2015. ISBN 978-3-0343-1576-0

Vol. 203 Maurizio Gotti, Stefania Maci & Michele Sala (eds)
Insights into Medical Communication.
422 pages. 2015. ISBN 978-3-0343-1694-1

Vol. 204 Carmen Argondizzo (ed.)
European Projects in University Language Centres. Creativity, Dynamics, Best Practice.
371 pages. 2015. ISBN 978-3-0343-1696-5

Vol. 205 Aura Luz Duffé Montalván (ed.)
Estudios sobre el léxico. Puntos y contrapuntos.
502 pages. 2016. ISBN 978-3-0343-2011-5

Vol. 206 Maria Pavesi, Maicol Formentelli & Elisa Ghia (eds)
The Languages of Dubbing. Mainstream Audiovisual Translation in Italy.
275 pages. 2014. ISBN 978-3-0343-1646-0

Vol. 207 Ruth Breeze & Inés Olza (eds)
Evaluation in media discourse. European perspectives.
268 pages. 2017. ISBN 978-3-0343-2014-6

Vol. 208 Vijay K. Bhatia & Maurizio Gotti (eds)
Arbitration Discourse in Asia.
331 pages. 2015. ISBN 978-3-0343-2032-0

Vol. 209 Sofía Bemposta-Rivas, Carla Bouzada-Jabois, Yolanda Fernández-Pena, Tamara Bouso, Yolanda J. Calvo-Benzies, Iván Tamaredo (eds)
New trends and methodologies in applied English language research III. Synchronic and diachronic studies on discourse, lexis and grammar processing.
280 pages. 2017. ISBN 978-3-0343-2039-9

Vol. 210 Francisco Alonso Almeida, Laura Cruz García & Víctor González Ruiz (eds)
Corpus-based studies on language varieties.
285 pages. 2016. ISBN 978-3-0343-2044-3

Vol. 211 Juan Pedro Rica Peromingo
Aspectos lingüísticos y técnicos de la traducción audiovisual (TAV).
177 pages. 2016. ISBN 978-3-0343-2055-9

Vol. 212 Maria Vender
Disentangling Dyslexia. VenderPhonological and Processing Deficit in Developmental Dyslexia.
338 pages. 2017. ISBN 978-3-0343-2064-1

Vol. 213 Zhilong Xie
Bilingual Advantages. Contributions of Different Bilingual Experiences to Cognitive Control Differences Among Young-adult Bilinguals.
221 pages. 2016. ISBN 978-3-0343-2081-8

Vol. 214 Larissa D'Angelo
Academic posters. A textual and visual metadiscourse analysis.
367 pages. 2016. ISBN 978-3-0343-2083-2

Vol. 215 Evelyne Berger
Prendre la parole en L2. Regard sur la compétence d'interaction en classe de langue.
246 pages. 2016. ISBN 978-3-0343-2084-9

Vol. 216 David Lasagabaster and Aintzane Doiz (eds)
CLIL experiences in secondary and tertiary education: In search of good practices.
262 pages. 2016. ISBN 978-3-0343-2104-4

Vol. 217 Elena Kkese
Identifying Plosives in L2 English: The Case of L1 Cypriot Greek Speakers.
317 pages. 2016. ISBN 978-3-0343-2060-3

Vol. 218 Sandra Campagna, Elana Ochse, Virginia Pulcini & Martin Solly (eds)
Languaging in and across Communities: New Voices, New Identities. Studies in Honour of Giuseppina Cortese.
507 pages. 2016. ISBN 978-3-0343-2073-3

Vol. 219 Adriana Orlandi & Laura Giacomini (ed.)
Defining collocation for lexicographic purposes. From linguistic theory to lexicographic practice.
328 pages. 2016. ISBN 978-3-0343-2054-2

Vol. 220 Pietro Luigi Iaia
Analysing English as a Lingua Franca in Video Games. Linguistic Features, Experiential and Functional Dimensions of Online and Scripted Interactions.
139 pages. 2016. ISBN 978-3-0343-2138-9

Vol. 221 Dimitrinka G. Níkleva (ed.)
La formación de los docentes de español para inmigrantes en distintos contextos educativos.
390 pages. 2017. ISBN 978-3-0343-2135-8

Vol. 222 Katherine Ackerley, Marta Guarda & Francesca Helm (eds)
Sharing Perspectives on English-Medium Instruction.
308 pages. 2017. ISBN 978-3-0343-2537-0

Vol. 223 Juana I. Marín-Arrese, Julia Lavid-López, Marta Carretero, Elena Domínguez Romero, Mª Victoria Martín de la Rosa & María Pérez Blanco (eds)
Evidentiality and Modality in European Languages. Discourse-pragmatic perspectives.
427 pages. 2017. ISBN 978-3-0343-2437-3

Vol. 224 Gilles Col
Construction du sens : un modèle instructionnel pour la sémantique.
292 pages. 2017. ISBN 978-3-0343-2572-1

Vol. 225 Ana Chiquito & Gabriel Quiroz (eds)
Pobreza, Lenguaje y Medios en América Latina.
362 pages. 2017. ISBN 978-3-0343-2142-6

Vol. 226 Xu Zhang
English Quasi-Numeral Classifiers. A Corpus-Based Cognitive-Typological Study.
360 pages. 2017. ISBN 978-3-0343-2818-0

Vol. 227 María Ángeles Orts, Ruth Breeze & Maurizio Gotti (eds)
Power, Persuasion and Manipulation in Specialised Genres. Providing Keys to the Rhetoric of Professional Communities.
368 pages. 2017. ISBN 978-3-0343-3010-7

Vol. 228 Maurizio Gotti, Stefania Maci & Michele Sala (eds)
Ways of Seeing, Ways of Being: Representing the Voices of Tourism.
453 pages. 2017. ISBN 978-3-0343-3031-2

Vol. 229 Dino Selvaggi
Plurilingual Code-Switching between Standard and Local Varieties.
A Socio-Psycholinguistic Approach
371 pages. 2018. ISBN 978-3-0343-2663-6

Vol. 230 Anca-Cristina Sterie
Interprofessional interactions at the hospital. Nurses' requests and reports of problems in calls with physicians.
371 pages. 2017. ISBN 978-3-0343-2734-3

Vol. 231 Xiaodong Zhang
Understanding Chinese EFL Teachers' Beliefs and Practices in the Textbook-Based Classroom.
189 pages. 2017. ISBN 978-3-0343-3053-4

Vol. 232 Manuela Caterina Moroni & Federica Ricci Garotti (Hrsg.)
Brücken schlagen zwischen Sprachwissenschaft und DaF-Didaktik.
345 pages. 2017. ISBN 978-3-0343-2667-4

Vol. 233 Dimitrinka Georgieva Níkleva
Necesidades y tendencias en la formación del profesorado de español como lengua extranjera
401 pages. 2017. ISBN 978-3-0343-2946-0

Vol. 234 Juan Santana-Lario & Salvador Valera (Hrsg.)
Competing patterns in English affixation.
272 pages. 2017. ISBN 978-3-0343-2701-5

Vol. 235 Francisco Salgado-Robles
Desarrollo de la competencia sociolingüística por aprendices de español en un contexto de inmersión en el extranjero
241 pages. 2018. ISBN 978-3-0343-2323-9

Vol. 236 Maria Chiara Janner
Sguardi linguistici sulla marca. Analisi morfosintattica dei nomi commerciali in italiano
345 pages. 2017. ISBN 978-3-0343-2667-4

Vol. 237 Bárbara Herrero Muñoz-Cobo & Otman El Azami Zalachi
La primavera del árabe marroquí.
192 pages. 2017. ISBN 978-3-0343-3104-3

Vol. 238 Consuelo Pascual Escagedo
El papel del oyente en la construcción de la conversación espontánea de estudiantes italianos en su interlengua y en su lengua materna
295 pages. 2017. ISBN 978-3-0343-3186-9

Vol. 239 Stefania M. Maci
The MS Digby 133 *Mary Magdalene*. Beyond scribal practices: language, discourse, values and attitudes.
336 pages. 2017. ISBN 978-3-0343-3256-9

Vol. 240 Eliecer Crespo-Fernández
Taboo in Discourse. Studies on Attenuation and Offence in Communication.
326 pages. 2018. ISBN 978-3-0343-3018-3

Vol. 241 Jana Altmanova, Maria Centrella, Katherine E. Russo (eds)
Terminology & Discourse / Terminologie et discours.
424 pages. 2018. ISBN 978-3-0343-2417-5

Vol. 242 Xavier Blanco et Inès Sfar (dir.)
Lexicologie(s) : approches croisées en sémantique lexicale.
442 pages. 2018. ISBN 978-3-0343-3056-5

Vol. 243 Yunfeng Ge
Resolution of Conflict of Interest in Chinese Civil Court Hearings.
A Perspective of Discourse Information Theory.
302 pages. 2018. ISBN 978-3-0343-3313-9

Vol. 244 Carla Vergaro
Illocutionary Shell Nouns in English
322 pages. 2018. ISBN 978-3-0343-3069-5

Vol. 245 Paolo Frassi
L'adjectif en français et sa définition lexicographique.
270 pages. 2018. ISBN 978-3-0343-3394-8

Vol. 246 Suwilai Premsrirat and David Hirsh (eds)
Language Revitalization. Insights from Thailand
328 pages. 2018. ISBN 978-3-0343-3497-6

Vol. 247 Wei Wang
Researching Learning and Learners in Genre-based Academic Writing Instruction
282 pages. 2018. ISBN 978-3-0343-3297-2

Vol. 248 Isusi Alabarte, Alberto & Lahuerta Martínez, Ana Cristina (eds)
La comprensión lectora de lengua extranjera
Estudio de los factores de familiaridad, interés, género y métodos de evaluación
336 pages. 2018. ISBN 978-3-0343-3493-8

Vol. 249 Mercedes Eurrutia Cavero
Approche didactique du langage techno-scientifique
Terminologie et discours
374 pages. 2018. ISBN 978-3-0343-3512-6

Vol. 250 Aurora Ruiz Mezcua (ed.)
Approaches to Telephone Interpretation
Research, Innovation, Teaching and Transference
268 pages. 2018. ISBN 978-3-0343-3330-6

Vol. 251 Morini Massimiliano
A Day in the News
A Stylistic Analysis of Newsspeak
188 pages. 2018. ISBN 978-3-0343-3507-2

Vol. 252 Ignacio Guillén-Galve & Ignacio Vázquez-Orta (eds.)
English as a Lingua Franca and Intercultural Communication
Implications and Applications in the Field of English Language Teaching
414 pages. 2018. ISBN 978-3-0343-2763-3

Vol. 253 Bianca Del Villano
Using the Devil with Courtesy
Shakespeare and the Language of (Im)Politeness
216 pages. 2018. ISBN 978-3-0343-2315-4

Vol. 254 David Hirsh (ed.)
Explorations in Second Language Vocabulary Research
252 pages. 2018. ISBN 978-3-0343-2940-8

Vol. 255 Tania Baumann (ed.)
Reiseführer - Sprach- und Kulturmittlung im Tourismus / Le guide turistiche - mediazione linguistica e culturale in ambito turistico
270 pages. 2018. ISBN 978-3-0343-3402-0

Vol. 256 Ariadna Sánchez-Hernández & Ana Herraiz-Martínez (eds)
Learning second language pragmatics beyond traditional contexts
376 pages. 2018. ISBN 978-3-0343-3437-2

Vol. 257 Albert Bastardas-Boada, Emili Boix-Fuster, Rosa Maria Torrens (eds)
Family Multilingualism in Medium-Sized Linguistic Communities
336 pages. 2019. ISBN 978-3-0343-2536-3

Vol. 258 Forthcoming

Vol. 259 Catia Nannoni
Participe présent et gérondif dans la presse française contemporaine
176 pages. 2019. ISBN 978-3-0343-3631-4

Vol. 260 Nieves Rodríguez Pérez & Bárbara Heinsch (eds.)
Contextos multilingües. Mediadores interculturales, formación del profesorado de lenguas extranjeras
289 pages. 2019. ISBN 978-3-0343-3768-7

Vol. 261 Forthcoming

Vol. 262 Laura Nadal
Lingüística experimental y contraargumentación
233 pages. 2019. ISBN 978-3-0343-3791-5

Vol. 263 Claudia Claridge & Merja Kytö (eds.)
Punctuation in Context – Past and Present Perspectives
288 pages. 2019. ISBN 978-3-0343-3790-8

Vol. 264 Maurizio Gotti, Stefania Maci, Michele Sala (eds.)
Scholarly Pathways
530 pages. 2020. ISBN 978-3-0343-3860-8

Vol. 265 Ruth Breeze, Ana M. Fernández Vallejo (eds.)
Politics and populism across modes and media
350 pages. 2019. ISBN 978-3-0343-3707-6

www.ingramcontent.com/pod-product-compliance
Ingram Content Group UK Ltd.
Pitfield, Milton Keynes, MK11 3LW, UK
UKHW021835100926
8556IPUK00004B/347

9 783034 337076